Praise for Joomla!: A Users Guide

W9-AVX-990

"A complete guide to the powerful features of Joomla! 1.5, this book takes a holistic approach to building a Joomla!-powered website—from the CMS itself to its many extensions, search engine optimization, and even building your own table-less template. The novice reader is eased into the subject and confidently guided through the basic principles and on to the more advanced features. This guide empowers the user not only to build a professional website, but to also make it a success."

—*Russell Walker, CEO, Netshine Software Limted (Joomla Development Consultancy)*

"If you've been using or following Joomla! in the past years you've most likely seen the name Barrie North or Joomlashack. Barrie has been a member of the community for a long time and as such, my expectations for this book where pretty high. Besides explaining how Joomla! works from a usability point of view, there is valuable information for people who want to learn serious template building and readers can stand out of the crowed by using Barrie's steps to make their (X)HTML and CSS optimized for accessibility and SEO. All in all, this book is a great guide that comes at the right time for newcomers and more experienced Joomla! users and developers, alike. Well-done, Barrie!"

—*Arno Zijlstra, Joomla! Cofounder, Custom Template Specialist, www.alvaana.com*

"In a time when solid, real-life Joomla! 1.5, information is rarely available, this book is a thirst quenching oasis of knowledge. The abundant and clear examples in the book make Joomla! 1.5 websites within anyone's reach. I heartily recommend, Joomla! a users Guide by Barrie North."

—*Tom Canavan, Dodging the Bullets: A Disaster Preparation Guide for Joomla! Web Sites*

"It's not easy to write a book about Joomla! there is just so much to talk about but Barrie North does an excellent job. It is suitable for both the first time user and those who have been using Joomla! for a very long time. The book is logically structured and will help you create a dynamic website in a very short space of time. There aren't many books that stay on my desk but this will be one of them."

—*Brian Teeman, Cofounder of Joomla! and OpenSourceMatters Inc.*

"Refreshing! After reading many how-to books, this one is a step beyond the rest because of its focus on examples based on live sites. This book is well-crafted for beginners to advanced users with a well-organized overview that walks you through the entire Joomla! CMS."

—*Steven Pignataro, corePHP, www.corephp.com*

"As a longtime Joomla! end-user and developer, I had low expectations for anything new I might learn from this book. However, I was pleasantly surprised to find it a great refresher course, especially since Joomla! 1.5 is a very different application from Joomla! 1.0. The book is logically organized, leading beginners from the most basic Joomla! concepts and continuing through to more complex ones, such as tableless template design and how to write a template for Joomla! 1.5. In summary, Barrie North has produced the gold-standard print reference for Joomla! 1.5. I highly recommend The Guide for novice and intermediate users if you want to make the most of Joomla!"

—*Victor Drover, http://dev.anything-digital.com*

Joomla!
A User's Guide

Joomla!
A User's Guide

Building a Successful
Joomla! Powered Website

Barrie M. North

PRENTICE
HALL

Prentice Hall
Upper Saddle River, NJ · Boston · Indianapolis · San Francisco
New York · Toronto · Montreal · London · Munich · Paris · Madrid
Cape Town · Sydney · Tokyo · Singapore · Mexico City

Many of the designations used by manufacturers and sellers to distinguish their products are claimed as trademarks. Where those designations appear in this book, and the publisher was aware of a trademark claim, the designations have been printed with initial capital letters or in all capitals.

The author and publisher have taken care in the preparation of this book, but make no expressed or implied warranty of any kind and assume no responsibility for errors or omissions. No liability is assumed for incidental or consequential damages in connection with or arising out of the use of the information or programs contained herein.

The publisher offers excellent discounts on this book when ordered in quantity for bulk purchases or special sales, which may include electronic versions and/or custom covers and content particular to your business, training goals, marketing focus, and branding interests. For more information, please contact:

U.S. Corporate and Government Sales
(800) 382-3419
corpsales@pearsontechgroup.com

For sales outside the United States please contact:

International Sales
international@pearsoned.com

This Book Is Safari Enabled
The Safari® Enabled icon on the cover of your favorite technology book means the book is available through Safari Bookshelf. When you buy this book, you get free access to the online edition for 45 days.

Safari Bookshelf is an electronic reference library that lets you easily search thousands of technical books, find code samples, download chapters, and access technical information whenever and wherever you need it.

To gain 45-day Safari Enabled access to this book:
- Go to http://www.prenhallprofessional.com/safarienabled
- Complete the brief registration form
- Enter the coupon code 61N3-2UVP-ISCU-L7PL-Q1M4

If you have difficulty registering on Safari Bookshelf or accessing the online edition, please e-mail customer-service@safaribooksonline.com.

Visit us on the Web: www.prenhallprofessional.com

Library of Congress Cataloging-in-Publication Data:

North, Barrie M.
Joomla! : a user's guide : building a successful Joomla! powered Website / Barrie M. North.
p. cm.
ISBN 0-13-613560-9 (pbk. : alk. paper) 1. Websites--Authoring programs. 2. Web site development. 3. Joomla! (Computer file) I. Title.
TK5105.8883.N67 2007
006.7'8--dc22
                2007039551

Copyright © 2008 Barrie M. North
All rights reserved except for Chapter 9 (see paragraph below). Printed in the United States of America. This publication is protected by copyright, and permission must be obtained from the publisher prior to any prohibited reproduction, storage in a retrieval system, or transmission in any form or by any means, electronic, mechanical, photocopying, recording, or likewise. For information regarding permissions, write to:

Pearson Education, Inc.
Rights and Contracts Department
501 Boylston Street, Suite 900
Boston, MA 02116
Fax: (617) 671-3447

Chapter 9 is released under a Creative Commons Attribution-Noncommerical-Share Alike 2.5 License. Please see http://creativecommons.org/licenses/by-nc-sa/2.5/ for more details.

ISBN-13: 978-0-136-13560-9
ISBN-10:   0-136-13560-9

Text printed in the United States on recycled paper at R.R. Donnelly in Crawfordsville, IN
Third printing March 2008

Editor in Chief
Mark Taub

Acquisitions Editors
Catherine B. Nolan
Debra Williams Cauley

Development Editor
Sheri Cain

Managing Editor
Gina Kanouse

Project Editor and Proofreader
Chelsey Marti

Copy Editor
Language Logistics, LLC

Senior Indexer
Cheryl Lenser

Technical Reviewers
Corey Burger
Kenneth Crowder

Editorial Assistant
Kim Boedigheimer

Cover Designer
Chuti Prasertsith

Composition
Gloria Schurick

For Sarah

Contents

Preface

Joomla! is an open source Content Management System (CMS) that anyone can download for free.[1] This makes it an ideal choice for small businesses. Don't let the price tag fool you—Joomla! is powerful and robust, and more big organizations are choosing to have open source software solutions all the time. This universal appeal has made Joomla! hugely popular as a CMS. This is evident by looking at how searches for Joomla! in Google have grown, roughly doubling every two months (see Figure P.1).

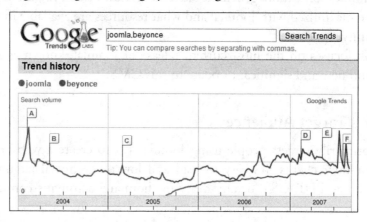

FIGURE P.1 Joomla!—as Popular as Pop

As Joomla! matures, it is being adopted by more and more organizations. Its greatest advantage is its flexibility. You can see it on a huge variety of sites:

- Corporations
- Schools and Universities
- Online Commerce Organizations
- Small Businesses

- Non-profit and Community Organizations
- Government Organizations
- Corporate Intranets and Extranets
- Personal or Family Home Pages
- Community-based Portals
- Magazines and Newspapers

The Purpose of This Book

This book is about Joomla!, the popular and award-winning[2] open source CMS. It will take you step-by-step through everything you need to develop a successful website powered by Joomla!. The book gives a general overview of management of a CMS and teaches you key concepts regarding content organization, editing, and templates. Last, the book examines some more general topics such as how Search Engine Optimization (SEO) can be maximized with Joomla! and what resources are available in the Joomla! web community.

This book focuses on the most current release of Joomla!, known as *Joomla! 1.5*. This is a brand new and significant update to this CMS.

This Book's Target Audience

This book primarily targets people using Joomla! 1.5 to create a website, either for themselves or their clients. It's easy to read and low on technical jargon. It doesn't assume you know PHP, CSS, or any other of the many acronyms common to web applications.

All of the concepts in the book are explained with clear, step-by-step contextual examples. If you follow all the steps in all the chapters, you will build seven separate Joomla! websites!

How Should I Use This Book?

You can use this book in several ways. You can start at the beginning and go chapter by chapter as you develop your own site. The book is carefully laid out so that introductory ideas in the earlier chapters are developed and built on to help you understand more advanced concepts later on. You can also use the book as a reference. If you need some quick ideas of what newsletter extensions are available, head to Chapter 6, "Extending Joomla!." Lastly, the Appendices contain valuable extra information about various aspects of Joomla!.

Chapter 1: Content Management Systems and an Introduction to Joomla!

In today's fast moving web, if you have a website that doesn't have rich functionality or fresh content, you will find yourself at a disadvantage to those that do. The idea of powering websites with a CMS has been around for some time, but it is only recently with the advent of high quality open source CMS scripts like Joomla! that we have seen these powerful CMS tools coming into the hands of you and me.

In this chapter, I explain in detail the difference between a "traditional" website and one using a CMS. We also look at the history of Joomla! and an overview of some of its features.

Chapter 2: Downloading and Installing Joomla!

Joomla! is one of the most popular open source CMS on the planet. The first step in becoming part of the "Joomla!sphere," the vibrant community that exists around the Joomla! Project, is to download Joomla! and install it on your web server.

This chapter shows you how to get up and running with a Joomla! site. The two steps are to find and download the latest files and to install them on a web server. This chapter describes both a local (your home computer) installation to use as you read this book (if you don't have a hosting account or have a slow internet connection) and real web server installations.

Chapter 3: Joomla! Administration Basics

The term "site administration" usually means the day to day tasks of adding content, managing users and making sure installed components and modules are running correctly. With a properly configured Joomla! site, the administration burden is relatively low. Most of the effort can be dedicated to generating that all important content.

In this chapter, we go on a whirlwind tour of the core administrative functions you need. I won't be going step by step explaining every last button in the admin backend, but rather picking out key functions, tips, and tricks that you'll need to know to keep your site humming.

Chapter 4: Content Is King: Organizing Your Content

As a CMS, Joomla!'s primary function is to organize and present all the content in your site. It does this through content articles. These discrete pieces of content must be organized into a two-level hierarchy called sections and categories.

This chapter provides an in-depth tutorial that explains how Joomla! displays its content articles and how you can organize the hierarchical structure of them. It details how to plan and organize the content and user experience for the site. It also explains the hierarchy structure currently used in Joomla!, sections and categories, and how to best structure content into them for small and large sites.

Chapter 5: Creating Menus and Navigation

Menus are perhaps the core of a Joomla! site. In a static HTML site, they merely serve as navigation. In a Joomla! site, they serve that purpose, but also determine the layout of what a dynamic page will look like and what content will appear on that page when you navigate to it. The relationship between menus, menu items, pages and modules is perhaps one of the most confusing in Joomla!. This chapter explains this relationship so that you can create a navigation scheme that works for your site.

Chapter 5 examines how the navigation (menus and links) is built for a Joomla! website and how the different aspects interact to produce a coherent navigation structure.

Chapter 6: Extending Joomla!

It's hard to find a Joomla! powered website that has not added functionality beyond the basics with some sort of extension. The word extension collectively describes components, modules, plugins, and languages. There are many hundreds available both free and commercially from 3rd party providers.

In this chapter, we look at some examples of core and 3rd party Joomla! extensions. We also examine how they are installed and managed in Joomla!.

Chapter 7: Expanding Your Content: Articles and Editors

There are two main ways to add and manage content to a Joomla! site: through the frontend or backend. Part of the biggest attraction of Joomla! is to easily add and edit content through a What You See Is What You Get (WYSIWYG) editor.

In this chapter, we start out looking at WYSIWYG and how it functions in the backend with Managers, Administrators, and Super Administrators. We then examine how authors, editors, and publishers manage content through the frontend.

Chapter 8: Getting Traffic to Your Site

Search Engine Optimization (SEO) might be one of the most maligned subjects on the web. From talk to black hat SEO, people who use unethical methods to gain rank in search engines, to their counterparts of white hat SEO, the good guys, how best to get traffic to your site is loaded with opinion and myth.

Trying to learn about SEO is difficult, to say the least. In this chapter, I emphasize **Search Engine Marketing** (SEM). I point out some obvious SEO tips and how they apply to Joomla!, but I'll also discuss a more holistic marketing plan including such strategies as Pay Per Click and blogging.

Chapter 9: Creating a Pure CSS Template

In this chapter, we go through the steps of creating a Joomla! template. Specifically, we create a template that uses Cascading Style Sheets (CSS) to produce a layout without use of tables. This is a desirable goal as it means that the template code is easier to validate to World Wide Web Consortium (W3C) standards. It also tends to load faster, be easier to maintain and perform better in search engines. We discuss these issues in detail later in the chapter.

Chapter 10: Creating a School Site with Joomla!

School websites tend to be medium to large in size. One of the defining characteristics of Joomla! is that it is very powerful and flexible, but can be quite time intensive to setup. This leads us of course to this chapter, hopefully an extensive guide to creating and setting up a school website using the Joomla! CMS.

Chapter 11: Creating a Restaurant Site with Joomla!

The chapter looks at the entire process of creating a restaurant website from scratch. We examine how to build a small business website, in this case a restaurant. Starting from an analysis of needs, this chapter shows you how to organize possible content all the way through to adding photos and considering further extensions.

Chapter 12: Creating a Blog Site with Joomla!

It seems like everyone has a blog these days. Many people still think of blogs as personal diaries, but more and more organizations and companies are using blogs as a way to shape perception of who they are and what they do. Chances are, if you go to a website today, you will find a link to their blog somewhere on their site. What is becoming more common on websites now, is a section of the site that is dedicated to the blog.

This chapter talks about blogs in a more general sense: a dynamic communication medium for a person or organization to interact with their stakeholders. We look at creating a blog site from scratch using Joomla!.

Appendix A: Getting Help

Stuck with Joomla!? There is a tremendous amount of information on the web, as well as many active communities to ask for help.

Appendix B: Joomla! Case Studies

Six real sites that are using Joomla!, taken from a wide range of industries and types of site.

Appendix C: A Quick Start to SEO

Need some quick tips to help your Search Engine Ranking? Implement these.

Appendix D: Install WAMP5

A quick guide to installing WAMP5 on your home computer. This package is important so you can follow along with all the site examples in the book.

What Is a Content Management System?

A CMS is a collection of scripts that separates content from its presentation. Its main features are the ease of creation and editing of content and dynamic web pages. CMSs are usually very sophisticated and can have newsfeeds, forums, and online stores—and are easily edited. More and more websites are moving toward a site powered by a CMS.

Most Content Management Systems are expensive, anywhere from $50,000 to $300,000, but there are an increasing number of open source alternatives becoming available. Open source CMSs have become increasingly more reliable and are now being used for important projects in many companies, non-profits, and organizations.

Why Use a CMS?

A CMS separates out the responsibilities of developing a website. The web designer can concern himself with the design, which means that nontechnical people can be responsible for the content.

The modern CMS is usually defined by its capability to manage and publish content. Most do far more, having the capability to add on a wide range of extensions or add-ons to increase functionality of the site.

What Is Open Source Software?

Joomla! is an example of open source software; its non-profit copyright holder is Open Source Matters.[3] An open source project is developed by a community of developers across the world, all volunteering their time. Some examples you might have heard of are Firefox, Apache, Wiki, Linux, or OpenOffice. All of these are open source and both have challenged and surpassed their commercial equivalents. If you are curious about how and why people should create powerful software for free, you can find more information on these sites:

- http://en.wikipedia.org/wiki/Open_source
- http://www.opensource.org/

Things To Look For

The following are specific elements to look for when reading:

> **TIP**
> The tip boxes give more advanced ideas about an aspect of Joomla!. You will usually be able to find more details at compassdesigns.net about the tip.

> **NOTE**
> The notes box denotes a caution about an aspect of the topic. It sometimes won't be applicable to all situations, but you should check if it would apply to your site.

> **The Least You Need to Know**
> The key critical concepts explained can be found in the LYNTK box. These are worth circling in a big red pen or writing out for yourself on a cheat sheet.

Joomla!

The full and proper name of the Joomla! CMS includes an exclamation point, as shown here. For the sake of readability, and a tree or two, I'll be dropping the exclamation in the text.

www.Joomlabook.com

You can find more information about this book, including complete browsable and downloadable versions of all the sites created in the chapters, at www.Joomlabook. com.

---

[1] http://forge.Joomla!.org/sf/go/projects.Joomla!/frs

[2] Joomla! won the award for the "Best Linux/Open Source Project" for 2005.

[3] http://www.opensourcematters.org

Acknowledgments

Without the continuing support of my wife, Sarah, this book would not have been possible. As we had our third son halfway through writing it, she let me frequently slip off to work on the manuscript while she kept them busy. Part of my thanks also goes to my three boys who (mostly) managed not to bug me while writing.

I'd like to thank the third-party developer community who I would frequently annoy on Skype with questions about this or that.

Last, all of my thanks to the guys who live on the trunk—the many developers who selflessly contribute code to the Joomla! project on a daily basis.

About the Author

Barrie North has over 15 years of experience with the Internet, as a user, designer, and teacher. He has spent over eight years in the education field, becoming steadily more involved in web technology and teaching web design classes to students and technology integration to teachers. Most recently he worked as an IT consultant for two new schools pioneering in the use of technology. As well as web design, he has provided web marketing/SEO, usability, and standards compliance expertise to his clients.

He is a partner of Joomlashack.com, providing templates and custom services. He also maintains a blog about all things Joomla! at compassdesigns.net.

When not working, he can frequently be found on the Joomla! community boards, and he has written many free tutorials for using Joomla!. His combination of Joomla! expertise, educational skills, and engaging writing has produced a book accessible to everyone.

Chapter 1

Content Management Systems and an Introduction to Joomla!

In This Chapter

In today's fast-paced world of the Internet, if you have a website that doesn't have rich functionality or fresh content, you will find yourself at a disadvantage to those that do. The idea of powering websites with Content Management Systems (CMS) has been around for some time, but it is only recently, with the advent of high-quality open source CMS scripts like Joomla, that you and I can now use these powerful CMS tools.

In this chapter, I explain in detail the difference between a "traditional" website and one using a CMS. I also provide a look back into the history of Joomla and give an overview of some of its features. Here are some of the topics this chapter covers:

■ What is a Content Management System (CMS), and how is it different from a "normal" website?

■ What is Joomla, and where did it come from?

■ What can Joomla do?

■ What are the basic elements of a Joomla web page?

What Is a Content Management System?

What exactly is a Content Management System? To better understand this, let's briefly look at your common, everyday web page. We will have to talk a little about some of the technology of web pages, but it's worth it to understand the power of a CMS.

To start, let's take a look at the historical development of web pages. Conceptually, there are two aspects to a web page: Its content and the presentation of that content. Over the last decade, there has been an evolution of how these two pieces interact:

- **Static web pages**—The content and presentation are in the same file.
- **Cascading Style Sheet web pages**—Content and presentation are separated.
- **Dynamic web pages**—Content and presentation are separated from the web page itself.

Static Web Pages

A web page is made up of a set of instructions—eXtensible Hypertext Markup Language (XHTML)—that tells your browser how to present the content of a web page. For example, the code might say, "Take this title 'This is a web page,' make it large, and make it bold." The results will look something like Figure 1.1.

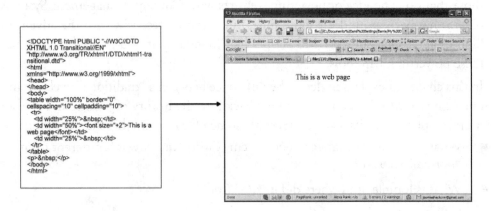

FIGURE 1.1 Results of code on a web page

This way of creating a web page is outdated, but it's astonishing how many designers still create sites using this outdated method. It has two main drawbacks:

- All of the content shown on the page ("This is a web page") and the presentation (big and bold) are tied together. If you want to change the color of all your titles, you have to go through all the pages in your site to do so.
- The pages have large file sizes. Because each bit of content is individually styled, the pages are big, which means it takes forever to load. Most experts agree that this also penalizes your search engine optimization efforts as large pages are harder for search engines to index.

Cascading Style Sheet Web Pages

The next step toward understanding content management is a recent (recent meaning in the last four or five years) development of web standards, a common set of "rules" that a web browser like Internet Explorer or Firefox uses to output a web page onto your screen. One of these standards involves using Cascading Style Sheets (CSS) to control the visual presentation of your web page. CSS is a simple mechanism for adding style (for example, fonts, colors, spacing, and so on) to web documents. All of this presentation information is contained in separate files from the content.

Now the web page generated might look something like Figure 1.2.

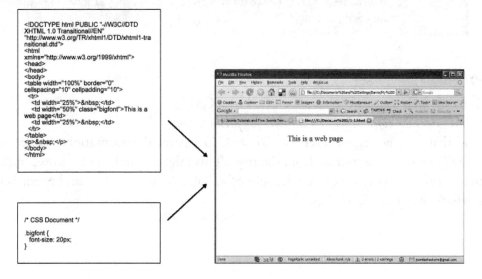

FIGURE 1.2 Modern web page using CSS

Now the file containing the content is much smaller because it does not contain presentation or style information. All the styling has been placed in a separate file that the browser reads and "layers" over the content to produce the final result.

Using CSS to control the presentation of the content has big advantages:

- Maintaining and revising the page is much easier. If you need to change all the title colors, you can just change one line in the CSS file.
- Both files are much smaller, which allows the data to load much more quickly than without using CSS.
- The CSS file has the additional advantage that it will be cached (saved) on a viewer's local computer so that it won't need to be downloaded from the Web each time the viewer visits a page.

> **NOTE**
> An example of this can be seen at www.csszengarden.com. Every page on this classic CSS site has identical content but has different CSS applied to each. You can browse through the designs and see the same content styled in hundreds of different ways.

> **The Least You Need to Know**
> Modern websites separate content from presentation using a technology known as Cascading Style Sheets (CSS).

Dynamic Web Pages

Dynamic web pages are what are created by a CMS.

A CMS does for content what CSS does for presentation.

Read that sentence again carefully. Where CSS separated presentation from content, a CMS separates the content from the page. This might seem like that leaves nothing, but in reality what is left can be thought of as "placeholders." This can be represented as what's shown in Figure 1.3.

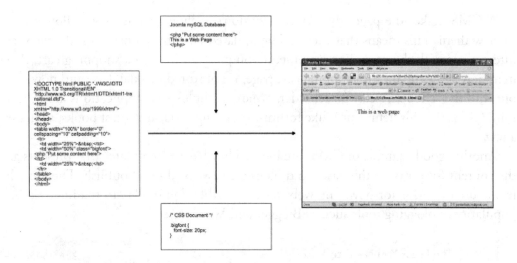

FIGURE 1.3 Structure of a CMS web page

The "put some content here" instruction tells the CMS to take some content from a database, the "pure content," and place it in a designated place on the page.

You might be thinking, "So what's so useful about that trick?" It's actually very powerful.

It separates out the responsibilities of developing a website. The web designer can concern himself with the presentation/design and the "placeholders." This means that non-technical people can be responsible for the content—the words and pictures of a website. Most CMSs have built-in tools to manage the publication of the content.

With this in mind, it's possible to imagine a workflow for content management that involves both designers and content authors (see Figure 1.4).

FIGURE 1.4 The CMS manages content publication

A CMS makes the pages dynamic: They don't really exist until you follow a link to view them. This means that they can be updated/customized based on the viewer's interactions with the page. For example, if you place an item in a shopping cart, that item now shows up on the shopping cart page. It got stored in a database and now gets put into the "shopping cart placeholder." Many complex web applications are in fact mini CMSs (by this definition), like forums, shopping carts, and guest books, to name a few.

Another good example of CMSs are blogs. They have a "template" that presents all the content (or posts, in this case), and blogs are easy to edit and publish. The growth in the use of CMSs for powering websites is probably due in part to the huge rise in popularity of blogging tools such as Blogger and Wordpress.

> **The Least You Need to Know**
> A CMS totally separates the content of the pages from their graphical design. This makes it easy to keep the site-wide design coherent and easy to change. It also makes adding content easy for non-technical people.

The range of available CMSs is extensive—from enterprise scale versions that cost $300,000 to open source versions, such as Joomla, that are free. Modern CMSs are usually defined by their capability to manage and publish content. They typically have workflow processes that start at content creation and move to publishing. Most do far more: They have the capability to add on a wide range of extensions or add-ons to give the site more functionality. From forums to newsletters, Joomla has over 2000 pluggable extensions available, many of which are free and are created by volunteer developers around the world. The official repository is at extensions.joomla.org and a repository specializing in commercial extensions can be found at www.extensionprofessionals.com. Both have a rating and review system (which is itself an extension!).

> **NOTE**
> The Joomla Extensions site and extensionprofessionals.com both have a rating and review system. It's worth being careful with how to use the ratings. The highest rated extensions are shown at the top level of the site. This means that they get more traffic and so tend to get rated more. There are often great extensions that are hidden away in the categories. It's worth taking an hour or two to browse all of them to find ones that might be of use to you.
> The quality of the extensions also varies widely. If you are using the extension on an important site, do the due diligence to check out the developer and visit his/her site.

There is one large drawback to using a CMS. They can be extremely complex, containing thousands of files and scripts that work together in concert with databases to present a website. Normally, this means that a CMS site will be designed and created by technical staff and managed and run by non-technical users. Joomla is probably the easiest to setup among currently available CMSs, allowing users of modest technical skill to harness its power. That's specifically the purpose of this book, to guide a non-technical user step-by-step in learning how to create and manage a website powered by Joomla.

This concept of "hard to set up but easy to grow" can be summed up in Table 1.1.

TABLE 1.1 Comparison of Static Websites and CMSs

Static Website	Content Management System
Easy to create initial web pages.	To create initial pages is time-consuming as a large script must be installed, databases set up, and templates created.
Content is static; changing it requires technical expertise.	Content is dynamic; it can be changed with no technical knowledge.
Difficult to add new functions, often needs custom code.	Most CMSs have many extensions that "plug in" easily.

Content Management Systems have been around for a while, but there is another factor that has contributed to their rise in popularity and ease of use: The growth of the open source software movement.

Open Source

In 1998, Netscape bucked the universal wisdom of how to release code by making its release of its browser, Netscape, freely available to anyone and everyone. This milestone was key in creating a philosophical movement among code developers where software would be created by large communities of developers and released openly to the world.

As the Web has grown explosively, we have seen open source software grow and mature to power the Web. The most significant has been four that are collectively referred to as "LAMP": Linux, Apache, MySQL, and PHP.

- **Linux**—An operating system
- **Apache**—Software to run a web server
- **MySQL**—Powerful database software
- **PHP**—A programming language used to write complex scripts that create interactive functionality with databases

LAMP has allowed developers to create powerful applications using the PHP programming language. One specific area of growth has been the development of CMSs that are written in PHP such asXoops, Post-Nuke, Wordpress, Mambo, Drupal, and Joomla.

> **The Least You Need to Know**
> Joomla is an example of open source software. It's created by a world-wide community of developers and distributed at no charge.

History of Joomla

Joomla is a powerful open source CMS that has grown in popularity since its rebranding from "Mambo" in 2006. Its two key features—ease of administration and flexibility of templating—have led to it being used to power everything from corporate Intranets to school district sites. Rather than try to explain the details, I'll provide a short excerpt from the Joomla website (dev.joomla.org/component/option,com_jd-wp/Itemid,33/p,79/), written by the former Lead Developer, Andrew Eddie, of Joomla:

> Mambo was originally developed by a Melbourne (Australia) based company, called Miro, in 2000.
>
> Miro publicly released its code under the names of Mambo Site Server and later Mambo Open Source at version 3 in April 2001 under the GNU GPL.
>
> In 2004 Linux Format awards Mambo "Best Free Software Project" of the Year and Linux User and Developer names it "Best Linux or Open Source Software." Above all other things, Mambo's template offerings become the most prolific and envy of any of the Content Management Systems of the Day.
>
> 2005 sees more major awards such as "Best Open Source Solution" and "Best of Show—Total Industry Solution" at LinuxWorld Boston and "Best Open Source Solution" at LinuxWorld San Francisco.
>
> Regrettably, in August 2005, a dispute develops involving the fulfillment of decisions within the Mambo Steering Committee. The entire Core Team decides to sever ties with Miro and leave the project. They regroup under the banner of Open Source Matters.

After a serious dust, polish and make-over, Open Source Matters gives birth to Joomla 1.0 in September 2005. Over the coming months, Mambo also reforms its own teams and support structures, abandoning the advanced work on the original version 4.5.3 and opting to continue to support the current stable code-base.

With the passage of time carrying us well into 2006, both Mambo and Joomla continue to win awards, both being heavily based on the original 4.5.2 code-base. At the time of writing, both projects are involved in heavy refactoring efforts of the new Mambo 4.6 and Joomla 1.5.

Mambo today—same name, same base code, different team.

Joomla today—different name, same base code, same team.

Joomla Community

The Joomla community is big, and it's active. The official forum at forum.joomla.org has (as of this writing) over 110,000 members, making it perhaps one of the largest forums on the Web. Along with that, there are many forums on Joomla's international sites. There are also many other third-party forums such as joomlashack.com (90,000 members). Although a crude measure, it's a useful way of seeing how large the community around Joomla might actually be.

A large and active community, measured here by the members of forums is an important factor in the success in an open source project.

Third-party Extensions Development

Joomla is perhaps unique among open source CMSs in the size and nature of the non-official developers that create extensions for it. It's hard to find a Joomla site that doesn't use one of these. The true power of Joomla is the astonishing range of extensions there are.

The nature of these developers is also interesting. There are an unusually high proportion of commercial developers and companies creating professional extensions for Joomla. Although the nature of open source and commercial development might seem unlikely bedfellows, many commentators have pointed to this characteristic of the Joomla project as a significant contributor to its growth.

Joomla's Features

Joomla has a number of "out of the box" features. When you download Joomla from www.joomla.org, you get a zip file of about 5MB that needs to be installed on a web server. Doing this extracts all the files and enters some "filler" content into the database. In no particular order, some of the features with the base installation include

- Simple creation/revision of content using a text editor from main website or hidden admin site
- User registration and ability to restrict viewing of pages based on user level
- Controlling editing and publishing of content based on various admin user levels
- Polls
- Simple contact forms
- Public site statistics
- Private detailed site traffic stats
- Built-in site search functionality
- Email a friend, PDF and print format capability
- RSS (and others) syndication
- Simple content rating system
- Showing newsfeeds from other sites

As you can see, there are tremendous features provided with Joomla. To have a web designer create all of these for a static site would cost tens of thousands of dollars, but it doesn't stop there. Joomla has a massive community of developers worldwide (over 30,000) that have contributed over 2000 extensions for Joomla, most of which are free. Some of the more popular types include

- Forums
- Shopping Carts
- Email Newsletters
- Calendars
- Document Managers
- Galleries
- Forms
- Directories

Each of these extensions you can install into Joomla to extend its functionality in some manner. Part of the popularity of Joomla has been the availability of a huge and diverse range of these extensions.

To customize your site even more, you can easily find highly specialized extensions for your needs:

- Recipe managers
- Help/support desk management
- Fishing tournament tracking
- AdSense placement
- Multiple site management
- Hotel room bookings

You get the idea!

> **The Least You Need to Know**
> Joomla has rich functionality in its default package. It can be further extended to almost any niche application through the availability of GPL and low cost commercial extensions.

Appendix B, "Joomla Case Studies," presents five case studies of a variety of websites that are powered by Joomla.

Elements of a Joomla Website

A Joomla website has several elements that all work together to produce a web page. The main three elements are content, modules, and the template. The content is the core aspect of the website, the template controls how the website is presented, and the modules add functionality around the edges.

Think of these three elements—content, modules, and templates—as three legs holding up a stool. Without one of these three key elements, the page (the stool) would topple.

In Figure 1.5, we can see the page of www.compassdesigns.net, a popular blog site about Joomla (OK, I'll admit, it's mine—a shameless plug!).

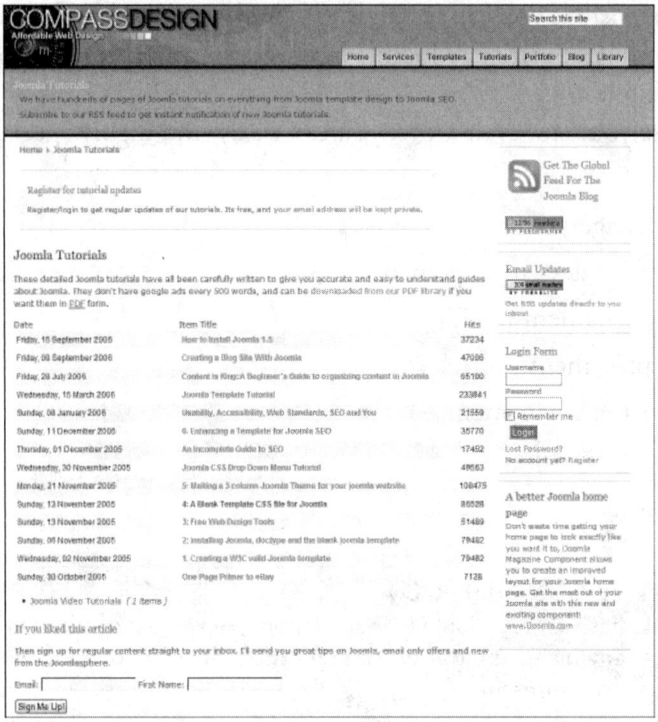

FIGURE 1.5 A Joomla website, www.compassdesigns.net

Figure 1.6 highlights two of the three elements of a Joomla page. The third, the template, is evident by the color, graphics, layout, and font (those being part of the template).

On this Joomla web page the content is a large column with a list of links to Joomla tutorials. Various modules are shown in the right-side column and at the top and bottom.

FIGURE 1.6 The elements of a Joomla web page

Content

The most important part of a website is the content; you have probably heard the phrase, "Content is King." Joomla, as a CMS, helps you efficiently create, publish, and manage your content. When I am talking about content here, I am talking about the meat and potatoes of your web page—the important stuff in the middle of the page that the viewer is looking at.

Joomla actually has a specific name for this core of the page; it calls it the main body of the page. This is usually the biggest column and is placed in the middle.

The content in the main body is generated from a component. The biggest and most important component in Joomla is the one that handles all your articles, the individual content items in the site. In fact, it's so important that often you will find these referred to as Content Articles. In the default Joomla installation there are also a few other components that will generate content in the main body, such as weblinks and contacts.

Many third-party components exist and will generate content in the main body. Examples include forums and shopping carts.

> **The Least You Need to Know**
> The main body of a Joomla web page loads content from components. The most important component is the one that manages all the articles.

Modules

Modules are smaller functional blocks that usually are shown around the main part of the page, like a poll/survey, login form, or a newsflash.

In the example in Figure 1.6, there are modules at the top: a search and a menu. In the right column is an RSS feed module and then a login form and a newsflash. At the bottom there's a signup form for an email newsletter.

Components and modules are usually both referred to as extensions because they extend the functionality of your site.

Templates

A *template* is simply a set of rules about presentation. For example, a template determines how many columns to use or what color to make titles. A template also determines the layout or positioning of the web page.

> **NOTE**
> You will find that templates are usually referred to as another type of extension, along with components and modules. Here I have separated templates from their brethren because I think the template forms a separate and distinct element of a Joomla page. The concept of the template is shown in Figure 1.7. Here you can see the raw content from the database that is presented through the template to the final viewed web page.

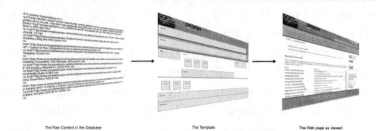

The Raw Content in the Database   The Template   The Web page as viewed

FIGURE 1.7 How a web page is built from the CMS database

> **The Least You Need To Know**
> A Joomla site is made up of content (articles or components), modules, and a template. The template acts as a filter (or lens). It controls all the presentation aspects of the web pages. It does not have any content, but it can include logos.

Summary

Joomla is a great low cost content management system that has the capability to power sophisticated websites. In this chapter we looked at the nature of a CMS, where Joomla came from, what it can do, and what makes up a Joomla web page.

- Modern websites separate content from presentation using a technology known as Cascading Style Sheets (CSS).

- A CMS totally separates the content of the pages from their graphical design. This makes it easy to keep the site-wide design coherent and easy to change. It also makes adding content easy for non-technical people.

- Joomla is an example of open source software. It's created by a world-wide community of developers and distributed at no charge.

- Joomla has rich functionality in its default package. It can be further extended to almost any niche application through the availability of GPL and low cost commercial extensions from extensions.joomla.org and www.extensionprofessionals.com.

- The main body of a Joomla web page loads content from components. The most important component is the one that manages all the articles.

- A Joomla site is made up of content (articles or components), modules, and a template. The template acts as a filter (or lens). It controls all the presentation aspects of the web pages. It does not have any content, but it can include logos.

Chapter 2

Downloading and Installing Joomla!

In This Chapter

Joomla is one of the most popular open source Content Management Systems (CMS) on the planet. The first step in becoming part of the "Joomlasphere," the vibrant community that exists around the Joomla Project, is to download Joomla and install it on your web server.

This chapter shows you how to get a Joomla-powered site up and running. The two steps are to find and download the latest files and to install them on a web server. This chapter describes both a local installation (your home computer) to use as you read this book (if you don't have a hosting account or have a slow Internet connection) and real web server installations. The topics covered in this chapter are

- How do I install Joomla?

- Where can I find the most current Joomla files?

- How do I unpack the Joomla files on my desktop computer?

- How do I unpack the Joomla files on a hosting account?

- How do I use the Joomla Installation Wizard?

- How can I support the Joomla Project?

17

How Do I Install Joomla?

The process of installing Joomla involves three steps:

1. Obtain the latest Joomla file package.
2. Unpack the package on a server.
3. Use a browser-based wizard to complete installation.

We will look at each of these in turn. There are two alternative paths you can take for step 2, either to unpack the Joomla file package on a remote hosting account or to create a web server that actually runs on your desktop/laptop computer. This second technique is a useful way to try out Joomla in creating a site and then transferring it to a hosting account.

Where Can I Find the Most Current Joomla Files?

The home of the Joomla Project is www.joomla.org. This is the website that acts as a focal point for the community of users and developers that are part of the "Joomlasphere."

The Joomla site is actually a collection of separate sections and sites for different aspects of the project—with one exception: They are all powered by Joomla.

- **www.joomla.org**—The main Joomla site and news. This lists the official news blog for Joomla. You can subscribe to news via RSS by clicking the link in the left-hand column.

- **help.joomla.org**—Documentation and help for Joomla. This section is full of guides, help screens, and FAQs to help you get up and running with your Joomla site. Also found here is the official Joomla manual, currently version 1.0.11.

- **forum.joomla.org**—At over 120,000 members at the time of this writing, the official Joomla Forum is one of the biggest forums on the Web. You can get help from the active Joomla community, whether it's for templates, translations, components, or just a general help question. When you are asking for help, remember that the forum is all volunteer, so provide as much detail on your problem as you can and be respectful.

- **extensions.joomla.org**—The Joomla extensions directory, packed with over 2,000 third-party extensions. Split into components, modules, and plugins, this is the place to come to extend the functionality of your Joomla website. It even includes useful reviews and rating tools so you can see what other people think of a particular extension.
- **shop.joomla.org**—Get your Joomla T-shirt here!
- **dev.joomla.org**—For developers, this is where you can find documentation on the Joomla API, blogs for the various developers of the core team, and various wikis and tutorials.

The last site is one that doesn't run on Joomla, but it's the one we are interested in right now. It's called *the forge* and is located at www.joomlacode.org. It serves as the code repository both for the main Joomla files and the hundreds of GPL third-party extensions.

As I am writing this book, the next generation of Joomla, the version known as 1.5, is still in a version known as a *Release Candidate*. This means that feature development has been frozen, and bugs are being fixed that were found in Beta ready for a stable release. Hopefully by the time you are reading this book, it will be a stable release. With that in mind, be aware that the following description of how to download the Joomla files is sure to change, but I'll try and explain the general concept of how the forge works so you should be able to find the files you need.

On the home page of Joomla, there will be some buttons that link directly to the forge files. Right now they look like Figure 2.1.

FIGURE 2.1 The download buttons on the www.joomla.org home page

When you click the button to download 1.5 RC 1, you are sent to the forge at joomlacode.org. We have actually drilled down a few levels into the site, and the files we need to download are shown in Figure 2.2.

FIGURE 2.2 Joomla 1.5 files

Here we see several different compression types/formats of the same file: zip, gz, and bz2. I usually download the zip file; it's slightly bigger but more universal. Just click the one you want and you'll get a dialog box asking you to save the file on your computer.

Before we move on, let's take a quick look at how the files are structured in the older version of Joomla, 1.0.12. It's more than likely that 1.5 will follow a similar format. If we click the button to download 1.0.12, we get a slightly different choice, as shown in Figure 2.3.

FIGURE 2.3 Structure of different file packages for Joomla

The bottom part of the screen shot has been cut off, the general idea is what we need.

You will see that halfway down are the files for the full package for this version; here it's called Joomla 1.0.12-Stable-Full_Package.zip. There are the same three compression options as for 1.5. There are also many packages that are updates based on what version you currently have installed.

The naming convention for Joomla versioning is "A.B.C," which represent the following elements:

- **A = Major release number**—Currently all versions of Joomla begin with "1" (1.X.X).
- **B = Minor release number**—This book is based on Joomla 1.5, as opposed to the previous version 1.0.
- **C = Maintenance release number**—Currently the 1.0 series is up to 1.0.13, so there have been 13 maintenance releases. We can expect 1.5 to follow a similar pattern starting at 1.5.0 for the stable release.

The Least You Need to Know

The core Joomla files are available for free at www.joomlacode.org. There are links directly to the files on the home page of www.joomla.org. When downloading them, make sure you are getting the correct version, either the full package or an update.

NOTE

Important: You cannot upgrade from Joomla 1.0 to Joomla 1.5. There are significant enough changes in the code that simply over writing files would break your site. The development team has carefully chosen to talk about migration (http://dev. joomla.org/component/option,com_jd-wp/Itemid,33/p,107/):

"Joomla 1.5 does not provide an upgrade path from earlier versions. Converting an older site to a Joomla 1.5 site requires creation of a new empty site using Joomla 1.5 and then populating the new site with the content from the old site. This migration of content is not a one-to-one process and involves conversions and modifications to the content dump."

This has been a deliberate choice to minimize the number of users who might attempt the "overwrite the files" technique. More can be found in the forum (David Gal, http:// forum.joomla.org/index.php/topic,63232.0.html):

"Joomla 1.5 is so significantly changed from 1.0 that there is no 'upgrade' path. This is the reason we are providing a migration path. The concept is to build a new site and to migrate data from the old site. Extensions need to be installed and configured as if the site is new. The core data migration does reconstruct menu items for core elements and also keeps core module records with configuration settings."

The development team is very aware of the migration needs of Joomla. By the time you are reading this, there will be a developed process for it.

So now that we have a compressed Joomla file package of several megabytes, what do we do with it?

> **NOTE**
> **Important**: Before you begin installing Joomla, you will need to have a MySQL database ready for Joomla to use.
>
> If you are installing locally (on your desktop) with WAMP5, it will have the permissions to create a database as you go through these steps.
>
> If you are installing on a web host, you will need to pre-create an SQL database. Make sure you note the username, password, and database name. The most common way to set up a database will be through some sort of button/link in your hosting admin panel. Look for something that talks about MySQL databases.

Unpacking Joomla on a Local Desktop Computer

If I unzip the Joomla file package I now have and try to run/open the main index.php file, it will open in some sort of editor by which you can see all the code. There will be no website. This is because Joomla is an example of client-server software.

Joomla is not a self-contained program, like Microsoft Word or Firefox. With these sorts of programs, you simply install them onto your computer by running an installation file. Joomla is very different by comparison.

Joomla is a complex series of Hypertext Preprocessor (PHP)[1] scripts that run on a web server. When you browse a Joomla site, these scripts are generated on the fly and create what you see on the pages of the site. The key term here is *web server*. This is an example of client-server scripting. The software is actually running on a different computer (the server), and you are interacting with it from a client (your web browser).

Thus you cannot download Joomla and try to run it on your computer like an EXE file. It has to have a server, which means you need to have a hosting account.

Now, before you shell out your hard-earned money for a hosting account, there is something else you can do first. You can actually run a web server on your local computer, in other words, your desktop or laptop. This is known as having a *localhost*. It may sound like I just contradicted myself from the previous paragraph but not quite. You can't "run" Joomla itself on your own computer, but you can install a localhost web server for it to "run on." In this scenario, your computer is acting as both the server and the client. One advantage is that your website will load very fast because it's coming from your own computer. One disadvantage is that you will have to move or "port" the site to a real web host later. It's still a great way to learn about Joomla before starting to develop your site.

> **The Least You Need to Know**
> Joomla needs a (web) server to run on. A good way to learn Joomla is to run a web server on your own computer, know as using a localhost. This makes the "website" blazingly fast.

To set up your localhost, you need some software that runs Apache, PHP, and MySQL on your computer. These are the component scripts of a remote web server on a hosting account. There are two popular packages that include all of these scripts, and both are free:

- **WAMP5**—(www.wampserver.com/en/index.php) for Windows
- **XAMPP**—(www.apachefriends.org/en/xampp.html) for Windows, Mac OS X, and Linux

I am going to quickly run through setting up WAMP5. Note that this package is Windows-specific. If you get stuck with this part of the process, you can refer to Appendix D, "Installing WAMP5," for how to install Wampserver.

1. Download WAMP5 from www.wampserver.com/en and then install it. It will create a folder called c:\wamp\www.

2. Extract/unpack the Joomla package you downloaded into a folder inside \www\. It doesn't matter what it is called. For example, c:\wamp\www\Joomla would work. Make sure that you don't unpack it in such a way that you end up with two folders, for example, c:\wamp\www\Joomla\Joomla-1.5-RC1.

3. Run WAMP5. You should get a handy icon in your system tray (the icons at the bottom right of a window's desktop), which will look similar to Figure 2.4. The figure shows three possible versions of the icon.

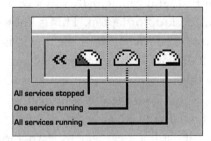

FIGURE 2.4 Wampserver icons in system tray (Windows)

4. You need the dial to be white to continue.

5. Now open a browser and go to http://localhost (no "www"), or you can left-click the icon and select localhost. You should see a page that looks like Figure 2.5.

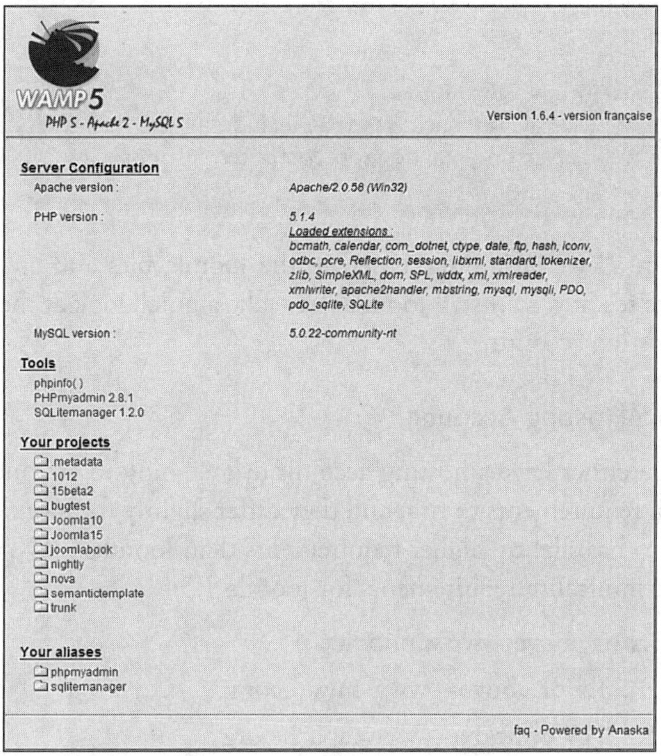

FIGURE 2.5 Browser view of Wampserver http://localhost

If you are not seeing this page, then you should stop and figure out why. You have to get this page before you can proceed. The WAMP5 site has some helpful troubleshooting FAQs and a forum. You should see your folder called "Joomla" in the list of Your Projects. Click that folder, and you will get taken to that website running locally on your computer.

NOTE

At some point, you will probably want to transfer your Joomla installation from your local computer to a host. Some guides on how to do this can be found on the Joomla forums: http://forum.joomla.org/index.php/topic,5556.0.html and http://forum.joomla.org/index.php/topic,5703.0.html.

The Least You Need to Know

There are several free packages that include all the files and scripts needed to run a web server on your desktop computer. Wampserver (WAMP5) is one for Windows.

At this point, all we have done is set up the Joomla files and are ready to install them. Before we see how to install Joomla, let's take a quick look at the upload process if you have a hosting account.

Unpacking on a Hosting Account

Let's assume you either have a hosting account or are going to get one. Joomla needs some minimum requirements to run, and they differ slightly for Joomla's different versions. Joomla 1.5 has slightly higher requirements than Joomla 1.0.X.

Here are the minimum requirements for Joomla 1.5:

- **PHP 4.3.x or above**—www.php.net
- **MySQL 3.23.x or above**—www.mysql.com
- **Apache 1.13.19 or above**—www.apache.org

You must ensure that you have MySQL, XML and Zlib support built into your PHP. For assistance in making sure you have the proper support, refer to the Joomla Help Forums (specifically, http://help.joomla.org/content/view/34/132/).

For Joomla 1.5, it's recommended you have PHP 4.4.3 or above (for enhanced security).

A thread on the Joomla forums lists various hosting companies who are active Joomla community members. The list can be found at http://forum.joomla.org/index.php/topic,6856.0.html.

Once you have a host that meets the requirements, you will need to upload the main Joomla files. There are two ways to do this:

- You can upload the entire zip file and then extract them on the server with a shell command or Cpanel file manager.
- You can extract the contents of the zip file onto your desktop and then upload them individually via FTP.

If you have Cpanel with your hosting company, the first method is perhaps the fastest way to do this, and almost all hosting companies provide it. Use this file manager to upload the zip file to public_html (or whatever you have on your host). You can then use it to extract the files. Just click the name of the file, and the option to extract will appear to the right as shown in Figure 2.6.

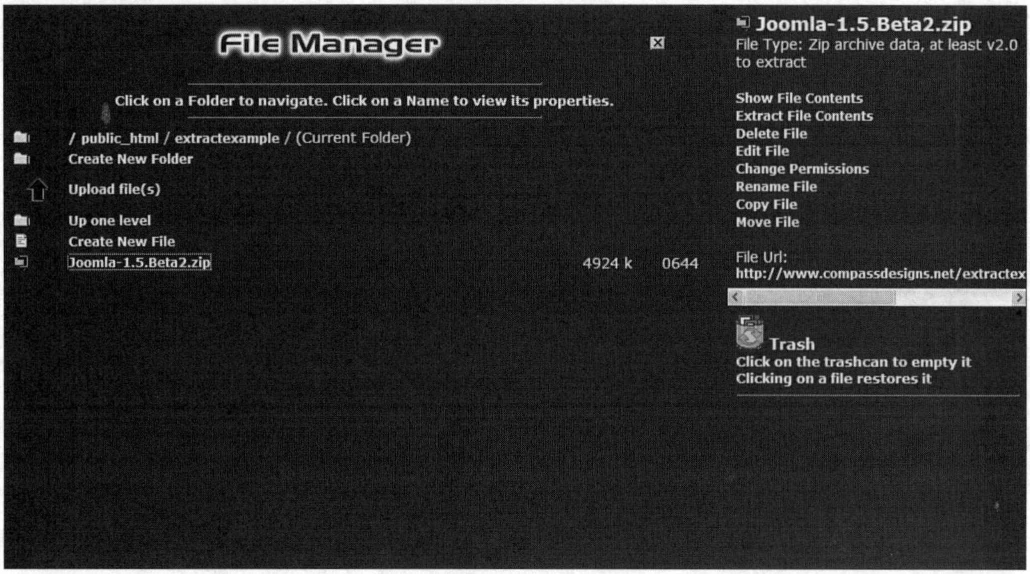

FIGURE 2.6 Extracting a file in Cpanel's file manager

Many web hosts will have a tool called Fantastico, which allows the instant creation of a Joomla website along with all the databases needed. I actually don't recommend using Fantastico. Although it makes the process easier, many hosts don't always have the most current file releases.

> **The Least You Need to Know**
> To install Joomla on a web host, your account will need to meet some minimum requirements. Make sure your host does; otherwise, it will cause problems later.

Running the Joomla Installation Wizard

If you have gotten this far, it means you have unzipped the Joomla package to either a remote web host or your local computer. Now for the fun stuff—actually installing Joomla.

This installation process is done via a browser and consists of several steps that set up and configure your Joomla site.

Step 1: Choose the Language

Using your browser of choice (mine is Firefox), navigate to the location of all the Joomla files. In my case, on a localhost, it is http://localhost/Joomla. You will see the first installation screen (see Figure 2.7).

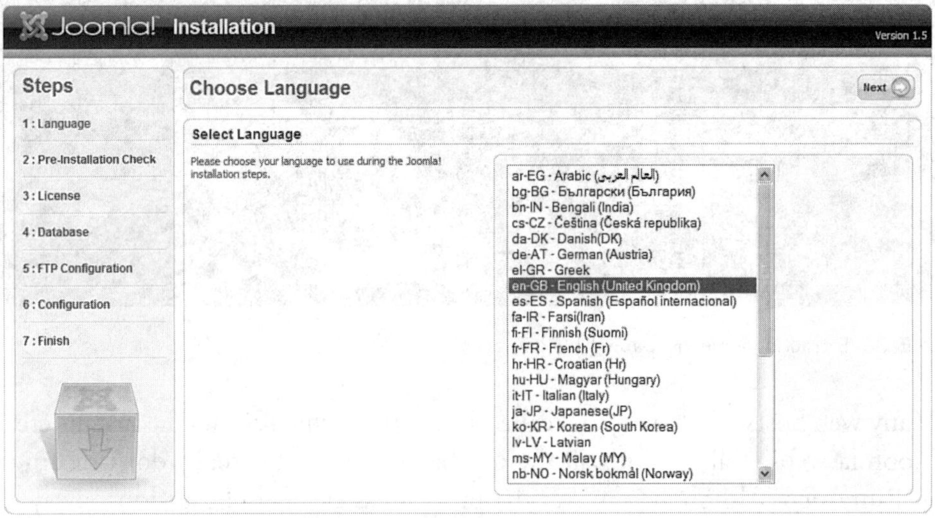

FIGURE 2.7 The Choose Language screen

Step 2: Pre-Installation Check

Figure 2.7 shows the first look at some of the internationalization features of Joomla 1.5. You can select among many languages for the installation instructions. After you have selected your language, the next screen you are presented with is the Pre-installation Check screen (see Figure 2.8).

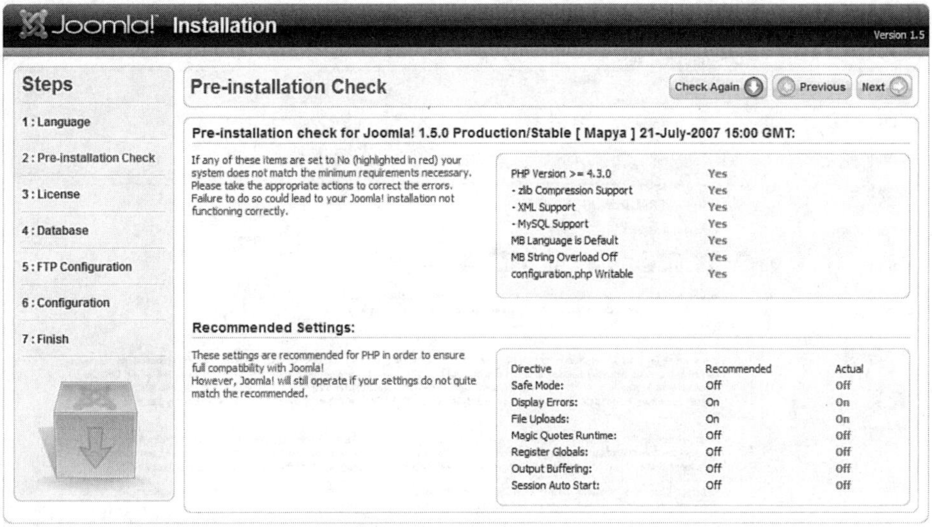

FIGURE 2.8 Pre-installation Check screen

A critical part in the installation process, this screen checks to see if all the minimum system requirements are met.

The first set are required minimums for installation. If they are red (not met), then you need to find a new environment (change hosts) or talk your hosting provider into changing their environment (upgrading PHP for example). Note that the last item, whether configuration.php is writeable, is a permissions issue on a file that is much easier to rectify. You can usually change permissions through the Cpanel provided by your host. This is a tool that is standard with almost all hosting companies.

The second set is recommended settings. If you don't meet them, you can still install Joomla, but you might experience problems with functionality and security.

Step 3: License

When all items are green, you are ready to proceed. Click Next, which will bring you to the License screen (see Figure 2.9).

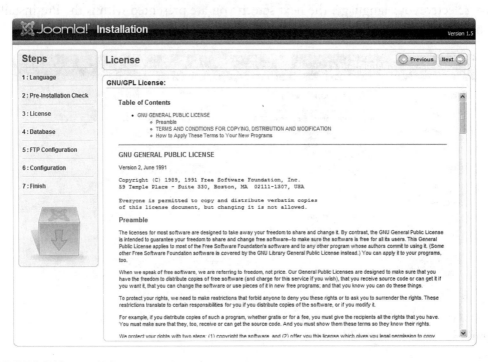

FIGURE 2.9 License screen

Joomla is released under a GNU/GPL license. One of the most common questions regarding this license is, "Can I remove the footer link that says Powered by Joomla." It's actually perfectly OK to do this; you just have to keep the copyright statement in the source code. However, I would recommend that you keep the link.

Why? Because Joomla is an open source project and is not sold, its development receives no funding. The bottom line is that hundreds of programmers around the world are developing this software that you are using right now. If you had to pay for that coding, it would cost over $2 million (www.ohloh.net/projects/20), but you get it for free. In return, keep the link; it will help the project gain in popularity and grow. Don't hide the fact that you are using Joomla—be proud of it! Don't be concerned about any kind of Search Engine Optimization (SEO) dilution with an extra link off your page. Links to authoritative sites actually help your SEO!

Joomla is a powerful piece of software. If you are using it for your website, take the time to make a donation, no matter how small. You can make a donation online at www.joomla.org/content/view/689/79/.

Step 4: Database Configuration

The next screen is Database Configuration (see Figure 2.10).

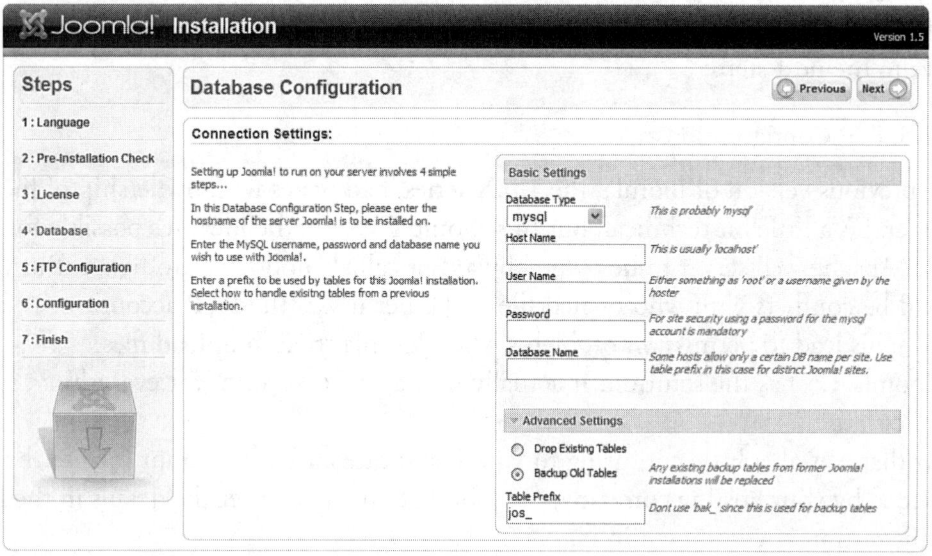

FIGURE 2.10 Database Configuration screen

The Database Configuration screen is one of the main pages of the installation process; it's where you need to enter important information about the database that your Joomla site will use. Note you will see a drop-down for the database type. Joomla 1.5 only really runs on SQL, but some of the foundation has been laid to use more types, for example Oracle, in the next release, 2.0.

The hostname will almost always be "localhost." The username and password are provided by your hosting company, usually in an email you got when you created the account.

If you are installing on a localhost using WAMP5 or XAMPP, the username is usually "root," and the password is nothing/blank.

Pick a database name for the SQL database that Joomla will use. Use some sort of name that is not confusing because other scripts use SQL databases, and before you know it, you might have several on your server and will need to tell them apart. Don't use spaces in the name.

If you are running several Joomla sites but only have access to one database, you will need to use table prefixes to distinguish them, which you need to enter in the advanced settings.

If you have an existing site and are reinstalling over the top of it, you need to select Drop Existing Tables. If you need to keep a backup of them, select Backup Old Tables. Using "jos" as a table prefix is conventional unless you have multiple sites in the same database.

If all was successful, when you click Next you will populate the SQL database and move to the next step.

Step 5: FTP Configuration

The previous version of Joomla, the 1.0.X series, had issues with ownership of files on a server. It's a little bit technical, but this should give you the idea: It's possible for files on an Apache web server to be owned by a user called "nobody." Go figure. But there would be conflicts with who owned files, whether it was the FTP account or Apache itself. This lead to permission problems when Joomla tried to upload files.

Joomla 1.5 has the solution: It actually uses an FTP account for everything, so no conflicts arise.

If that was all a little confusing to you, just create an FTP account (or use the one provided by your hosting company) for Joomla to use and enter the details in the FTP Configuration screen shown in Figure 2.11.

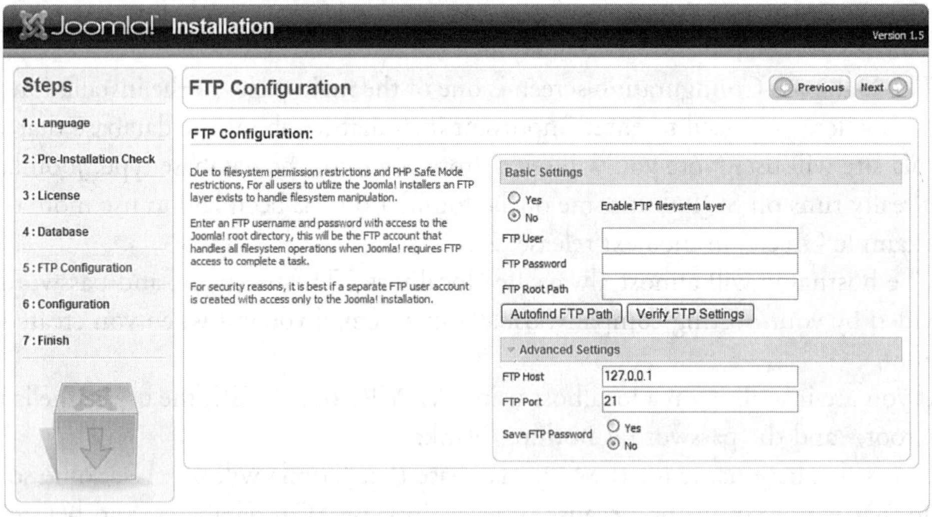

FIGURE 2.11 The FTP Configuration screen

Step 6: Main Configuration

The Main Configuration page is where you enter some information about your new site and determine how you will insert content into your site (see Figure 2.12).

Give your site a name (pay attention to SEO keywords) and then enter the super administration information. The first user in the site will use this information and will automatically get super administrator status. Note that if you don't change the password, it will use the one shown on the left. **Make sure you write it down!** Feel free to eat the sticky note you wrote it on once you have committed it to memory, but if you forget it immediately (which I have done) you will need to reinstall.

When it comes to the content of your sparklingly new site, you have three choices:

- **Install default sample data**—This installs the default Joomla content that you have probably seen all over the Web with "Welcome to Joomla." Note that it also includes all the menus, navigation links, and sections/categories. If you are learning how to use Joomla, this is highly recommended. It's easier to adapt and revise than to start from scratch. **If you don't click the Install Sample Data button, you'll be starting out with a blank site!**

- **Load local Joomla 1.5 SQL script**—This is an SQL file that might have a customized set of content.

- **Load migration script**—This is a special function that is part of a process to migrate a Joomla site running on 1.0 to 1.5 and requires a special component to do so.

> **The Least You Need to Know**
> If you are new to Joomla, you should install the sample data. But realize its only a suggestion of how you can organize content.

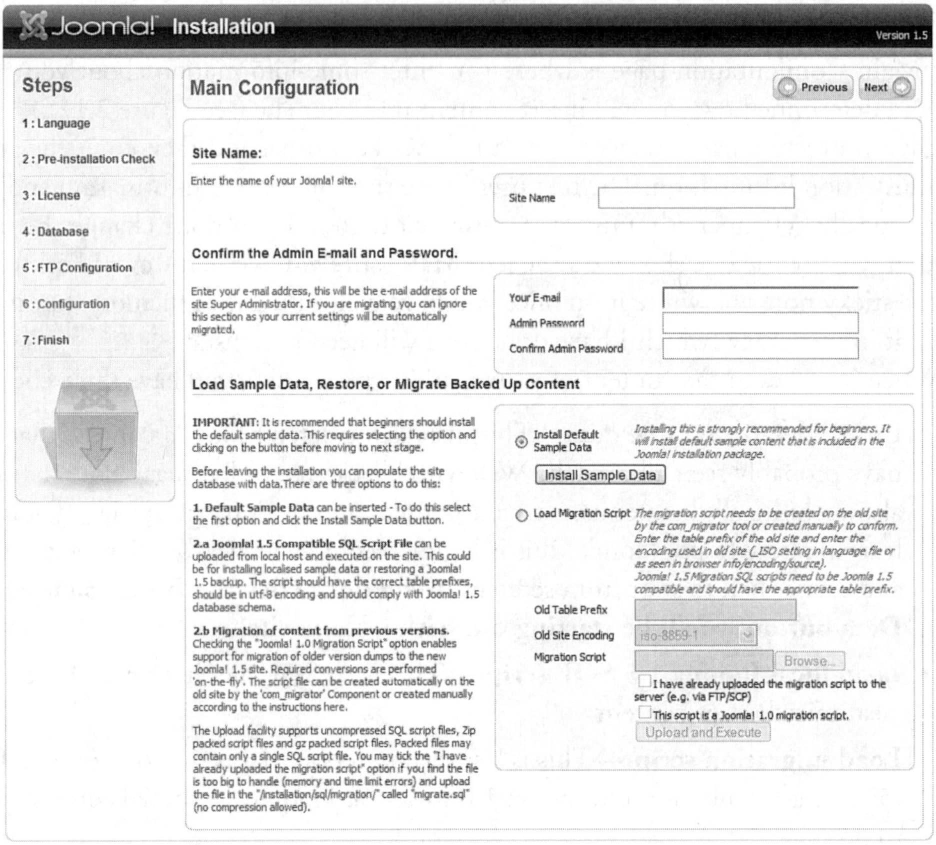

FIGURE 2.12 Main Configuration screen

Step 7: Finish

Cross your eyes, close your fingers, and click Next. Hopefully you will see the screen shown in Figure 2.13. You now have a website "Powered by Joomla."

If you do get this result, you can investigate different language options, view the site, or jump right to the administration of your site.

> **NOTE**
> **Important**: Make sure you remove the installation directory as directed on the Finish page.

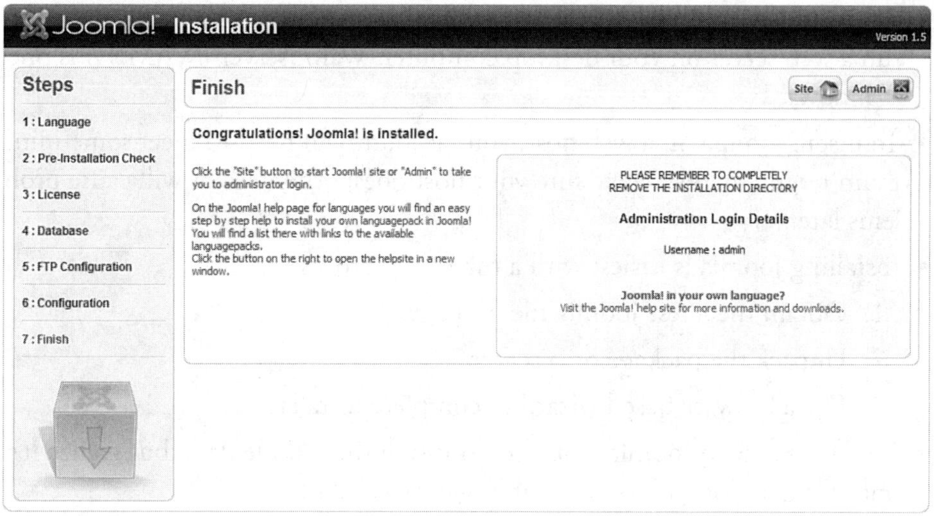

FIGURE 2.13 Finish!

If you don't get this page, then you have some work to do. Often issues arise because of server environments. If the solution is not obvious, a useful step is to copy the error message or the main part of it and then search for it on the Joomla help forums, forum.joomla.org, and Google it. Chances are that someone else has already run into this error and has posted the solution online. (*Useful trick:* Include the message in double quotations in the search box so you search for the exact phrase.)

Summary

Installing Joomla is perhaps the biggest hurdle to getting starting on your website. You'll need to create a MySQL database for Joomla and upload all of the files to a server. After these two steps are complete, it's relatively easy to use the Joomla Installation Wizard that runs in a browser.

- The core Joomla files are available for free at www.joomlacode.org. There are links directly to the files on the home page of www.joomla.org. When downloading them, make sure you are getting the correct version, either the full package or an update.

- Joomla needs a (web) server to run on. A good way to learn Joomla is to run a web server on your own computer, known as using a localhost. This makes the "website" blazingly fast.

- There are several free packages that include all the files and scripts needed to run a web server on your desktop computer. Wampserver (WAMP5) is one for Windows.

- To install Joomla on a web host, your account will need to meet some minimum requirements. Make sure your host does; otherwise, it will cause problems later.

- Installing Joomla is easiest with a three-step process:

  1. Obtain the latest Joomla file package.

  2. Unpack the package on a server.

  3. Use a browser-based wizard to complete installation.

- If you are new to Joomla, you should install the sample data, but realize it's only a suggestion of how you can organize content.

---

[1]Yes, the acronym doesn't quite match the words. It used to stand for Personal Home Page. PHP is principally a programming language for web pages/servers.

Chapter 3

Joomla! Administration Basics

The term *site administration* usually means the day to day tasks of adding content, managing users, and making sure installed components and modules are running correctly. With a properly configured Joomla site, the administration burden is relatively low, and most of the effort can be dedicated to generating that all-important content.

In This Chapter

In this chapter we go on a whirlwind tour of the core administrative functions you'll need. I don't go step by step, explaining every last button in the admin backend, but rather pick out key functions, tips, and tricks that you'll need to know to keep your site humming. I highly recommend getting the official user manual from joomla.org, which does have that wide level of detail.

- What is the difference between the frontend and the backend of a Joomla-powered website?

- What are the main administrator menu functions?

- What types of users are there, and how do they relate to the frontend and backend?

What Is the Frontend and Backend of a Joomla-powered Website?

After you install Joomla, you actually have two sites:

- The public site (commonly called the *frontend*) that people view at www.yoursite.com
- The administration site (commonly called the *backend*) whose URL is www.yoursite.com/administrator

While some administration is possible via the frontend of the site, it's most efficient to manage your site through the backend.

The Least You Need To Know

A Joomla website consists of two sites: the public frontend and a private administrative backend.

When you browse to the backend, you are greeted by a login prompt (see Figure 3.1).

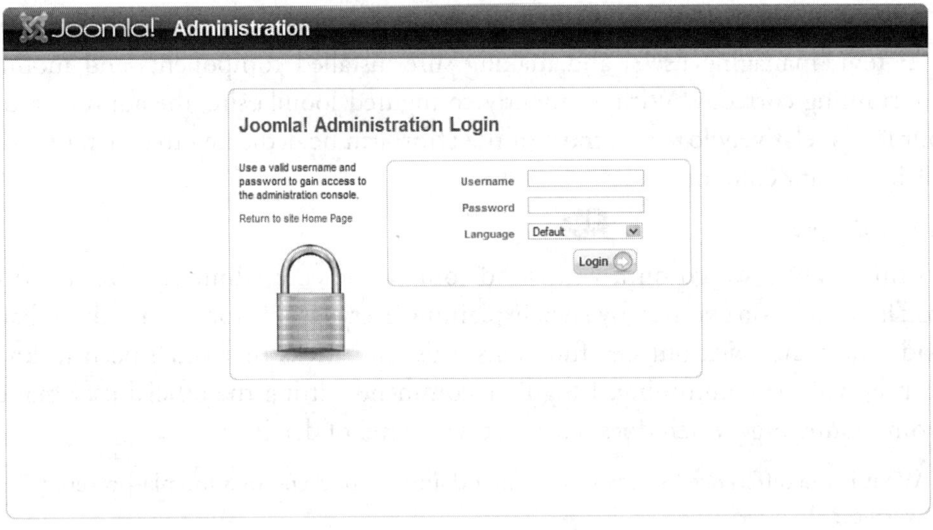

X Joomla! Administration

Joomla! Administration Login

Use a valid username and
password to gain access to
the administration console.

Return to site Home Page

Username	
Password	
Language	Default

Login

FIGURE 3.1 Backend login screen

To get any further, you'll need an administrative password. I hope you remembered it!

I know you never will, but should you ever lose your administrative password, there is a post about how to recover it on the forums: forum.joomla.org/index.php/topic,10985.0.html.

When you installed Joomla, on the final screen, you were asked for an admin password. That is the first account created, and it is given an Access Control Level (ACL) group of Super Administrator. The username is "admin," and the password will be whatever you entered.

Assuming you log in with a super administrator account, you'll be presented with the administrative backend of your site. It looks slightly different based on what level of administrator you are.

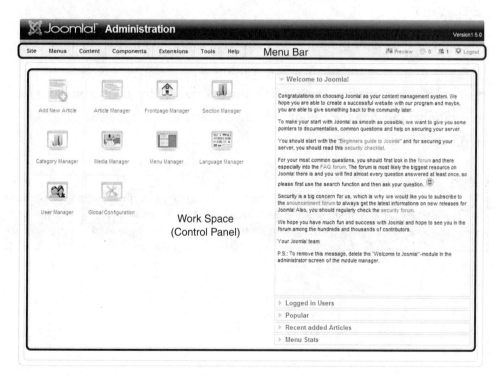

FIGURE 3.2 Initial Administrative view

At the top of the page is a *Menu Bar*, immediately under that is a *Toolbar* (in Figure 3.2 it is not visible), and then the large area is the *Workspace*. The initial page when you first log in to the backend is called the *Control Panel*.

Menu Bar

The Menu Bar is the main navigation for the admin backend. The horizontal menu accesses all the functions of administration:

- Site
- Menus
- Content
- Components
- Extensions
- Tools
- Help

On the right of the Menu Bar are some additional information and functions:

- A link to preview the site in a new window
- A link to your private messages (the number shows how many you have)
- A number showing the amount of viewers currently on the site
- A button/link to logout

> **NOTE**
> If you are logged in as an administrator or manager (as opposed to a super administrator), fewer menu options are available. The different levels of administrator access are discussed later in this chapter when we look at the User Manager.

Toolbar

Immediately under the Menu Bar is the Toolbar. It's collapsed in the initial Control Panel view, but it appears when you navigate to a particular function, like the Article Manager, as you will see in the rest of this chapter's screenshots.

The Toolbar displays various context-sensitive icon buttons for that function. For example in Figure 3.3, we can see the toolbar from the Article Manager.

FIGURE 3.3 Toolbar from Article Manager

While on the Article Manager screen, we have the options of Unarchive, Archive, Publish, Unpublish, Move, Copy, Trash, Edit, New, Preferences, and Help.

In Figure 3.4 we can compare this to the Toolbar that is shown in the Menu Manager. Here we have only Copy, Delete, Edit, New, and Help.

FIGURE 3.4 Toolbar shown in Menu Manager

> **NOTE**
> Although the icon buttons displayed are different for each function, the actual button itself always does the same thing. For example, the publish button will also do the same thing in whatever manager screen you are on.

Workspace

The main body of the admin page is the Workspace, not to be confused with the Control Panel, which is the first view you get after you log in. You will see several different themes of how this is structured. One common format is a basic table, usually used for various managers, articles, menus, and so on.

> **⊃ CAUTION**
> There is no current set of layout standards for third-party extensions. The creator of an extension is free to make his administrative interface look however he likes. This can sometimes lead to inconsistency, though, and most developers usually take the lead from the core Joomla for their design.

> **The Least You Need To Know**
> The Workspace is the main tool in administering a Joomla site. Different parts of it are visible to different administrators. Third-party extensions will often have Workspaces that are organized differently than the core Joomla functions.

Let's quickly take an overview of all the functions in the backend. Rather than regurgitate the information already available at help.joomla.org, I'll only pause to point out things that are worth noting or cautions I think you should know.

Administrator Functions in the Menu Bar

As just described, the Menu Bar contains all the functions involved in controlling and managing your Joomla website. I'll try to make this book useful by adding to the basic information available in the Joomla documentation. I'll briefly touch on each one in turn, pointing out important roles of each.

> **The Least You Need To Know**
> The best place to go for information about the specific functions of all menus and buttons is help.joomla.org. It's much more accurate and up-to-date than a book can be!

Site Submenu

The Site Menu contains several functions that are site-wide, including the very important Configuration screen. Figure 3.5 shows the submenus in the Site Menu.

FIGURE 3.5 Site submenu

Control Panel

The Control Panel is displayed when you first log in to the backend. It has icon buttons on the left to access common functions and a series of lists on the right that are Ajax-powered (the cool-looking thing where stuff slides out when you click it).

What is visible in the Control Panel (and in the Menu Bar) depends on what type of admin user you are when you log in.

There are three administrator levels:

- Super administrator (highest permissions)
- Administrator (medium permissions)
- Manager (lowest permissions)

Each administrator level sees slightly different options in the backend. For example, a manager, with the lowest levels of permission, cannot see or have access to the Configuration.

The super administrator view was shown in Figure 3.2. The manager (top) and administrator (bottom) views are shown in Figure 3.6.

FIGURE 3.6 Administrator and manager differences

The Administrator view does not have global site-wide functions such as configuration. The Manager view does not have extensions or tools. In both cases the number of accessible functions is less than what's available in super administrator view.

> **The Least You Need to Know**
> Depending on which level of Administrator you log in to on the backend with, you see different options in the functions you can perform.

> The navigation of the backend depends on JavaScript. You must have it enabled to use the site fully. Some software such as Norton Internet Security has also been known to cause problems such as menus not expanding properly.

User Manager and Access Control Levels

Access Control Levels (ACL) is the grand sounding name given to assigning different functions to different user types. Joomla has nine user levels. You assign these different ACL roles to users through the User Manager in the Site Menu. A list of user types and ACLs can be found in Table 3.1.

Selecting the User Manager will bring up a table with all the users that have an ACL of registered or higher, including administrators. An example site with just a few users is shown in Figure 3.7.

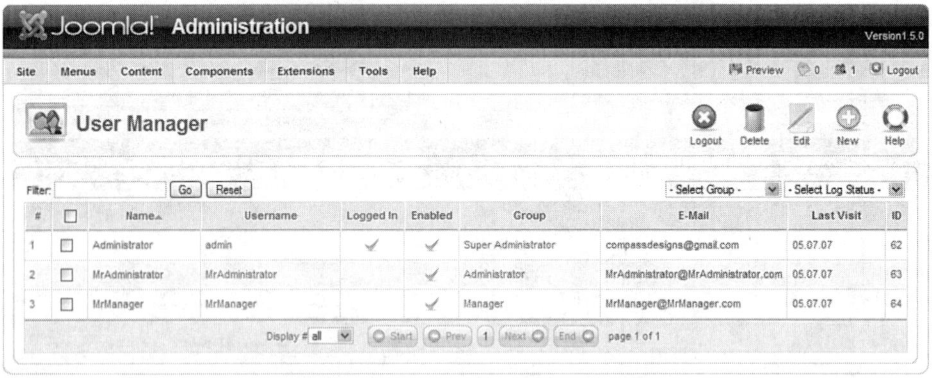

FIGURE 3.7 User Manager

Simply put, the User Manager manages users, and only administrators and super administrators can view it.

The filter, shown in Figure 3.7 on the left side, is your search tool for Joomla (it probably should be called "search"). You can enter a name, username, or an email, and it will find all users that have what you typed present in their fields. You can also select a specific group or see only users that are logged in.

> **TIP**
> You can't currently export or import users into Joomla without either a third-party component or accessing the SQL tables directly through a tool such as PHPMy-Admin.

There are nine user levels in a Joomla-powered website. Each level has different permissions and capabilities in the frontend and the backend of the site. Table 3.1 describes each user level.

TABLE 3.1 Joomla Access Control Levels

User	Frontend	Backend Functions/Menus
Public Frontend	Browse Only	No Access
Registered	Can view restricted content	No Access
Author	Can create content	No Access
Editor	Can edit content	No Access
Publisher	Can publish content	No Access
Manager	As publisher	Media Manager Menu Manager Content Managers Frontpage Manager Component Manager Help
Administrator	As publisher	As Manager User Manager Install/Uninstall Extensions Module Manager Plugin Manager Global Checkin
Super Administrator	As publisher	As Administrator Configuration Language Manager Template Manager Template Installer Language Installer Mass Mail

These permissions are additive, so an editor can do everything an author can—that is, edit and create content.

Guest, registered, author, editor, and publisher are termed *frontend users*. Very often a Joomla site will have many of these users. This makes it possible to establish content publication workflows. It also allows the responsibility of content publication to be distributed, one of the advantages of a CMS.

If you want lots of content, have lots of authors, editors, and publishers!

Manager, administrator, and super administrators are termed *backend users*. Usually there is only one super administrator. These users are designed to control the site rather than just focus on content.

> **The Least You Need to Know**
> There are two main types of users: frontend and backend. The frontend users manipulate content; the backend users manage the site.

Users are either created automatically though the registration link on the frontend log-on form, or they can be created manually in the backend.

> **TIP**
> The automatic registration function can be turned on or off in the Global Configuration. If you want your site to grow quickly, offer something of value for free and ask people to register to view it. Make sure you prominently display your privacy policy and that you adhere to it!

Media Manager

The Media Manager is a one-stop shop to manage all the media that might be used on a site; it includes all types of media, not just images (see Figure 3.8).

The Media Manager shows a basic file manager type view of all files that are in the /images folder. The Media Manager automatically points to this folder; you can't browse to any other folders in the Joomla installation.

FIGURE 3.8 Media Manager

The Media Manager is used to change/add/edit folders and upload or delete media in them. It's a handy place to put some organization onto your media storage so all your images (for example) aren't dumped into one big folder, which would make them difficult to locate.

> Make sure you have a logical structure for your media. Your actual structure doesn't matter, but creating folders for certain sections or categories or types of images will make it easier when you have several to handle. It's worth documenting them too if multiple administrators are on your site.

Configuration

The Configuration screen is important for your site. It's only available to super administrators and contains critical settings to keep your site running (see Figure 3.9).

It was formerly called Global Configuration on the menu but has been shortened on the submenu to just Configuration. The following list describes the three tabs within Configuration.

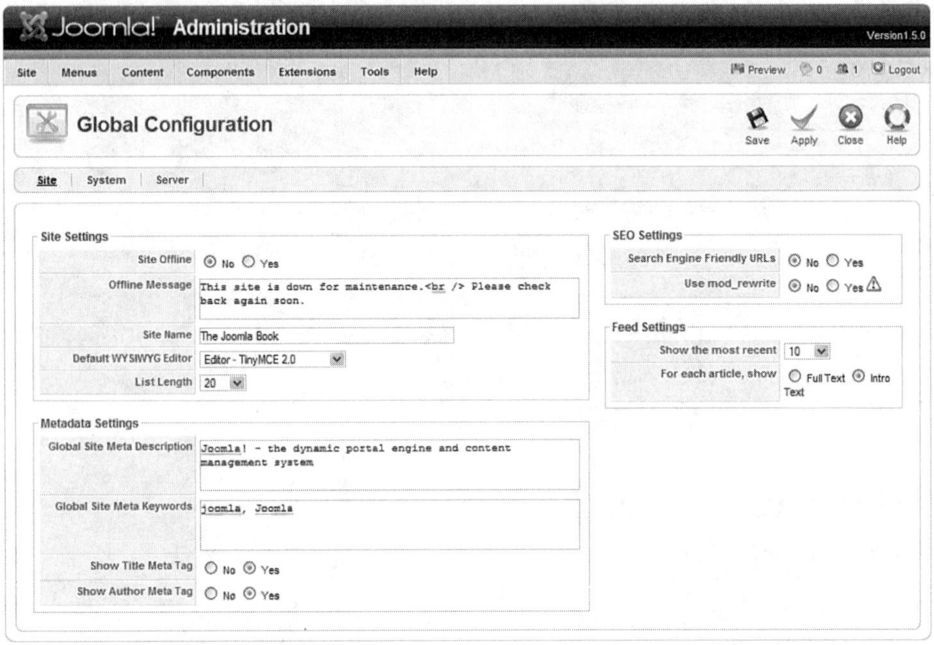

FIGURE 3.9 Initial Global Configuration screen

> **NOTE**
> New in Joomla 1.5 is the layout of Global Configuration. It has now been split into only three tabs as opposed to the previous ten.

- **Site**—The initial active tab that contains some very general things about your Joomla website:
  - **Site Offline**—If you take the site offline, visitors will get an offline message. You can customize the offline message with HTML, images, logo, and so on.
  - **Site Name**—Your site name is really vital for SEO in that it always starts any page title (what goes in the blue bar). I cover this in more detail in Chapter 8, "Getting Traffic to Your Site."

- **SEO Settings**—This is a new feature in version 1.5: Human readable URLs that are part of the default Joomla installation. These are often described as search engine friendly URLs (SEF). Be careful with these settings. There are changes that need to be made with the .htaccess file in order to get mod-rewrite SEF to work. I'll talk more about SEF in Chapter 8.

- **Metadata Settings**—You should keep these very short as they will appear on every single page/article of the site. I recommend using only three to five global site keywords.

- **Feed settings**—RSS has been greatly improved in 1.5, and you now have finer control of the nature of the feeds. Being able to show the full text for an article means you can syndicate complete articles to other sites.

- **System**—Most of these settings, such as the debug and cache, you should never need to change. Be certain you have your secret password! If you do manage to lock yourself out, this page will help: forum.joomla.org/index.php/topic,10985.0.html.

  - **User Settings**—Probably the only setting you might want to change is the user settings. Here you can decide whether to allow users to register themselves from the frontend.

  - **Cache (options to set site cache, hopefully speeding it up)**—If you are making a lot of revisions to your site, especially on the template, it's worth turning the cache off while you do. If you don't, you will make changes and scratch your head why they don't take any effect.

- **Server**—Again, most of the settings in the server tab you should not need to change.

  - **Database (settings about the MySQL database running the site, handle with care)**—I often find myself looking here to remind myself what I called the database. I always seem to forget!

  - **Mail (email options for how the site will send email)**—Some hosts don't support PHP mail; make sure the mailer matches what your host offers.

Menus

Menus are a critical part of a Joomla site. They not only provide navigation but also determine the layout of a page that is linked to through the menu. Menus are difficult to understand, and we examine them in much more depth in Chapter 5, "Creating Menus and Navigation." For now we will just take a quick overview to provide some context for the more challenging concepts later on.

Figure 3.10 shows the Menus submenu with the sample content installed.

FIGURE 3.10 Menu drop-down options

The Menus option has all of the menus that are used in the website. In Figure 3.10, you can see the Menu and Trash Managers and the six menus that are created in sample content of a default Joomla installation.

> **NOTE**
> These menu names are totally arbitrary; they are just names given to menus in a "fake" set of content as an example.

Clicking the Menu Manager will take you to a summary table of all the menus used in the site, shown in Figure 3.11.

> Clicking the Menu Items icons in the Menu Manager is the same as just clicking that menu in the drop-down main menu. Using the drop-down menu just skips a step.

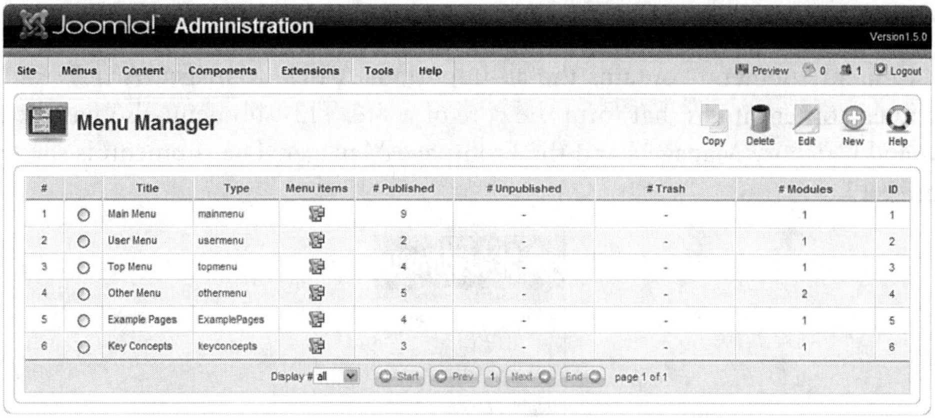

FIGURE 3.11 Menu Manager

Clicking the menu name allows you to change the name of that menu. Clicking the small Menu Items icons shows you what actual links are on that menu. Figure 3.12 shows the Menu Manager when you click "mainmenu" (of the sample content menus).

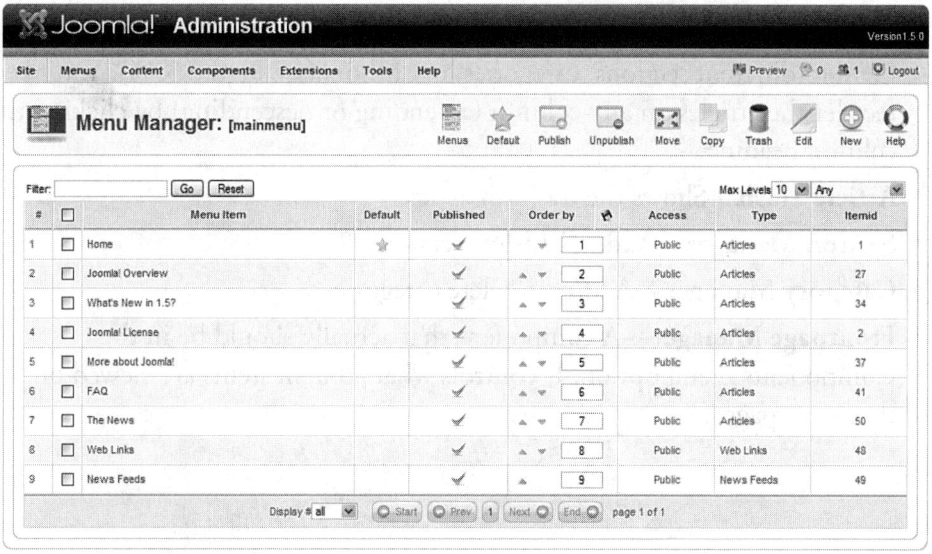

FIGURE 3.12 A menu within Menu Manager

We revisit menus in much more detail in Chapter 5.

Content

The Content submenu contains the all-important Article Manager. Articles are the individual content items that form the core of a site. This submenu also has the Sections and Category Managers and the Frontpage Manager. The submenu is shown in Figure 3.13.

FIGURE 3.13 Content submenu

The Content menu option can be thought of as a big component that presents your articles (content items) in various ways. It contains six different functions:

- **Article Manager**—Displays all your content items with various ways to filter them to different sections, categories, or authors (see Figure 3.14). You can reorder the articles on any column (ascending or descending) by clicking that column heading.
- **Article Trash**—Shows the trash for articles.
- **Section Manager**—Add/edit/delete sections.
- **Category Manager**—Add/edit/delete categories.
- **Frontpage Manager**—A component that actually should be in the Components menu option. It controls what content items are viewed on the home page.

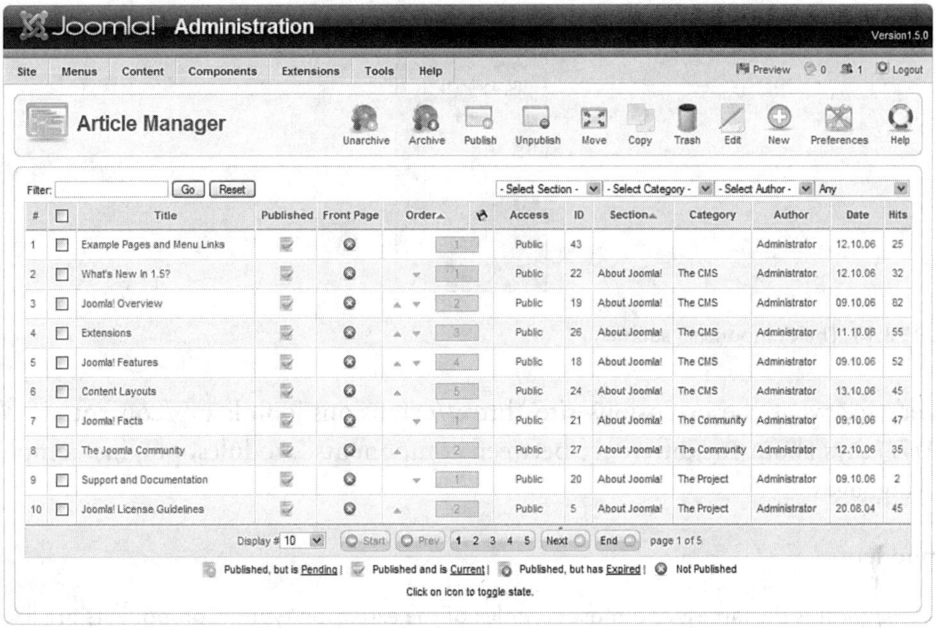

FIGURE 3.14 The Article Manager

> Notice that the first article in Figure 3.14 has no section or category. This is because they are uncategorized. This system has completely replaced static items that are in Joomla 1.0.X but no longer exist in Joomla 1.5.

The Component Menu

Components are the most important extensions for a Joomla site, the others being modules, plugins, templates, and languages. We will go into more detail on each of these in dedicated chapters. The component menu is where you can administrate the functionality of components that are part of the Joomla core and ones you have installed (see Figure 3.15).

FIGURE 3.15 The Components submenu

Let's see what the extensions site (http://extensions.joomla.org/content/view/15/63/1/7/) says about the difference between components, modules, plugins, templates, and languages:

Components

A *component* is the largest and most complex of the extension types. Components are like mini-applications that render the main body of the page. An analogy that might make the relationship easier to understand would be that Joomla is a book, and all the components are chapters in the book. The core content component (com_content), for example, is the mini-application that handles all core content rendering just as the core registration component (com_registration) is the mini-application that handles user registration.

Modules

A more lightweight and flexible extension used for page rendering is a *module*. Modules are used for small bits of the page that are generally less complex and able to be seen across different components. To continue in our book analogy, a module can be looked at as a footnote or header block or perhaps an image/caption block that can be rendered on a particular page. Obviously you can have a footnote on any page, but not all pages will have them. Footnotes also might appear regardless of which chapter you are reading. Similarly, modules can be rendered regardless of which component you have loaded.

Plugin

One of the more advanced extensions for Joomla! is the *plugin*. In previous versions plugins were known as "mambots." Along with the development of Joomla 1.5, mambots have been renamed plugins, and their functionality has been expanded. A plugin is a section of code that runs when a pre-defined event happens within Joomla. Editors are plugins, for example, that execute when the Joomla event "onGetEditorArea" occurs. Using a plugin allows a developer to change the way her code behaves depending on which plugins are installed to react to an event.

Language

New to Joomla 1.5 and perhaps the most basic and critical extension is a *language*. Languages are packaged as either a core language pack or an extension language pack. They allow both the Joomla core as well as third-party components and modules to be internationalized.

So a component is a specialized mini-application that runs in Joomla as part of its core. There are many hundreds available for free and commercially from third-party providers. You can find out more about them at extensions.joomla.org.

> **NOTE**
> Some components make use of modules and plugins as well as the component itself to achieve full functionality.

The default components that ship with Joomla are

- Content
- Banners
- Contacts
- Newsfeeds
- Polls
- Web Links

Extensions

Extensions come in several types: components, modules, plugins, templates and languages. Components are fundamental to the functionality of a Joomla site and have their own menu. The rest can be found in the Extensions submenu as shown in Figure 3.16.

FIGURE 3.16 Extensions submenu

The Extensions menu holds all the, well, extensions you might have installed into Joomla to extend its functionality. Each of the smaller extensions has its own manager.

> **NOTE**
>
> In the Extensions menu, there are managers for modules, plugins, templates, and languages. The manager for components, however, is in a separate menu item. This is because components are more complex than the aforementioned extensions, and it would make navigation difficult if they were all in together—so they are given a menu item of their own.

Install/Uninstall

The Install/Uninstall menu link takes you to the Extensions Manager. Here you can install new extensions and uninstall ones you don't want any longer. The manager is shown in Figure 3.17.

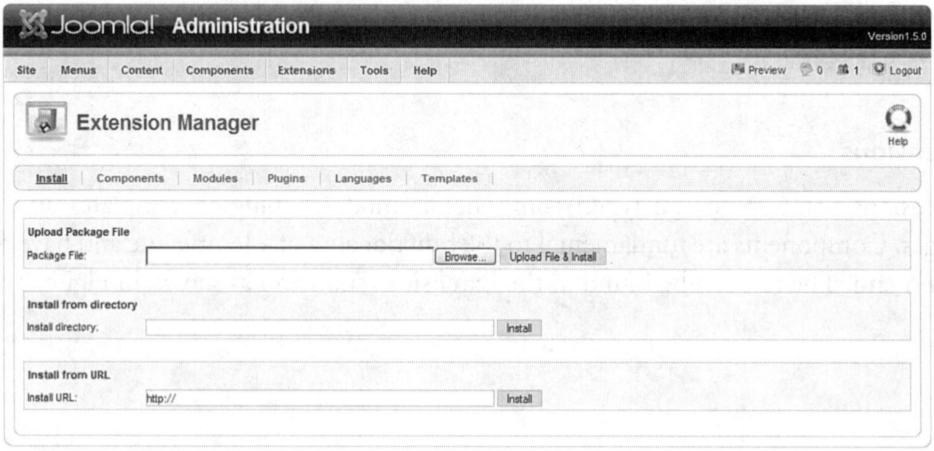

FIGURE 3.17 Extensions Manager

Joomla allows the installation of extensions from their packaged installable zip files. Joomla 1.5 will automatically detect what type of extension is being installed. The Install/Uninstall page also details individual extensions on their own pages so they can be uninstalled.

To be able to be installed automatically into your Joomla site, the package must be zipped up and have an XML file with instructions to Joomla about how to unpack it.

> **NOTE**
> Sometimes third-party developers have a zip file that contains the real installable zip file as well as files like documentation. It's a zip file in a zip file. If you get an error installing things, check that this isn't happening. Usually a filename like UNZIPME is a giveaway.

Module Manager

The Module Manager controls the parameters (options) and placement of all of the modules in a Joomla site, shown here in Figure 3.18.

FIGURE 3.18 Module Manager

Modules can be thought of as mini-components. Where a component always displays its content in the main body, modules display their content in designated places.

For example, the Log In module might have its location set as "left" (in most templates this would be in the left column).

Often a component will have a number of modules bundled with it. For example Virtuemart, a popular shopping cart component, has a module that shows the latest items for sale.

> **TIP**
> The module locations are totally arbitrary, based on the template designer's whims. If I wanted to, I could have all my "left" modules be in a column located on the right. This is not something to be concerned about, though. Most designers generally follow reasonable conventions. It's worth noting, however, if you are using a free template from who knows where.

Plugin Manager

The Plugin Manager is where you can control the options of all the plugins you have installed. Formerly called mambots, these plugins add small site-wide functionality. The Manager is shown in Figure 3.19.

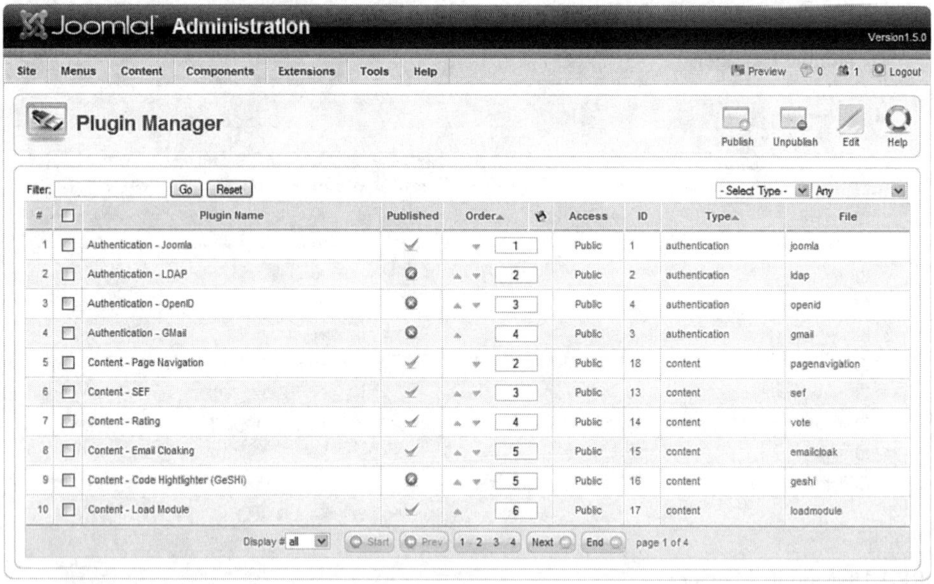

FIGURE 3.19 Plugin Manager

Many of these plugins don't have options; they simply provide some function. Some examples are

- **Content—mail Cloaking**—Automatically checks all pages for email addresses and replaces them in the code by JavaScript so email spam bots can't harvest them.
- **Content-Load Module**—This allows you to load modules into the middle of a content article.

Template Manager

The Template Manager shows all templates currently installed (see Figure 3.20).

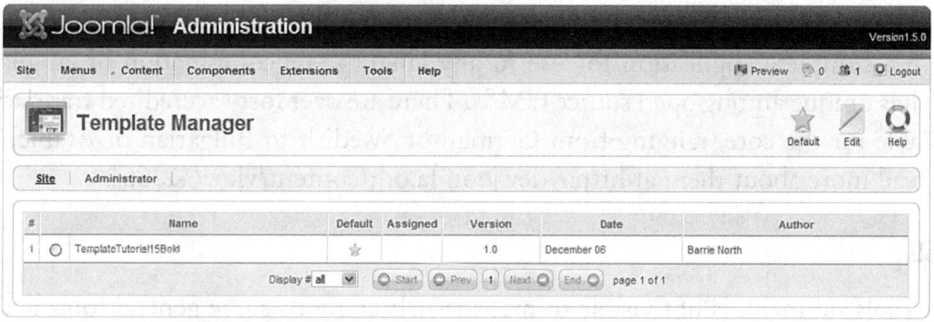

FIGURE 3.20 Template Manager

The Template Manager controls how a template is implemented on your site. You can edit the HTML or CSS files, assign a template to specific pages, and preview it with the module positions shown.

Some of the new features in Joomla 1.5 allow templates total control over how the Joomla core, components, and modules are outputted without having to make any hacks. This is a very versatile and powerful feature, and we'll look at it again later in Chapter 9, "Creating a Pure CSS Template."

Language Manager

Joomla 1.5 has several powerful new features with respect to internationalization. The Language Manager shows all language packs currently installed (see Figure 3.21).

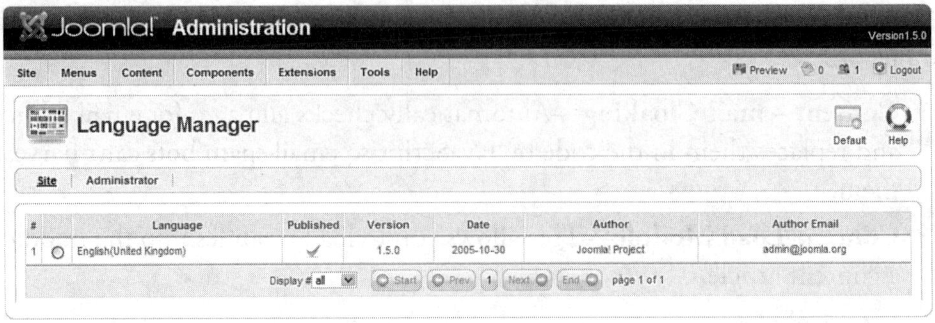

FIGURE 3.21 Language Manager

Joomla 1.5 has a UTF-8 character set, which means you have RTL (right to left) support and language packs for backend, installer, and help systems. This makes Joomla 1.5 a complete application for use in any language or combination of languages, which is unique among open source CMSs. There are over forty accredited translations available for the core, ranging from German or Swedish to Bulgarian or Arabic. You can read more about them at http://dev.joomla.org/content/view/42/66/.

Tools

The Tools submenu is not visible to managers. It contains some general tools used in administering your site (see Figure 3.22).

FIGURE 3.22 Tools submenu

The Tools menu appears for administrators and super administrators only. It has a very basic private message system (PMS) and a basic mass mail. The PMS receives notification when a piece of content is submitted (for example), and the mass mail function allows you to email all your users. It should be used with extreme caution, however, as sending emails in this way is likely not to conform to modern CAN-SPAM regulations. To send bulk email, you will need an appropriate third-party extension. Some reviews can be found at my blog, compassdesigns.net.

Global Checkin

The Global Checkin tool checks in all content items that might be open or have been opened for editing. Joomla has a built-in function that allows only one person to edit a content article at a time. This is very important for content management. It does this by "checking out" items so no one else can open them. However, if someone uses his back button or closes his browser while editing, the item can remain checked out. The Global Checkin provides a function for the super administrator to make all content items available for editing again. Needless to say, the super administrator would need to make sure that no one was editing at the time.

Help

The Help submenu contains links to the official Joomla documentation that will open in the backend in a wrapper (see Figure 3.23). This means you always have access to the most current documentation.

FIGURE 3.23 Help submenu

Joomla has a useful Help function built into the administrative backend. It's a searchable knowledge base of most basic functions and is a mirror of the Help documentation at help.joomla.org.

> **NOTE**
> At the time of writing, the Help site for 1.5 was not completely set up. Depending on when you are reading this book, you might well find the documentation for 1.5 still in development.

Another great place to get questions answered of a more troubleshooting nature is the official Joomla forums, forum.joomla.org. It's a large community, and there are many users that are immensely helpful.

Site Preview

When you use the Preview function, Joomla opens a new browser window with the frontend of the site shown. The preview link is in the right of the Menu bar, as shown in Figure 3.24.

FIGURE 3.24 Site offline setting in Global Configuration

Joomla contains a useful feature that involves taking the site offline. You can find it at **Site>Configuration**. When you make the site offline, visitors are greeted with the simple message shown in Figure 3.25.

The useful part of this is if you now log in as an administrator, you get to see the site as outside visitors would see it. This is tremendously useful as you can work on a site before going live and see your edits, but the public will be unable to see it.

This is made even more useful in that you can adjust the offline message to your taste. Maybe you want to include a brief message about your site and that it is coming soon. You can also add as much HTML to the Site Offline message as you like, even more than you think might fit into the box in the Global Configuration. You can even include images using an <img> HTML tag.

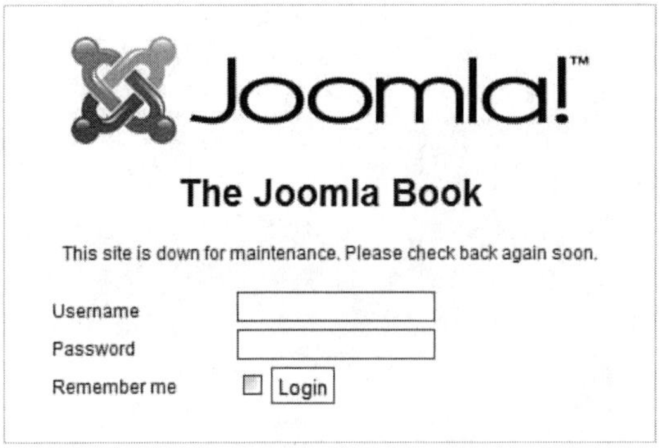

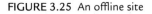

The Joomla Book

This site is down for maintenance. Please check back again soon.

Username

Password

Remember me   ☐ Login

FIGURE 3.25 An offline site

Summary

This chapter described both the frontend and backend of a Joomla-powered website and quickly toured how to navigate the administrative backend. The menus we have covered thus far are referred to often throughout the rest of this book, and submenus to be navigated will be represented in this format: **Site>Configuration** (this example takes you to the Global Configuration screen).

As we looked at our overview of the backend, we saw that

- A Joomla website consists of two sites: the public frontend and an administrative backend.
- The best place to go for information about the specific functions of all menus and buttons is help.joomla.org. It's much more accurate and up-to-date than a book can be!
- The Control Panel is the main tool to administer a Joomla site. Different parts of it are visible to different administrators. Third-party extensions will often have Workspaces that are organized differently than the core Joomla functions.
- There are two main types of users: frontend and backend. The frontend user types manipulate content, while backend user types are responsible for site management.

Chapter 4

Content Is King:
Organizing Your Content

As a Content Management System, Joomla's primary function is to organize and present all the content in your site. It does this through content articles. These discrete pieces of content must be organized into a 2-level hierarchy comprised of *sections* and *categories*.

In This Chapter

This chapter provides an in-depth tutorial that explains how Joomla displays its content articles and how you can organize their hierarchical structure. It details how to plan and organize the content and user experience for the site. It also explains the hierarchy structure currently used in Joomla—sections and categories—and how to best shape content into them for small and large sites.

- How does Joomla generate web pages?

- In what different ways can I present content items?

- How can I organize my content?

- How do components and modules present information?

How Does Joomla Generate Web Pages?

For those new to Joomla, one of the most difficult things to figure out is how content is organized. The relationship between sections, categories, blogs, and tables can be very confusing.

The key to understanding how to organize content is in how Joomla generates pages. I addressed this in detail in Chapter 1, "Content Management Systems and an Introduction to Joomla," and am bringing it up again. If you have a firm grasp of PHP-served dynamic pages, you can skip to How Joomla Organizes its Articles, but if part of your brain still harkens back to static HTML pages, it's worth a quick revisiting!

To get a better idea of how a Joomla site can be organized, let's make a sitemap for an imaginary site. It will be for a company called Widget Inc., which sells widgets in both blue and green. This example could easily be generalized into any sort of "brochure" site for a small company.

A sitemap is a standard planning tool used by web designers and is critical for a Joomla website. It's often shown as a tree diagram that shows all the pages in the site. Figure 4.1 shows an example.

> **The Least You Need to Know**
> A sitemap is critical to having a well organized site. You must make an effort to draft one before you start working in the administrator backend.

In this sitemap, each web page is represented by a box, and the lines are links within the site. A sitemap represents the architecture (links) of a site rather than its content organization. It is still a useful planning tool for organizing the site, however. In Figure 4.1, there are seven pages; from an organizational point of view, it seems as if there are four main paths in the site:

- About Us
- Services
- Contact Us
- Widget Blog

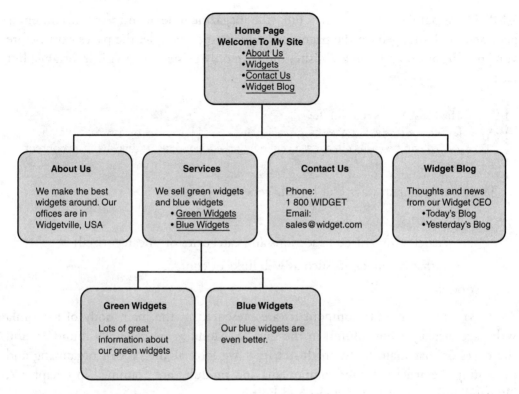

FIGURE 4.1 Website sitemap

The first step in trying to understand how Joomla structures its content is to realize that *there are no pages!*

OK, so what does that mean?

In Chapter 1, we talked about the idea of "placeholders" for the content. Remember, the content is stored in the database and needs to be placed onto the pages by Joomla. The Content Management System (CMS) has spaces on its pages to place content, and it needs to know what content it should put there. Joomla only knows what content should be used after the viewer clicks a link. When he has done this, Joomla then knows what page to generate, gets the content, and puts it into place.

Consider a different example—a magazine. You turn to the index, look something up, get the page number and turn to that page. For that page to be filled with content, the magazine author/designer needed to have chosen the content and arranged it as they wanted on that page. So you turn to that page and you see the content. This seems like an overly simple example, but it illustrates clearly how pages are generated in a

CMS. On a Joomla site, you click a link (the magazine index), and *then* the content is generated and arranged on the page. In the magazine example, the pages exist before you go to it, but on a Joomla website, the page only exists as you visit it. Strange but true.

> **The Least You Need to Know**
> Joomla generates a page the instant you click its link. This means that the pages viewed can be easily changed by changing the menu links rather than the content itself.

There are two main ways that Joomla generates content:

- Components
  - Articles (organized in sections and categories or uncategorized)
  - Other components such as web links or contacts
- Modules

As we saw in Chapter 1, components are presented in the main body of a Joomla web page, usually a big column in the middle. Modules are generally found around the edges of that main body. In this chapter we look at the task of organizing and presenting the articles. Other components and modules are examined in Chapter 7, "Expanding Your Content: Articles and Editors."

How Does Joomla Organize Content Articles?

Joomla gives you two options for how to organize all your content articles. Remember that each article is a discrete piece of content; for example, it might be a two-paragraph news announcement about your company. While a small site might only have five to ten articles, a big site could have thousands. The size and complexity of your site are a huge consideration for how to organize your articles.

Let's take a conceptual look at these two organizational options, and then we will see how they apply to our imaginary Joomla website for Widget Inc.

Uncategorized Articles

Uncategorized articles are by far the simplest way to organize a Joomla website. As the name implies, there is basically no hierarchical structure.

Let's consider an analogy to help us understand. Imagine we are trying to organize a stack of papers on a desk. Each piece of paper represents a single content article, and our website is represented by a filing cabinet next to the desk.

If we were to organize our articles as uncategorized, we would simply place them in a drawer of the filing cabinet. If there aren't many articles, this is a fast and easy way to organize them. I can easily find what I want by just picking up the small stack of papers and flipping through the sheets (that is, following links to the different articles).

Sections and Categories

If I have many more articles than a dozen, using uncategorized articles isn't going to work. If I pick up the stack, I might have to flip through a thousand pieces of paper.

As with almost all Content Management Systems, Joomla provides a hierarchy to organize large amounts of content articles. Joomla offers two levels: the highest is called sections, and below that are categories. In the most general case you will have the kind of structure (sections and categories) shown here.

- Section 1
  - Category A
    - Article i
    - Article ii
  - Category B
    - Article iii
    - Article iv
- Section 2
  - Category C
    - Article v
    - Article vi
  - Category D
    - Article vii
    - Article viii

> **NOTE**
> You can't put content items in a section; they must go in a category. This means that each section needs at least one category.

To return to our filing cabinet analogy, in the cabinet you have drop-down folders, and inside them you have manila folders, and inside those are sheets of paper that are the articles. This is shown in Figure 4.2.

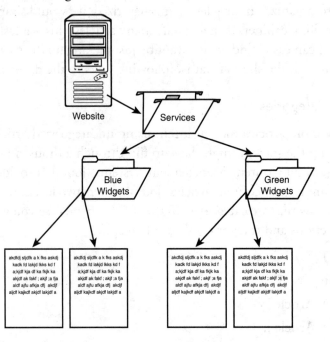

FIGURE 4.2 How Joomla stores its content

The filing cabinet is the website, the drop-down folders are the sections, the manila folders are the categories, and the papers are the articles.

Sections

The highest tier of the Joomla content hierarchy is made up of *sections*. The best way to think of sections is as containers that provide the largest set of items in the hierarchy. Sections are the parents of categories. A section can have one or more children (categories). A section can also be an empty set with no children (categories), but in that case, it will not be visible to site visitors.

Categories

Categories make up the middle tier of the hierarchy. Categories are children of their parent sections. A category must be assigned to a section; it cannot exist without one.

Categories are also the parents of content items. A category can have one or more children (content items). A category can also be an empty seat with no children (content items), but as with a section with this setup, it will not be visible to site visitors.

Articles

Content articles are the lowest tier of the hierarchy and are the most important. They are what most people think of as "pages" of their website—that is, content articles are what you create to add content to display to site visitors. A content article must be assigned to a category; it cannot exist without one.

Sample Hierarchy

Let's say we want to create a website that discusses Classic American Automobiles.

Plan the Sections

Let's also assume that we have decided that one type of automobile we wish to discuss on the website is the Muscle Car group—those big beefy performance autos that were so popular in America in the 1960s and 1970s. We will make this type of automobile our highest tier—a section. So first we create a new section and name it "Muscle Cars."

Plan the Categories

A logical subset of Muscle Cars (parent item) would be a list of the manufacturers who made Muscle Cars. So next we create categories for each manufacturer: Chevrolet, Chrysler, Pontiac, and Ford. We assign each of these categories to the section "Muscle Cars."

Plan the Articles

Now we get to the meat of the matter: Building the pages for each car model. The models of cars are, in other words, the lowest level of our hierarchy. To create pages for each model, we create content items that represent each. We then assign each model (content item) to the proper manufacturer (category). Let's look at one specific category: Ford. For this manufacturer, we want to create pages for each of the following models: Mustang, Fairlane, Falcon, and Galaxy. In this case we create content items for each model and assign each to the category named "Ford."

Visually, we have created a content hierarchy that looks like the following:

- MUSCLE CARS [Section]
    - Chevrolet [Category]
    - Chrysler [Category]
    - Pontiac [Category]
    - Ford [Category]
        - Mustang [Content Item]
        - Fairlane [Content Item]
        - Falcon [Content Item]
        - Galaxy [Content Item]

Let's return to our imaginary widget company and go through two examples of organizing the content using the two methods that were just explained, uncategorized and sections/categories.

> **The Least You Need to Know**
> Joomla offers two methods to organize articles. The first is to use uncategorized articles, which are suited for very small sites. For larger sites the second method of sections in categories needs to be used.

Creating the Widget Inc. Website with Uncategorized Content

So we can better understand how to set up content on a site, let's not organize our content into sections and categories, but just make all the content items uncategorized.

The simplest way to create a site with Joomla is with uncategorized content. It's much easier to understand how a Joomla site is driven, so it is a good place to start. The uncategorized method is not much use if you have more than a dozen pages, however, because the content gets too difficult to manage. A single uncategorized content item in the database will correspond to a single page of content on the website—nice and easy.

> **The Least You Need to Know**
> Making your pages with uncategorized content items is the simplest way to build a Joomla site, but it is difficult to manage with more than a dozen pages.

If you want to follow along as we create this site, you will need to install Joomla (see Chapter 2, "Downloading and Installing Joomla") somewhere. I would advise installing it as a localhost.

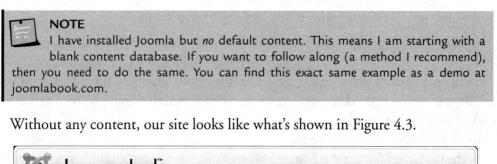

NOTE
I have installed Joomla but *no* default content. This means I am starting with a blank content database. If you want to follow along (a method I recommend), then you need to do the same. You can find this exact same example as a demo at joomlabook.com.

Without any content, our site looks like what's shown in Figure 4.3.

FIGURE 4.3 Fresh installation of Joomla with no content

To make this example we are working through more appropriate, we need a slightly simpler sitemap of Widget Inc. Let's say we have a simple website that consists of three pages: a "Home" page, an "About Us" page, and a "Services" page. This is shown in Figure 4.4.

FIGURE 4.4 Simple sitemap of Widget Inc.

First, we need to create some articles for this example site.

Creating Content Articles

If you haven't already, you should go back and review Chapter 3, "Joomla Administration Basics." You will need to have a good sense of how to navigate the backend as you work through this example.

Read it? Excellent, let's move on.

In the Content Menu is the Article Manager. We have two content items we need to create, About Us and Services. These are created simply by clicking the New button.

Go to **Content>Article Manager**.

The Article Manager with no articles yet added is shown in Figure 4.5

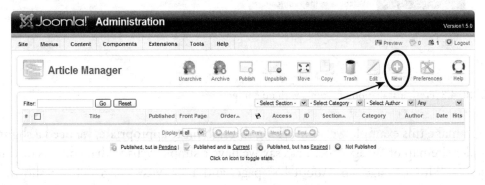

FIGURE 4.5 Article Manager

When we click the New button an editor appears, and we can fill in the desired content. In Figure 4.6, you can see where I have added a sentence into the editor.

We will look into adding content and the editor in much more detail in Chapter 7. For now we are examining site organization. Notice that I put in the title and have the section and category as uncategorized; in Figure 4.7 you can see the drop-down boxes showing this.

You might have noticed if you are following along with an empty content Joomla installation that there was only one choice for section and category in the drop-down box—uncategorized. This makes sense because we have not created any; you create sections and categories as they become available as options in this drop-down. Also if you select a particular section, a drop-down will automatically be populated with the categories that are in that section.

FIGURE 4.6 Adding an uncategorized article

Click the Save icon and then add another article with the title "Services." After adding Services in a similar way, we have two articles in our manager as shown in Figure 4.7. Notice how the section and category columns are blank.

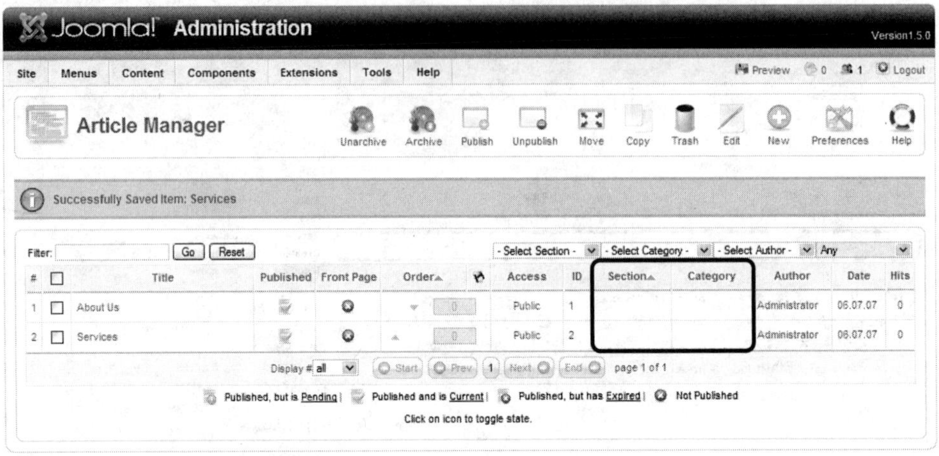

FIGURE 4.7 Article Manager with About Us and Services content articles

So now that we have added our content, let's look at the frontend of our website. If you are following along carefully (there will be a quiz later!), you should see a screen like the one shown in Figure 4.8.

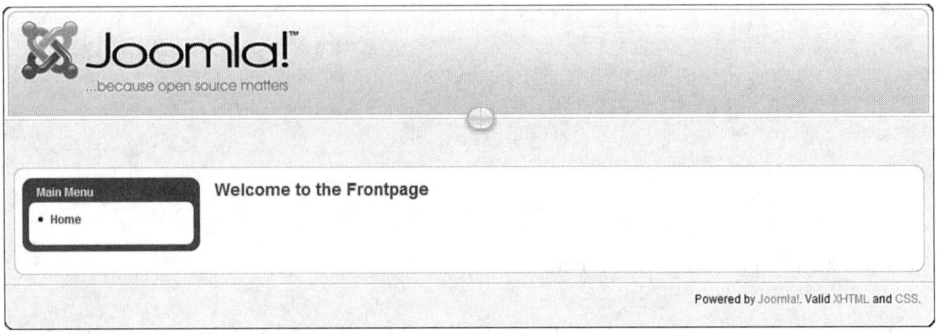

FIGURE 4.8 Frontend with two content articles

"Wait a second," I hear you say. "Where's my content?!"

As we just discussed, the hardest thing for users to realize about Joomla is that content does not exist by itself on the pages of the website, only in the database. It is only shown on the website when it is linked to in a menu—that is, the menus determine the content of a Joomla site, not the content items. Sure, they will be there in the database, but they will only appear when we link to them in a menu somewhere. A consequence of this is that you have to create the content first and then create the links to it.

This is true for all content that is in the main body of your pages.[1] They must have a link to them to cause them to appear on the site. Just to increase the confusion, they must also be "published" in the Content Item Manager. Our two items are published, so let's add links to these content items in the menu.

> **The Least You Need To Know**
> Menu links determine both what will be on a page and how it will be laid out.

> **TIP**
> You can use an advanced menu technique I like to call a *landing page menu* because the menu that causes the content item to be shown on a page does not need to be published or visible itself. I can create a menu that is not itself published but links to various other pages. I can then use these in various situations without having to link to them off my site. Maybe I want a special page that offers one of my products at a discount and gives the URL in an offline newspaper ad or a landing page for my Google AdWords campaign. To find these URLs, just look at the URL line in the menu item.

Creating Menu Items

Let's head over to the menu that is in this site; it's called the *mainmenu*. If you look back at Figure 4.7, you will see this menu in the left-hand column. It has only one link in it to start, one that links to the home page of the website.

Go to **Menus > Main Menu**. In the Menu Manager we see a screen like in Figure 4.9. Currently it's showing only our single link to the home page.

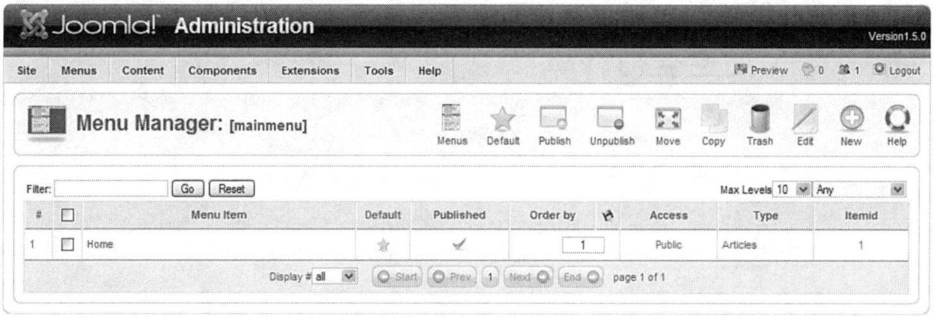

FIGURE 4.9 Initial main menu

We create a new menu by clicking the New button. We then see a screen from which we can add a new menu item, shown in Figure 4.10.

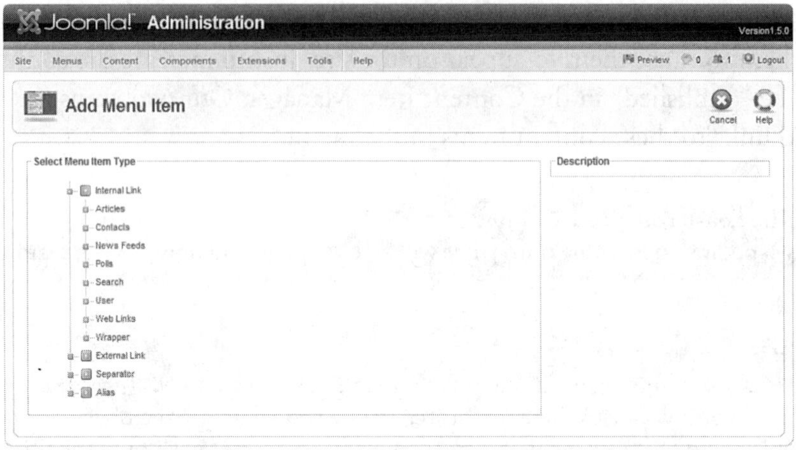

FIGURE 4.10 Add Menu Item admin screen

The process to add a menu is all new in Joomla 1.5 and is presented as a tree structure. Because we want an internal link to a single article, let's expand the tree by clicking **internal link > articles**. The tree expands with all the viable options for us to link
to for our menu item. This is shown in Figure 4.11.

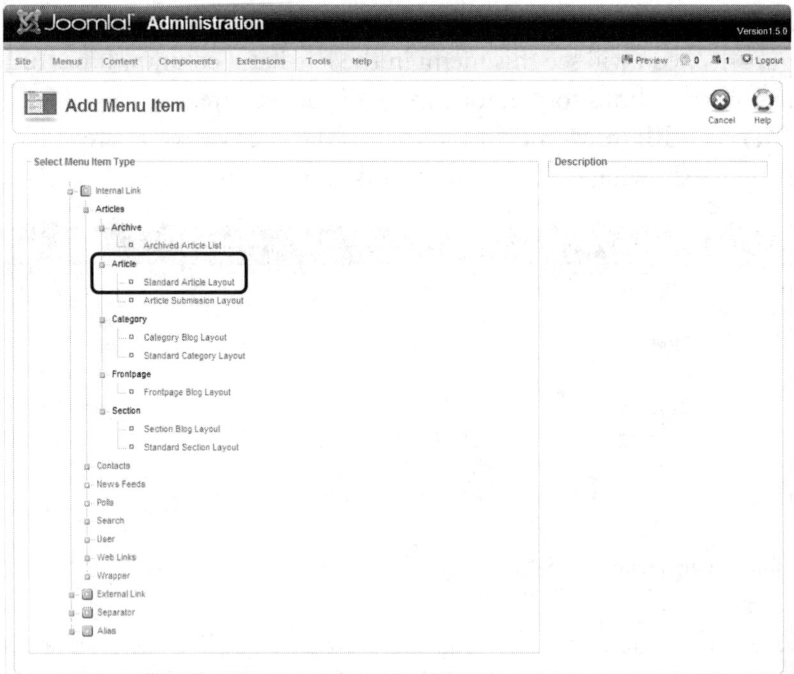

FIGURE 4.11 Creating a link to a single content article

Note that we could have a link to a whole section or a category. As we don't have any of those, let's go for the article and click Standard Article Layout, shown in Figure 4.11.

On the next screen, New Menu Item (see Figure 4.12), we need to fill out the various parameters for a new link. It's not immediately obvious how to select the article we want to link to it. Under menu item parameters on the right-hand side there is a button to select the article (shown in the figure).

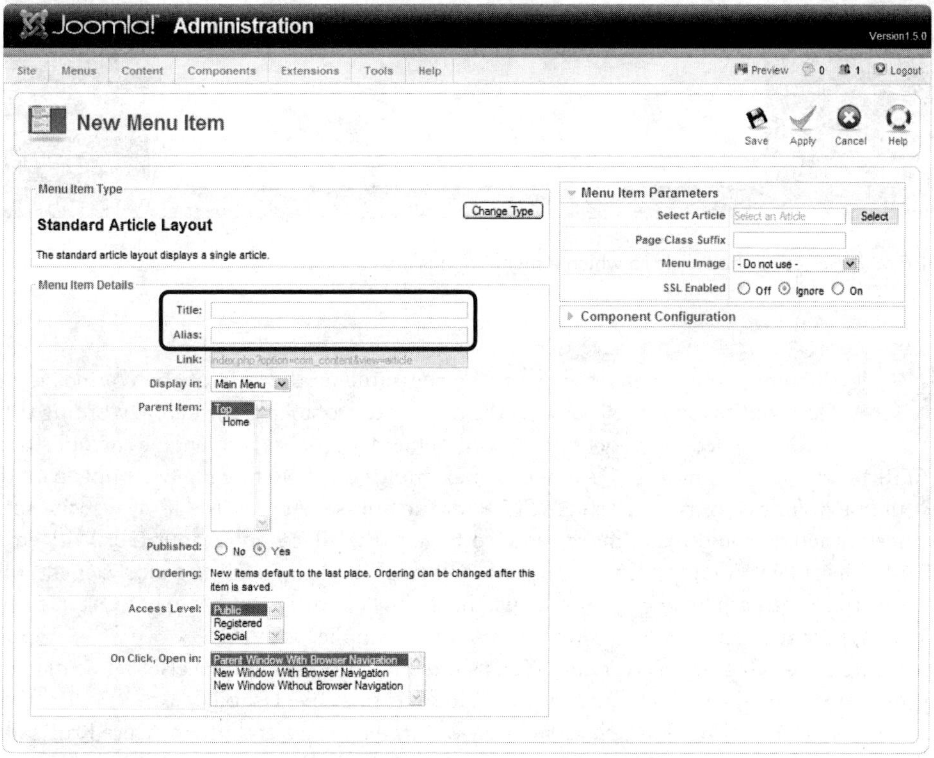

FIGURE 4.12 Adding new menu item parameters

Clicking Select makes a pop-up box appear where we can select the article we want to link to, shown in Figure 4.13.

Last but not least, give your link a name. The name given will be the words that are displayed as the link. This is a critical point for search engine optimization (SEO).

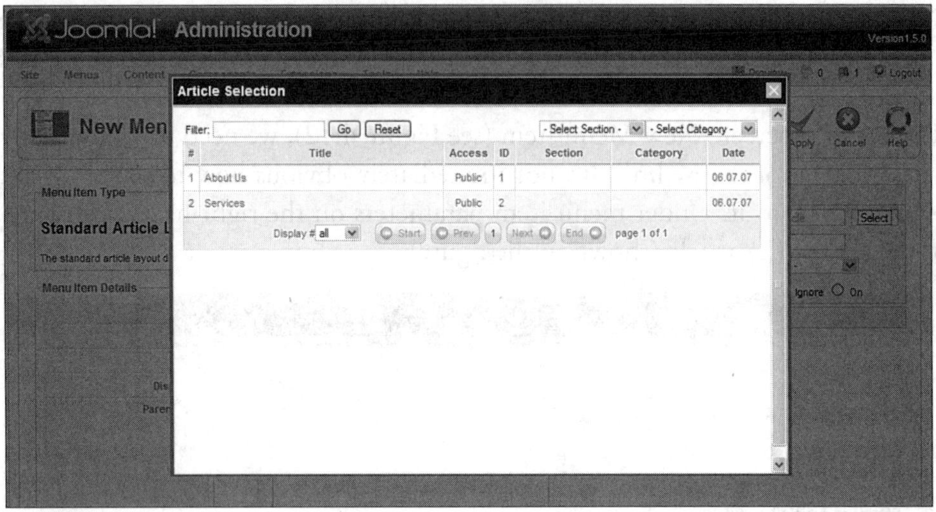

FIGURE 4.13 Selecting the article to which a menu item is linked

NOTE

The link name does not have to be the same as the title of the content item. Now, SEO wisdom tells us that the anchor text of a link, the actual wording that is "underlined," is very important to achieve a good search engine rank position (SERP) with that key phrase. This makes our example good for showing what not to do. It would be pointless to try and achieve SERP for the phrase "About Us." If my website sold widgets, then it would make more sense to have a link that said "About Our Widgets." Then at least I get Google points for having "widgets" in the link. For the most benefit, the title of the page I am linking to should also have the keyword phrase/anchor text in some version, perhaps "About Widget Inc., Your Quality Supplier for Widgets."

While we are discussing link text and SEO, I should mention something else. When making a site, care should be taken to make it as "usable" as possible. Usability experts tell us that the words in a link should match very closely with the page we end up on. Steve Krug talks about this in his book *Don't Make Me Think*, saying, "If there's a major discrepancy between the link name and the page name, my trust in the site will diminish."

Taking both these factors into account, trying to place important keywords in the link text along with making the link usable is a balancing act. Often, doing better at one means that the other is worse. Don't think you can dismiss usability. What's the point of having substantial traffic if visitors leave your site out of frustration? Needless to say, it takes work and some careful thought to decide on link text. Fortunately, however, it's easy to change later; you just go in and edit the menu item!

The Least You Need to Know
You can create links to a content item, but the content needs to exist first. The names of a link (anchor text) need to be chosen very carefully.

Back to making our sample site. After creating another link to Services in the same way, our main menu will look like Figure 4.14.

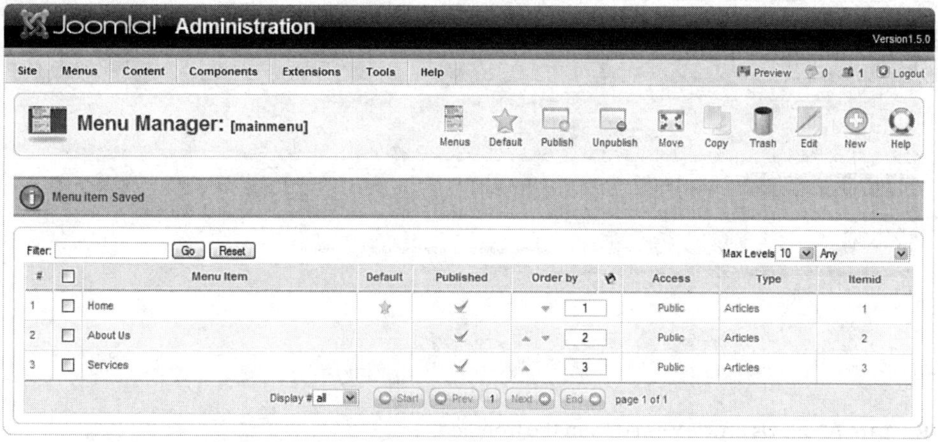

FIGURE 4.14 Main menu with Home, About Us, and Services menu items

When we go to the frontend now, we see these three menu items in our main menu in the left column (shown in Figure 4.15). Clicking any of those three links will navigate us around our simple, three-page Joomla website.

FIGURE 4.15 Frontend of a three-page Joomla website

Notice that the names of the menu items in the main menu (in Menu Manager) are what appear on the page in the same order. You can actually change the order on the page by changing the order in the backend (by clicking the small arrows in the Menu Manager).

Click the links, and you get the pages with the content that we entered. For example, if we click About Us, we see the content article as shown in Figure 4.16.

FIGURE 4.16 About Us article viewed from the frontend

When we click the Home link we are again greeted by the blank page shown in Figure 4.8. But why is the home page blank? For that, we need to look at the Front Page component.

Front Page Component

We now have two content articles, About Us and Services. We also have two menu items in the main menu that link to those articles. Now we need to set up the last page of the Widget Inc. website, the home page. We start getting to some of the aspects of Joomla that are more difficult to understand now. When freshly installed, the home page is not a simple link to content articles; it's actually a special component called the *Front Page component*.

As discussed in Chapter 1, content in the main body is generated by any number of components. Up until now in this chapter, we have been discussing com_content, the component that deals with the articles and presents them in various ways. There are several components in the Joomla core that generate main body content in this way:

- Contacts
- Newsfeeds
- Polls
- Web links
- Front Page

The first four of these do not use articles but pull their content from various places, either within the Joomla site database (contacts) or even other sites (RSS newsfeeds). The Front Page component does use articles and presents them in a specialized way. Basically, a *component* is a mini-application that presents data in the main body of a Joomla site in some fashion. A good example of a component is a forum. The content presented is highly specialized and different from the rest of the site.

In almost every case (except the Front Page component), all components installed are in the Components menu. The Front Page component is unique in Joomla in that it is not managed from anything in the Components menu, but rather in the Front Page Manager, the Article Manager, and from within content articles themselves. Quite simply, the Front Page component allows the publishing of *any* content item in a Joomla site's database on the front/home page regardless of where it appears on the site.

> **The Least You Need to Know**
>
> Components are mini-applications that present content in the main body in a special way.
>
> The home page of a Joomla site is a component. It allows you to pull content from anywhere in your site for its use.

Looking at the Front Page Manager, we see what's shown in Figure 4.17.

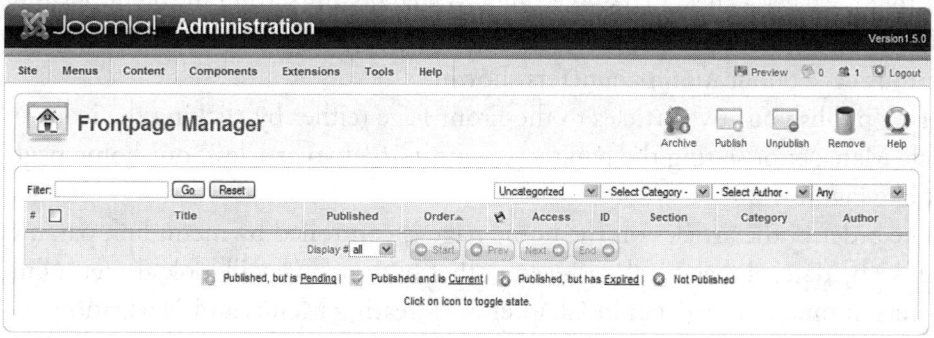

FIGURE 4.17 Front Page Manager with no articles

We don't have anything in the Front Page Manager yet. Maybe that's why our home page is blank!

> **NOTE**
> You cannot add content articles to your home page with the Front Page Manager; it only arranges them. You have to add from the Article Manager or from the article parameters.

If we look closely at the Article Manager, we can see a column about the Front Page. Here it is shown in Figure 4.18.

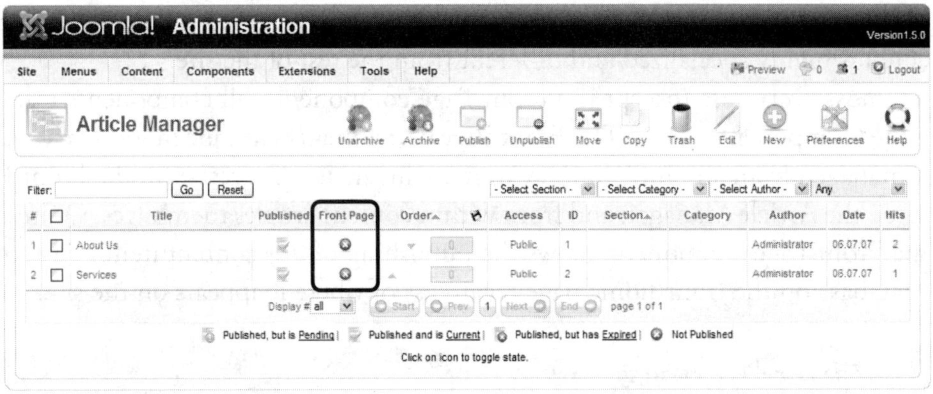

FIGURE 4.18 Front Page publishing icons in the Article Manager

These publishing icons in the Front Page column control whether an item appears on the home page of the site. We can simply click these crosses and check marks to have the items included on the front page. Note that the two articles have red Xs. If we click them, we get a checkmark. We can also change this setting in the publishing tab in the actual content item itself. In Figure 4.19, we can see the About Us article with the Front Page publication parameters shown.

If we publish our two articles to the Front Page (either by clicking the icons in the Article Manager or setting the parameter within the two articles), our home page will look like Figure 4.20.

The order of the articles on the home page is controlled by menu link parameters. It can be by date, alphabetical, or several other options. We will look at menu link parameters in much more detail in Chapter 5, "Creating Menus and Navigation."

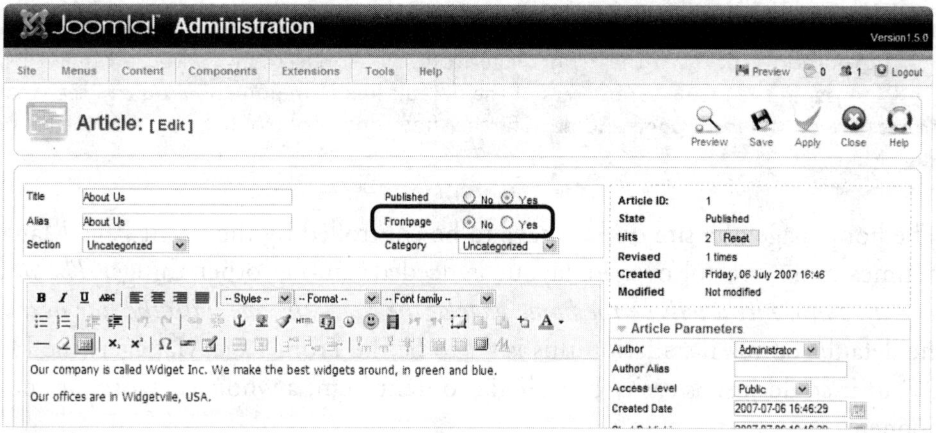

FIGURE 4.19 Front Page publishing parameter in an article

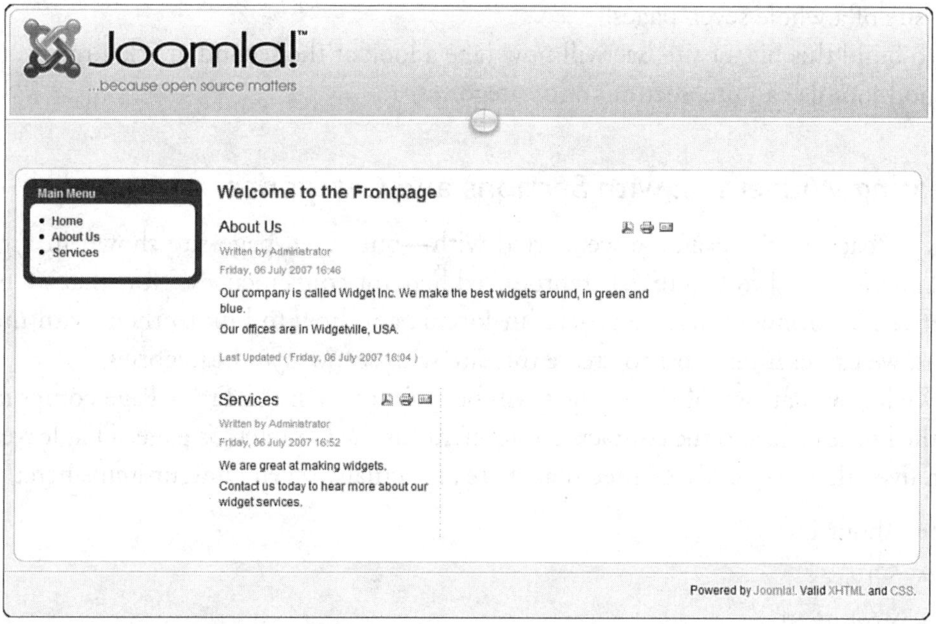

FIGURE 4.20 Home page with two Front Page published articles

> **NOTE**
> You add articles to the Front Page from the Article Manger. You arrange their order in the menu parameters of the default link in mainmenu. You can see what articles are on the front page and have further fine-tuned control over them in the Front Page Manager.

The home page of a site doesn't have to be controlled by the Front Page Manager. Sometimes more control over its layout is needed, among other things. *The default item in the main menu will be the home page of the site—the one with the star next to it.* In the default Joomla installation this is set to be the Front Page Manager (the Home link), but it could just as easily be a single content item, a whole category, or another component.

Figure 4.20 shows a very simple three-page Joomla website based on the sitemap in Figure 4.5. At the beginning of this chapter, we had considered a slightly more complex site of a whole seven pages!

To build this bigger site, we will now take a look at the second article organization method Joomla can use, sections and categories.

Creating Widget Inc. with Sections and Categories

Let's go back to the example we started with—our seven-page site shown in Figure 4.21 (it's identical to Figure 4.1, reproduced here for convenience). Now that we have a better idea of how to create articles in Joomla and how to link to them with menu items, we can examine how to create this site with sections and categories.

We know that two of these pages will be components: the Front Page component for the home page and the contacts component for the Contact Us page. That leaves us with five other pages. We can see that there are actually seven content items here:

- About Us
- Services
- Widget Blog
- Today's blog
- Yesterday's blog
- Green Widgets
- Blue Widgets

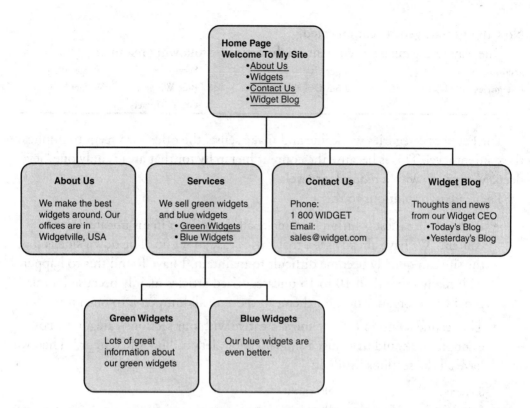

FIGURE 4.21 Seven-page Widget Inc. sitemap...again

Joomla gives us two organizational levels: First are *sections*, and then inside them are *categories*.

> **TIP**
> In the Joomla roadmap (the details of future releases at joomla.org), there are plans to change the hierarchical structure to be infinite categories.

At first glance, our structure might seem obvious. Leaving out the two components, we have three sections:

- About Us
- Services
- Widget Blog

Now things start getting complicated...

One way to organize our content might be in the following manner:

Sections	About Us	Services	Widget Blog
Categories	About Us	Blue Widgets	Widget Blog
		Green Widgets	

The Services categories work fine and make sense; the other two seem to duplicate the content level. This is because the content hierarchy for that area is only one "level" deep. We end up with a redundant level.

There are two solutions to this:

- Perhaps the easiest solution is to make all single-level items uncategorized content. We have already seen that this is easy to set up. The down side is that the site can quickly become difficult to maintain. I have found this to happen with many more than 10 to 15 uncategorized articles mainly because Joomla provides no organization for them, so they are all lumped into one group.

- The second solution is to be more creative with our sections/categories. For example, we could have just a single section; let's call it "AllContent." Then we have all the sections inside it:

Sections	AllContent
Categories	About Us
	Blue Widgets
	Green Widgets
	Widget Blog

This problem of a redundant level often occurs with smaller sites that have little content. In those instances you have to get creative. In our example it might be good to use a mix of both solutions—a single uncategorized article for About Us and then two sections for Services and the Widget Blog. The Widget Blog is a good candidate for its own category and section because this type tends to have several entries. Even though there is a redundant layer of structure, it will be easier to keep the site organized.

> **The Least You Need to Know**
> Joomla only has two hierarchy levels for organizing content sections and categories—no more, no less.
> A content article must be in a category, which must be in a section. This can lead to a redundant organizational level for small sites.
> There are many ways to organize the same set of content in a Joomla site.

To let our example go through, let's use the "middle of the road" solution in which About Us is uncategorized with two sections. We will choose to have two sections and three categories:

- Services
- Blue Widgets
- Green Widgets
- Widget Blog
- Widget Blog
- About Us (uncategorized)

Now it seems as though the Widget Blog will have a redundant level. If I am the site designer, I might as well do this, however. If the site grows, as hopefully it will, I will have the ability to add more categories. It's easier to do this if I already have the structure built in, even if it does not seem to make sense at first.

To start setting up our content, it's easiest to start in the following order:

1. Create the sections
2. Create the categories
3. Create the articles

Creating Sections

In going to the Section Manager (**Content > Section Manager**), we see that it is blank. This is because we installed our site with no content in the installation process. Click New, and we see the editor screen for a new section as shown in Figure 4.22.

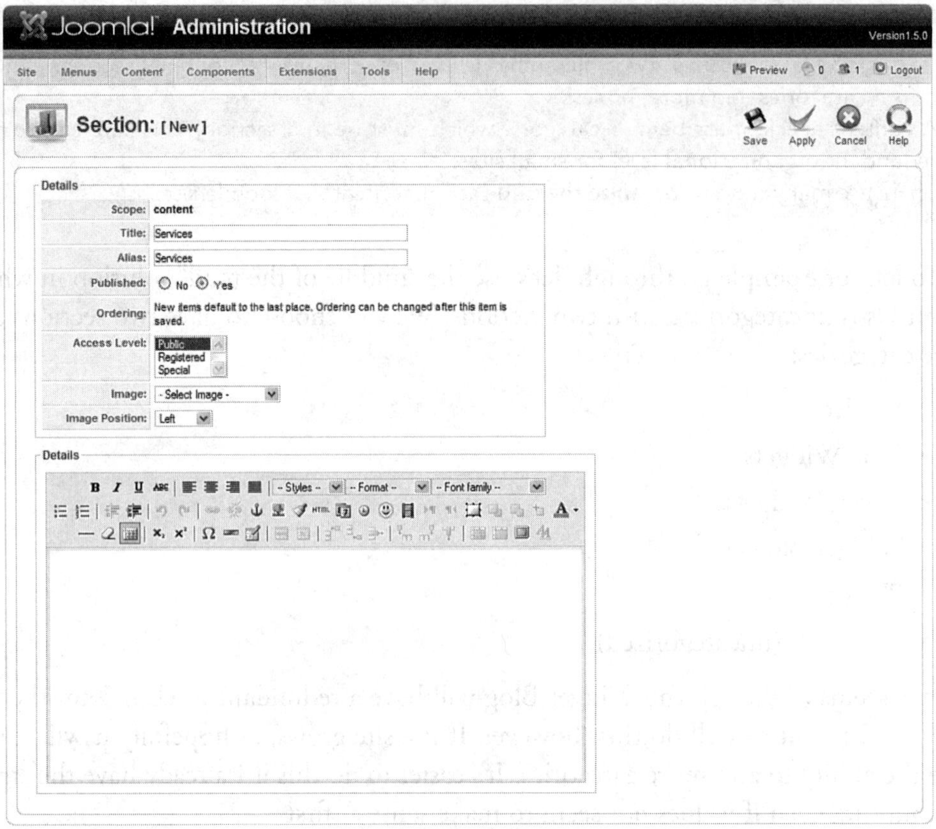

FIGURE 4.22 Adding the Services section

In Figure 4.23, we can see the title and section name. After we have set up the section for the Widget Blog, our Section Manager should look like Figure 4.23.

Note that there are no categories or active articles yet.

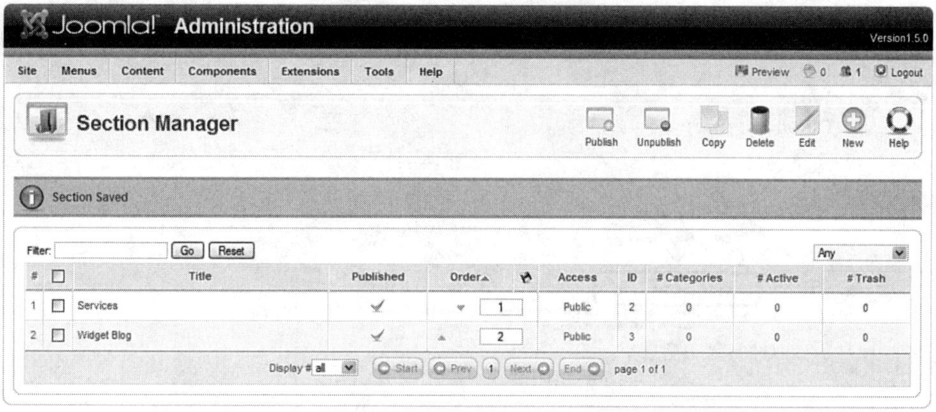

FIGURE 4.23 Section Manager with two sections created

Creating Categories

Next, we go to the Category Manager (**Content > Category Manager**) and set up the categories we need.

In Figure 4.24, the category **Blue Widgets** has been added. Notice we have to make sure we put it in the correct section (Services in this case) and save it as before. (I find myself doing this a lot—creating categories and not paying attention to which sections they were saved to. And then I can't find them!)

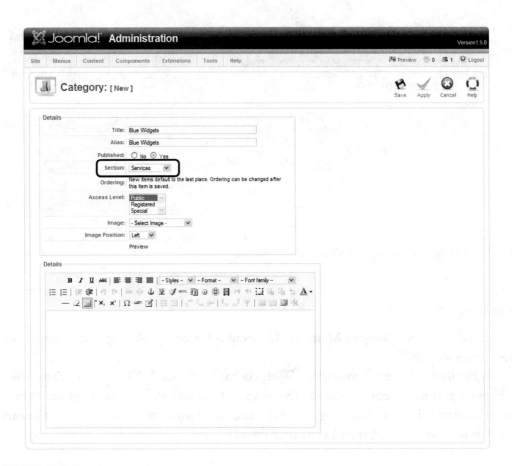

FIGURE 4.24 Creating a category

In the same way, we can create categories for Green Widgets and one called Barries Blog. After we have done this, our Category Manager should now look like the screen in Figure 4.25.

The Category Manager is similar to the Section Manager. It shows if the category is published, its order (more about that in Chapter 6 "Extending Joomla"), the id, what section it is in, and how many content articles are in it *and* in the trash.

Notice the name we gave to the single category for the blog: "Barrie's Blog." It would be reasonable to assume that maybe a few people in Widget Inc. might have blogs. I used the apostrophe to point out something important, though. You should not, if at all possible, use punctuation in any title for a section, category, or article. Two problems can arise: It can *sometimes* cause error in the URL and when you are trying to validate the page, and some third-party extensions use the name to generate a URL that needs to be easily readable.

Take this URL for example: www.widgetinc.com/blog/barrie's-blog/somepost. html.

Punctuation is not understood, so a browser would show it as follows: http://www. widgetinc.com/blog/barrie%92s-blog/somepost.html.

Notice what the apostrophe got replaced by "%92." Hardly rolls off the tongue, now, does it? Let's go back in and change "Barrie's" to "Barries."

Now that we have our section and category structure created, let's add some articles.

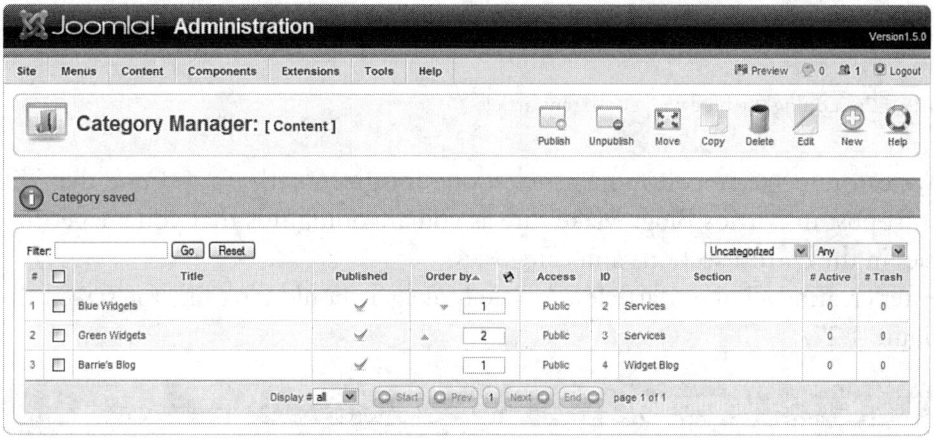

FIGURE 4.25 Category Manager with three categories

Creating Content Articles

Assuming you have been following along with our example with your own fresh installation of Joomla, you will already have two articles in your site. The About Us article can remain as it is—uncategorized. Rather than just delete the Services article, let's move it into the correct category. This will give us a chance to examine those Joomla functions.

Let's go to the Article Manager (**Content > Article Manager**) and open the services content article. Let's turn this article we made already into one about blue widgets. We can change the title to "Blue Widgets" and then make sure that its section is Services and its category is blue widgets. These drop-down boxes are shown in Figure 4.26.

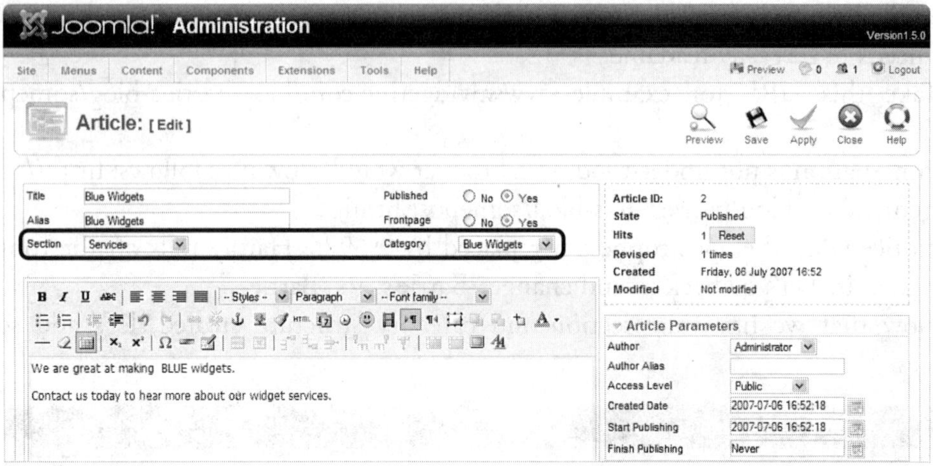

FIGURE 4.26 Editing the blue widget content article

We can now create two more articles, one for green widgets and one that will be our first post in Barrie's Blog. Make sure as you are doing this that you are getting the articles in the correct sections and categories.

After creating all of our articles, Article Manager should look like the screen shown in Figure 4.27.

FIGURE 4.27 Article Manager with four content articles

You'll notice in looking at Figure 4.27 that the two articles from before, About Us and Blue Widgets (formally Services) are shown on the front page. Before we move on, let's make sure that About Us is the only front page article.

If we take a look at the frontend of the website after making that Front Page adjustment, we should see a screen as shown in Figure 4.28.

FIGURE 4.28 Front page after adding content

If we navigate around a little, we quickly see that the links we created are still pointing to the individual content articles. Although we have set up our content, we haven't set up our menu items. Let's do that now.

Creating Menu Items

In Chapter 5, I go into much more detail about the relationship between menus, menu items, modules, and the content presented on the page. Right now I want to go through a complete process of creating a very simple site. We revisit the same process in the next chapter, but the repetition will help you understand a difficult concept in two different contexts.

First let's go to the main menu (**Menu Manager > main menu**) and delete the link to Services, leaving the link to About Us.

Then we can create two links to our blog and services. Clicking the Menu button in the Menu Manager as before, we go to the Add Menu Item screen shown in Figure 4.29. We will create a menu item to a blog layout for our two sections.

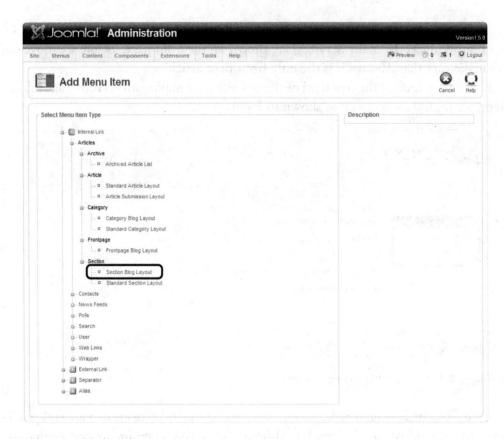

FIGURE 4.29 Adding a link to a section

This time we will link to a section blog layout, shown in Figure 4.29. I'll explain in more detail the various other options here in the next chapter. For now, just click away!

When you select the menu item type, you get the New Menu Item screen as before, as shown in Figure 4.30.

As we did when we were creating menu items that linked to single content articles, we have to choose where the link points to from the drop-down box. This time, however, we are selecting a section rather than a single content item, which is shown in Figure 4.31.

We can then create another menu item in exactly the same way that links to the Widget Blog section.

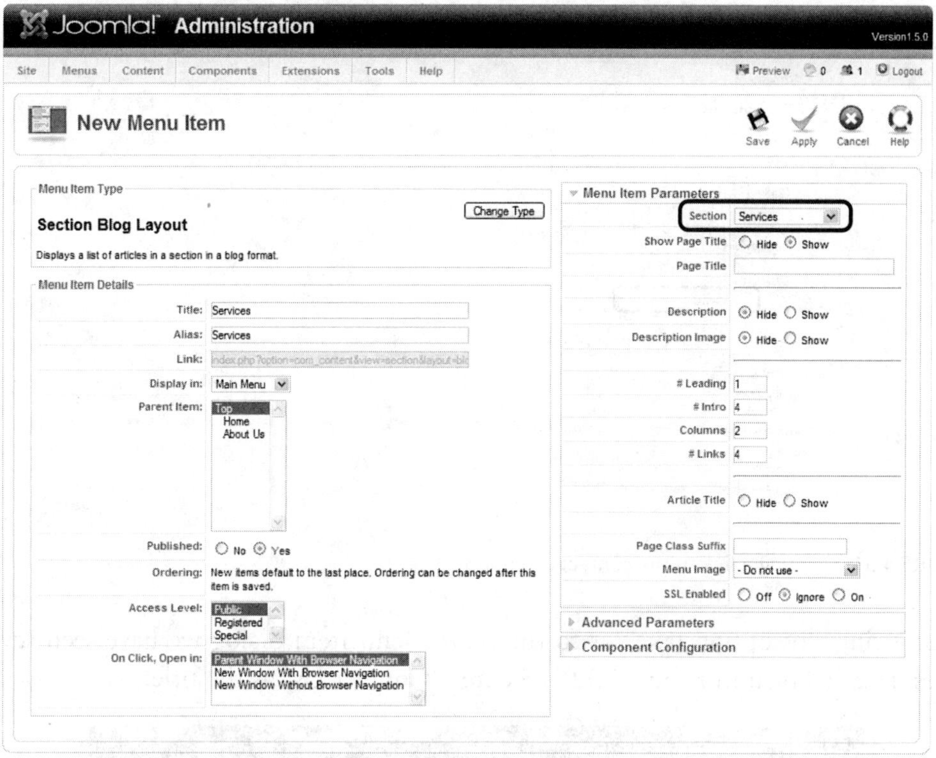

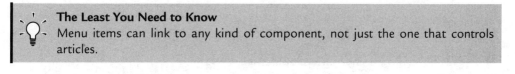

FIGURE 4.30 Selecting the section for a new menu item

Linking to Components

We now need a link to the Contact Us page. As explained previously, this link will be to the contacts component. This component will show a form in the main body that visitors can use to contact the administrator of the website.

> **The Least You Need to Know**
> Menu items can link to any kind of component, not just the one that controls articles.

Creating this link is relatively simple. We go to the main menu in the Menu Manager, and on clicking, we select a link to a standard contact layout, shown here in Figure 4.31. The link we want is circled in the figure.

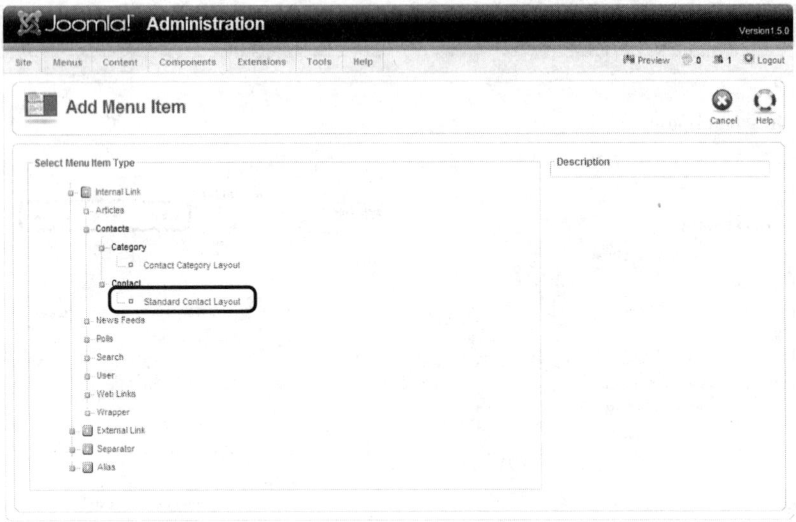

FIGURE 4.31 Creating a link to the contacts component

Selecting this option takes us to the New Menu Item dialog we have seen several times. Here (shown in Figure 4.32) we enter "Contact Us" as the title.

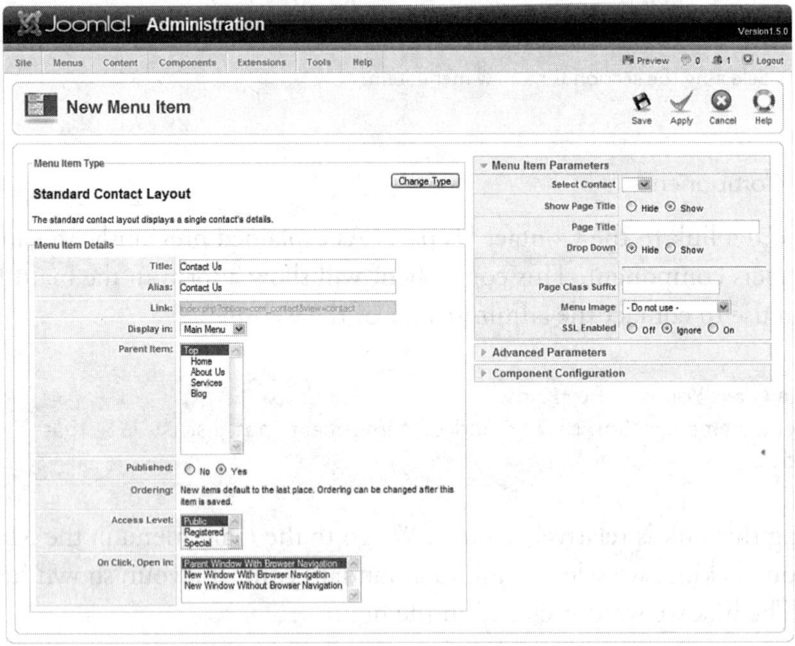

FIGURE 4.32 New Menu Item dialog for component link

If we click the new Contact Us link in the frontend, we get an error message. This is because we haven't set up any contacts yet in this new site (if we had installed the sample content, this would have been done for us).

To set up a contact we first need to set up a category for our contacts.

Go to **components > contacts > categories**.

This takes us to the contact Category Manager. We create a new category by clicking New and filling in the name for the category, as shown in Figure 4.33. The name for the category is Site Administrators.

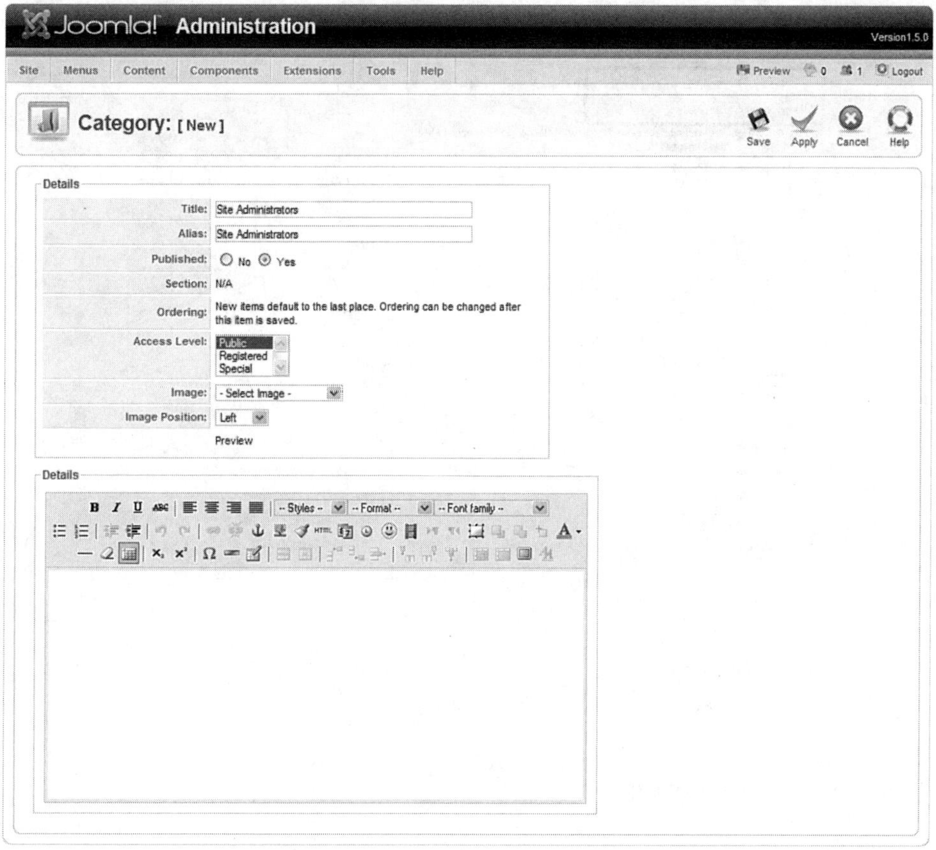

FIGURE 4.33 Contacts Category Manager

Next we need to add a contact that will be shown when you follow the menu item link, Contact Us.

Go to **components > contacts > contact.**

This takes us to the Contacts Manager, which should be empty. To create a new contact, we click New and get the Contact screen shown in Figure 4.34.

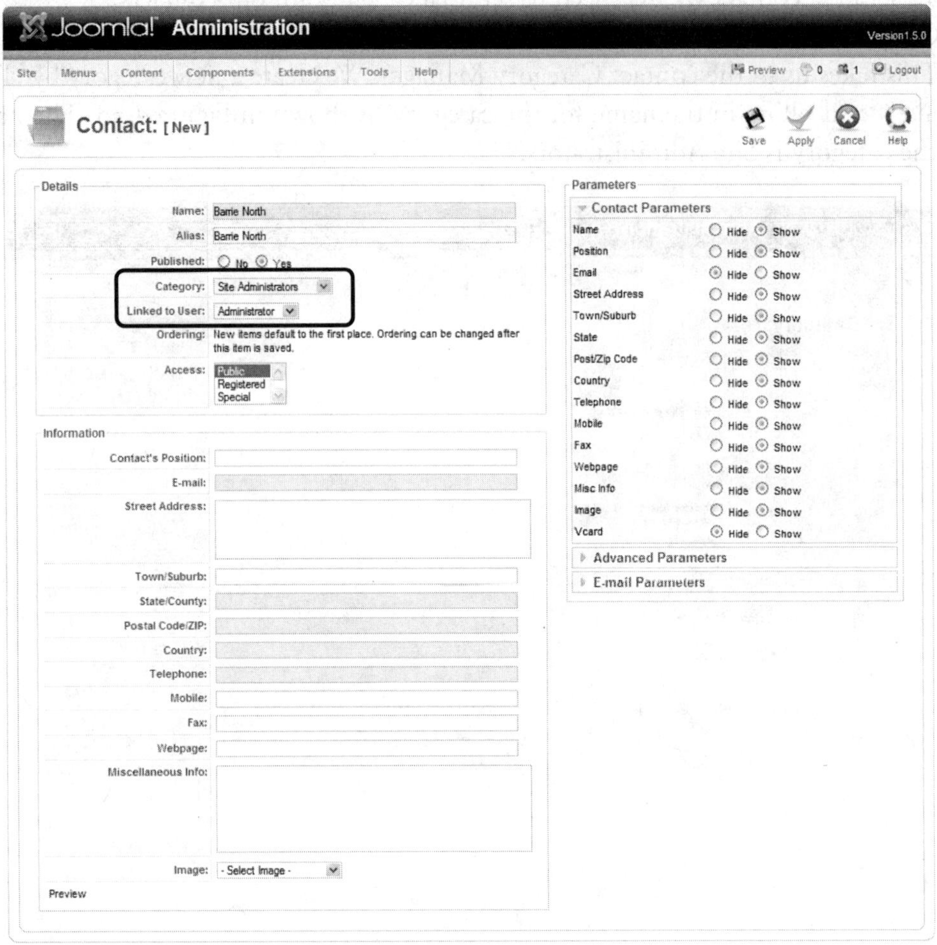

FIGURE 4.34 Creating a new contact

The most important step here is to make sure we link this contact to a user. The only user we currently have in this site is Administrator, so the drop-down box will only show that user. The same applies for the category we have to choose; we have only created one, Site Administrators, and that is what is in the drop-down box.

Now we can go back into our Contact Us menu item in mainmenu (**menus > mainmenu> contact us**), and we see Barrie North as an option for what the menu item links to. The frontend of the site should now look like Figure 4.35 when we follow the Contact Us menu item link.

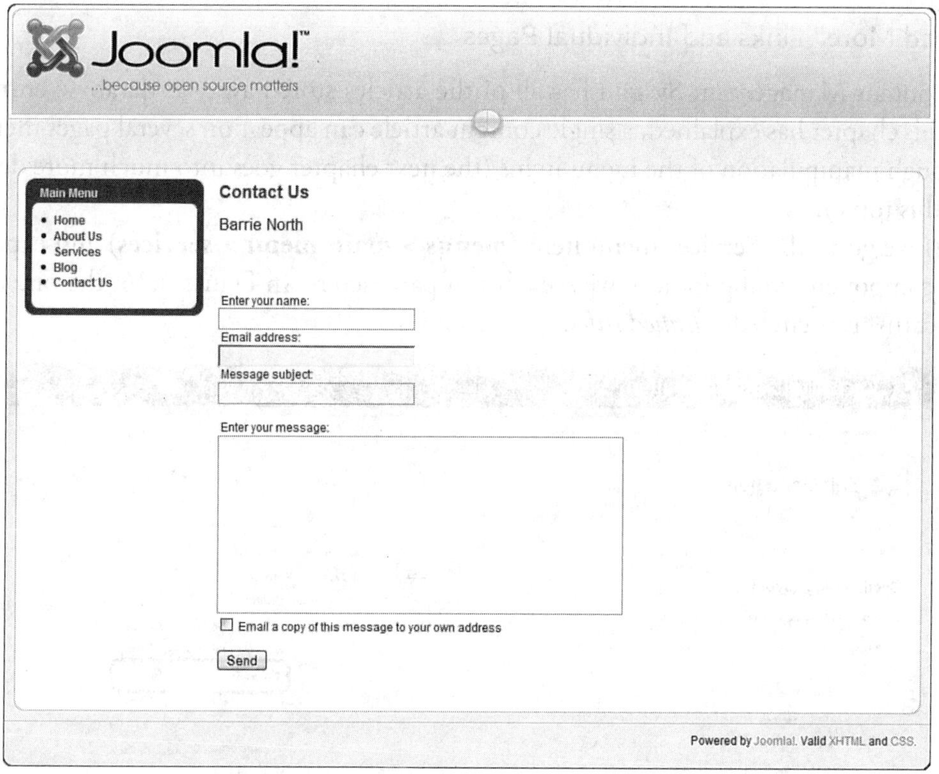

FIGURE 4.35 Contact Us page from the frontend

> **NOTE**
> If you noticed, each time we created a menu item, we had to select what the menu item links to in a parameter on the right-hand side drop-down box. This is common with all menu items, whether articles or components.

If we look back at our sitemap, we see that we had one link for each article, green widgets and blue widgets, each on their own page. Currently we have a link called Services that shows content from both of those articles.

How do we get two more pages for each of those articles?

This is very easy, in fact, and gives us a glimpse into how powerful a dynamic CMS can be. All we need to do is change a parameter on that menu item, and we instantly create two new web pages.

"Read More" Links and Individual Pages

A Content Management System has all of the articles stored away as database entries. As this chapter has explained, a single content article can appear on several pages merely through manipulation of the menu items (the next chapter goes into much more detail on this topic).

If we go to the Services menu item (**menus > main menu > services**) and expand the component configuration, we see a list of parameters. In Figure 4.36, the one that concerns us is circled—*linked titles*.

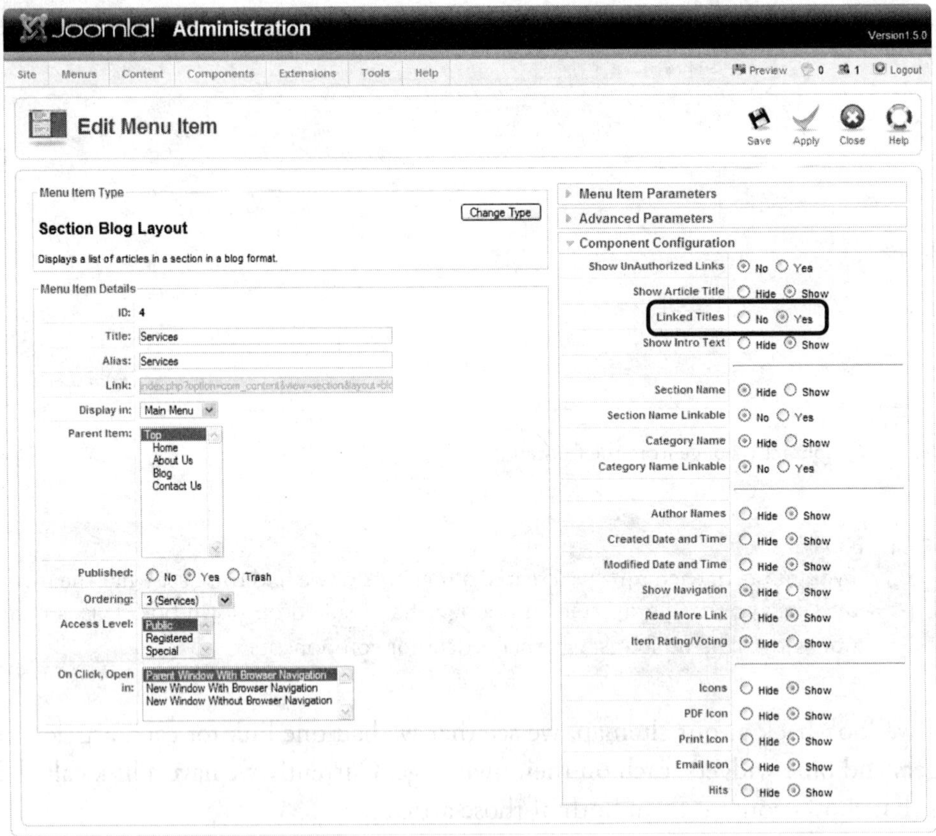

FIGURE 4.36 Component configuration parameters for a menu item

When we change this to Yes and save the menu item, this has the effect of turning all of the titles in the Services section blog into links that go to the individual content articles represented as a single page. As shown in Figure 4.37, there's a subtle difference: The title now has a hover effect, and there is also a Read More… link.

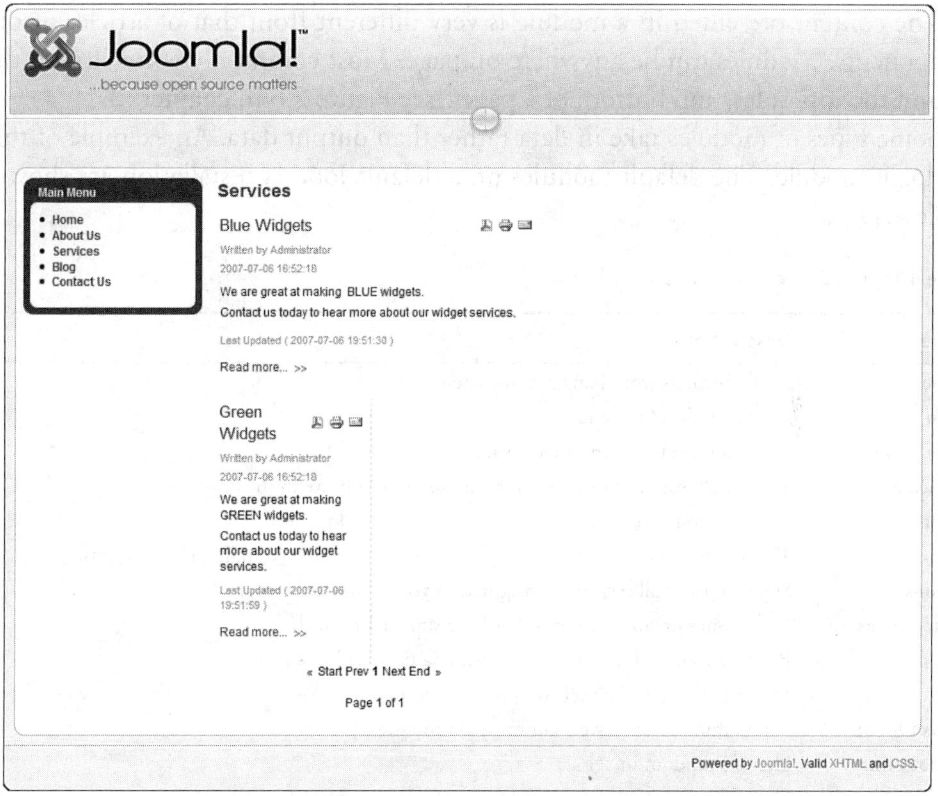

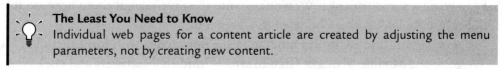

FIGURE 4.37   Frontend linked titles

Following these links will now take us to individual pages for the articles. We could have had a large number of articles showing in that section blog layout and could have created instant links to new pages by changing that simple parameter.

> **The Least You Need to Know**
> Individual web pages for a content article are created by adjusting the menu parameters, not by creating new content.

Module Content

Until now in this chapter we have been looking at how content can be organized and presented in the main body of a web page. It's also possible to have snippets of content appear around the edges of the main body by using Modules.

The content presented in a module is very different from that of articles or other components. Modules can be anywhere on page. Most commonly you will find them around the top, sides, and bottom of a page[2] (see Figure 2.6 in chapter 2).

Some types of modules take in data rather than output data. An example of this is the login module. The default modules on a default Joomla installation are shown in Table 4.1.

Table 4.1   Default Joomla Modules

Name	Description
Banner	Shows banners from banner component
Menu	Presents links of a menu
Login Form	Shows a form to log in or create account
Syndicate	Shows RSS feed links that viewers can use to syndicate to the home page
Statistics	Shows various site stats
Archive	This module shows a list of the calendar months, which contain archived items.
Sections	Shows a list of all sections configured in your database
Related Items	Shows links of content items that have similar keywords
Wrapper	Presents another URL inside an iframe (a page within a page)
Polls	Shows polls from the poll component
Who's Online	Shows number of viewers currently on the site
Random Image	Shows a random image
Newsflash	Shows a random content item from a chosen category
Latest News	Shows link list of most recently published content items
Popular	Shows link list of most popular content items (by page view)
Search	Shows a search box
Custom	A special module that is created by the administrator, which can contain any sort of HTML

The Custom module is very flexible. You can think of it as a tiny module article that can go on a particular page. We won't go into too much detail about how modules work because we look at them in detail in Chapter 6.

For now, we will add a Custom module to the home page with some text in it.

We go to the Module Manager (**Extensions > Module Manager**) and click New. This takes us to the New Module screen, shown in Figure 4.38.

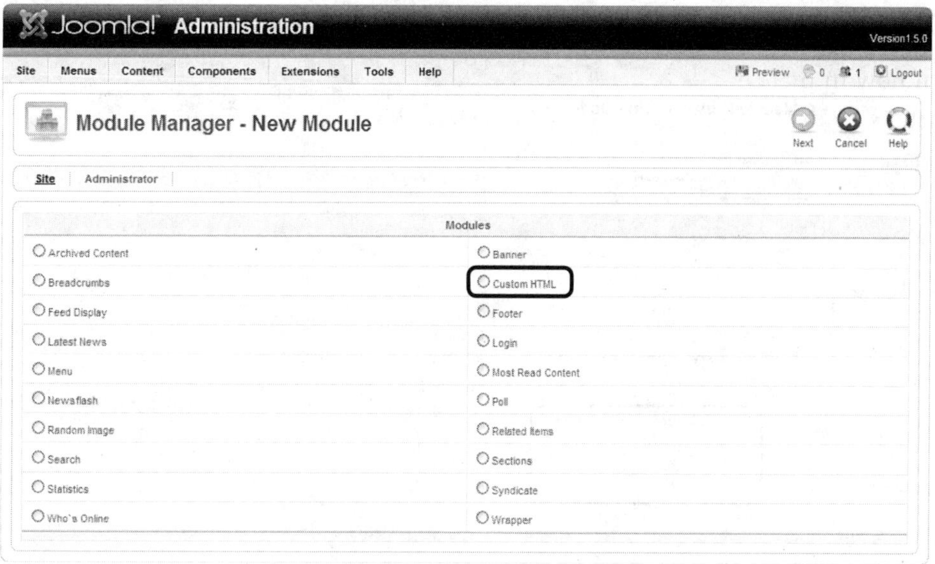

FIGURE 4.38 Creating a new custom module

We select the Custom HTML module shown in Figure 4.39 and click Next.

This takes us to the Edit Module screen (see Figure 4.39). Here we enter a title and some content in the editor, as well as make sure that it's in the correct position (we will use right) and has the correct menu assignment (all of them).

This will place a small snippet of content in the right-hand column.

Our small example site is now finished; hopefully it should look something like the screenshot shown in Figure 4.40.

We have organized our content and used some uncategorized content and a link to a component. The result to the viewer is a dynamic site that has a logical navigation scheme and some interactivity with a Contact Us form. In later chapters we will see how to set up much more complex sites such as a school website.

> **The Least You Need to Know**
> Creating a Joomla website from a sitemap will always require a combination of content articles, other components, and modules. From the backend they are administered in different ways (that is, articles versus other components), but in the frontend they appear seamless.

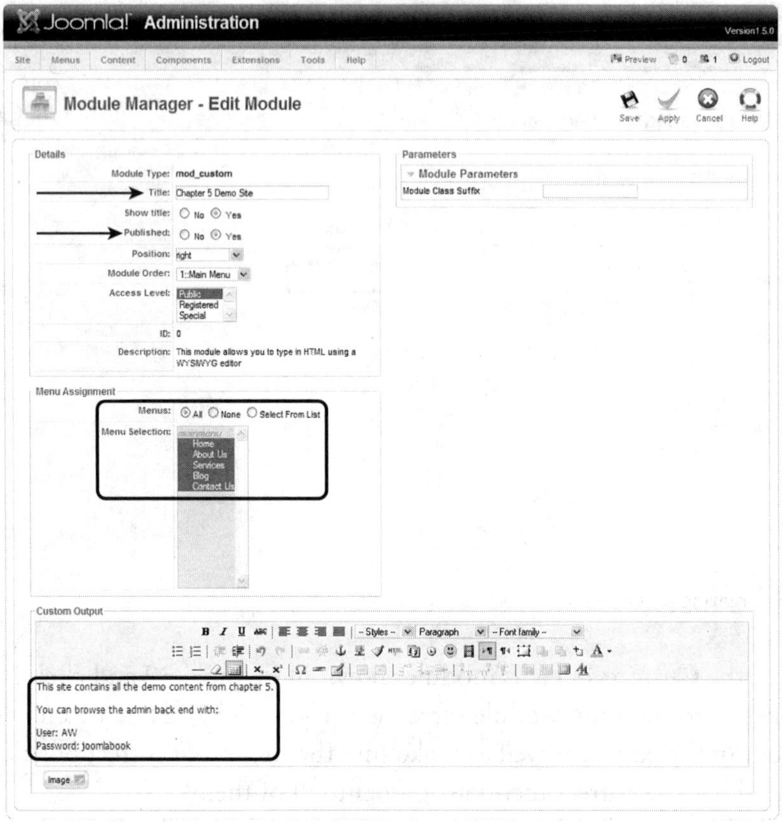

FIGURE 4.39 Editing a custom module

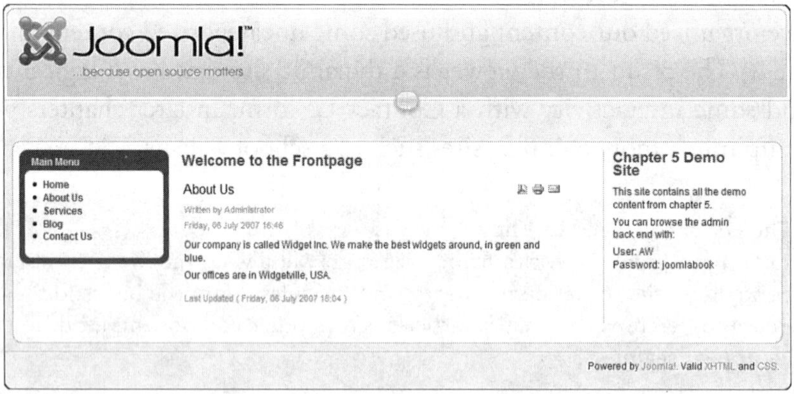

FIGURE 4.40 Completed seven-page Joomla site

User's Guide Chapter 4 Demo Site

Demos of the two sites created in this chapter are available at www.joomlabook.com. They are an exact copy of what you should have if you followed all the steps in this chapter. You can log in to the administrative backend so you can see the site framework and the sections, categories, and menus that were set up.

Summary

In this chapter, we tackled one of the trickiest parts of creating a Joomla site—taking a sitemap and content and organizing it into Joomla's content hierarchy.

- A sitemap is critical to having a well organized site. You must make an effort to draft one before you start working in the administrator backend.

- Joomla generates a page the instant you go to visit it. This means that the pages viewed can be easily changed by changing the menu links rather than the content itself.

- Joomla offers two methods to organize articles. The first is to use uncategorized articles, suited for very small sites. For larger sites the second method of sections and categories needs to be used.

- Making your pages with uncategorized content items is the simplest way to build a Joomla site, but it is difficult to manage with more than 10 pages.

- Menu links determine both what will be on a page and how it will be laid out.

- You can create links to a content item, but the content needs to exist first. The name of a link (anchor text) needs to be chosen very carefully.

- Components are mini-applications that present content in the main body in a special way. The home page of a Joomla site is a component. It allows you to pull content from anywhere in your site for its use.

- Joomla has only two hierarchy levels for organizing content sections and categories. A content article must be in a category, which must be in a section. This can lead to a redundant organizational level for small sites.

- There are many ways to organize the same set of content in a Joomla site.

- Menu items can link to any kind of component, not just the one that controls articles.

- Individual web pages for a content article are created by adjusting the menu parameters, not by creating new content.
- Creating a Joomla website from a sitemap will always require a combination of content articles, other components, and modules. From the backend they are administered in different ways (that is, articles versus other components), but in the frontend they appear seamless.

---

[1] This isn't true for content that is in a module. These do appear on pages without having to be linked to. They do have to be told what pages to appear on however, and by pages, we of course mean links! More on modules later.

---

[2] Note that the layout is totally dependant on the designer of the template, 1, 2, or 3 columns, footer, no footer, you get the idea.

Chapter 5

Creating Menus and Navigation

Menus are perhaps the core of a Joomla site. In a static HTML site, they merely serve as navigation. In a Joomla site, they serve that purpose but also determine the layout of what a dynamic page will look like and what content will appear on that page when you navigate to it.

The relationship between menus, menu items, pages, and modules is perhaps one of the most confusing in Joomla. This chapter explains this relationship so that you can create a navigation scheme that works for your site.

In This Chapter

This chapter examines how the navigation (menus and links) is built for a Joomla website and how the different aspects interact to produce a coherent navigation structure. We look at each of the follow questions.

- How do menus and modules work together?

- What do menu items do?

- What is a blog layout?

- What is a standard layout?

- How can I change a menu's appearance through the Module Manager?

- How do I get submenus or drop-down menus?

How Do Menus and Modules Work Together?

Each menu has a module that controls where and how the menu appears on a page. There are currently six menus that are installed in a default Joomla installation. If we go to the Menu Manager, we can see these six, as shown in Figure 5.1. One quick thing to point out in the Menu Manager is that you edit the menu by clicking the small menu item icon, not the title, as you might think.

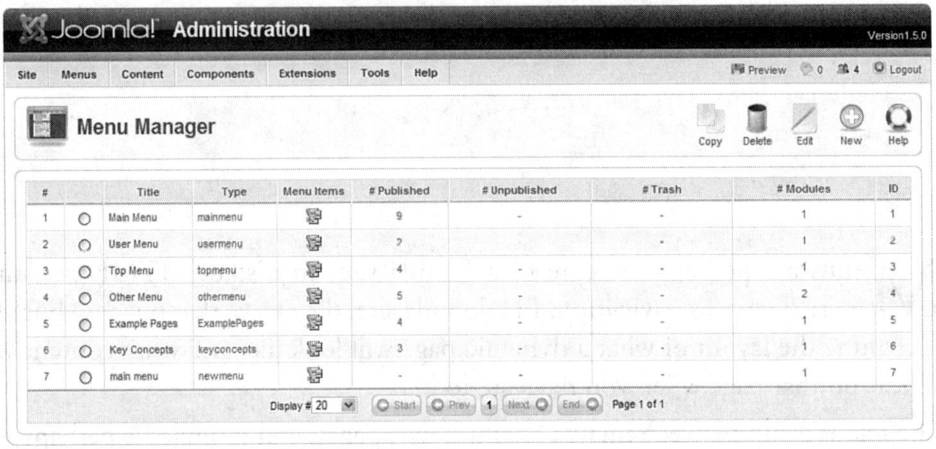

FIGURE 5.1 Six default menus

The six menus are as follows:

- **Main menu**. Contains the main navigation for the default content.

- **User menu**. A special menu that contains some functions for users when they are logged in.

- **Top menu**. A duplication of some links that are in the main menu.

- **Other menu**. Contains four offsite links to sites related to Joomla.

- **Example Pages**. Links demonstrating the different layouts.
- **Key Concepts**. Links to pages explaining layouts and extensions.

> **The Least You Need to Know**
> This menu structure is only Joomla's suggestion or example. I actually personally created the example pages and key concepts menus and content as part of a team working on Joomla sample content. It's very likely that the sample content will change and evolve over time and releases.
> These six menus get installed when you choose to "install sample data" during the installation. In most cases you will need to create your own or revise these. You could even just delete them and start over again.

The first thing to understand is that each menu has at least one module associated with it. This module controls where and how the menu appears. For example, you could have a module that only appears on the home page and in the left column.

Flip to Chapter 1,"Content Management Systems and an Introduction to Joomla," and read over the part about how a Content Management System is dynamic. The content gets pulled from the database and put into "placeholders" or "buckets" on the pages. A way to understand the previous paragraph is that the menu is the content in the database, and the module is a placeholder for it. If you want to position the menu, you move around its *placeholder* (the module) from the left-hand to the right-hand column for example. If you want to manage the *content* of the menu (the links), then you go to the Menu Manager.

The appearance of a menu is managed through the Module Manager, for example, whether a link gets an underline when you hover, what color the link is, and whether it looks like a button. All of these characteristics would be defined in the template's Cascading Style Sheets (CSS) file (more on that in Chapter 9, "Creating a Pure CSS Template") and are controlled in the Module Manager by using a module suffix (also explained further in Chapter 11, "Creating a Restaurant Site with Joomla").

Figure 5.2 shows one of the default menus installed, the *mainmenu*. Shown is the menu in the Menu Manager, its corresponding module in the Module Manager, and how it is presented in the frontend.

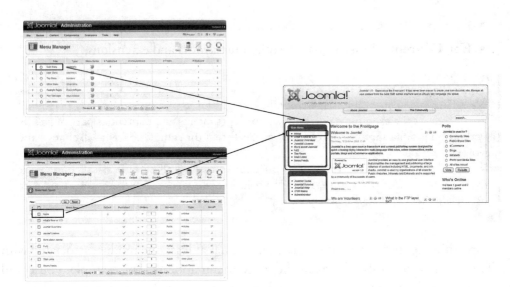

FIGURE 5.2 Interrelationship between menus and modules

The basic building blocks of these menus are the menu items. Each menu item corresponds to a single link in the frontend. Next we look at the importance of these menu items and what they do.

> **The Least You Need to Know**
> The backend part of a menu, where the links go and what they do, is controlled by the Menu Manager. The frontend part of a menu, where it is, and what it looks like, is controlled by a menu's module.

What Do Menu Items Do?

Answer: A lot!

In a Joomla site, all pages are generated dynamically. Joomla uses information from whatever link the site visitor just clicked to decide what the web page will contain and look like when he gets there.

You can think of a menu link as having three parts:

- Where the link goes
- What the Joomla page looks like after following the link
- How the menu link's appearance is controlled

The links on the menu are controlled by the menu item in that menu (here mainmenu) in the Menu Manager. This determines what pages they go to and the appearance of those pages. This is the "where" and the "what."

In this example, the menu's appearance (left column, brown background, and so on) is controlled by settings in the mainmenu module. This is the "how."

> **TIP**
> You can actually have more than one module for a menu. For example, you could have a menu appear in the left column on the home page and in the right column on other pages in the site.

We saw in Chapter 4, "Content Is King: Organizing Your Content" menus and links have some important characteristics:

- Menus control the site. Pages are dynamic and so don't exist until linked to.
- Menus/links and content are completely independent of each other in the database; content must be created and then linked to.
- Menu links can be created as you are creating the content after it is saved.
- Menu links can link to content or components.
- Menu links determine the appearance of the page linked to.

Let's look in more detail at the three parts of a menu item: the what, where, and how. To do this let's create a menu item.

Creating a Menu Item

The Menu Manager contains all the menus on a site. Each menu controls where links go to and what the page looks like when you get there within a specific module.

To better understand the where and the what, let's create a menu item (a link) within a menu. It doesn't matter which menu at this point; you can pick any to try this out.

When you create a menu item, as we saw in Chapter 4, you get a screen where you are presented with a tree-like structure. You click the option to drill down to further choices. The top level of the tree is shown in Figure 5.3.

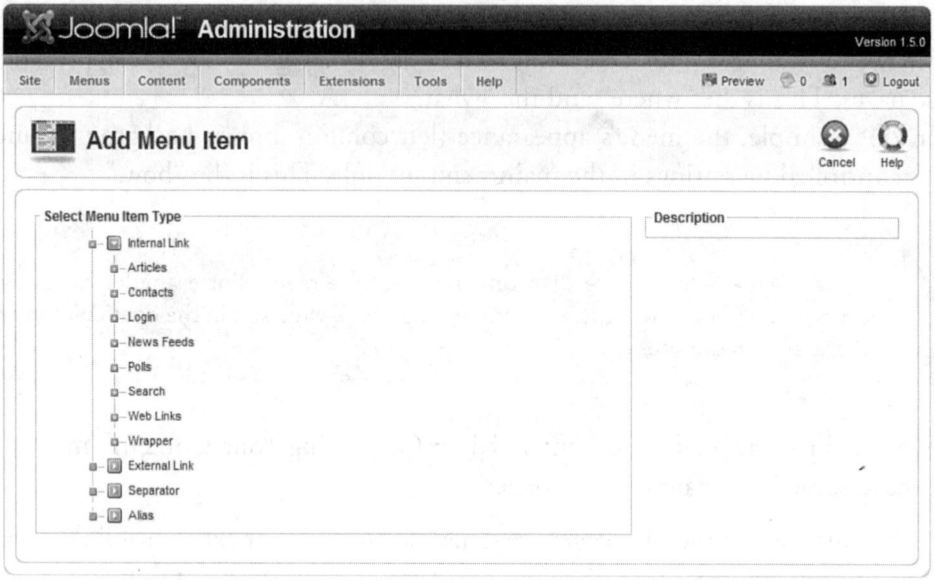

FIGURE 5.3 Menu link options

The purpose of this first screen is for you to decide what the page will look like when the link is followed. Joomla calls this a page's *layout*. Different layouts combine one or more articles based on their section or category in a selection of styles. Let's look at some of the main ones.

There are many choices, and you can only see one at a time, so I have created a compilation of them all, shown in Figure 5.4. If you have installed any components that can be linked to, such as Mosets Directory, they will also be shown as menu options.

Now, this list is intimidating, but don't panic. Right now, we only need to consider four of these options:

- Articles→Category→Category Blog Layout
- Articles→Category→Standard Category Layout
- Articles→Section→Section Blog Layout
- Articles→Section→Standard Section Layout

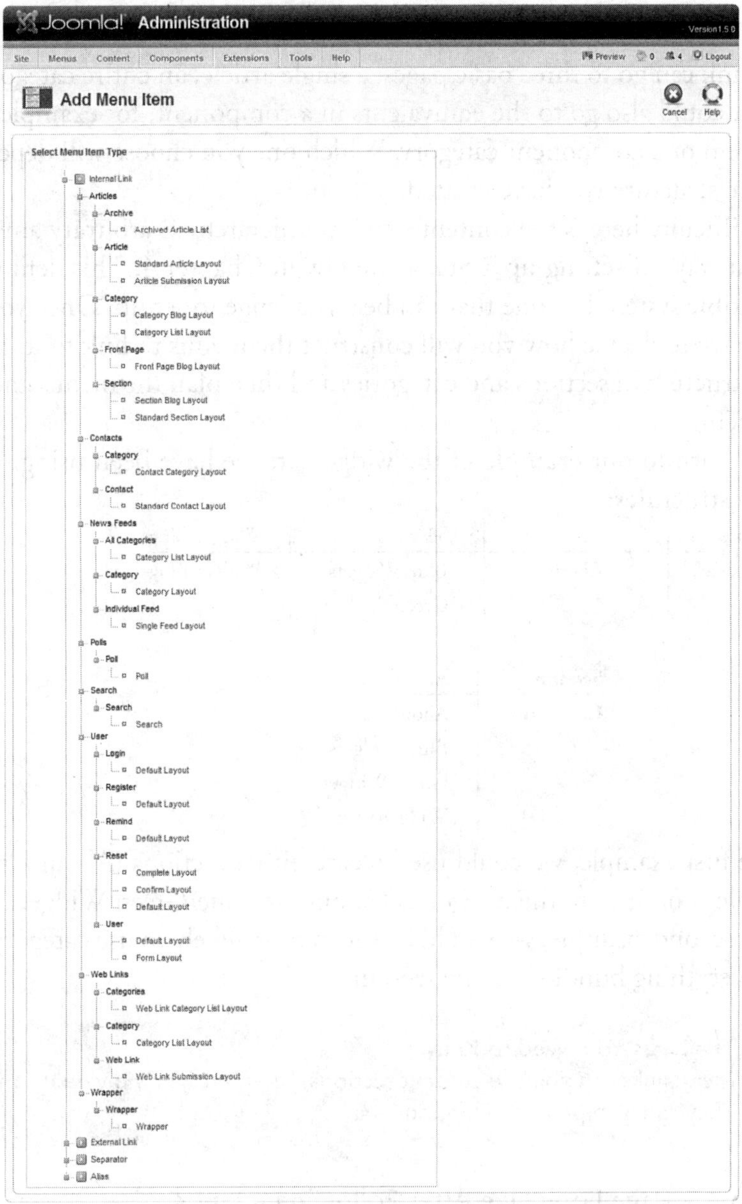

FIGURE 5.4 All possible menu options

Where Does a Menu Item Link To?

A menu link can go to three basic pages: a single article, an entire category, or an entire section. It could also go to the equivalents in a component, for example, a single component item or a component category. Which one you choose will depend completely on the site structure you have created.

The difficulty here is the content structure/hierarchy is arbitrary anyway, and there are several ways of setting up a site, as we saw in Chapter 4. This definitely makes for a very flexible system but one that can be a challenge to set up. Once you have set that up, you have to decide how you will construct the menus to link to it. So plan the site content structure in sections and categories and then plan the menus and how you will link to them.

Let's return to our example of the widget site we have been using. We considered these two structures:

Sections	About Us	Services	Widget Blog
Categories	About Us	Blue Widgets	Widget Blog
		Green Widgets	

And

Sections	AllContent
Categories	About Us
	Blue Widgets
	Green Widgets
	Widget Blog

In the first example, we could use links to either sections (About Us, Services, and Widget Blog) or links to the categories (About Us, Blue/Green Widgets, Widget Blog).

In the second example, we would be much more likely to use category links because we had everything bundled in one section.

> **The Least You Need to Know**
> Menu links can point to content sections, categories, or individual content articles. They can also point to components.

What Does a Page Look Like After Following a Link?

Now that we've briefly looked at the *where*, let's look at the *what* (what the pages look like). There are two basic layouts you can have when you follow a menu item: a *blog* and a *standard* layout. A blog is so named because it is similar to that seen on many blogs, a series of paragraphs with the opportunity to "Read More." A standard layout is a table with all the articles listed as titles only.

> **NOTE**
> It is possible to create your own customized layouts of articles by creating overrides in the template. We will look at this in more detail in Chapter 9.

Thus we have two basic options of how to present content:

- The blog layout shows content articles with the option of showing some "intro" or "teaser" text. There are also more presentation options; you can have one column or ten. The first few items can have summary text, and the rest could be just links. The blog format is much more flexible than the standard layout.

- The standard (table) layout shows all content items with titles only. The titles are links to the items themselves.

> **NOTE**
> We have been talking about two types of blogs (sorry). The Widget Blog, discussed in our widget site, is a blog that we see all over the Web, blogspot.com, for example. Joomla, however, uses the word to describe a specific article *layout*. Of course, the name is taken from "blogs," but just be aware that the word has a specific meaning in Joomla.

Continuing our Widget Company Site Example

Let's develop our site a little bit more so we can see what these layouts look like.

When we last left our widget site in Chapter 4, we had four articles in two sections (see Figure 5.5).

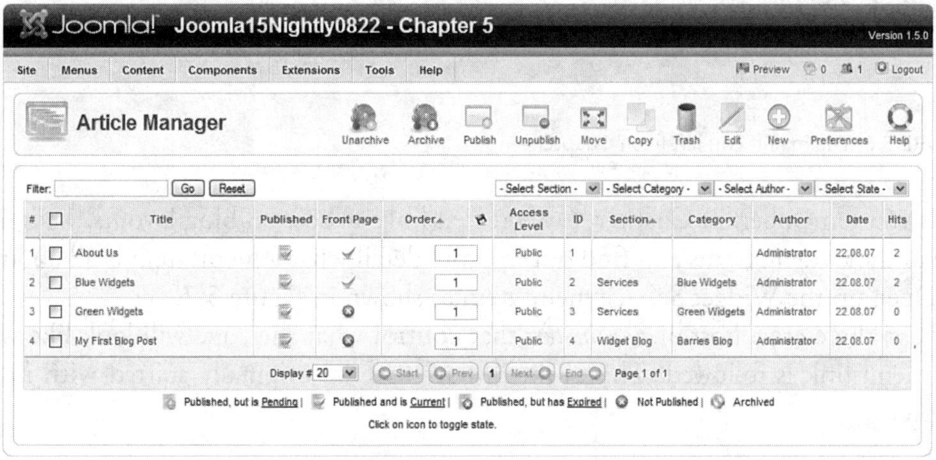

FIGURE 5.5 Our articles from Chapter 4

Now we have a few articles, we are going to create some menu links to them in blog and standard formats. We will actually have them pointing to exactly the same content; the layouts will simply be different. This also serves as a good example of how a one to one relationship does not exist between menu links and content.

> **The Least You Need to Know**
> There are two main layouts of a Joomla page, blog and standard. The blog shows intro text with a "Read More" link. The standard layout shows a table of linked titles. Which layout is used is determined by the menu link parameters.

Blog Layout

Go to the Menu Manager and open the mainmenu. If you were following along in Chapter 4, you will have a few menu items that we created, as shown in Figure 5.6.

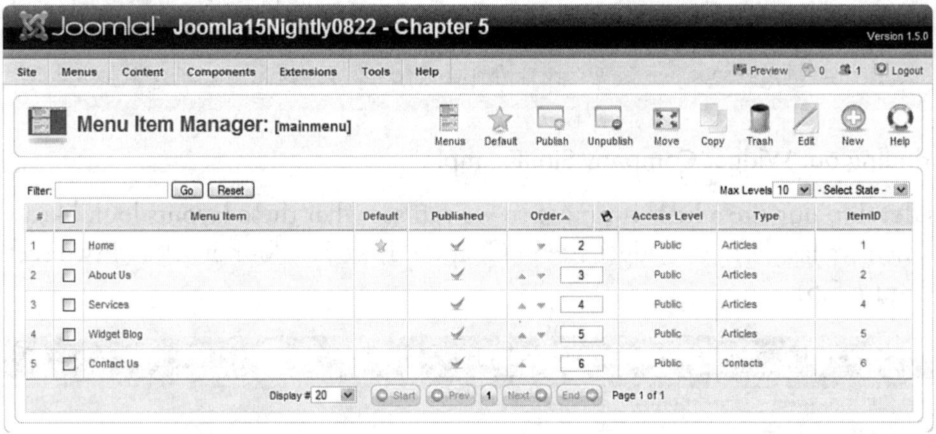

FIGURE 5.6 The mainmenu left from Chapter 4

If you remember, in Chapter 4 we created links to section blog layouts. Let's open one of these menu items and find out in more detail what a menu item is all about.

Open up the Widget Service menu item as shown in Figure 5.7.

Last, there are a host of *parameters* that control what the page will look like when the menu link is followed. This is the "what" that we originally started with in this chapter.

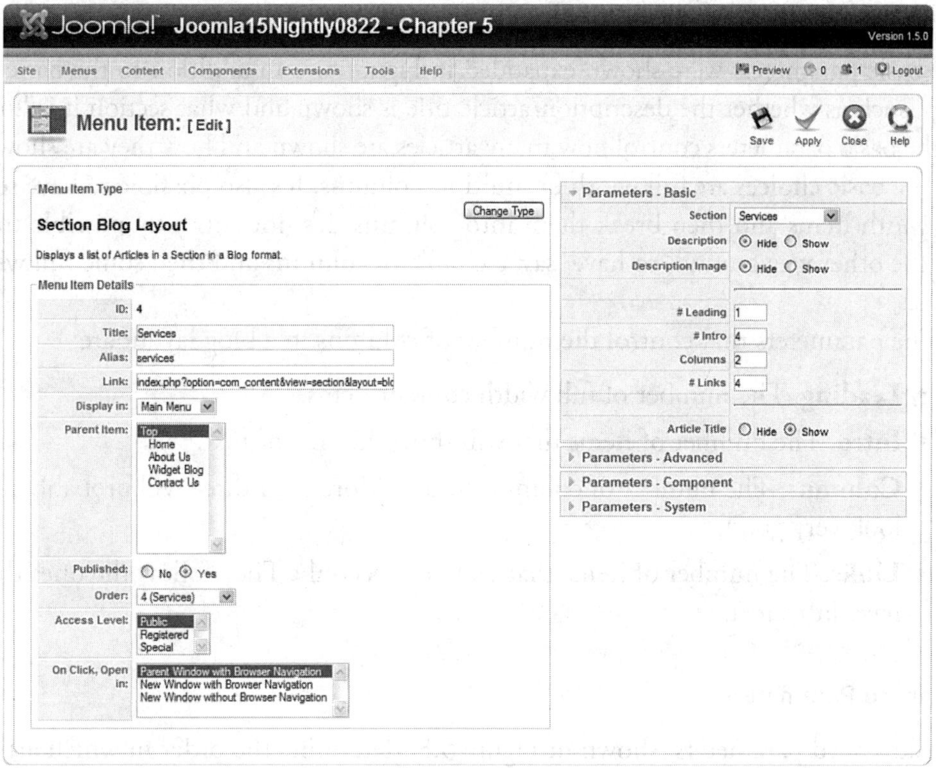

FIGURE 5.7 Section Blog Layout Menu item

There are many parameters that can be set: basic, advanced, component, and system.

The choice of blog or table, and then the parameter settings in the menu item are the biggest factors in controlling the look and flow of a Joomla site. Note this description for a blog layout applies whether we are linking to a section or a category.

Blog Layout Parameters

Rather than regurgitate the information on the Help site, let's look at some of the more common or important parameters shown on the right side in Figure 5.7. The most important settings are those that determine how many items will be shown and in what format.

Basic Parameters

The basic parameters were shown expanded in Figure 5.7. In addition to the basic settings, such as whether the description/article title is shown and what section it is linked to, the basic parameters control how many articles are shown and how they are shown.

The basic choices are full width or multiple columns. It's also possible to have some full width items and then break them into columns. It's not currently possible to do this the other way around, to have, say, a couple of columns and then some full width items.

The parameters that control the number of columns in a blog layout are:

- **Leading**. The number of full width content items.
- **Intro**. The number of items that will show the "intro" text.
- **Columns**. The number of columns to use. More than three will probably not look very good.
- **Links**. The number of items that will be links only. They follow the ones that have intro text.

Advanced Parameters

The advanced parameters, shown in Figure 5.8, determine the order in which articles appear.

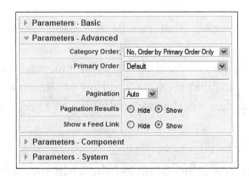

FIGURE 5.8 Section Blog Layout advanced parameters

The actual order in which content items appear can be quite complicated. They could be listed by date, alphabetically, as selected in the content manager, to name a few. There are basically two overarching options:

- You can sort (if you have more than one) the content into categories first by selecting anything other than "No, order by Primary Order only." You can sort the categories alphabetically or by "Ordering," which means the order that they appear in the Category Manager. Then the content items will get sorted by what you select in the Primary Order.

- You can bundle all the items together by selecting the "Primary Order Only" and then whatever you desire in the Primary Order.

Obviously, these are only meaningful if you have items from more than one category in the link.

Component Parameters

The component parameters, shown in Figure 5.9, are duplicates of ones in the Article Manager preferences, such as whether to show author names. Having these options allows you to override the global settings on a menu item (page-by-page) basis.

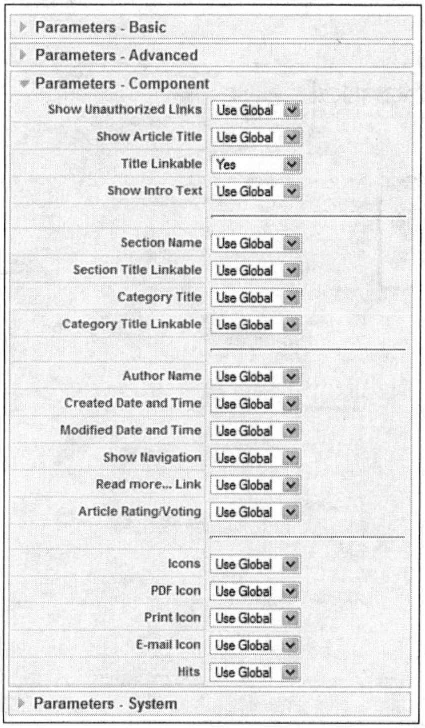

FIGURE 5.9 Section Blog Layout component parameters

System Parameters

Last, the system parameters include settings such as whether the page title is to show, as shown in Figure 5.10.

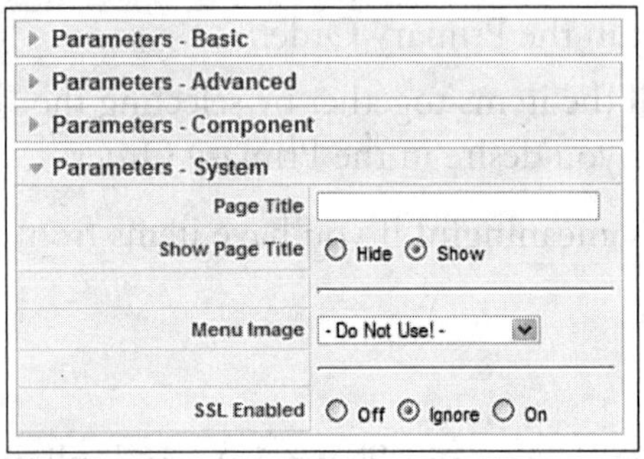

FIGURE 5.10 Section Blog Layout system parameters

If we keep all of the default parameters, our live site will look like that shown in Figure 5.11.

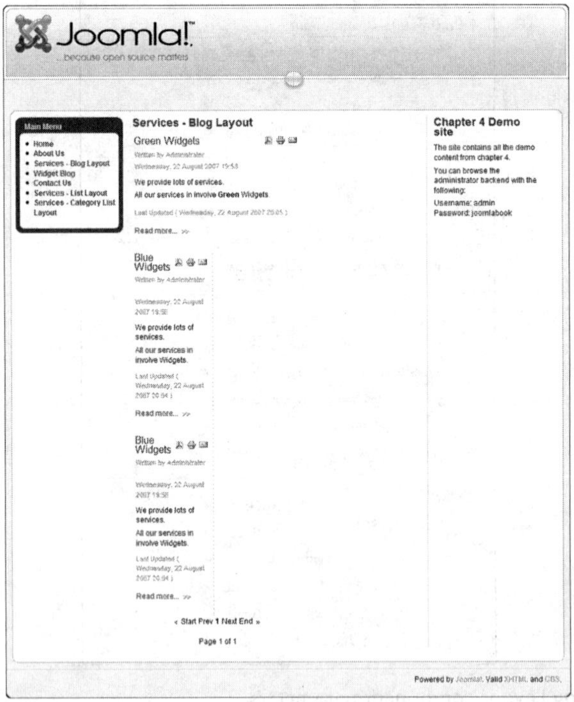

FIGURE 5.11 A basic blog layout of a section

This screenshot is the blog that is shown with our two content articles. It's a blog of a section. Here you can see there is one full width leading content item, and four are shown in two columns.

> **The Least You Need to Know**
> A blog layout presents content items in any number of columns, with the option to show intro text along with a "Read More" link.

List/Standard Layout for a Section

Next we create a page with the same articles from the services section, but shown in a *list layout*. Sometimes this is called a *table layout* or a *standard layout*. Let's create a second menu item that links to the same content but presents it in a different format. In addition to showing the second main layout option in Joomla, this will also illustrate the concept that the content is dynamic and that the same content in the database can appear on many pages.

Going to the mainmenu in the Menu Manager, we click New and this time select the Section Layout from the option tree circled in Figure 5.12.

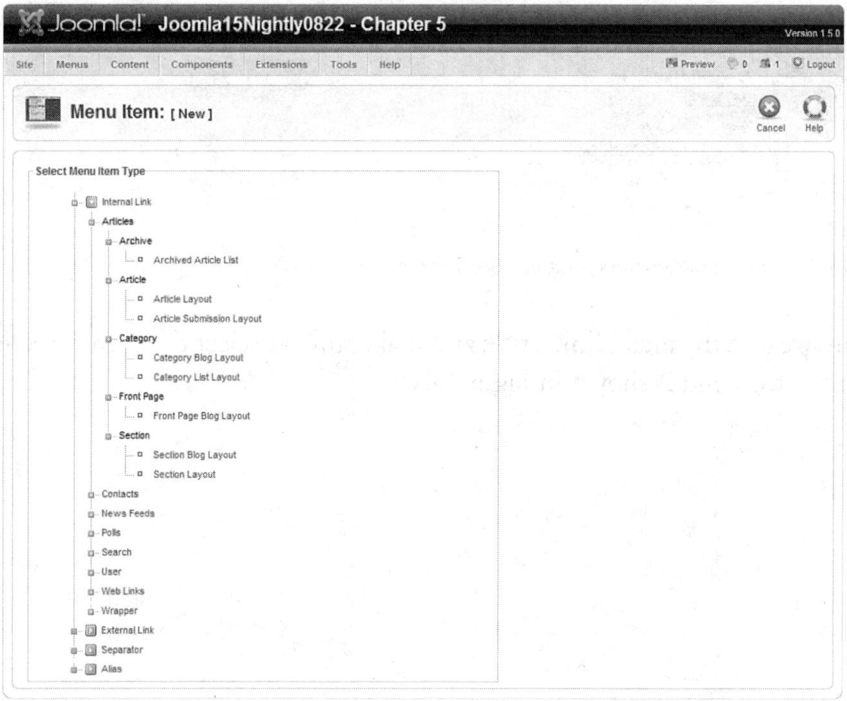

FIGURE 5.12 Selecting a Section List Layout

The New Menu Item screen is more or less the same as before except the parameters are different (see Figure 5.13).

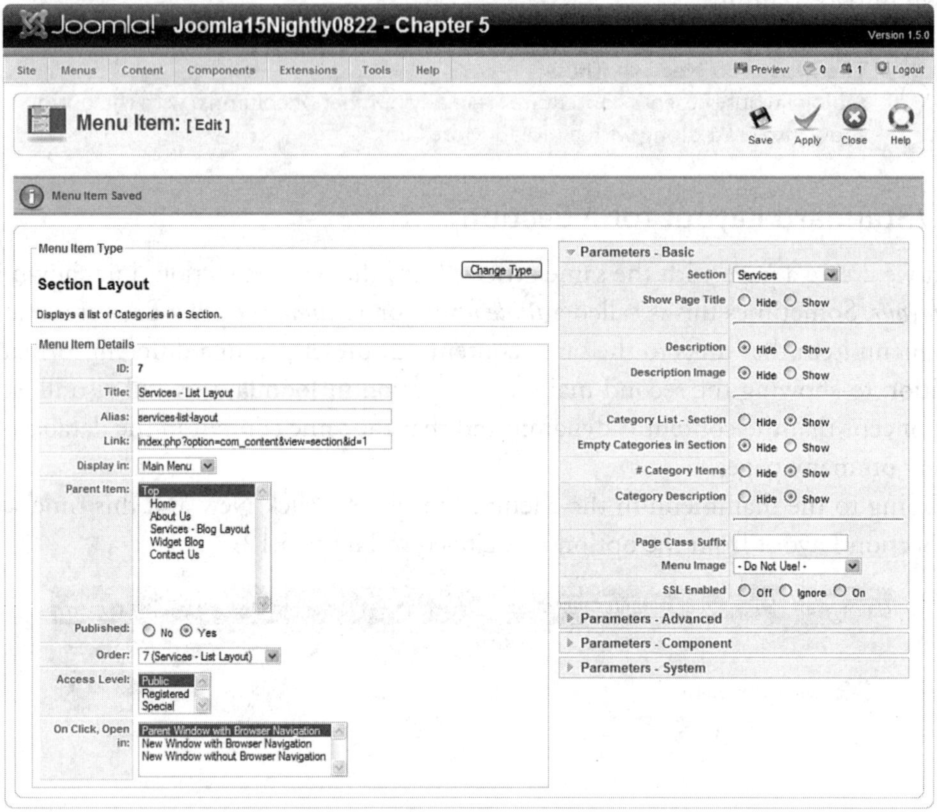

Figure 5.13 Menu item parameters for a List Section Layout

Again, we give the menu link a title and make sure we select the correct section. The result in the frontend is shown in Figure 5.14.

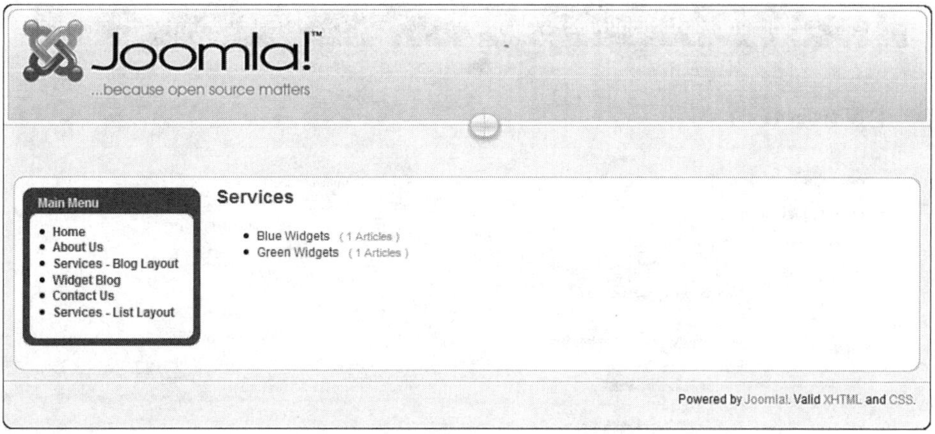

FIGURE 5.14 Frontend view of a List Section Layout

Section List/Standard Layout Parameters

The main difference in parameters from the blog layout is in the basic settings. As you can see in Figure 5.13, you can set various options for how the categories are listed.

There is little difference with the blog layout whether you have a menu item linking to a section or a category, but the parameters and presentation for the list/standard layout is a little different. Let's create a list/standard layout to a category to see this in action.

List/Standard Layout for a Blog

Going to the mainmenu in the Menu Manager, we click New and this time select the Category List Layout from the option tree.

The New Menu Item screen is more or less the same as the Section List Layout, except the parameters are different (see Figure 5.15).

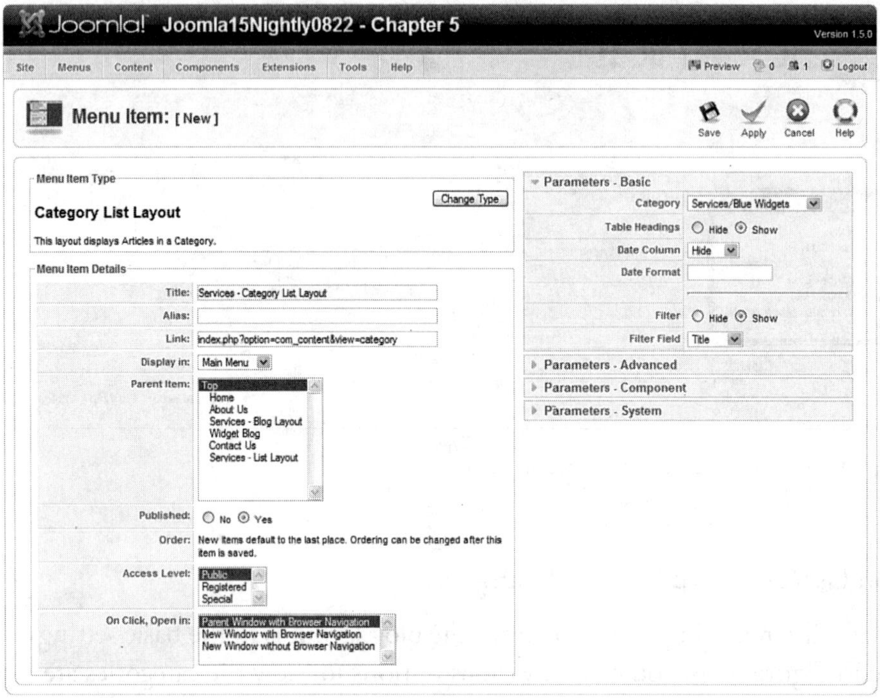

FIGURE 5.15 Menu item parameters for a Category List Layout

Again, we give the menu link a title and make sure we select the correct category. The result in the frontend is shown in Figure 5.16.

FIGURE 5.16 Frontend view of a List Category Layout

Category List/Standard Layout Parameters

The main difference in parameters between this and the blog layout is in the basic settings. As you can see in Figure 5.15, you can set various options for how the articles are listed.

> **The Least You Need to Know**
> A Standard layout shows articles as linked article titles in a table. The presentation for a section is slightly different than a category.

Module Manager

The Module Manager controls the placement and appearance of a menu, for example, whether you want the menu to be in the left or right column or if the links have a hover effect.

As mentioned previously, when you create a menu, a corresponding module is created for it. The module will be called whatever was used for the menu name.

> **NOTE**
> Any visual look and feel, like a hover effect, you want for a menu must be present in the CSS files of a template. Most templates have a number of options pre-created, and you select between them using the module suffix parameter.

As an example, let's check out some templates. I am going to use some of the demos from www.joomlashack.com; you can find these four templates at

- demotemplates.joomlashack.com/lush
- demotemplates.joomlashack.com/element
- demotemplates.joomlashack.com/simplicty
- demotemplates.joomlashack.com/lightfast

Their menus are shown in Figure 5.17.

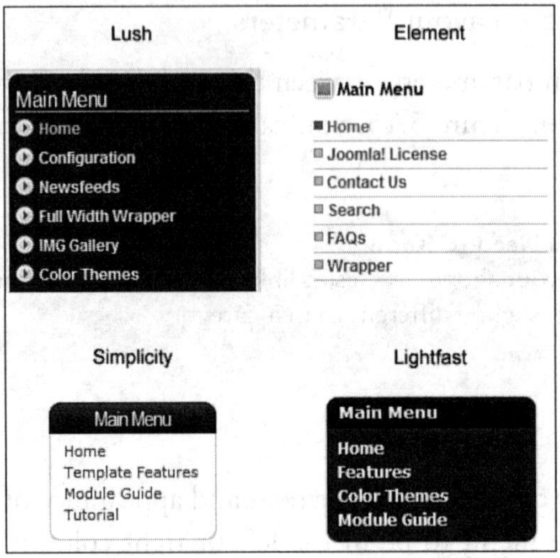

FIGURE 5.17 Four different styles of menu in different templates

The underlying XHTML code outputted by Joomla is identical in these four examples. The difference is that slightly different menu links are used (which I consider content), and the CSS is different. All of that CSS is controlled by the template. The point to emphasize here is that the module and the template CSS are controlling the appearance of the menus.

Let's see how this is done. If we go to the Module Manager (**Extensions>Module Manager**), we see a list of all the modules currently on the site (see Figure 5.18).

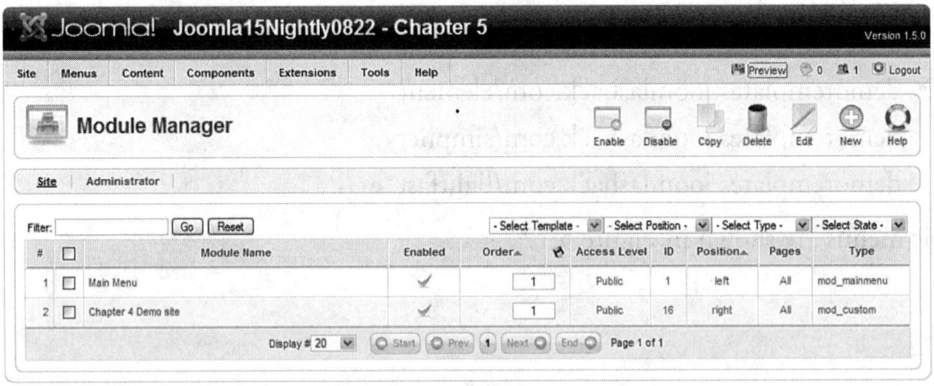

FIGURE 5.18 Module Manager showing Main Menu

You can see in Figure 5.18 that we have a module called Main Menu, which corresponds to the…mainmenu. The module type for this is a mod_mainmenu.

> **NOTE**
> Joomla is talking about two different things for mainmenus! One is the name of the main menu of the site that serves as the main navigation in a default install. The second use of the term is that mod_mainmenu is the type of module that controls a menu, any menu. It probably should be called just mod_menu.

Let's look closer at how we can control the menu. Clicking the Main Menu module gives you the parameters for that menu (see Figure 5.19).

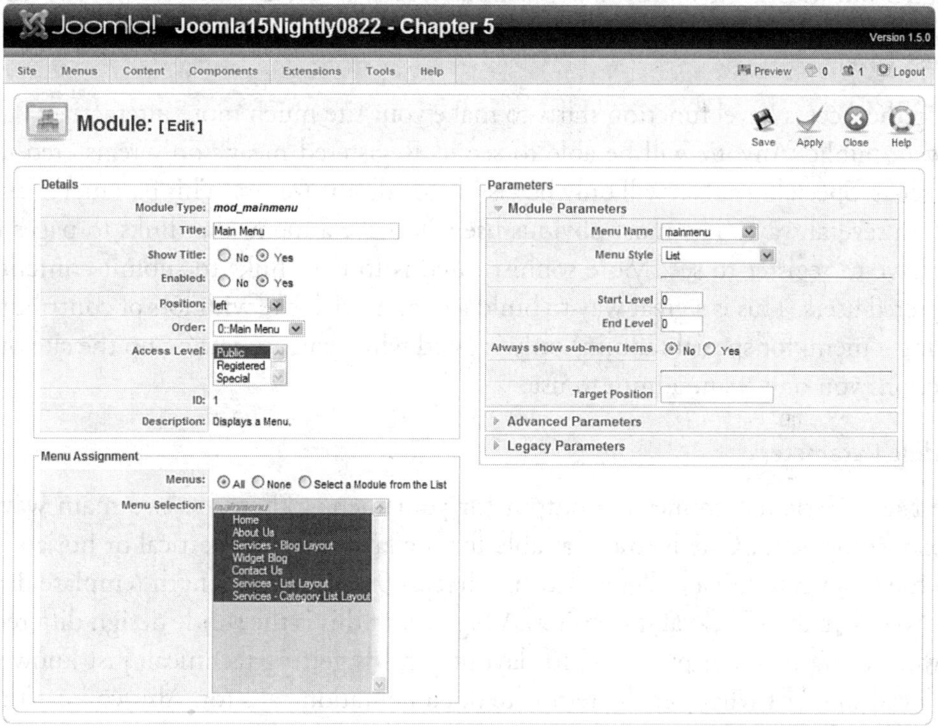

FIGURE 5.19 Menu Module parameters

Module Parameters

There are many options here for the parameters of the module. Let's look at some of the more important ones.

Show Title

Show Title determines whether the title is shown on the page output. This will be an H3 tag unless overridden in the template.

Position

The Position option controls what module location the menu appears in. This is set by the designer of the template you are using. Note the descriptive location of a module, for example, left doesn't have to actually be on the left. It will depend on where the designer put it. If using a third-party template, refer to the documentation provided.

Access Level

Using the Access Level function starts to make your site much more interactive. Public is, well, public. Anyone will be able to see it. Registered means only registered users will see it. Special means it will only be visible to administrators. This parameter can be used in several ways. The most obvious use is to have a menu that links to pages that you have to register to see. More sophisticated is to have links to submit content for registered users. This is a great way to build a content rich site with lots of contributors. Setting a menu for special (admin) only is good while you are setting up the site or for functions you only want admin to use.

Module Parameters

The Menu Style determines the output for your menu. There are two main ways to display your menu: One is to use a table for the layout (either vertical or horizontal), and the other is to use a bulleted list. In Chapter 9 I discuss at length template design and how to make W3C-valid websites. A big part of this is the subtle design differences between using tables or pure CSS for layout. This is getting technical; just know that you need to select whatever the template documentation calls for. Also you can't have sublevels currently in 1.0.X with a flat list.

At the time of writing, Joomla 1.5 has legacy support for the previous way that a bulleted list was rendered (flat list) and a new way that allows more flexibility (list).

Thus there are four current options:

- **List**. New method of showing a bulleted list
- **Vertical**. Uses a vertical table
- **Horizontal**. Uses a horizontal table
- **Flat List**. Old method of showing a bulleted list

The key improvement to the new list is that you can now have submenus that will have flat/bulleted lists `<ul>` inside each other. This makes design tricks such as suckerfish drop-down menus possible without any third-party extensions.

Menu and Module Class Suffixes (Advanced Parameters)

The Menu Suffix and Module Class Suffix control the appearance of the menu. All of the menus will use CSS in the template to style how they look. By carefully coding the CSS, the menu's appearance can be quickly and easily changed based on the suffixes used. An example of how this works might be different colored rounded boxes, as shown in Figure 5.17, with our Joomlashack examples.

Menu Assignment

Perhaps the most important parameter is the Menu Assignment. This controls which pages the menu will appear on. Now remember that a "page" only exists if a link points to it, so the list here is really a list of menu items (links) rather than pages. You can select All, None, or Select. You can also CRTL+click to select multiple pages…I mean links!

> **NOTE**
> You can have more than one module corresponding to the same menu; just copy the module. For example, you could have a side menu (or any other module) that was in the left column on the home page but in the right column through the rest of the site.

> **The Least You Need to Know**
> The module for a menu controls its placement on a page and its appearance. It also controls what pages the menu will appear on and what access level can see them, that is, guest or registered user. The menu's appearance is determined by code in the template's CSS.

Submenus

Joomla 1.5 has a feature with which you can create submenus, and they can be displayed in various ways. In the previous version of Joomla, it was not possible to have submenus if you were displaying your menu as a flat list. This was an issue because a flat list is a more standards-compliant method of displaying links.

In 1.5, this functionality was added to menus. It allows you to have submenus and flat lists. This is very important, as in the hands of a skilled template designer it allows you to do things such as have drop-down menus and images for links without having to resort to JavaScript or tables, both of which are bad for accessibility, SEO, and W3C compliance.

If "always show submenu items" is set to "yes," you get the following output. Note that you *must* have the menu style selected as List, and I usually have the end level set to 99 to make sure it's always expanded.

```html
<ul class="menuthreelevel">
  <li id="current" class="active item1"><a href="#"><span>Home</span></a></li>
  <li class="parent item27"><a href="#"><span>1st Link 1st level</span></a>
    <ul>
      <li class="parent item34"><a href="#"><span>1st Link 2nd level </span></a>
        <ul>
          <li class="item52"><a href="#"><span>1st link 3rd level</span></a></li>
          <li class="item53"><a href="#"><span>2nd Link 3rd level</span></a></li>
        </ul>
      </li>
      <li class="item2"><a href="#"><span>2nd link 2nd level</span></a></li>
      <li class="item37"><a href="#"><span>3rd link 2nd level</span></a></li>
    </ul>
  </li>
  <li class="parent item41"><a href="#"><span>2nd link 1st level </span></a>
    <ul>
      <li class="item50"><a href="#">1st Link 2nd level</a></li>
      <li class="item48"><a href="#">2nd Link 2nd level</a></li>
      <li class="item49"><a href="#">3rd Link 2nd level</a></li>
    </ul>
  </li>
</ul>
```

Notice this output. There are multiple classes on the `<li>` tags allowing advanced templating.

The Least You Need to Know
Various submenus are possible using advanced CSS techniques. These could be expandable menus or drop-downs.

Summary

In this chapter, we looked at menus and navigation for a Joomla website. It's important to realize that the menu links actually control the appearance of the page that is linked through the menu link's parameters in the Menu Manager.

We saw that

- The initial four menus—main menu, other menu, top menu, and user menu—are only Joomla's suggestions or examples. In most cases you will need to create your own or revise them.

- The "backend" part of a menu, where the links go and what they do are controlled by the Menu Manager. The frontend part of a menu, where it is and what it looks like, is controlled by a menu's module.

- A menu link can point to content sections, categories, or individual content articles. They can also point to components.

- There are two main layouts of a Joomla page, blog and standard. The blog layout displays intro text with a "Read More" link. The standard or list layout shows a table of linked titles. Which layout is used is determined by the menu link parameters.

- A blog layout presents content items in any number of columns, with the option to show intro text along with a "Read More" link.

- A standard layout shows articles as linked titles in a table. The presentation for a section is slightly different than for a category.

- The module for a menu controls its placement on a page and its appearance. It also controls which pages the menu will appear on and what access level can see them (guest or registered user). The menu's appearance is determined by code in the template's CSS.

- Various submenus are possible using advanced CSS techniques. These could be expandable menus or drop-downs.

User's Guide Chapter 5 Demo Site

Demos of the two sites created in this chapter are available at www.joomlabook.com. They are an exact copy of what you should have if you followed all the steps in this chapter. You can log in to the administrative backend so you can see the site framework and the sections, categories, and menus that were set up.

Chapter 6

Extending Joomla!

As you will recall from Chapter 1, "Content Management Systems and an Introduction to Joomla," it's hard to find a Joomla-powered website that has not added functionality beyond the basics with some sort of extension. The word extension collectively describes components, modules, plugins, and languages.

There are several hundred extensions available both free and commercially from third-party providers. You can find out more about them at extensions.joomla.org and www.extensionprofessionals.com.

Currently, most extensions work with the 1.0.X version of Joomla. Because it is so new, there are currently not many third-party extensions that run natively on 1.5. As it goes though its roadmap cycle of Beta to Release Candidate to Stable, we will hopefully see third-party extensions upgraded to work on the new version.

In this chapter we look at some examples of core and third-party Joomla extensions. We also examine how they are installed and managed in Joomla.

■ What are extensions?

■ How do I install Joomla extensions?

■ Where can I get third-party extensions?

■ What are components?

■ What are modules?

What Are Extensions?

Extensions are installable packages that extend the core functionality of Joomla in some way. There are five types of extensions:

- **Components**—A component is the most complex type of extension. It is some sort of mini-application that usually renders content in the main body (large middle column) of the page. The core content component (com content), for example, is the mini-application that shows all your articles in some way. Another example might be a forum component that shows boards, threads, and so on. Not all components are about content; some handle a complex function. For example, the registration component (com registration) handles user registration.

- **Modules**—Modules are usually much smaller and less complex than components. They also usually appear around the edges of the main body, in the header, side columns, or footer and are small extensions that do small tasks. For example, the Latest News module shows links to the most recent articles that have been added to the site. Often, a module will work with a particular component. For example, the login form module allows site visitors to log in to the site.

- **Plugins**—A plugin (formerly called mambot) is a special piece of code that can be used across the site and runs when a page is loaded. An example is the email cloaking plugin, which hides email addresses with JavaScript so spam robots cannot see them.

- **Templates**—Templates control the graphical look and feel of the site. They usually include colors, graphics, and typography.

- **Languages**—By installing a language pack, it is possible to internationalize Joomla to a different language. All of the words that are part of Joomla (like where it says "Read More") will be displayed in the chosen language.

Installing Extensions

All extensions will come in the form of compressed zip files and are installed via the same process. To install, you simply use the Extension Manager.

Go to **Extensions>Install/Uninstall**. This will show the Extension Manager, as shown in Figure 6.1.

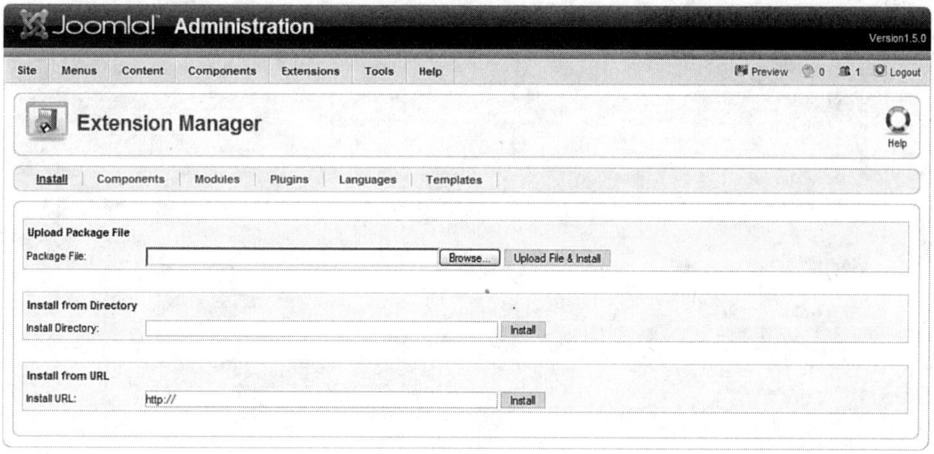

FIGURE 6.1 Extension Manager

On the first tab labeled Install, there is a tool to upload the installation package (the zip file of the extension). When you browse to the file and upload it, Joomla automatically detects what type of extension it is and installs it. You will then be shown a screen that tells you the installation has been successful. Often, depending on the third-party extension being installed, you will also be shown some more details about the extension, such as set-up instructions or where to seek support.

> **NOTE**
> If you have an error in the installation, the most common problems are permissions and ownership of folders. Joomla can't write or create a folder needed for the installation of the extension. The easiest way to solve this is to use the FTP layer. This is set up in the Global Configuration.

The Extension Manager is also used to uninstall components. In Figure 6.1 you see tabs for Components, Modules, Plugins, Languages and Templates. If you click Components (Figure 6.2), you see a list of components that can be uninstalled.

FIGURE 6.2 Component Extension Manager

Notice in Figure 6.2 that many of the components are grayed out. These are core components of Joomla that cannot be uninstalled.

Managing Extensions

Each type of extension *except components* has its own manager in the Extensions menu. The drop-down of the Extensions menu is shown in Figure 6.3.

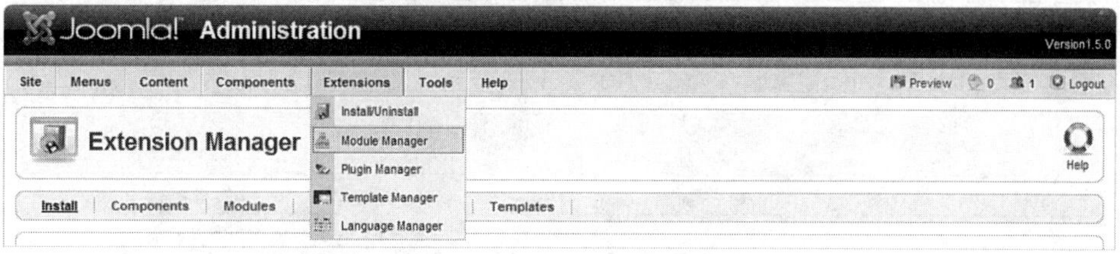

FIGURE 6.3 The Extension submenu

Components has its own menu because of the complexity of a component compared to, say, a module.

The Module and Plugin Managers follow the same format (similar to the Article Manager). The Module Manager is shown in Figure 6.4.

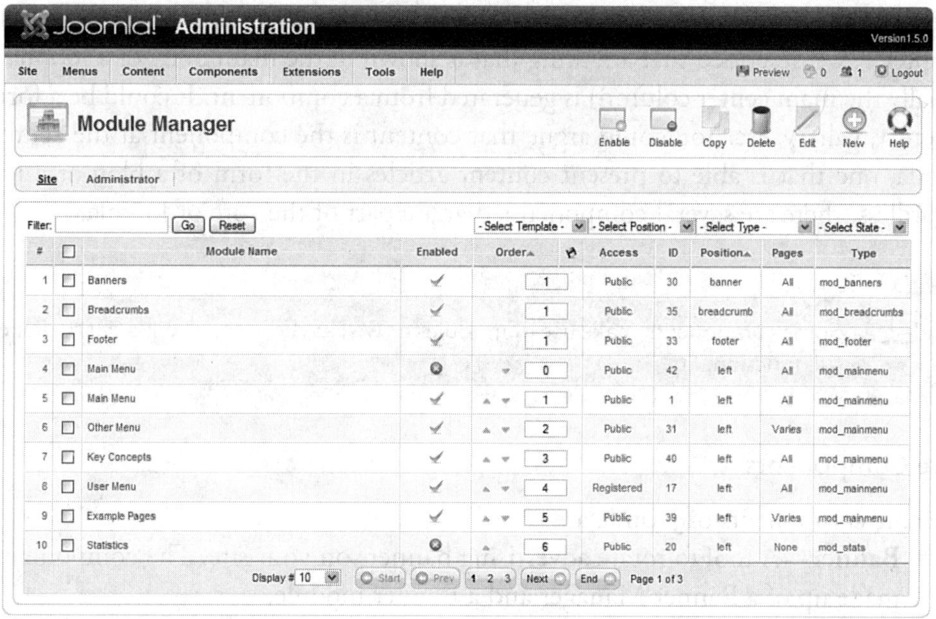

FIGURE 6.4 Module Manager

The Template and Language Managers are slightly different mainly because you can only have one active at any one time. The Template Manager is shown in Figure 6.5.

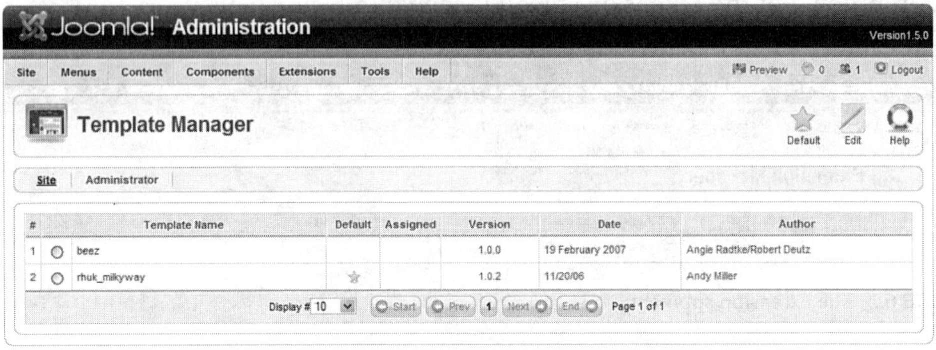

FIGURE 6.5 Template Manager

Components

A component is a specialized mini-application that runs in Joomla. If you flip back to Chapter 1, we described that anything that is shown in the main body of a Joomla site (usually the main center column) is generated from a component. It could be a forum, directory, gallery, etc. You could argue that content is the component at the center of Joomla, one that is able to present content articles in the form of a blog or a table. Regardless, there are several components that are part of the core of Joomla.

> **NOTE**
> Some components make use of modules as well as the component itself to achieve full functionality.

Core Components

The core components of Joomla are

- **Banner**—A tool to rotate advertising banners on your site. The component is made up of a Banner Manager and a Banner module.
- **Contacts**—By using this component, you can present a list of contacts on the site. A manager also has the ability to set categories for contacts. When linking to the component, you can link to individual contacts or a whole category.

- **Newsfeeds**—The newsfeed component is a great way to effortlessly build relevant content for your site. It makes use of RSS technology. If another website has an RSS feed, you can present that feed on a page of your site.

- **Polls**—If you want to increase the site visitor interactivity, polls are an easy way to do so. Polls are created using the Poll Manager and then presented using the Poll module.

- **Search**—Joomla has a powerful built-in search function. Along with its corresponding module, it allows visitors to search all the articles of the site with keywords.

- **Web Links**—Any web page can have links to other sites. The web link component takes this a step further by storing the links and showing a count of how many times they have been clicked. Its most useful feature is that it allows site users to submit links by creating a corresponding menu item. This type of tool is commonly called a *directory*.

- **Massmail**—This tool allows emails to be sent to all registered users. It is a very simple tool and does not approach the functionality of third-party email components. It is difficult to ensure that emails sent conform to the CAN-SPAM act, but it is useful for sending out a quick email to a user group, such as administrators.

Third-party Components

One of the exciting things about Joomla is the huge range of extensions available for it. Joomla is unique in the open source world where open source GPL advocates and commercial vendors work side by side to grow the project. The two main repositories for third-party extensions are extensions.joomla.org and www.extensionprofessionals.com.

With more than 2,000 extensions, it's impossible to provide any generalities on how they work. Each one tends to have a slightly different admin structure in the backend based on the decisions of the creator.

The following sections comprise a short list of 1.0.X extensions that I have found and have used time and again for my own sites and our clients at Joomlashack. The descriptions are quoted directly from the extensions directory. At Joomlashack we have used every one of these extensions at least 10 times (that was my threshold for inclusion) for individual projects. We have tested each and found them all to be "best of class" and have come to depend on them for our own and client projects. Some of them are commercial, and some are GPL. If you find yourself using a GPL extension, visit the creator's site and see if there is a donation feature to donate a pizza!

Jom Comment (Comments)—http://www.jom-comment.com

Jom Comment is the comment system chosen by the pros! A powerful, Ajax-based comment system for your Joomla website. Jom Comment ensures comments appear slick and smooth with Ajax while saving server bandwidth. Protect your website from unwanted spam with powerful Captcha image challenge. Templatize your entire comment module to look and feel like the rest of your website. Jom Comment is easy to use and install and has superb developer support. If you've got AkoComment or Combo-Max data, just import them to Jom Comment. You'll be up and running in no time.

joomlaXplorer (File Manager)—http://joomlacode.org/gf/project/joomlaxplorer/

joomlaXplorer is a file and FTP manager. It allows you to edit files, delete, copy, rename, archive, and unpack files/directories directly on your server. You can browse directories and files; edit, copy, move, and delete files; search, upload, and download files; create new files and directories, change file permissions (chmod), and more. This script is based on QuiXplorer 2.3.1.

Community Builder (User Management)—http://www.joomlapolis.com/

The Community Builder suite extends the Joomla user management system. Key features are extra fields in profile, enhanced registration workflows, user lists, connection paths between users, admin defined tabs and user profiles, image upload, frontend workflow management, and integration with other components like PMS, Newsletter, Forum, and Galleries. Release 1.0.2 stable is compatible with Joomla 1.0 and 1.5 Beta 1 and mambo 4.5.0-4.6.1. See announcement on home page.

SlideShowPro for Joomla (Gallery)—http://www.joomlashack.com

SlideShowPro is a popular Flash-generated image gallery, which can be loaded into Joomla by use of this module. The module allows users to control all the normal Flash component settings within the administration of Joomla The module may be duplicated to run more than one instance using the same SWF under a completely different set of parameters. This module requires Flash MX or greater to generate and requires the SlideShowPro Flash component from www.slideshowpro.net. FLA source help file and module is bundled with the module.

VirtueMart (Shopping Cart)—http://virtuemart.net/

VirtueMart is a complete shopping cart solution (formerly known as mambo-php-Shop) for Joomla. It's popular, widely used, and can also be used as a catalogue. With its powerful administration tool, you can handle an unlimited number of categories, products, orders, and customers.

Joomap (Sitemap)—http://joomlacode.org/gf/project/joomap/

Joomap is a sitemap component for Joomla that shows the normal Menu Structure, Content Categories, Sections, and Virtuemart Categories in a hierarchical list. A plugin system and translation support make it easy to expand the range of supported content and localization! The new version also supports the generation of a Google Sitemap conformant XML list.

Mosets Tree (Directory)—http://www.mosets.com/tree/

Mosets Tree is a directory extension for Joomla. This is the extension that powers the Joomla Extensions Directory at http://extensions.joomla.org. You can use Mosets Tree to run a complex Yahoo! style directory directly inside your Joomla website. Mosets Tree is designed to handle any data that requires a directory structure such as a Business Directory, Links Directory, and Scripts Directory.

perForms (Forms)—http://joomlacode.org/gf/project/performs

perForms is the forms component for Joomla. perForms aims to be simple and fast: Create forms in seconds, capture data to your database, email data on submit, view captured data in administrator, full CAPTCHA support (with com_securityimages), file upload security, captured data can be downloaded in the form of a spreadsheet for analysis, utf-8 Native, and 14 languages. perForms includes a plugin (mambot) so you can embed your forms directly into Joomla content, and a Module showing response data in summary or report form.

Remository (File/document Manager)—http://www.remository.com/

A neat file remository with a good range of functions and an attractive user interface. Close to release of version 3.40 with a range of advanced facilities—Remository 3.40 RC2 is currently available from the Remository site.

JCal Pro (Calendar)—http://dev.anything-digital.com/

JCal Pro is a W3C-validated events calendar component with a gorgeous, CSS-based frontend display. Feature highlights include Event and Category import from Ext-Calendar, native Joomla permissioning for event creation/management, WYSIWYG event descriptions, administrative theme installation and management, backend event management, native Joomla permissioning for event viewing (i.e. private categories), integrated search mambot, and feature-rich mini-calendar and latest events modules.

Modules

Modules can be thought of as the little brother of components. They are much smaller but still add some sort of functionality or interactivity to a page. As just discussed, a component might actually have several modules bundled with it. For example JCalPro, a calendar component, has a module that shows a small version of the calendar in a sidebar.

Module Display

All modules have some common options available for how they are presented (see Figure 6.6).

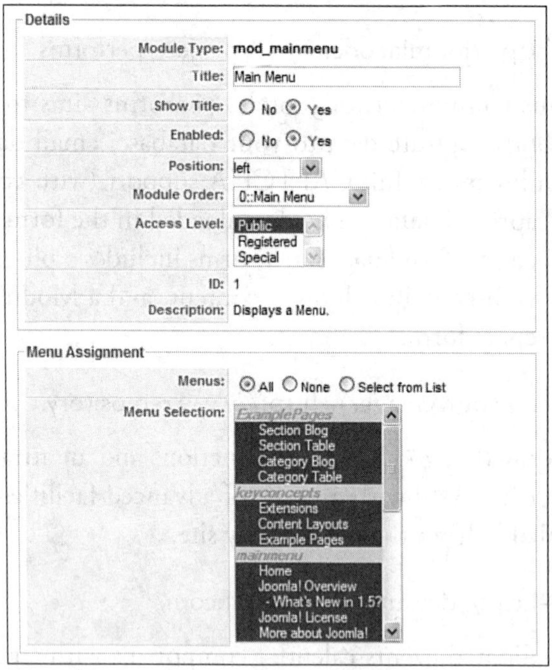

FIGURE 6.6 Module details and menu assignment options

At the top left side are the module details:

- the title
- whether enabled/published
- the position (as determined in the template)
- the order among modules in that position
- the access level

These are fairly self-explanatory. The one that is of particular note is access level. It is possible to create almost completely different versions of your website for different user groups, such as guests, registered users, and administrators.

The bottom left shows the menu assignment and is potentially harder to understand. Chapter 5, "Creating Menus and Navigation," introduced this complex idea of assigning modules to menu items rather than pages.

This controls which pages the menu will appear on. Now remember that a "page" only exists if a link points to it. So the list here is really a list of menu links rather than pages. You can select All, None or Select from List. You can also CTRL+click to select multiple pages (I mean menu items!).

In Figure 6.6, the Main Menu module is presented on all of the pages of the site.

Obviously, figuring this out can quickly become confusing. I recommend actually resorting to pen and paper and mapping out what your main pages will look like and what modules will be located on those pages.

Usually modules are placed and controlled by the site administrator, considering they are site-wide.

Core Modules

Like components, a number of modules exist in the core default installation of Joomla. They can be split into several types: core content modules, core component-related modules, and core miscellaneous modules.

Core Content Modules

Joomla has a number of modules that are part of the default installation.

- **Archived Content**—This module shows a list of months that link to all archive content on the site. As mentioned previously, archiving content on your site has advantages and drawbacks. The main drawback is that the URL is changed.

- **Latest News**—The Latest News module is very useful. It displays a linked list of the most recent content items created on the site. Although called Latest News, which is one of the categories in a default install, it can be set to only take content from specific sections or categories. This is a great way to dynamically show recently added content on your home page.

- **Newsflash**—Next in the series of modules that show content dynamically (Latest News and Most Read), the Newsflash module shows *random* content items. Slightly different from the other two, it can show the intro text of the content item as well as just the title. Again, it can show content from any section or category, not just the Newsflash category, one of the default categories of a Joomla install.

- **Random Image**—Another content presentation module, it's the equivalent of the Newsflash module but is for images.

> **TIP**
> With some careful planning in the design of the template, it's easy to have the Random Image module actually be the header of your site. This has the effect of showing randomly alternating images as your header.

- **Custom HTML**—This module accepts XHTML content through an editor. This makes it one of the most flexible of all the modules. As well as text/graphics, you can insert web-based code, like JavaScript or XHTML.

- **Most Read Content**—This is another useful module to easily show dynamic content; it shows a linked list of the most popular content currently on your site. As with the Latest News module, it can show content from specific sections and/or categories.

> **NOTE**
> There is currently no module in the core of Joomla that combines the ability to show intro text but not have it be random. There are third-party modules that achieve this, but they are not completely reliable.

- **Related Items**—This module shows a linked list of all items related to the one currently being displayed. Joomla decides whether a content item is related based on what has been entered in the *metatag keywords* for that content item.

Note it's not possible to limit the number of items displayed as it is in other modules. We talk more about metatags at length in Chapter 8, "Getting Traffic to Your Site."

- **Sections**—Shows a linked list of all sections of your site. Unfortunately there is no equivalent to show categories.

Core Component-Related Modules

The default Joomla installation also includes a number of modules that work with core components.

- **Syndicate**—The module counterpart to the syndication component. It is an RSS feed of the Frontpage component. This means that it does not matter where the syndicate module is; it will only provide a feed to content published by the FrontPage component.

> **TIP**
> The Frontpage component doesn't actually have to be on the front page of the site. Confusing, I know, but Joomla uses whatever link is first in the mainmenu as the home page. You could actually move the link to the Frontpage component deeper into the site. This is handy for blogs you don't want to show on the home page.

- **Poll**—A companion to the poll component, this module actually shows the poll questions.

Core Miscellaneous Modules

Last, there are a number of modules that provide other functionality to the site.

- **Login**—A critical module for most Joomla sites. It displays a simple form for users to log in or to create a user name/retrieve password. Note that a log in form can also be linked to from a menu to display on the main body. The module is not used in this case.
- **Menu**—Another vital module. The main menu module shows menus of the site.

- **Who's Online**—A simple module that shows the number of registered users and guests currently at the site.

- **Statistics**—Shows simple visitor stats with the option of showing more technical server stats.

- **Feed Display**—This module's ability to show an RSS feed makes it the module equivalent of the Newsfeed component, which can show a feed in the main body.

- **Wrapper**—This module will load an external page into a module, much as the wrapper component does for the mainbody. Its usefulness is limited in a module, as it can only load small amounts of content as modules are usually placed in columns and other smaller places of the page.

Third-party Modules

Like components, a diverse collection of third-party modules has been created for Joomla. As I described for components, we are still in a transition period, but here I have outlined some modules for 1.0.X that I have "tried and tested."

JPG Flash Rotator 2 (Image Rotator)—http://www.joomlashack.com

JPG Flash Rotator 2 (X)HTML Flash module allows you to select from a series of images for use of a fading slideshow/banner on your Joomla site. Here are its features: Validates (X)HTML, Supports WMODE=Transparent, Displays up to 5 different Flash transitions (Circular, Fluid, Background Fade, Cross Fade, Flying Squares, Linear Blinds), Random display option, Individual frame linking, Fully integrated back-end administration (no knowledge of Flash needed), Custom movie size, Customizable background color, and Tab navigation on/off feature.

Jumi—http://www.vedeme.cz

Jumi is a universal multipurpose module and plugin for Joomla and Mambo. With Jumi you can include php html JavaScript scripts into the modules position and content articles, you can include thousands of your scripts into the modules and content articles with just one module and/or plugin installation, you can even include static html or txt pages into your pages without using wrapper component, and you can easily set up, change, and pass to the php script unlimited number of argument values and thus modify the behavior of the content.

AdSense Module— http://www.joomlaspan.com

The best simple solution for implementing Google AdSense ads in Joomla ADVANCED FEATURE: Option to block certain IP numbers from seeing Google Ads. Now you can block those "unsafe" clicks that could potentially disable you from Google AdSense! We suggest that you insert your own IP number there, to block your own accidental clicks, except when you want to test the appearance of the ads on your page. When an IP is blocked, you can assign some other ad to be shown there. It also has chameleon codes that can make the ad colors automatically.

As you can see, I tend to use far more components than modules. This is attributed partly to the fact that often the components are bundled with several modules that work with them.

Plugins

Plugins offer some form of site-wide functionality. Most Joomla users will find that they do not need to manage plugins as often as components or modules.

Core Plugins

- **Authentication**—Joomla has several plugins that can be used to allow authentication (login) integration with different systems. Included are Gmail, OpenID, and LDAP.
- **Content-Code Highlighter**—This plugin will highlight code in content (when you use the <cpre> tag) according to GeSHi standards.
- **Content-Email Cloaking**—This plugin converts any email address written in an article to JavaScript. This makes it undetectable by spam email harvesters.
- **Content-Load Modules**—This plugin allows you to load a module into a content article by putting [**loadposition user1**] where you want the module to load.
- **Button: Image, Pagebreak and Readmore**—This plugin controls the images, readmore, and pagebreak buttons in the article editor.
- **Editors**—There are three editors shipped with the Joomla core: No Editor, TinyMCE, and XStandard Lite. Other more advanced or commercial editors can be installed.
- **Search**—This plugin controls the indexing and thus searching of content.

- **System–Legacy**—This plugin will allow the possibility to run extensions (templates, components, and modules) that are coded for 1.0.X to run on 1.5. Note that an extension developer will have to have upgraded his code to run on 1.5 legacy from 1.0.X.
- **System–Cache**—This plugin controls the new caching features of 1.5.
- **XML-RPC**—These plugins allow for the administration of a Joomla site remotely.

Third-party Plugins

As with components and modules, many third-party plugins exist. The one I have used most consistently is an editor plugin. Although there are currently no editors available for 1.5, I have frequently used a commercial one for 1.0.X.

WysiwygPro (Editor)—http://www.wysiwyg-pro.com

WysiwygPro replaces the default editor. WysiwygPro is a commercially supported WYSIWYG editor with advanced features, such as an image and document manager and a link manager, so you can easily create links to pages and articles. You can control every aspect of WysiwygPro from the administrator panel where you can set which buttons and tools should be available, which fonts and classes can be used, etc.

Plugin Googlemaps—http://joomlacode.org/gf/project/mambot_google1/

Plugin (Mambot) for displaying one or more googlemaps within content-items of Joomla. You can set width, height, latitude, Longitude, zoomtype, initial zoom level, text displayed in a marker and of course the Google api key. These parameters can also be set as default in the administrator of Joomla at the plugin. Version 2.8 is available and has new features like show a kml-file, use mousewheel zooming, and let a user enter his address and show a route to/from your location in maps.google.com.

Templates

Chapter 1 examined how a template controls the look and feel of a Joomla site. In Chapter 9, "Creating a Pure CSS Template," we look in much more at detail how to create your own template.

Core Templates

Joomla currently ships with three core templates:

- **Khepri**—This is the administrator template in the backend. Yes, you can make new administrator templates to customize the look and feel of the administrative interface!
- **Milkyway**—This is the default template.
- **Beez**—This is a special proof of concept template that serves as an example of a template that uses the new template override feature in 1.5. We briefly discussed these features in Chapter 9.

Third-party Templates

There are thousands of templates available for Joomla 1.0.X. With the launch of 1.5 as a Release Candidate in the summer of 2007, more and more 1.5 templates are becoming available. Perhaps the easiest way to find a template for your site is to Google "Joomla 1.5 templates" or "free Joomla 1.5 templates."

Third-party template providers are of two types, clubs and per template. Clubs charge an annual fee and are good if you like to frequently update your site design, considering templates are generally added monthly. Per template providers offer templates on an individual basis and are usually slightly cheaper.

Summary

Joomla has an extension for every possible need for a website. They are available from a variety of places, for a variety of prices. Many are licensed under the GPL and are available for free. Here are some recap points for this chapter:

- Joomla is supported by a diverse community of developers that create the critical extensions needed to increase the basic functionality of Joomla.
- Many of these extensions are available for free under a GPL license; others are commercial.
- Specific details about the functionality of extensions can be found on the official help site at help.joomla.org.
- A short list of extensions that have been tested and used by the author are available in this chapter.

Chapter 7

Expanding Your Content: Articles and Editors

There are two main ways to add and manage content to a Joomla site: through the frontend or through the backend. Part of the biggest attraction of Joomla is to be able to easily add and edit content through a What You See Is What You Get (WYSIWYG) editor.

In This Chapter

This chapter begins with looking at WYSIWYG and how it functions in the backend with Managers, Administrators, and Super Administrators. It then examines how authors, editors, and publishers manage content through the frontend.

- What is WYSIWYG editing?

- How do you manage articles in the backend?

- How should you use metadata?

- How do you add images and other media to articles?

- How do you manage content from the frontend?

- What is the difference between authors, editors, and publishers?

- What is article checkin?

WYSIWYG Editors

You've probably used a What You See Is What You Get (WYSIWYG) editor, but you might not even be aware that you have. If you've ever used some sort of editor where you can highlight words, change their formatting, and have those changes be instantly visible to you, then you've used a WYSIWYG editor. Even Microsoft Word is a WYSIWYG editor (albeit a complicated one)!

WYSIWYG is different than a markup language, such as (X)HTML. When you use a programming language, you must assign styles instead of just using a button. Joomla and web-based email, such as Yahoo and Gmail, use simple editors. Figure 7.1 shows an example editor taken from a Yahoo email account.

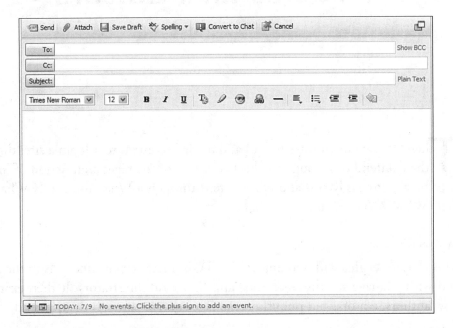

FIGURE 7.1 A Yahoo webmail WYSIWYG editor

The default Joomla editor follows similar principles, along with various formatting buttons that will be familiar to you from Microsoft Word. Figure 7.2 shows the default Joomla editor, TinyMCE.

FIGURE 7.2 Default Joomla editor—TinyMCE

Joomla ships with two options for an editor, TinyMCE and XStandard, but many other Joomla editors are available.

- TinyMCE is a platform-independent web-based Javascript HTML WYSIWYG editor (http://tinymce.moxiecode.com/).
- XStandard is the leading standards-compliant plug-in WYSIWYG editor for Windows desktop applications and browser-based Content Management Systems—IE/Mozilla/Firefox/Netscape (http://www.xstandard.com/).

Managing WYSIWYG Editors

It's possible to have any number of editors installed as plugins to Joomla. There are three main aspects to managing the editors that you have installed.

First, you need to set your site-wide global editor. This is done in the backend in the Global Configuration dialog box.

Go to **Site > Configuration**. You will see a drop-down box for your default WYSIWYG editor (see Figure 7.3).

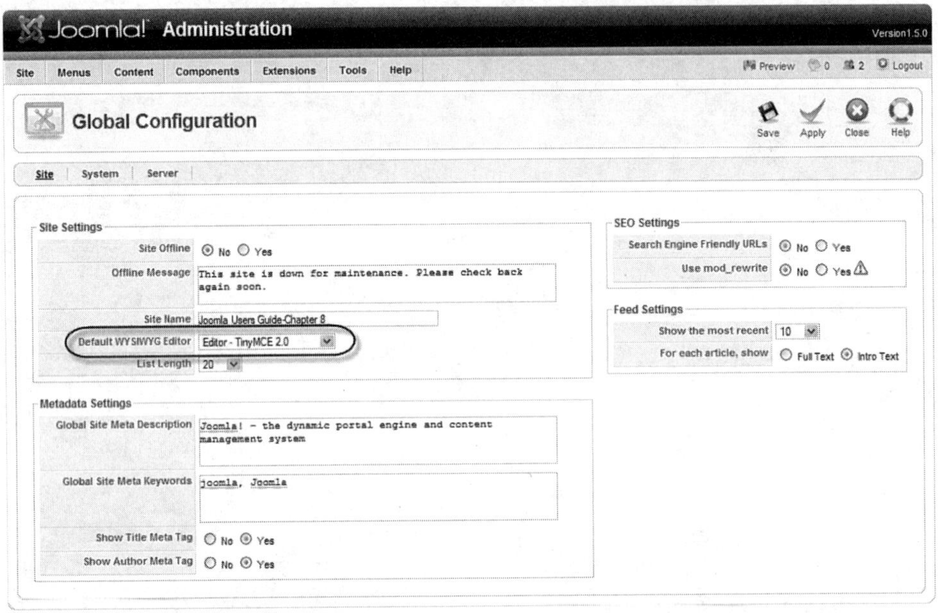

FIGURE 7.3 Default WYSIWYG editor setting

After deciding what your site-wide default editor will be, you also have the option to set a different editor (leave another tool) for individual users. This is done in the User Manager.

Go to **Site > User Manager**. Click the user to open up the User Manager—Edit screen. Circled in Figure 7.4, you see the setting to select a different editor. If the User Editor drop-down box is simply left as Select Editor, the global editor will be assigned to that user.

The last aspect of managing WYSIWYG editors is within the editors themselves. In the Plugin Manager, some editors have special parameters that you can set to achieve varying functionality. In Figure 7.5, you can see the parameters available for the TinyMCE editor.

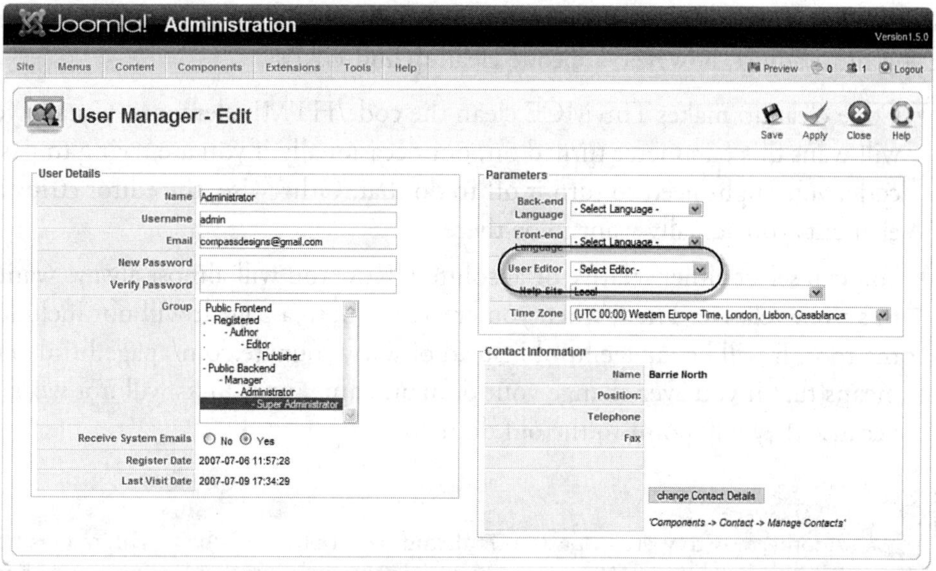

FIGURE 7.4 Individual user WYSIWYG editor setting

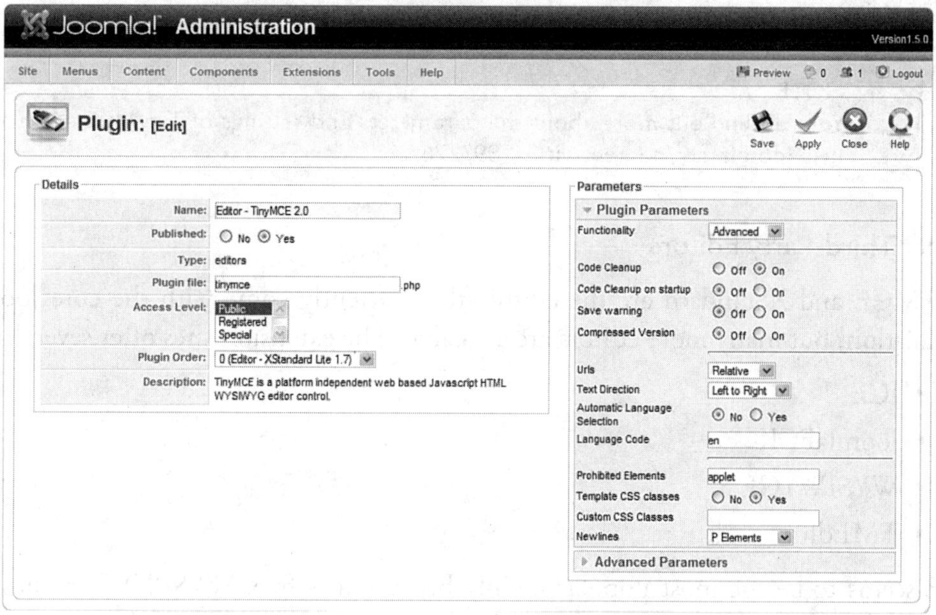

FIGURE 7.5 WYSIWYG editor parameters

Most of these parameters do not need to be adjusted. Two important parameters that you must adjust, however, are code cleanup and URLs:

- Code cleanup makes TinyMCE clean the code/HTML elements. Usually you will want this parameter turned on, but occasionally if you are trying to paste code, you might need to turn it off to do that. Otherwise, the editor strips out elements you actually want to be there.

- You can select either relative or absolute URLs. You will almost always want this to be relative. Then, when you create a link to a page it will not include the root. It will be /apage.html instead of www.yoursite.com/apage.html. This means that if you ever change your domain name, your links will not work because they will point to the old domain.

> **NOTE**
> Another way to write or paste HTML and be sure that it is being entered properly is to turn the WYSIWYG editor off, either at a site-wide level or on a user basis. Sometimes I will create a special admin user called "noWYSIWYG," which has its editor turned off (set to No WYSIWYG Editor). This allows me to log in and work in pure HTML if I need to.

> **NOTE**
> You can find out more about the parameters and settings of TinyMCE at http://help.Joomla.org/content/view/189/276/.

Other Third-Party Editors

TinyMCE and XStandard are the editors that currently come with the core Joomla installation, but many more editors are available. The extension sites offer several:

- JCE
- JoomlaFCK
- WYSIWYGPro
- TMEdit

JCE seems to be the most popular mainly because it is free. WYSIWYGPro has the edge in features/stability, but it is a commercial editor, currently costing $47 (www.wysiwyg-pro.com).

NOTE

This list of editors shows those that currently have products developed for the 1.0 version of Joomla. To date, there are very few editors in released versions that will work with Joomla 1.5, the topic of this book. Hopefully at the time of publication, new versions will have been released, and you will be able to find them on the Joomla extensions site, extensions.Joomla.org.

If you are working on a website in which you will be editing a large amount of content, you should consider the commercial editor options. You will save the price in the time saved.

All of the editors work more or less in the same way. There are several small icons for various functions along the top. Rather than go over this in too much detail, let's examine some critical points and some common problems:

- **You must click Save, Apply, or Cancel to leave the editor.** This is especially important while editing from the frontend.

- **Don't apply font style, such as making a font smaller, to big sections in the editor.** This should be done in the CSS file of the template. That was the whole point of separating content from presentation (see Chapter 1, "Content Management Systems and an Introduction to Joomla")!

- **Always make sure you have the correct section and category.** I have lost count of the times I left this as the first one on the list and then couldn't find my content.

- **If something happens to your connection while you are editing, *you'll lose everything*.** I recommend that you write longer pieces offline and copy/paste.

- **Be careful copying and pasting from MS Word.** When you paste from Word, it uses lots of daft CSS peculiar to Microsoft. Unfortunately it gets pasted in too. An easy way to strip it all out is to paste into Notepad (or other pure text editor), copy again, and then paste into Joomla. Note, if you do this, paragraph returns `<p>` will be turned into line carriage returns `<br>`.

- **If you have a lot of writing to do, an efficient way to do it is to actually write in an HTML editor.** Sure, you usually use them for creating web pages, but in this situation they make pretty good word processors. A great open source choice is available at www.nvu.com.

- **If the site administrator installs a new editor, he should set it to default in the global configuration.**
- **You have to set up the sections and categories before adding content.**
- **The Title Alias is an optional field.** It is used by third-party SEF components to produce meaningful URLs.

If you get a colored background that makes the editor unreadable, that's because it's using the same background that is on the main site. A simple fix is to add this to the template's CSS in the main template CSS file (template.css):

```
body.contentpane{background-color: #fff; background-image: none;}
```

We'll look in more detail at the actual editor itself and the various extra Joomla options it uses later in this chapter. For now let's move on to looking at how to add content articles.

> **The Least You Need to Know**
> WYSIWYG stands for What You See Is What You Get. It allows editing of content without knowledge of (X)HTML. Several editors are available for Joomla and can be installed as plugins.

Creating and Managing Articles

Adding content to a website is relatively easy. We have already done most of the hard work: understanding sections and categories, tables and blogs, and menus. Now that the setup is finished, Joomla starts to show its CMS power—adding content quickly and simply.

This chapter continues with the sample site that we set up in Chapter 4, "Content Is King: Organizing Your Content." That site was an example of a fictitious company called Widget, Inc. If you followed that chapter and built the site, you will be able to follow on exactly where we left off as we learn how to create and manage content articles.

If you did not create that site, you might want to go back and do so; otherwise, you can follow along with a default Joomla installation.

There are two main ways to create and manage content articles in Joomla:

- **Backend editing** is for managers, administrators and super administrators. It allows these users to manage the articles through the Article Manager. It also allows for the management of images (and other media) through the Media

Manager. Generally, backend article management is much more efficient than doing so through the frontend.

- **Frontend editing** is for authors, editors, and publishers. It allows for these users to manage content articles on the actual page where that content article exists. When logged in, a special icon will appear that allows editing of that article while you are looking at it in the frontend. Management of media is more difficult through the frontend.

> ☀ **The Least You Need to Know**
> Backend editing is more efficient, but generally not as many users are given backend access.
> Frontend editing allows more users to be involved in managing the content. It also allows for the quick and easy editing of single articles.

Managing Content Through the Backend

Let's go to the backend of our Chapter 5 Widget Inc. website.

We log in as a manager (*Username*: MrManager; *Password*: Joomlabook), so we have fewer menu choices. The manager access level is useful if you have many people managing your content in the backend. It gives access to everything they need but not to any other administrative functions that might do something more drastic to the site.

Let's look at the Article Manager (see Figure 7.6). Go to **Content > Article Manager**.

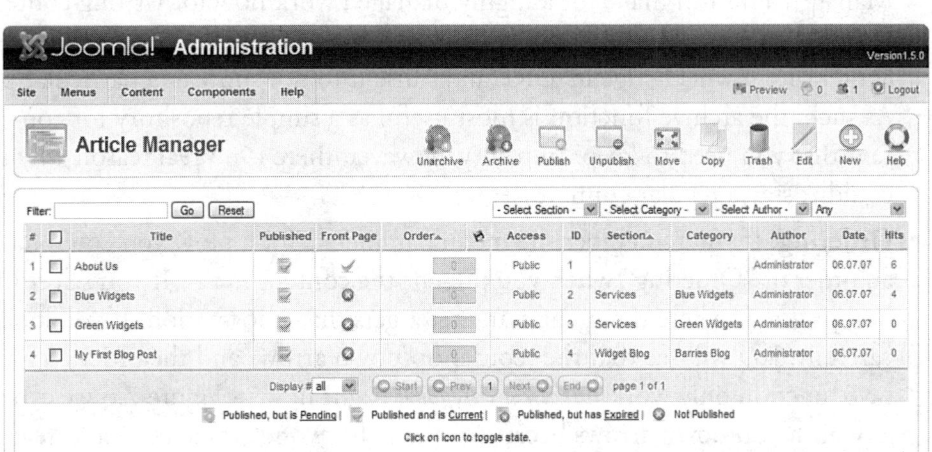

FIGURE 7.6 The Article Manager

Here, we see the four content articles that we created in Chapter 4. All are published, and one is on the Front Page. Again, some guides (for the 1.0.X help) are at the Joomla help site (help.Joomla.org/content/view/68/153/ and help.Joomla.org/content/view/69/68/).

Let's quickly look at some important features that the Article Manager offers:

- **Multiple select checkboxes**. The column on the far left with all the check boxes allows multiple selections of content items. You can select any one you want and then use the icons in the tool bar: publish, copy, delete, and so on en masse.

- **Column Sorting**. You can click any of the column headings and sort the table in ascending or descending order.

- **Icons and links in the Manager**. The small icons in the Published, Front Page, and Access columns are clickable toggles. If you click, say, on something that is unpublished, that will publish it. The Title, Section, and Category columns are links. Clicking them will take you to relevant pages where you can edit that item.

- **Filters**. In a big site you can easily have thousands of content articles. Using the Menu Manager starts getting difficult unless you use filters. You can filter by section, category, author, or a variable of your choice.

- **Archiving**. You can archive any content item. Once archived, it cannot be changed and gets moved to the Archive Manager rather than the Content Manager. This can make for a highly managed work flow for writing content: write > review > publish > archive. However, one problem is that archiving a content item will change its URL and cause it to not show in a particular page. As such, the archive function is most useful as a simple repository for content that you need to keep. In reality, however, there is no real reason why it couldn't stay a regular content item.

- **Ordering**. If you remember the menu parameters for a blog, you could have an order of "Ordering" when you present the content items. If you select that option, *this* is where the menu parameter gets that information. If you look carefully, you will see that the reorder up/down arrows and the order column save function only work *within a category*. Right now in Figure 7.6 we can't see any of the up/down arrows because we only have one article in each category. As we add more, we will see this function appear.

Let's add a content item and see the content editing interface. This is done with a WYSIWYG editor.

Adding Content from the Backend

To add content to our site from the backend, click New in the Article Manager, which takes us to the Article Edit screen, as shown in Figure 7.7.

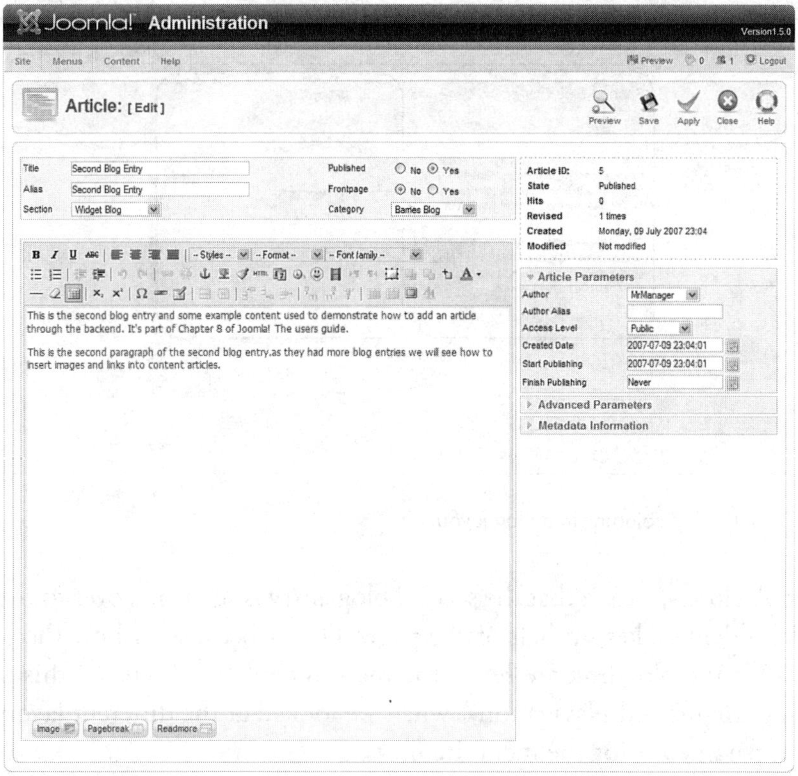

FIGURE 7.7 Article editing screen

If we click Save, the article is saved, and the screen closes, taking us back to the Article Manager. Clicking Apply saves the article but leaves the article editor open. Let's click Save and then look at the result in the frontend.

Clicking the blog link shows all of the articles that are in the blog. Figure 7.8 shows the blog page.

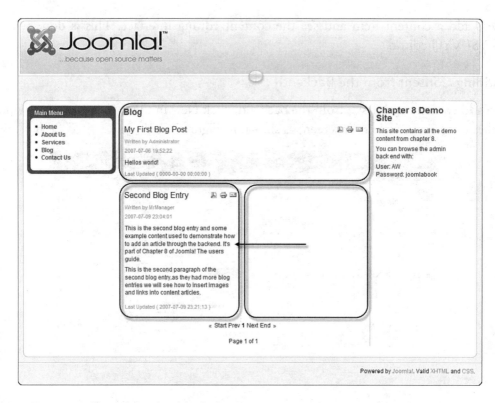

FIGURE 7.8 Controlling columns in a blog layout

If we look closely, we see that the second blog entry is squashed over to the left-hand side, so it suddenly takes up half of the page. This is because of how the menu item parameters for the blog link are set in the main menu. We discussed this in Chapter 5, "Creating Menus and Navigation," when we looked at the different layouts and the blog layout parameters for the menu item.

To make this look a little cleaner, let's change the number of columns to just one. Go to **Menu > Menu Manager > mainmenu > Blog**. In the Menu Item Parameters, change the Columns to 1 and save the menu item. Now our blog posts take up the full width.

If we have a longer article, we need to make use of a Read More link. This allows just introductory text to be shown in the blog layout, and the full article is displayed only when you click the Read More link.

Longer Articles and the Read More Button

Let's open up the second blog entry in the Article Manager and add another paragraph. After adding a third paragraph, place the cursor at the end of the second paragraph (or the beginning of the third) and click the Read More button at the bottom of the editor. When you do this, you see a line appear between the two paragraphs (see Figure 7.9).

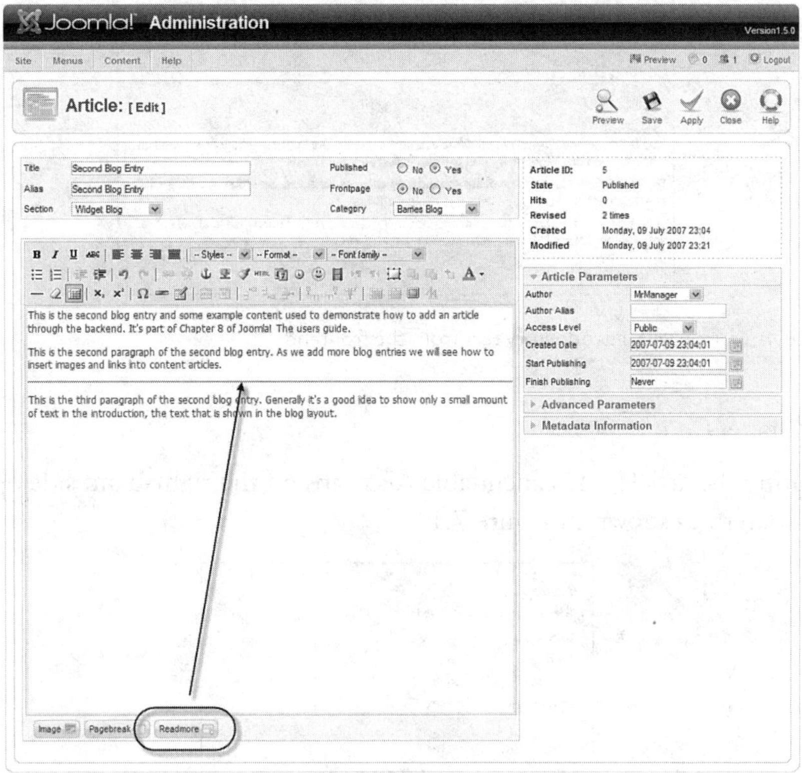

FIGURE 7.9 Creating a Read More link

This line separates the introductory text from the rest of the longer article. The effect of clicking the Read More link in the two different versions of the content article can be seen in Figure 7.10.

Second Blog Entry

Written by MrManager

2007-07-09 23:04:01

This is the second blog entry and some example content used to demonstrate how to add
an article through the backend. It's part of Chapter 8 of Joomla! The users guide.

This is the second paragraph of the second blog entry. As we add more blog entries we will
see how to insert images and links into content articles.

Last Updated (2007-07-09 23:41:48)

Read more... >>

Second Blog Entry

Written by MrManager

Monday, 09 July 2007

This is the second blog entry and some example content used to demonstrate how to add an
article through the backend. It's part of Chapter 8 of Joomla! The users guide.

This is the second paragraph of the second blog entry. As we add more blog entries we will
see how to insert images and links into content articles.

This is the third paragraph of the second blog entry. Generally it's a good idea to show only a
small amount of text in the introduction, the text that is shown in the blog layout.

Last Updated (2007-07-09 23:41:48)

FIGURE 7.10 An article with introductory text from the frontend

Basic Parameters

When editing the article, the expendable Ajax tabs on the right-hand side open to the
basic parameters, as shown in Figure 7.11.

Article ID:	5
State	Published
Hits	2 Reset
Revised	3 times
Created	Monday, 09 July 2007 23:04
Modified	Monday, 09 July 2007 23:41

▼ Article Parameters

Author	MrManager
Author Alias	
Access Level	Public
Created Date	2007-07-09 23:04:01
Start Publishing	2007-07-09 23:04:01
Finish Publishing	Never

▶ Advanced Parameters

▶ Metadata Information

FIGURE 7.11 Basic article parameters

NOTE
The help screen information (for Joomla 1.0.X) can be found at http://help.
Joomla. org/content/view/263/222/.

When creating an item, a backend user can have it instantly published and/or shown on the Front Page. Note that frontend users must have their content approved.

You can use the access level to create content viewable only to registered users. Combined with a component that can create payment-based subscription, this is a powerful way to create a website that has a subscription to premium content.

You can change the creator of a content item. This gives someone else permissions to edit it, given that some user levels can only edit their own work.

You can set a start date in the future to have articles appear automatically. An example where this might be useful is writing a series of blog posts in advance before you go on vacation!

You can also use the Finish publishing setting to unpublish articles that are time-sensitive, for examples some sort of special offer only available for a week.

Advanced Parameters

Clicking the Advanced Parameters tab expands those settings, as shown in Figure 7.12.

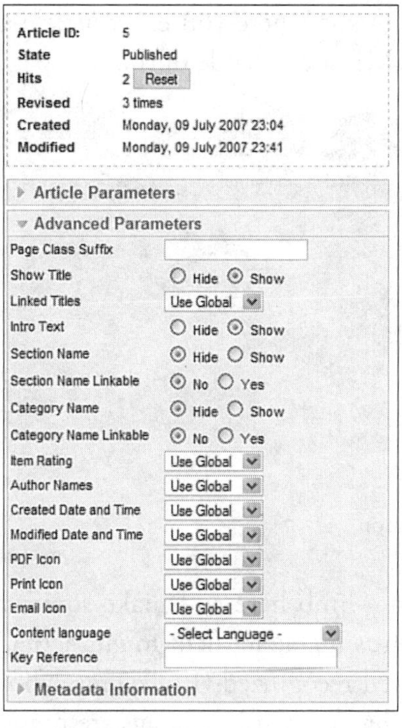

FIGURE 7.12 Advanced article parameters

The setting I find myself using most frequently here is the Show/Hide Intro Text parameter. This allows me to have better control over the presentation of an optical when it appears with others in a blog layout. For example, I could use a smaller thumbnail of an image in the intro text but then have a larger image (which would look bad in the blog layout) when the full article is viewed.

Again the rest of the parameters are explained in detail on the Joomla help site.

> **NOTE**
> Most of these parameters are contained in the preferences in the article manager. The button for this is in the toolbar. You should always try to set the global preferences to have the settings you most often need; then you can customize individual menu link and content item parameters from there.
> If you have several pages that need the same settings, make a blank content item first with filler content and then set the parameters as you need them. When you copy that page, all the parameter settings are carried over as well.

Metadata Information

As shown in Figure 7.13, this is where you enter article-specific metadata (the meta tags that appear in the HTML source code of the web page).

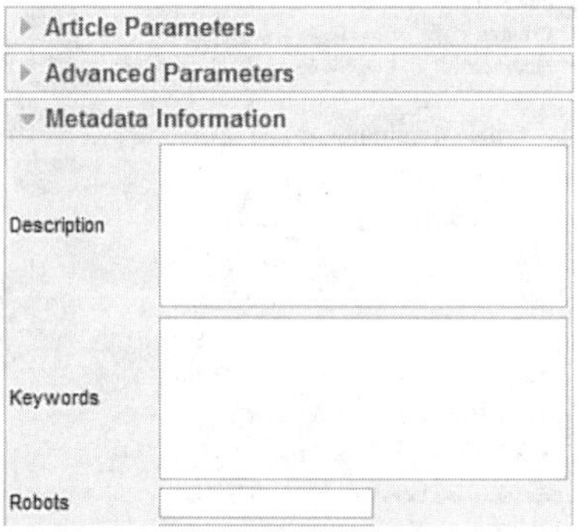

FIGURE 7.13 Metadata information

I'm going to go out on a limb here and make somewhat of a radical suggestion: The best use of the keywords metadata field might actually not be for search engine optimization (SEO). It's well recognized (I talk more about this in Chapter 8, "Getting Traffic to Your Site") that keyword metatags are pretty much ignored by modern search engines.

However, it's possible for Joomla to use these keywords to perform different functions than just appearing in the HTML source code.

For example, Joomla has a module called *related items*. This module displays other content items that are related to the item currently displayed. These are based on the keywords metadata. If you take care and attention in choosing a small amount of article-relevant keywords, this module will function very well. If you decide, however, that there is a keyword you are going to put in every single article, then every single article is going to be related in this module, and it will be useless to you.

One thing to be aware of is that this data is appended to data set in the global configuration. For pages that have several content items, such as a blog presentation, the data from each content gets added. Again, needless to say, small is better—a one sentence description and two to three keywords is adequate.

> **The Least You Need to Know**
> The Article Manager lists all articles in a Joomla site. When creating/adding articles, care must be taken as to the content, what section/category it goes in, whether it's published, and various article parameters (such as metadata).

Inserting Images into Content

Managing your images presents some of the biggest problems you might face in creating a website. The most common problem is that the image has a resolution that doesn't work well for web pages. If you take a photo with your digital camera and then upload it to the Web, you'll find it could easily be a megabyte in size and several times the size of your computer screen. First and foremost, images need to be optimized with some sort of graphics program for presentation on the Web—this means 72 or 96 dpi.

Three excellent online tools to do this are

1. www.snipshot.com
2. www.webresizer.com
3. www.picresize.com

Joomla can help you get your images into your content articles quickly and easily. Let's create a new blog post and insert an image into it.

Go to the Article Manager and click New to create a new article. At the bottom of the editor screen is an Image button, circled in Figure 7.14. You might notice among the buttons of the editor (TinyMCE in this case), there is another button you can click to insert an image (also circled in the figure). We don't use that one, however. We use the one at the bottom of the editor box actually labeled "Image."

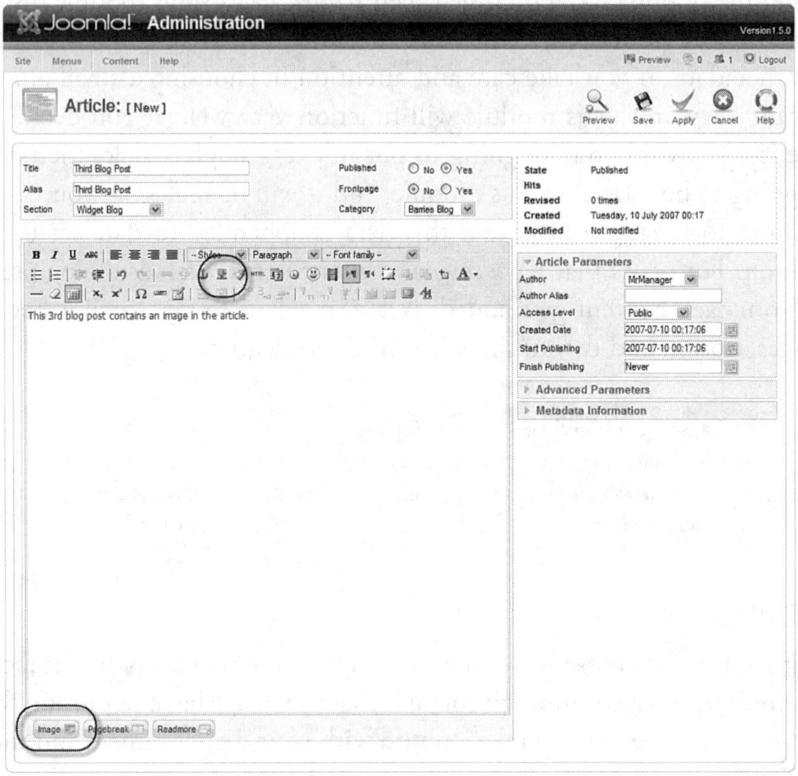

FIGURE 7.14 The Joomla Image button

> **NOTE**
> Remember that TinyMCE is a third-party editor. It's used in many applications, which is why it has its own insert image button.

If you put your cursor where you want your image and then click the Image button, a pop-up box will appear from which you can select the image you want to insert from the Joomla images folder. This pop-up box is virtually identical to the Media Manager available in the backend. The pop-up box is shown in Figure 7.15.

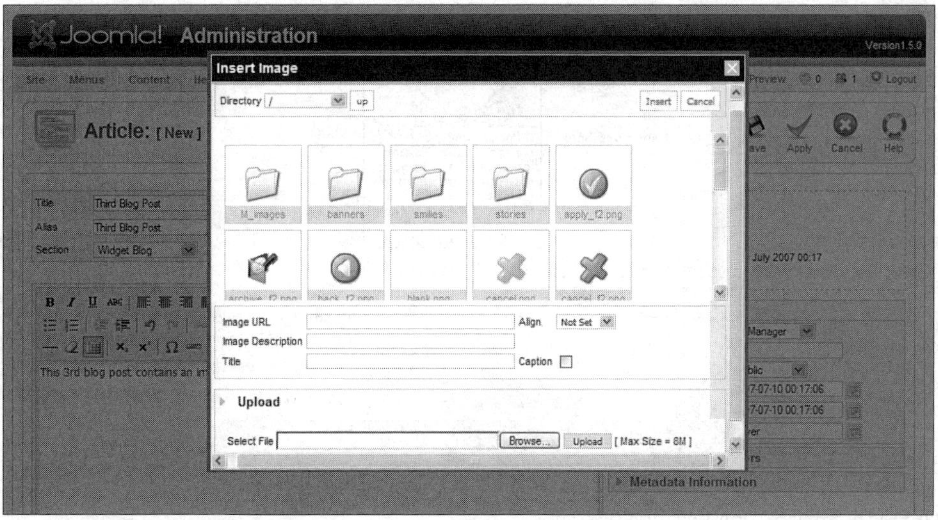

FIGURE 7.15 Insert Image dialog box

Navigate to the folder that holds the image and then click it. Next, click the insert button at the upper right. The image then appears in the content article.

> **The Least You Need to Know**
> Images are inserted in content articles through Joomla's own insert image function and not ones provided by WYSIWYG editors.

If your image isn't uploaded yet, you can also use this insert image dialog to upload your image before using it. Make sure, however, that you have optimized your image for the Web so that its resolution is appropriate.

> **NOTE**
> If you are inserting several images, you will find it easier to pre-upload them using the main Media Manager (or even FTP) rather than using the article editor media tool.

Editing Image Properties

If you want to edit the properties of the image you just inserted, for example to align it to the left or right, once inserted, you can adjust its properties by clicking it and then clicking the insert/edit image button of the TinyMCE editor. This brings up the property dialog box as shown in Figure 7.16.

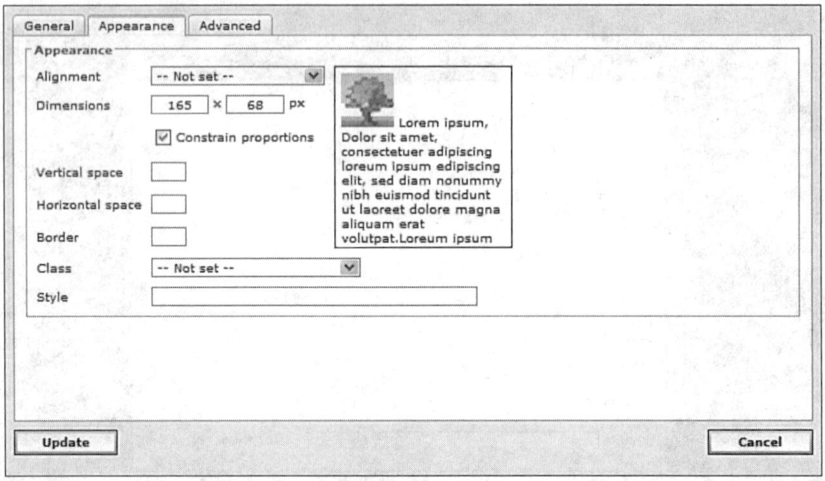

FIGURE 7.16 Image Property dialog box

Most useful here is the ability to adjust the margin around the edges of the image. Unfortunately it does this using vspace and hspace, which are both depreciated HTML tags and do not meet CSS web standards. Some other editors such as XStandard and WYSIWYGPro correctly use margins that meet standards.

> **NOTE**
> Regardless of whether your source code does or doesn't meet web design standards, you should always make sure that you have a healthy amount of white space around your images. You should aim for at least a 10-pixel margin around the four edges. It's all very well having clean standards-based HTML but not if your webpage itself looks terrible because the images are all squashed together. I call this real-world web design!

Creating an Article Table of Contents

If you have a very long article, you might find it useful to break it up into several pages. Joomla can do this automatically for you using its *pagebreak* function.

Let's open our third blog post article, insert a Read More link/break after the image, and then enter some more text.

To add a page break after the sentence, click the Pagebreak button at the bottom of the editor next to the Joomla Image button. A dialog appears where you can enter the title of that page, shown in Figure 7.17.

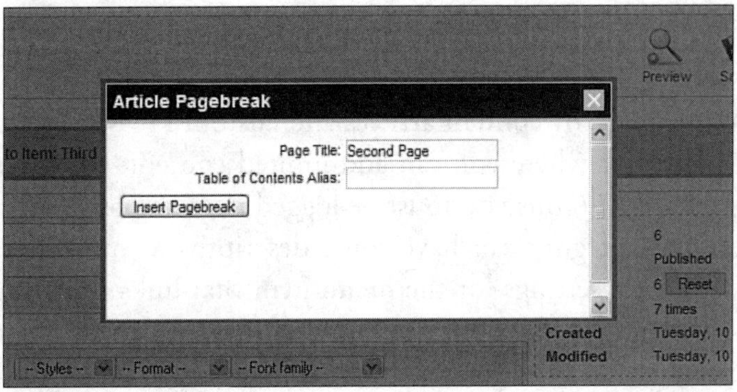

FIGURE 7.17 Pagebreak Dialog Box

When viewed from the frontend (see Figure 7.18), the table of contents is displayed in a small box at the upper right portion of the article with links to the different pages. The visual appearance of the table of contents box can be styled through the template CSS files.

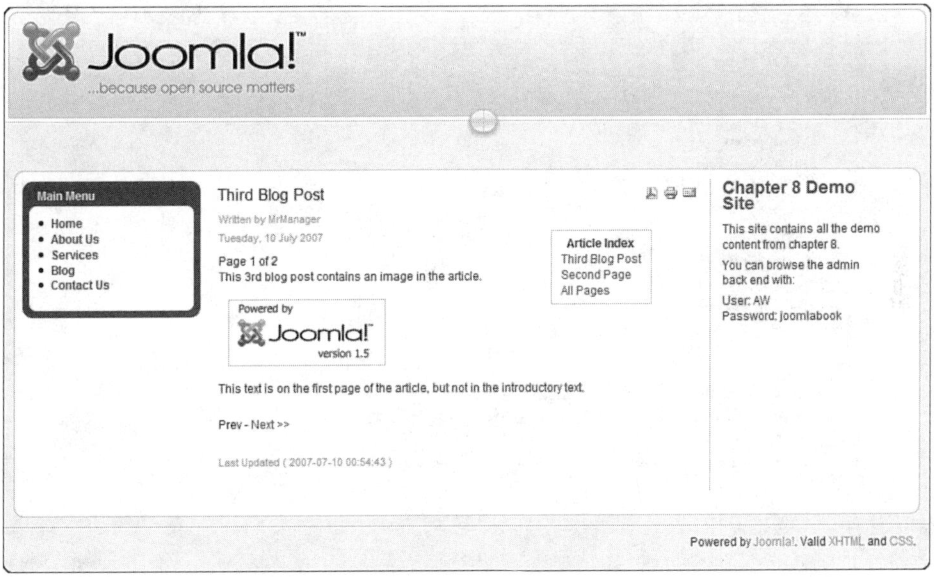

FIGURE 7.18 Joomla article table of contents view from the frontend

Section and Category Descriptions

So far we have looked at two main vehicles for you to add your content in Joomla: the main body as represented by content articles and custom HTML modules.

There is a third place where you can add limited content: the descriptions of sections and categories. To do this you must be logged in to the backend of the site.

Each section and category can have some descriptive content associated with it. Based on the parameter settings for the menu item that links to it, you can have this description show or not. If the description is set to be shown, it is shown at the top of the page for that section/category but only on that top-level page. If links are connected to individual articles, the descriptions are not shown.

Sounds confusing, but let's look at an example. First, let's add a description to the Widget Blog section.

Go to **Content > Section Manager > Widget Blog**. This brings up the Section Editor (see Figure 7.19).

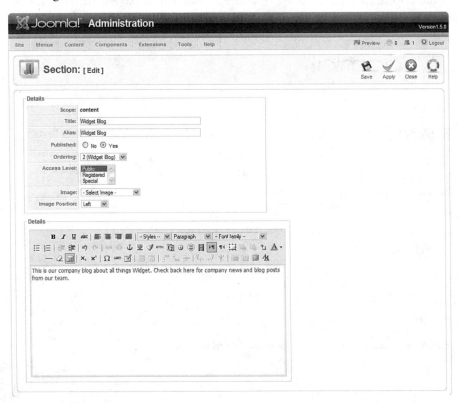

FIGURE 7.19 Editing the Section Description

In the WYSIWYG editor labeled Details, you can add content, images, and/or text that will appear as the description for that section.

Save this screen. We now need to go to the menu item and set the parameter to show the description. Go to **Menus > Menu Manager > mainmenu > Blog**.

In this Edit Menu Item screen (see Figure 7.20), on the right-hand side in the Menu Item Parameters, you see the settings to Show/Hide the description (circled). Set them to Show.

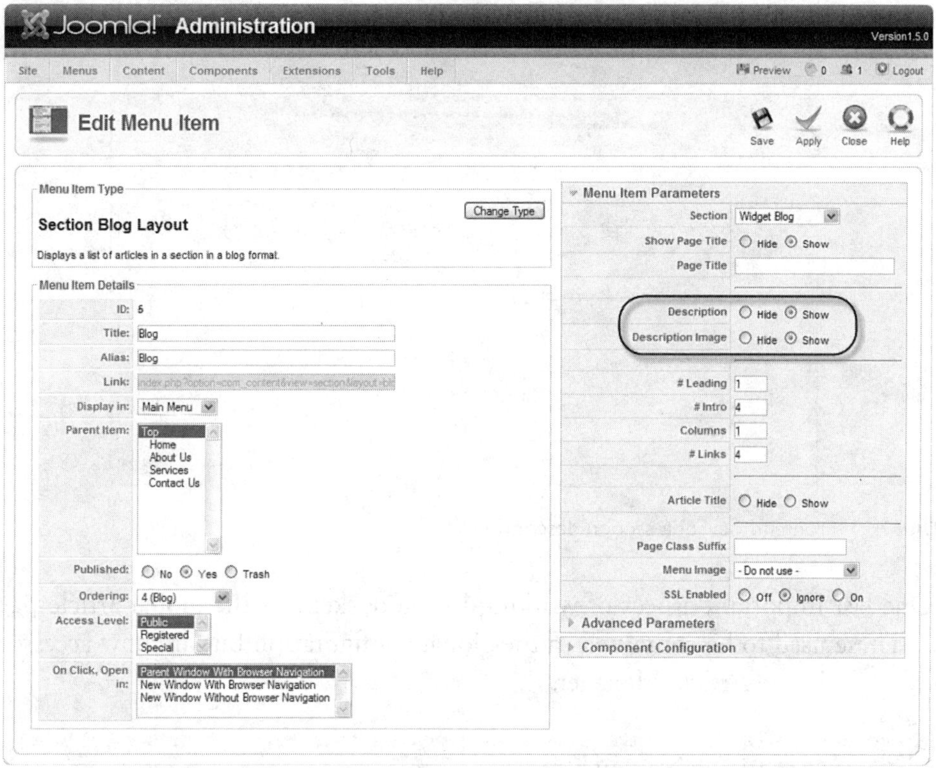

FIGURE 7.20 Show Description Parameter in Edit Menu Item

I rarely use the description image. This is a specific Joomla setting that shows an image that is designated in the Section/Category Edit screen (refer to Figure 7.19). When I want to place an image here, I do it in the HTML editor, so I find that I very rarely use the description image function.

Viewed from the frontend, our blog now looks like the screen in 7.21.

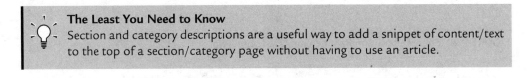

FIGURE 7.21 Frontend view of a section description

One last important aspect of working in the backend is the global article parameters. These used to be contained in the global configuration but are now accessed (in Joomla 1.5) in the Article Manager.

> **The Least You Need to Know**
> Section and category descriptions are a useful way to add a snippet of content/text to the top of a section/category page without having to use an article.

Article Content Preferences

When logged in as a super administrator, the Article Manager has an additional icon in the toolbar for preferences, as circled in Figure 7.22.

Clicking the Preferences icon will bring up a pop-up dialog box with the various site-wide settings available for articles, shown in Figure 7.23.

FIGURE 7.22 Preferences in the Article Manager

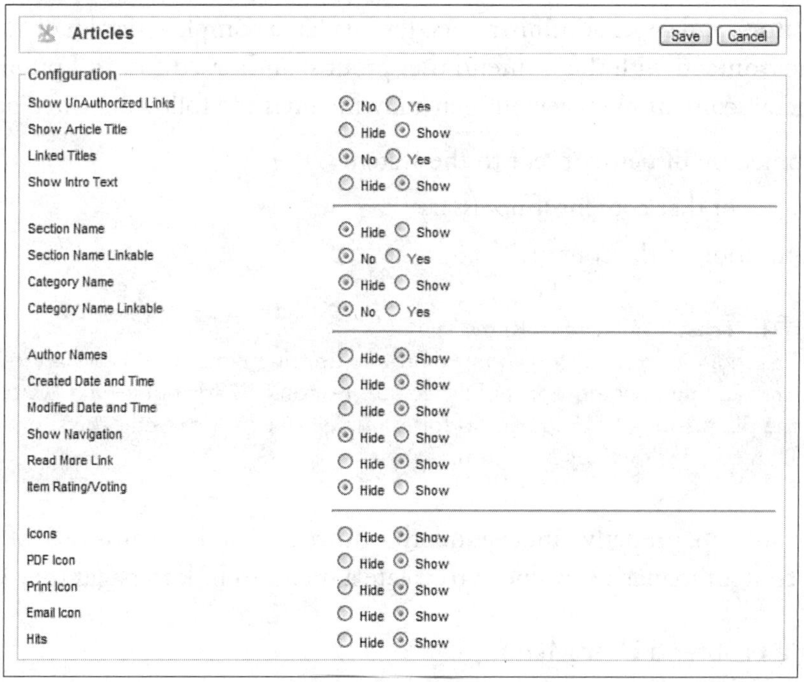

FIGURE 7.23 Article Global Configuration

> **The Least You Need to Know**
> Article Global Configuration should be set to what you think you want most often.
> It is possible to override them on a menu item or article level.

> **NOTE**
> More explanation (for 1.0.X) can be found at http://help.Joomla.org/content/view/
> 51/224/1/3/.

As we initially discussed, it's more efficient for a single person to manage content from the backend. If you have several content contributors, however, you might not want to give them all backend access. The answer in this scenario is to let them manage the content from the frontend.

Managing Content Through The Frontend

As we have already seen, the backend of a Joomla site is only available to managers, administrators, and super administrators. Joomla has a complete system of adding content to the frontend with the frontend user groups: author, editor, and publisher.

In general, content management generally includes the following three operations:

1. Submission of new content to the system

2. Editing of that content if necessary

3. Publication of the content

> **The Least You Need to Know**
> Authors are generally responsible for submitting content; editors are responsible
> for editing content; and publishers are responsible for publishing content. How-
> ever, the permissions are additive, so for example, an editor can edit the submitted con-
> tent of an author as well as their own.

Before we can properly understand the functions and permissions of the three frontend content managers, we need to create a menu to link to pages they will need.

Creating a Frontend User Menu

To create a frontend user menu, we must first create a new menu (which we did in Chapter 5, "Creating Menus and Navigation"). Go to **Menus > Menu Manager > New**. This brings up the New Menu Details screen as shown in Figure 7.24. Note that in the first field, the Module Name should not contain spaces.

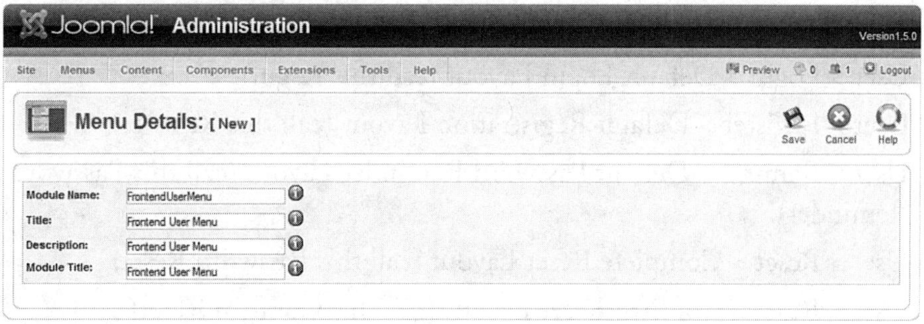

FIGURE 7.24 Creating a new user menu

By clicking Save, we return to the Menu Manager. Open the Frontend User Menu we just created by clicking the Menu Items icon for that menu. We should get a menu that has no items.

We now need to add menu items as we have before, but this time we are not linking to articles, sections, categories, or components, but to the *User* menu item type. Clicking that option expands the tree structure as shown in Figure 7.25.

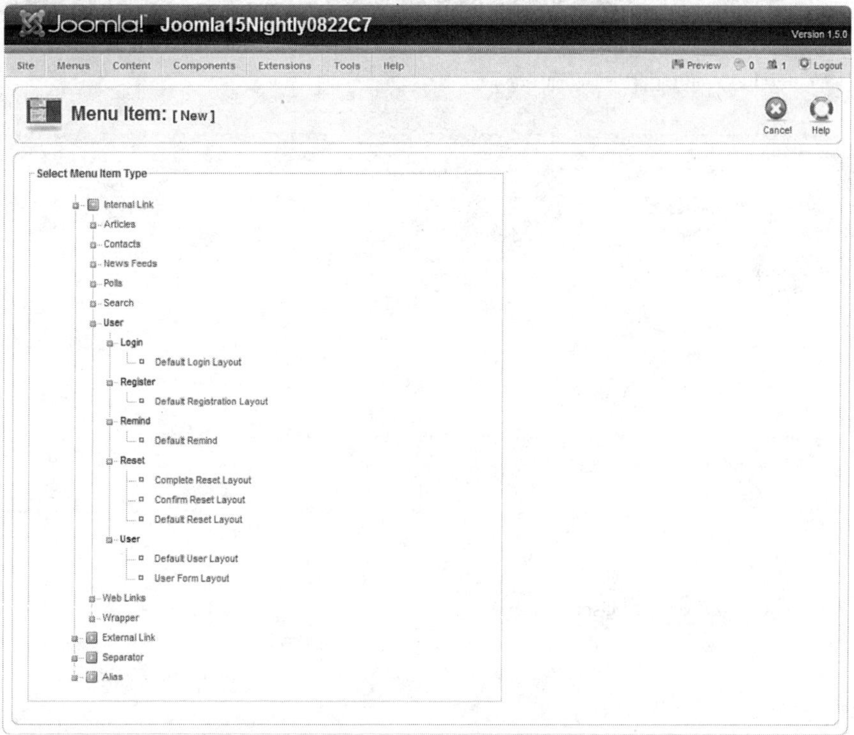

FIGURE 7.25 The User menu item tree

We should now create menu links for the following:

- User > Login > Default Login Layout (call this Login)
- User > Register > Default Registration Layout (call this Register)
- User > Remind > Default Password Reminder Layout (call this Password Reminder)
- User > Reset > Complete Reset Layout (call this Password Reset)
- User > Reset > Confirm Reset Layout (call this Confirm Reset)
- User > Reset > Default Reset Layout (call this Default Reset)
- User > User > Default User Layout (call this Default User)
- User > User > User Form Layout (call this User Form)
- Articles > Article Submission Layout (call this Submit Content)

After adding these nine menu items, the menu in the backend should look like Figure 7.26.

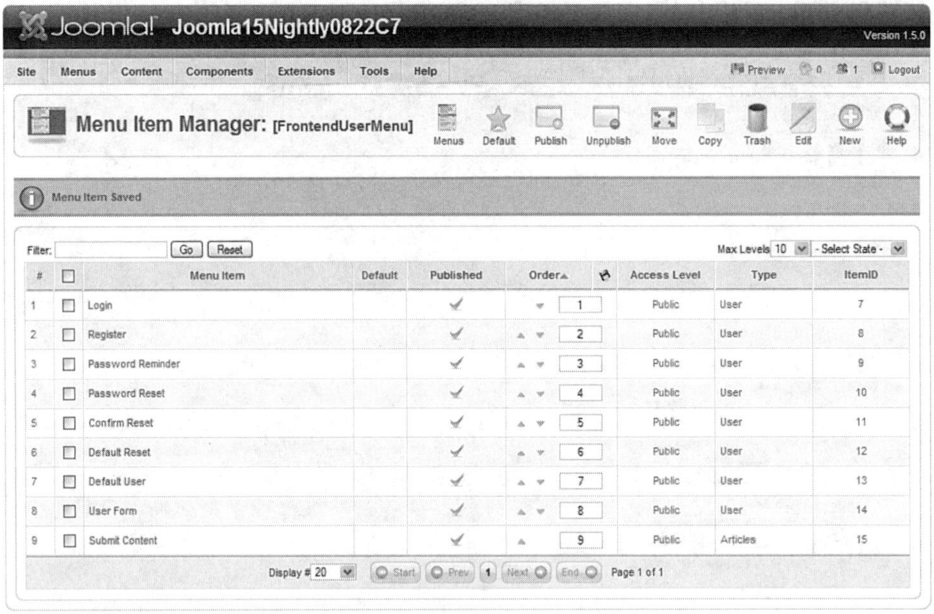

FIGURE 7.26 The new Frontend User menu

From the frontend, the module of the menu will be presented as in Figure 7.27.

FIGURE 7.27 Frontend view of complete user menu

Remember that the *presentation* of a menu is controlled by its corresponding *module*. Its *functionality* and where the menu items link to is controlled by its *menu* in the Menu Manager.

To give the menu the same style as the main menu and to move it, we need to find its module.

Go to **Extensions > Module Manager > Frontend User Menu**. In the advanced parameters you need to enter the Module Class Suffix as **_menu**. This allows Joomla to apply the predetermined CSS styles as defined by the template.

Also you can set the Module Order to be 2::Main Menu so it will appear after the Main Menu in the left column.

Now, the user menu we have set up here shows all the possible links you can have. We would not use all of these for a real site. You'll notice that there are links to register and to recover the password on the login form. What menu items you choose depend on the functionality you want to offer users.

The last step to setting up this menu is to make use of the access control features of Joomla so that some of the menu items are only seen by logged-in users.

Limiting Access to Menus by User Level

If a visitor goes to our site, we probably don't want them to see the menu items for Your Details and Submit Content; it would just confuse them. Even more so, the Submit Content link will only work if a visitor is logged in.

Fortunately, Joomla allows the easy control of what is visible and what is not. For any Joomla item, whether its an article, module, or menu item, you can set the access (whether you can see it) to be one of three levels.

- **Public**. Anyone can see it.
- **Registered**. Registered users and above can see it.
- **Special**. Any administrator (author and above) can see it.

This is done either by toggling the Access column in any of the managers, article, module or menu, or by changing the parameter when you are editing that specific item.

With this in mind, we want to have the Login and Register menu items be public and all of the rest of the links to be registered. We'll also change the Submit Content menu item to be Special.

Go to **Menus > Menu Manager > Frontend User Menu**. Click the Access column words (where it says Public to start), and you will notice it toggles through the three options. Click until Your Details and Submit Content menu items are set to Special access. The menu should look like Figure 7.28.

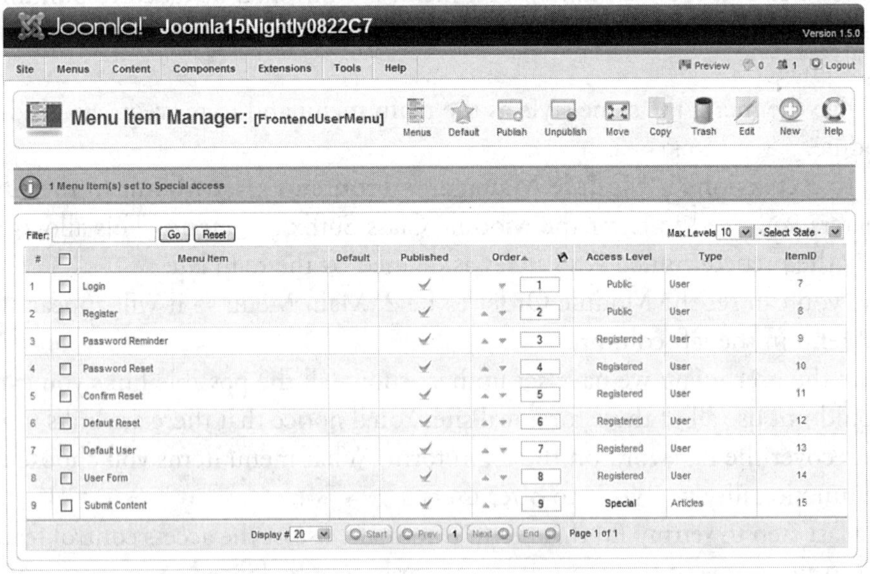

FIGURE 7.28 Changing menu permissions

Now if someone visits the site, he sees only the Login link. If he logs in and is a frontend or backend administrator, two more links magically appear!

Now we have a means to add articles through the frontend. When a frontend administrator logs in, she can go to the Submit Content page and see a form. To better understand how this works, we need to look at each—author, editor, and publisher— in turn.

Let's make three users to do this. Go to **Site > User Manager** and create three users for the three access levels. I called mine MrAuthor, MrEditor, and MrPublisher.

Your User Manager should look like Figure 7.29 when done.

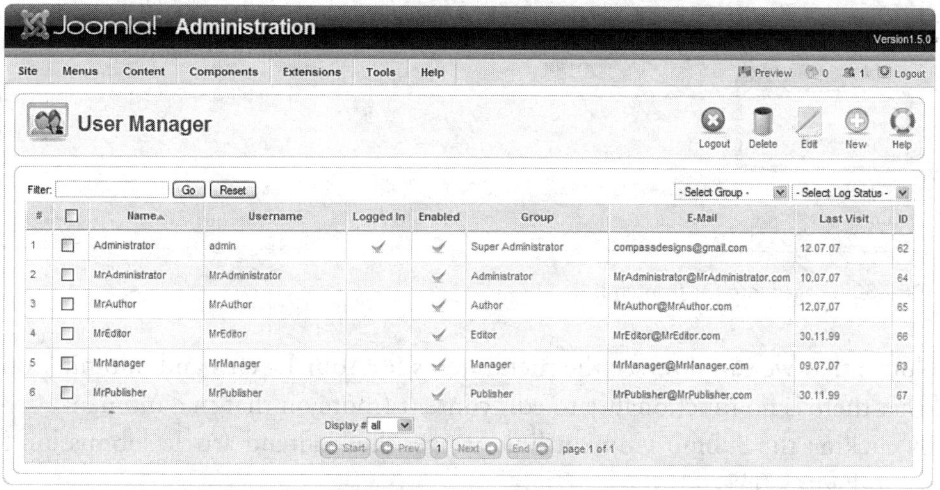

FIGURE 7.29 Creating users in the User Manager

Notice that there is some confusion here as I have an Administrator and a MrAdministrator. That's because the administrator name is the default one created by Joomla on installation. MrAdministrator is the one I added at an administrator access level. If that confuses you, open up the Administrator user (the original one) and change his name to MrSuperAdministrator to match our scheme.

Now let's take a look at how an author can manage content.

Authors

Authors are the lowest level of frontend content administrators in Joomla. The concept of the author is that they can submit content but cannot edit it or publish it.

Let's go to the frontend of the site and log in as MrAuthor. In doing so, we see the home page shown in Figure 7.30.

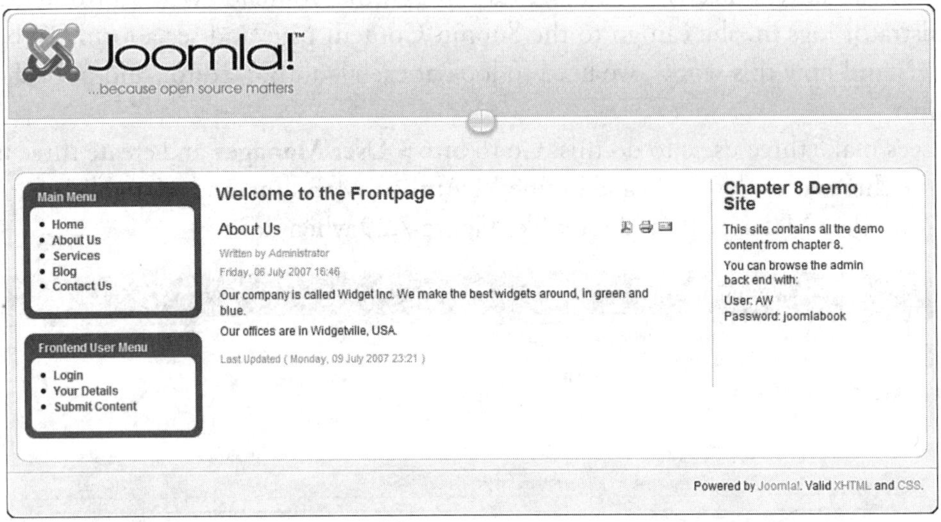

FIGURE 7.30 Logged into the frontend

Notice that we can now see the menu items for Your Details and Submit Content and that there is no functionality to edit content (more on that in a moment).

By clicking the Submit Content link, we get the frontend article submission form shown in Figure 7.31.

We need to fill in some information and make sure that we put the article in the Widget Blog section. If you have been keeping count, this has been the fourth blog post! Save the article.

On saving the item, we get this message: "Thanks for your submission. Your submission will now be reviewed before being posted to the site."

After saving, we quickly find that the article is nowhere to be found in the frontend. That's because authors cannot publish articles. When an author creates an article, it is automatically flagged as unpublished.

Now let's log in to the backend as a super administrator and see what is going on. Log in as Admin (or MrSuperAdministrator if you changed the name). Go to **Content > Article Manager**.

We see the fourth blog post as unpublished. This status is circled in Figure 7.32.

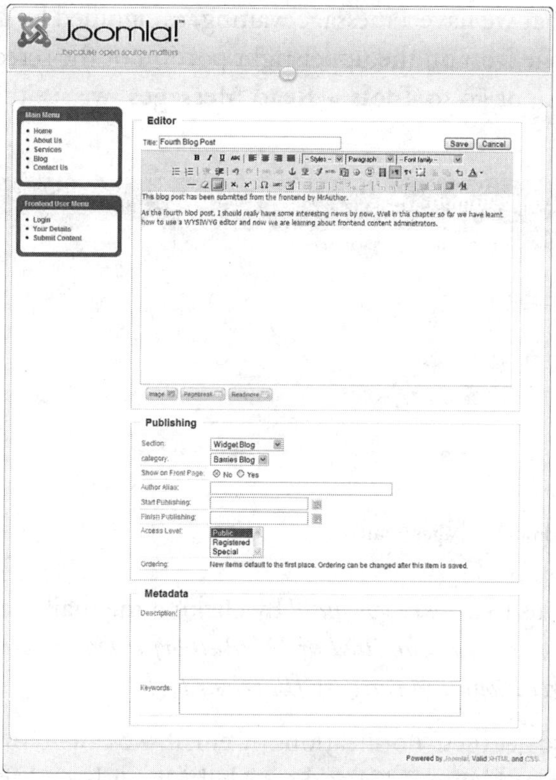

FIGURE 7.31 The frontend Editor screen

FIGURE 7.32 Approving content articles

We also notice that we have a message waiting, as signified by the number "1" next to the Private Message icon on the upper right portion of the screen (circled).

If we click the "1" or go to **Tools > Read Messages**, we see the inbox as shown in Figure 7.33.

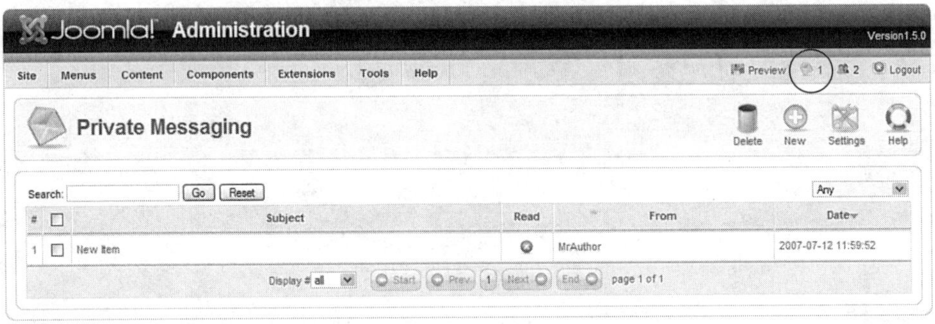

FIGURE 7.33 Getting admin messages/mail

Joomla is telling us that *we've got mail!* By clicking the mail message, we read that
A new article has been submitted by [MrAuthor] titled [Fourth Blog Post] from section [Widget Blog] and category [Barries Blog].

If we want to also get these notifications by email, we can go to Settings (the icon in the upper right area of Figure 7.33) and set Mail Me on New Message to Yes. *Publish the new article in the Article Manager* by toggling through the Published icon in the Article Manager.

If we go to the frontend of the site and into the Widget Blog, we can see our new article, shown in Figure 7.34.

Note that there is still no way to edit the content for the author until it is published. For that, we need to see what editors can do.

> **The Least You Need to Know**
> Authors can create but not publish or edit articles. They are useful when you have several users able to add content to a site in a controlled way as their submissions are reviewed by another administrator.

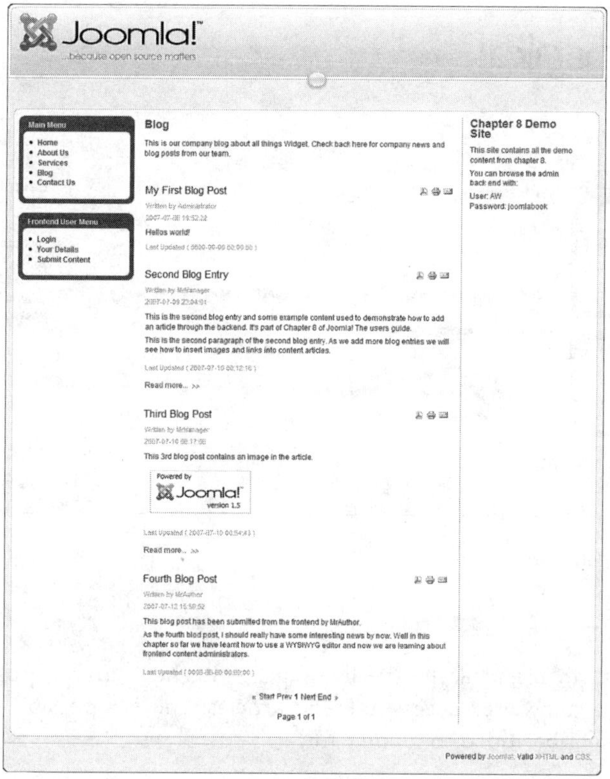

FIGURE 7.34 Widget Blog with new articles

Editors

An editor can submit content exactly the same as an author. They can submit it, but they cannot publish it. They also can edit any content on the site.

Let's log in to the frontend as MrEditor. As soon as we do this, we see the home page has a small but important difference, shown in Figure 7.35.

If you are watching carefully, you'll see the tiny icon next to the article title. This is a button that will now be throughout the whole site for each article. Clicking it brings up an Article Edit screen almost identical to the submission form.

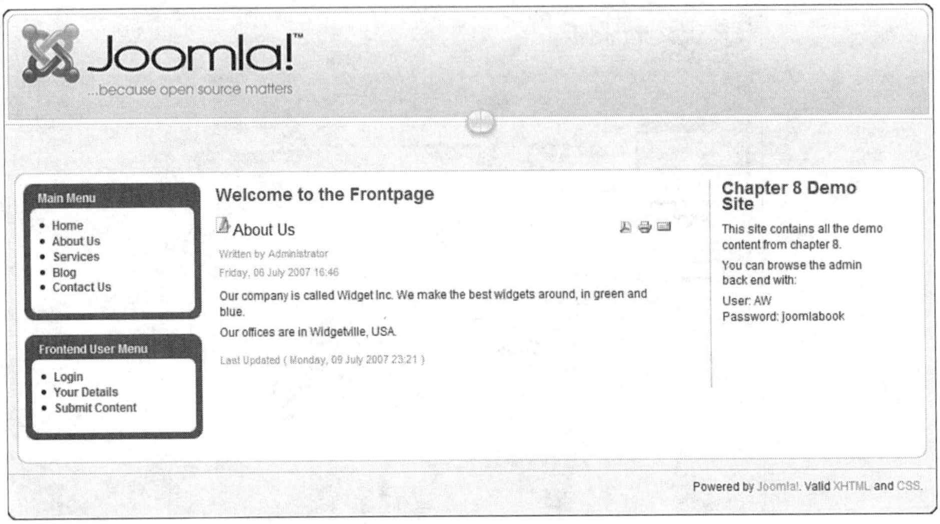

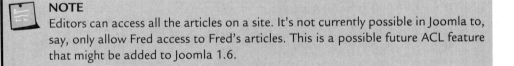

FIGURE 7.35 Logging in to edit articles

> **NOTE**
> Editors can access all the articles on a site. It's not currently possible in Joomla to, say, only allow Fred access to Fred's articles. This is a possible future ACL feature that might be added to Joomla 1.6.

So editors can edit articles but not publish them. How could this be implemented in a real site?

From my experience in helping many clients build Joomla sites, it's only very big ones that have authors. Most sites will have a dozen or so *content producers* who are set at the editor level. Clients have found it more useful for these content producers to be able to create and edit their articles. Then they are passed for final review to a publisher or above for publication.

> **The Least You Need to Know**
> Editors can create and edit articles. They cannot publish their own content, but they can edit any article whether published or not.

For the last step in building content articles from the frontend, we need to look at publishers.

Publishers

Publishers have all the same abilities of editors plus the ability to actually publish articles on the website. All the same controls that we just saw for submitting and editing content are also available to publishers. Publishers may author their own content, edit the content of other authors or editors, and cause articles to be published on the website.

Let's log in as MrPublisher and see the difference. Upon logging in, almost everything is identical. The same Edit button is next to the titles, and the same form is shown to create or edit an article. The minor difference is a couple of extra parameters in the create/edit form, here circled in Figure 7.36.

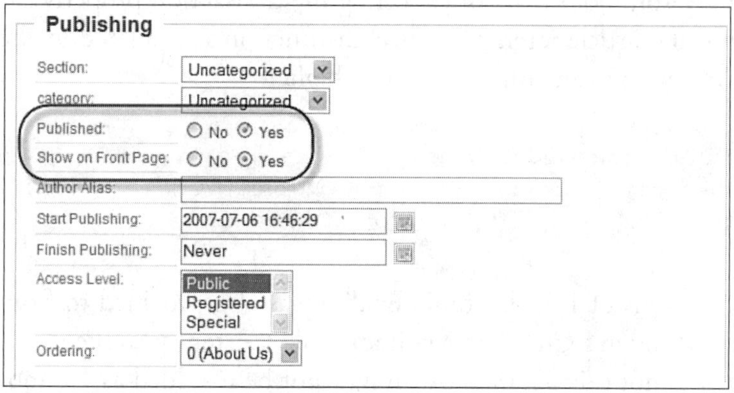

FIGURE 7.36 Frontend publisher functions

Publishers effectively have exactly the same rights regarding content as backend administrators. They cannot, however, log in to the backend.

> **The Least You Need to Know**
> Publishers can create, edit, and publish any article.

Article Checkin

When working in one of the edit windows, such as when an author is creating new content, you should always click the Cancel or Save icons to exit the page. The reason for this is that Joomla locks the content while you are editing it, preventing other users such as editors and publishers from accessing it at the same time. This function is referred to as Global *Checkin*, which is managed with the global checkin tool in the backend.

There are times when exiting these edit windows improperly could result in content being locked to others. The following are just a few cases in which this could occur:

- The user accidentally closes his or her browser window before canceling or saving the transaction.
- The user uses the browser navigation functions to move away from the site before canceling or saving the transaction.
- A power failure knocks your PC out at the wrong time.

Whatever the reason, not saving or canceling the transaction properly can block users from accessing the article later. The checkin function is available in the backend in Tools when logged in as an administrator or higher.

> **The Least You Need to Know**
> Joomla has a system for only allowing one user at a time to edit articles. It's managed through the global checkin tool in the backend.

In earlier versions of 1.5, this functionality was also provided to frontend content administrators through a Check-In My Items link. Currently, in the Release Candidate version, this does not exist. It might or might not be re-added as 1.5 moves towards a Stable release.

User's Guide Chapter 7 Demo Site

A demo of this site is available at www.joomlabook.com. It is an exact copy of what you should have if you follow all the steps in this chapter. You can log in to the administrative backend so you can see the site framework and the sections, categories, and menus that were set up.

Summary

In this chapter, we looked at how we can manage our content articles from the backend and frontend. Defining some plan or process in your organization for this is critical to leveraging the power of Joomla as a Content Management System. Leaving the generation of content in the hands of one person will mean a site that is infrequently updated and stale.

- WYSIWYG stands for What You See Is What You Get. It allows editing of content without knowledge of (X)HTML. Several editors are available for Joomla and can be installed as plugins.

- Backend editing is efficient but often not as efficient when many users are given backend access. Frontend editing allows more users to be involved in managing the content. It also allows for the quick and easy editing of single articles.

- The Article Manager lists all articles in a Joomla site. When creating/adding articles, care must be taken as to the content, what section/category it goes in, whether it is published, and various article parameters, such as metadata.

- Images are inserted in content articles through Joomla's own insert image function and not ones provided by WYSIWYG editors.

- Section and category descriptions are a useful way to add a snippet of content/text to the top of a section/category page without having to use an article.

- Article Global Configuration should be set to what you think you want most often. It is possible to override it on a menu item or article level.

- Authors are generally responsible for submitting content; editors are responsible for editing content; and publishers are responsible for publishing content. However, the permissions are additive, so for example, an editor can edit the submitted content of an author as well as their own.

- Authors can create but not publish or edit articles. They are useful when you have many users adding content to a site in a controlled way as their submissions must be reviewed by another administrator.

- Editors can create and edit articles. They cannot publish their own content. They can edit any article whether published or not.

- Publishers can create, edit, and publish any article.

- Joomla has a system for only allowing one user at a time to edit articles, called global checkin, and it's managed through the global checkin tool in the backend.

Chapter 8

Getting Traffic to Your Site

Search engine optimization (SEO) might be one of the most maligned subjects on the Web. If you talk to *black hat SEO* (people who use unethical methods to gain rank in search engines) to their counterparts, *white hat SEO* (the good guys), how best to get traffic to your site is loaded with opinion and myth.

Trying to learn about SEO is difficult, to say the least, because there are a few problems:

- No one knows for sure what works; the search engines won't reveal their algorithms.
- Some people pushing SEO information are in business only to make easy money from poor services.
- The whole thing is so complex (see the first point).

In this chapter, I emphasize something slightly different from SEO, known as *search engine marketing (SEM)*. I point out some obvious SEO tips and how they apply to Joomla, but I also discuss a more holistic plan including such strategies as Pay-Per-Click and blogging.

- Why do I want traffic to my site?

- How can I get traffic to my site?

- How can I get organic traffic with SEO?

- How can I get referral traffic?

- How can I get Pay-Per-Click traffic?

- How can I use email marketing to get traffic?

- What is SEF?

Start at the Beginning: Site Goals

Why do you want traffic? Before you go anywhere, you need to answer this question. You can break it down into

- What is your website about?
- Who will visit it?
- What will they gain?
- What will you gain?

Write the answers on a piece of paper...no, really!

Unless you have a clear idea of why you are building a site, you'll struggle to make decisions later in the process of designing and publishing it. It's especially important to think about what your viewers will gain from visiting your site. The answer to this question will form the underpinning of your SEM efforts.

Now that you have thought some what about who is going to visit your site, we can talk about the "how."

Publishing your site is only a small step in the path to getting traffic. Unless you do something else, your site will just sit there, and no one will know it exists. Unfortunately, unlike the Kevin Costner film *Field of Dreams*, "If you build it, they will come," is not true on the Web.

When we consider the bigger concept of SEM, we can split the different ways to get traffic into several main categories:

- **Organic**. What was traditionally known as SEO, organic marketing is the idea of having your website visible in various search engines when people search for keywords.

- **Referral**. Quite simply, the idea of having links from other sites to yours. A robust SEM plan will have a comprehensive link building strategy. These can be natural through attracting links to your high-quality content, or can be paid links or other techniques.

- **Pay-Per-Click (PPC)**. This strategy involves bidding for placement on search results. Submitting an ad to a search engine such as Google also means that it appears on its distributed ad network, for example in Google's case, AdSense. So your ads will appear both in search results and on content sites.

- **Email**. Building an email subscription list is a key part of a modern SEM plan. It's important to know who your website viewers are and if appropriate to capture their emails so that you can present them with information that might draw them back to your site.

If you want your website to be successful, it is absolutely critical that you have a balanced plan that addresses these four components. Just focusing on one will put you at a disadvantage to competitors that have a more balanced approach. It's exactly the same principle that your financial consultant might tell you: Have a diversified portfolio.

> **NOTE**
> Disclaimer! I am not an "SEO guy," and I don't play one on TV. What I describe here are things I have read, observed, and, in most cases, implemented that seem to be successful.

Organic Traffic (SEO)

Let's search Google for the keyword "Joomla." Figure 8.1 shows the results of this search in September 2007 (I wonder if 58 million websites are really using Joomla).

This search greatly illustrates the difference between organic and PPC marketing. The results that appear on the left are ones produced by the Google algorithm (more on that later in our section about how Google calculates PageRank). These are ranked by an insanely complicated formula used by the search engine. The search engine is trying to find the most useful sites connected to the keyword that you used in your search. Here we can see that www.joomla.org is number one. (My commercial template site, joomlashack.com comes in at number 7, and my blog compassdesigns.net at number 10. I thought I would just note that observation partly to show that I do have some clue what I'm talking about in this SEM chapter—and partly just to make a shameless plug!)

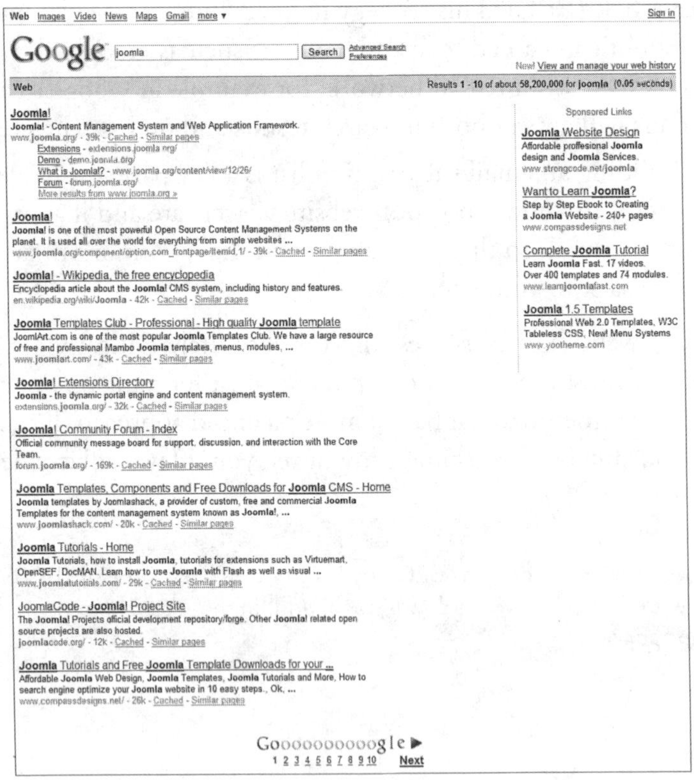

FIGURE 8.1 Google results for Joomla

The results on the left are what would be called organic (or natural) results, and the results on the right (and sometimes along the top) are the PPC results. These people pay to appear in this listing. Interestingly enough, you can see that Adobe is now paying to be advertised on Joomla searches. As we will see later on, there are some huge implications in where your website appears on this page.

So let's start learning about how to increase your organic search engine ranking position (SERP). There is a massive amount of information about SEO, SEM, and SERP. You have to be careful, though, about the quality of the information you get. There are huge numbers of people who would be happy to take your money for some e-book and run. Here is an example.

How to earn $1,000s a day with Search Engine Optimization and Joomla.

"How you can profit from the EXACT SAME search engine optimization strategies that I used to charge clients $3,590 a day to implement!"

In this web-based, no-hype guide, I'll reveal my simple step-by-step search engine optimization strategy that I have been using for two years on over 350 clients and that anyone can use to get a front page ranking on Google.

See what I mean? That is an actual example of one of the millions of people selling these services on the Web. The real truth about search engine optimization is that there is no "silver bullet" anymore. It used to be true that you could stuff a few keywords into some metatags and get lots of traffic. Now search engines are much smarter. Google recently released its patent #20050071741 on its "Information Retrieval Based on Historical Data" (that's that little search page to you and me). In the document were over 118 factors[1] that affected a website's position in the search engine's rankings!

This is the real truth about SEO: There is no such thing as search engine optimization anymore. The only reality now is having a long-term web marketing strategy and a commitment to building a site full of quality information.

Having said that, assuming that your site is one with quality content, SEO still has its place. Look at the statistics shown in Table 8.1.

TABLE 8.1 Use of the Internet among adults

% U.S. Adults Online	
Total Adults	73%
18–49 Year Olds	86%
% Commonly Using	
Email	91%
Search	91%

Source: Pew Internet 04/06

Trying to get high organic ranking through SEO is important as we can see in the Pew Internet statistics. The search engine is the first step for the vast majority of people trying to find information on the Web.

SEO used to be about trying to game the system. This worked three years ago, but now search engines are much more sophisticated. Attempts to stuff metatags or put lots of hidden text on a page are more than likely going to get you penalized. This next point is very important to understanding SEO: *A search engine tries to find high-quality content based on a keyword search.*

To be most successful at organic SEO, you need to meet this need. Create a site with lots of high-quality content and make it easy for both search engine spiders and human Web visitors to find and read.

> **TIP**
> If you are serious about SEO, you should probably think about allocating some budget to a professional. If a potential vendor you are looking at has any sort of guarantee with regard to results, run to the hills. It's impossible to predict results in this industry, and claims like this are recognized as being associated with cowboys (or cowgirls).

Let's look next at the steps in a roughly chronological order that you might take as you launch a new site.

Now a little word about some software called "Information Retrieval Based on Historical Data" (Google).

Introduction to Google

Google is *the* Internet search engine. Over 150 million searches are conducted daily. Among Google, Yahoo!, and MSN, these three account for about 90% of all searches made on the Web.

With these millions of Google searches everyday, even if your business or product is currently listed on Google, do you think that a boost in ranking to the first or second page would increase the number of potential customers coming to your website?

> **TIP**
> Google isn't the only player in town, but surprisingly most search engines get their results from only a handful of main engines. Bruce Clay made a handy chart to show the relationships. You can view it at www.bruceclay.com/searchenginerelationship-chart.htm.

How Does Google Calculate Page Relevance?

Although I don't know how the Google algorithm works exactly (no one does)—it's a closely guarded secret—I do know that Google relies on over 118 different calculations to work out the relevancy of any particular page for a search. The big one is *link popularity*.

Link Popularity

If you have downloaded the Google toolbar (toolbar.google.com), then you will have seen the green bar that Google uses to rank every site you visit. This ranking is Google's PageRank and is indicated on a scale of 1 to 10. Generally, sites with a PageRank of 7 to 10 are considered excellent in terms of quality and popularity.

Google's main criterion for the calculation of relevancy for a page is based on the number of websites that link back to that particular site. Each site that links back to you must in itself contain quality content and have a high PageRank for it to impact positively on the PageRank of your website.

If Google's PageRank technology sounds confusing, just try and remember that Google's PageRank is the number one criterion for calculating the relevancy of any web page in relation to the specified search term. We will come back to link popularity later.

There are supposedly over 118 factors involved in exactly how Google calculates Search Engine Rank Position (SERP). As mentioned before, Google places more emphasis on PageRank than other engines.

Creating Keywords

It's critical to know exactly why you are building your site and who your site's audience is.

Remember this question? Let's talk about the first step in using this information: keywords.

Keywords drive search engines. The idea is that a search engine wants to return a page in a search about something that the searcher is looking for. It's doing this by looking at what was entered into the search box (the keywords) and then trying to match those keywords with pages in its database.

A *key phrase* is just a few keywords put together. Researchers tell us that very few people just use one word to search anymore and are getting more sophisticated, using three or more keywords in a search.

Imagine you are a potential visitor to your site. What keywords or phrases will you type in to find it? Take a blank piece of paper and write down as many words or phrases as you can that you, as a potential visitor, would search for to find a site like yours in a search engine.

Here's an example. For a site about baby names, you might have

- Baby names
- Popular baby names
- Most popular baby names

Notice how I didn't use the single word "baby." People who are searching on that term might be looking any number of things. At this point we don't want to be too general.

Try to write 20 to 30 keywords or phrases on your piece of paper. If you're having trouble coming up with keywords, ask your partner, friends, or family members which keywords they would use to find your site. At this point, you should have a list of no less than 20 keywords or phrases at your disposal.

Right now, some research is called for. You need to find out how many people are searching for your keywords and phrases, and you need a tool to tell you this information. The big gun here is something called Wordtracker (www.wordtrackerkeywords. com). It costs just under $10 for a one-day subscription, but the information it gives is worth it. If your site depends on traffic, I recommend this tool.

> **NOTE**
> Three other free tools also work, but they don't give the detail that Wordtracker does:
> - www.digitalpoint.com/tools/suggestion/
> - inventory.overture.com/d/searchinventory/suggestion
> - www.yourseobook.com

TIP

These tools will only tell you how many searches are being made. Another piece of information is how many sites you are competing against. Even if there are several searches for a given term, if there are also many competing websites, then getting a high SERP will be challenging. This is where Wordtracker shines. It also gives a factor called the Keyword Effectiveness Index (KEI). This is basically a measure of how effective (easy in terms of competition and useful in terms of number of searches) a particular key phrase will be.

Using any of these tools, start at the top of your keyword list and enter each one into the text box. As you can see, the term suggestion tool returns a list of keywords and how many times they were searched for during the last day. As you type each of your keywords into the text box and see the number of searches, write that number down next to your keyword on the page.

As you are doing this, you'll also come across key phrases that people are searching that you didn't think of. Include them too.

You should now have a list of keywords with the number of searches for that keyword from last month on your page. To get the five most popular keywords, simply take the five keywords with the highest number of searches. Write them down in order of most popular to least popular. You should now have your list of five most popular keywords, maybe something like this:

778231	baby name
68325	baby girl name
63222	baby boy name
38285	odd baby name
33583	top 100 baby name

NOTE

"Odd baby name." How odd is that for a search term? At this point, it's worth being creative on your search terms. Who would have thought this would be getting almost 40,000 searches a month, and this is just on Yahoo!.

It's possible to optimize your pages for both single and plural. Some engines differentiate between the two. If you depend on traffic for your site, optimize for both.

Next, you need to get an idea of the competition. Go to Google and enter in your first key phrase in quotes like this:

"baby name"

Looking at the right-hand side of the Google search, you'll see what the competition is (see Figure 8.2).

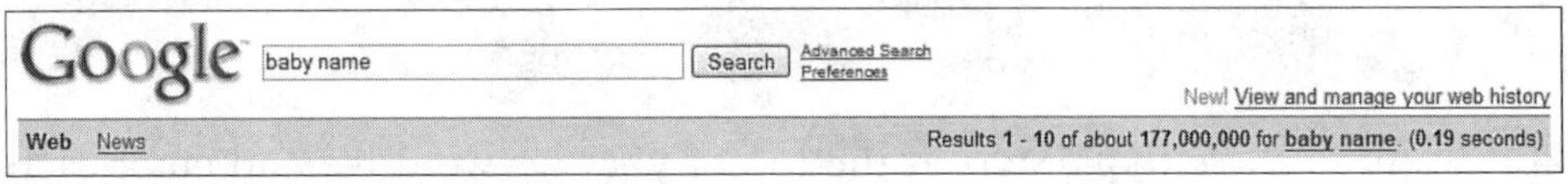

FIGURE 8.2 Number of Google pages returned on a search

Not bad, only 177 million sites to beat! Well, you didn't think this would be easy, did you?

Take the search terms you have narrowed down to find out your competition and add them as a third column. Make sure you remember to search in quotes because the search looks for these words as a phrase rather than just the individual terms at any place.

These keywords are going to form the basis for all your site optimization strategies. Keep your keyword list with you as you read through the rest of these articles.

Now that's somewhat of a labor-intensive process. Tools like Wordtracker automate much of it for you. If you think you really need to have a solid SEO strategy, you should probably invest in a sub for a day or two.

Keywords and Domain Name

Engines use your domain name as a factor in the Search Engine Results Page (SERP). Now, there is a lot of debate here: Some think that branding for the viewers is more important than having a keyword in the URL—it's google.com, not searchengine.com! But if you can combine both, great! (Notice my domain is www.compass**design**s.net. This will get me a little boost if someone searches for "web **design**" but still retains some branding.)

You can't easily change your domain after you have made your site, so this is why it's best to think about SEO before starting on the site design. If you can use a keyword in the domain, go for it, but don't dilute your brand to do so.

Again, this is an area where there is significant disagreement; the current wisdom seems to be that domain name is not so important.

NOTE
We will discuss anchor text—that's the text that appears in the link to your site—when we look at the basic factors that influence SERP. It's astonishingly important. One way that a keyword-based domain can help here is that you can just paste your URL into a page, and the keywords will already be there—a lazy man's way of linking perhaps, but not especially effective.

Designing Your Site for Organic Traffic

Ready for the techie stuff? OK, grab your coffee/beer/herbal chai.

As I mentioned before, designing your site for traffic, both human and search engine spider, is very different than it was a few years ago. It's now about what is on the page that people can see. There's no more having a 200 keyword list that is set to the same color as the background at the bottom of the page.

Web Standards and Accessibility

Now, it might seem as if I am going off-topic here in a chapter about web traffic, but I am going to talk about two things seemingly unrelated to SEO: designing to web standards and accessibility.

Designing a website to *standards* means having a site that will benefit the greatest number of web users while ensuring the long-term viability of the site itself. This means that a site can be viewed in an array of browsers or other Internet devices such as PDAs. The World Wide Web Consortium (W3C) is the international organization that develops web standards, directed by Tim Berners-Lee, the inventor of the World Wide Web.

Specifically, meeting web standards for design essentially means separating content from presentation with Cascading Style Sheets (CSS). One advantage of the CSS-based layout is its flexibility—the content can be accessed regardless of the type of browser that is being used. It allows sites to work on many kinds of devices instead of just the personal computer. Other advantages include

- smaller file sizes and faster page loads
- less bandwidth usage
- faster development and maintenance
- ease of redesign

It is worth noting that the design principles contained within web standards also lead to sites that are more *usable* (along with credibility, usability is a major factor in why viewers return to a site).

> **NOTE**
> Most Content Management Systems (CMSs), Joomla included, have challenges when trying to get their sites to validate for web standards and accessibility. The problem is complicated; content is generated dynamically through PHP (for Joomla), so sometimes either the PHP code or the content itself can cause issues.

Fortunately, this difficulty has been significantly addressed in Joomla 1.5 with the ability added for template designers to completely override the CMS output.

Accessibility, sometimes mistakenly called *usability*, is an attempt for a page to be accessible to all possible viewers. Usually this is chosen to mean such examples as someone who is blind (uses a screen reader) or old (struggles with small fonts/delicate mouse-based navigation). I use these two as examples as they are the ones quoted most often (don't shoot the messenger!).

OK, so why did I bring those up?

Many of the factors involved in SEO, standards, and accessibility overlap. For example, designing a site with CSS makes for leaner, faster pages that will be indexed by search engines more effectively. Another example would be designing a site with accessibility in mind so that it works just as well for someone using a screen reader as it does a search engine spider.

As a piece of roving software, the Google spider is effectively blind and will read your site exactly as someone would with a screen reader.

The implication here is you can get the most effective results by designing a site that meets web standards and is accessible first. Its optimization for search engines will come as a natural consequence. A well designed site will have a large overlap in the middle of these three areas; a poorly designed site might have no overlap at all.

The relationship between SEO, standards-based design, and accessibility is an important one. A tutorial is available on this topic at compassdesigns.net.

Basic Things that Influence SERP

First and most important: You need lots of content—*lots* of it. Before you have even considered site design and such, you should have 100 odd pages of actual content. Yes, there are supposed to be two zeros on the end of that: 100. I mean it. A page of content means about 200 to 500 words.

Of course, no one does this— even I don't! But if you are serious about getting lots of traffic, and you have a lot of rich content to publish, just think how far ahead you will be of poor schmuks like me.

> **The Least You Need to Know**
> You should have some sort of search engine friendly URL (SEF) enabled. It's thought that search engines don't like dynamically generated pages, and that's the whole point of Joomla Joomla has a built-in SEF that replaces long URLs with shorter ones without variables.

According to the "SEO guys,"[2] the following are the most important factors in deciding SERP, along with a number to show relative value. The research conducted tried to assign a weight to a particular factor's influence on SERP, shown here as a percentage. This shows you the actual relative value between, say, having good anchor text links compared to keywords in the H1 tag. These ten factors add up to 21% of the SERP based on these estimates.

(Incoming) Anchor Text of Links—2.3% and Up

The phrasing, terms, order, and length of an incoming link's anchor text is one of the most important factors taken into account by the major search engines for ranking. Specific anchor text links help a site to rank better for that particular term/phrase at the search engines. In other words, it's the actual text that represents the link on a web page. The process of finding links to your site is sometimes called "off-site optimization." It's possibly the most important factor in achieving high SERP.

If you want proof of this, search for "miserable failure" in Google and look carefully at the number one result. Ponder a little on the implications of that (it's called Google Bombing).

Title Tag—2.3%

This is what appears in the blue bar at the top of your browser; it comes from a tag called `<title>`. As well as being used as a pure factor in SERP, it also boosts rank in other ways. Some engines use "click-through" rates as a factor. Sites where the title closely matches the content tend to get better click-throughs (searchers see it's not a spam site). When words in the title are also used as anchor text in a link to the page, you get more benefit.

Joomla easily allows you to manipulate the title of a page. With built-in SEF enabled, your title will reflect the content of the page. If you install a third-party SEF, then you can set the page title to be the title alias of that page.

Keyword Use in Document Text—2.2%

Your keywords must appear in the actual copy of the page. Supposedly, search engines pay more attention to the first and last paragraphs. The idea here is that your page is supposed to actually be about what the search keywords were!

Usually, the way to go about this is to have your keywords firmly in your mind as you write your copy. I don't know about you, but I find this really hard. I prefer a different approach.

There is a simple trick here: Write your quality content and then use a keyword density tool to find the keyword density. *Then* take the top words and use these as the keywords you might use in a link or a metatag. It might seem a little backwards, but it's surprisingly effective at creating pages that will appear in search engines.

There are a number of free tools for checking keyword density. The one I use the most is at www.ranks.nl.

One disadvantage here is linked to the fact that Joomla is dynamic. The code is not very lean; that is, there is a lot of HTML compared to actual copy text. This in turn reduces your keyword density (indirectly). Using CSS instead of tables means leaner code. It's also possible with CSS to have your page "source ordered." This means that the real content (the middle column to you and me) comes before the side columns and/or navigation. This also goes back to the previous discussion about the link between SEO and web standards.

> **NOTE**
> In the header (the code you can't see but a search engine can), there are a few lines that are called tags. One of them is for keywords. It's widely recognized that search engines no longer use these to calculate SERP. It *is* still thought that they can be negative. If you have keywords in your tag that are not on your page, you can get penalized for it. Some engines also pull meta description for ranking text. Personally, I don't bother with them much.
> If you do want to use these, it's easy to add keywords to the keywords tag for that page. You just go to the meta info when you are editing the content and plop them in. Joomla also has a button that will put in the section, category, and article title. Note that the global metatags are added as well, those specified for the site in the global configuration. It's good to only have your most important two to three words there and put the rest in the pages.

A few extensions help you generate keywords, note these are Joomla 1.0 extensions:

- iJoomla Metatag Generator
- metaFly
- MetaTags NX (revision of above)
- OpenSEF (actually a full SEF component)

I am not sure that spending too much time on metatag extensions is efficient. As just mentioned, they are not really used much by search engines, so their contribution is negligible.

Accessibility of Document—2.2%

Here is my definition of accessibility for SEO: Accessibility is anything on the page that impedes a search engine spider's ability to crawl a page. There can be a number of culprits:

- **Avoid Splash Pages**. Flash and heavily graphic introductions prohibit engines from crawling your site.

- **Avoid Frames**. Never use pages with frames. Frames are too complex for the crawlers and too cumbersome to index. Joomla uses something called a wrapper that has the same problems. Avoid it when you can.

- **Avoid JavaScript When Possible**. Though JavaScript menus are very popular, they disable crawlers from accessing those links. Most well-indexed websites incorporate text-based links primarily because they are search engine friendly. If necessary, JavaScript should be referenced externally. JavaScript menus are very popular because they look great. As good as they look to people however, they look equally as bad to spiders. Try using CSS to style your menus; you'll be surprised how good they look. You can even have drop-down submenus. There is a tutorial on this at www.compassdesigns.net.

- **Utilize Your Error Pages**. Too often Webmasters forget about error pages (such as 404 errors). Error pages should always redirect "lost" users to valuable, text-based pages. Placing text links to major site pages is an excellent practice. Visit www.cnet.com/error for an example of a well-utilized error page.

- **Avoid Tables for Layout**. This is part of the interrelationship between accessibility and SEO. An excellent description is at www.hotdesign.com/seybold/everything.html.

Links to Document from Site-Internal Pages—2.1%

Almost as useful as the holy grail of external links is internal links—and certainly a lot easier to implement. Who knew?! This is easily the most underrated criteria, but it's important to make sure you are making good use of anchor text. A well-linked to document is considered more important than an obscure page, even if the links are coming from the site itself. The easiest way to ensure proper internal linking is *with nav bars and sitemaps.*

Primary Subject Matter of Site—2.1%

What your website is about is determined through analysis of the content. It's critical that it correlates to keywords, anchor text, and so on.

One strange off-shoot of this is perhaps it's not worth spending much effort trying to build the page rank of the home page. This strange concept is explained in the idea of Search Engine Theme Pyramids[3].

A related factor is having a good sitemap. Not only is it good spider food, you can also load it with lots of quality anchor text for those internal links as well as relevancy text (that which appears near a link). Also important is the invisible Google sitemap, which is an XML file for the Google spider only. There are also some extensions for a Google sitemap, though I find it's best to upload a Google sitemap independently.

You can set up sites for viewers to add their own content, so it's effortless to add tons of content quickly and easily. Remember, it's a Content Management System after all.

External Links to Linking Pages—2.0%

These are the links from other sites to you. Note that it's much better to have specific pages linked rather than your home page because of the idea of Search Engine Theme Pyramids. Don't bother with link farms or anything you see advertised for a link. You are much better off finding links from sites that have similar topics to yourself.

Want a neat trick to find other sites to link to you? Use PR Prowler, of course.

Take advantage of other Joomla sites that share your topic. Most Joomla sites use the same "Contact Us" page in the CMS. This page has this in the URL:

"option=com_contact"

So go to Google and do a search for your topic along with this text. For example:

"option=com_contact baby names"

Use your keywords because you want links from your topical community.

Link Popularity of Site in Topical Community—2.0%

The search engine is trying to figure out what your page is about so it can decide if it's relevant to a user's search. Links from pages with similar topics add credence to your page. Use the "related:" tag in Google—for example, type "related:www.cnn.com" in, and Google will search for sites related to the topic of www.cnn.com. Then spend some time emailing Webmasters and asking for links. There is software out there that will do this automatically for you; I would advise against using any of them, however. They are pretty easy to spot and usually get a one way trip to the trash bin. PR Prowler was made to be able to create personal emails quickly and easily.

Global Link Popularity of Site—1.9%

This means that links from sites that are "important" (that is, have a high SERP) are more valued than those from a lower SERP. A factor worth considering when searching out links—get the ones from sites with a high PageRank first and not just high page rank, but high "Trust Rank." Google has actually trademarked this term, so most people are pretty confident they are using it in their optimization. Trust Rank is a site's value in terms of how authoritative it is on a subject/keyword.

Keyword Spamming—1.9%

Careful, spamming is a negative factor! This means having a keyword density in text or tags so high that the engine decides you are stuffing. Your rank will go from #1 to #10,000 in a heartbeat. Want to know the best part? No one actually knows what percent density this is, and it's probably different for different engines! Between you and me, I am not going above 5–10% on my pages.

There are many factors that determine search engine page ranking. Rather than tweak minor tags, it's better to leverage Joomla's true power of being a fully fledged CMS to gain rank by efficiently adding lots of quality content. Uh, and don't use flash. (OK, I admit I am biased.)

Advanced SEO Techniques

One of my favorite expressions is "maximum efficiency, minimum effort." It's sometimes known as the 80/20 rule. Do the 20% of things you need to get 80% of the result. What we discussed in the "Basic Things that Influence SERP" section is the 20% effort. If we really want to try and squeeze everything we can from SEO, then there are some more advanced techniques we can try. Remember, we are not being very efficient here. To be honest, your time would be better spent adding content, but let's assume you have hired someone to do that or are very bored!

Boosting Your Site's Keyword Density

Your site's keyword density is one criterion that search engines will judge your site on when deciding where to index you on a per search-term basis. Keyword density refers to the number of times a keyword appears through a particular page on your website. Using your top five keywords from the Overture term suggestion tool, you can boost the keyword density of your website in four ways:

- Keyword placement in the `<title>` tag
- Using `<h1>` and `<h2>` tags to emphasize keywords
- Naming your website and pages with keywords
- Incorporating keywords into body text

Let's now take a look at each of these methods in more detail.

> **NOTE**
> Make sure you have your top five keywords handy.

Keyword Placement in the `<title>` Tag

Overall, you are aiming for a 10% keyword density per page on your website. That means that for every page on your website, you need to incorporate your top five keywords/phrases to achieve a 10% keyword density.

When a web page is chosen by Google as a match to a search term, the title and first few lines of "readable" text are shown from that website in Google's results. Google also weighs these two pieces of text highly when calculating the relevance of a website.

> **NOTE**
> We are talking about the title of the web page here, not to be confused with the title of the article in Joomla. *But*—be aware that Joomla will take the article title and use it in the web page title if you set the Show Meta Title Tag to Yes in global configuration.

You can use your top 5 keywords/phrases to construct your titles. Each page/article on your website needs to have a different, slightly reworded title that uses some of your top five keywords in each one. As you will soon see, each title needs to relate to that page's name and heading tags to create the ideal keyword density.

Let's say that I run a website about those baby names again. Here were my top five keywords/phrases:

- baby name
- baby girl name
- baby boy name
- odd baby name
- top 100 baby name

Let's also say that my site has four pages:

- A home page
- A page about baby names
- A services page
- A "fast facts" page

I need four differently worded page titles. Using my keywords and the "no more than 40 characters in a title" rule, here's what I came up with:

Title #1: <u>Baby names</u>

Title #2: <u>Baby Girl Names</u> and <u>Baby Boy Names</u>

Title #3: <u>Baby Name Services</u>

Title #4: <u>What Are the Top 100 Baby Names?</u>

In each of the titles I've underlined where my top five keywords/phrases are. Notice how every title is different, yet between them they contain a mix and match of every one of my keywords/phrases?

Here are two tips I stress when creating the content of title tags:

- Use every single one of your top five keywords/phrases in various mix-and-match combinations through each of your web pages title tags.
- Keep the length of each title's text under 40 characters.

> **TIP**
> One of the best ways to check the effectiveness of the phrasing of your keywords is to compare them to those of your competitors. Use Google to search for one of your top five keywords/phrases. Look at how the top five ranked search results word their titles. Are you using your keywords in a similar fashion? Maybe you could rearrange a word or two? Analyze these results and make sure your web page titles are the same—if not better—than your competitors'.

`<h1>` and `<h2>` Tags to Emphasize Keywords

Heading tags have been used for years in HTML to improve the formatting of a particular word or sentence on a web page. Heading tags range from `<h1>` (bigger text, signifying more importance) to `<h2>`, `<h3>`, `<h4>`, `<h5>`, and `<h6>` (smaller text, signifying less importance).

Heading tags are generally used to emphasize a page or paragraph heading to search engines for importance. You should stick to only `<h1>` and `<h2>` tags. If you had a normal piece of HTML code that looked like this:

```
<p> <strong>Joomla Rocks!</strong> </p>
```

…then output from this would simply be bolded text:

Joomla Rocks!

However, if you use an `<h1>` tag instead, like this:

```
<h1>Joomla Rocks!</h1>
```

…then the text would now look like this:

Joomla Rocks!

Not only is text between heading tags more visually appealing, but if worded correctly, it will boost your Google ranking significantly, as Google picks up keywords between headings tags as having a higher relevance than any other text around it.

Here is where things start to get tricky.

Unfortunately, some of the most important keywords are output by the Joomla core as somewhat random CSS styles. For example, an article title when it is shown on the page is shown in the code as

```
<td class="contentheading" width="100%">Welcome to Joomla</td>
```

Not only is this not viewed as important to Google, but being placed in a table dilutes the text density. Fortunately there is a solution. In Joomla 1.5, there has been a significant improvement in how the template is rendered. This makes it possible to override the way Joomla outputs the code. So it would be possible for a template designer to create a template that rendered the title as

```
<H1>Welcome to Joomla</H1>
```

> **TIP**
>
> As lucky readers of this wonderful book, you can get a specially developed SEO template to maximize the leverage of some of the techniques described here by going to www.joomlabook.com and registering. You'll then be able to download a special template override file that you can use in your own template.

Now that you have clearly defined page and paragraph heading tags, you need to optimize the actual text between the heading tags because this is the text that Google will pick up and use as part of your site's keyword density.

The trick here is keyword density. Using your top five keywords/phrases, you should create heading tags for each page that relates to the title of that article. For example, if an article title were Baby Names, and Joomla generated the page, the title tag would look like this:

```
<title>Baby Names</title>
```

Then you would want to concentrate on including these words throughout your page enough times to produce a 10% keyword density (that is, for every 10 words on the page, one would be a word in the page title tag).

Taking this into consideration, you might create a page heading that looks like this:

```
<h1>Baby Names and more, find out what are the most popular names for your baby</h1>
```

See how you can use the same keywords but in a different sentence that makes sense (that is, conforms to proper grammar standards)? You could continue this by setting up various headings for your paragraphs with `<h2>` tags:

```
<h2>Girl Baby Names<h2>
<h2>Boy Baby Names</h2>
```

Using Keywords in Your Article Titles

The next thing that you can do to boost your keyword density is to name your articles effectively. How do you do this? Well, you guessed it—by using your top five keywords/phrases in your actual domain name and file names of your web pages.

Keeping with the earlier example, if one of your phrases was "baby names" and you had a page with these heading tags setup:

```
<h1>Baby Names and more, find out what are the most popular names for your baby</h1>
<h2>Girl Baby Names<h2>
<h2>Boy Baby Names</h2>
```

…then you would save this article as "Possible Baby Names."

Incorporating Keywords into Body Text

We've already seen how to use your top five keywords in both the title and headings of your web pages. The last thing that you can do to boost keyword density is to include keywords throughout the actual content of your web page. As was already mentioned, you should aim for a keyword density of 10%—but where do you put your key-words?

Well, it's simple actually. My general rule of thumb is to place keywords in a ratio using this rule:

number of keywords per paragraph = number of paragraphs / number of key-words

For example, if you have two keywords and four paragraphs on one of your web pages, then you would include two keywords per paragraph. Yes, this totals eight keywords (2 keywords×4 paragraphs), but you can rearrange keywords as well.

> **NOTE**
> If you end up with a "number of keywords per paragraph" value of less than one, then just round it up to one.

If you use these correctly, your content should have an average keyword density of 10%. It is OK to have one paragraph with a keyword density of 13% and another with 7%, just as long as they all average out. When used in combination with the keywords in the title tag and headings on your website, you now have a perfect keyword density setup for Google, which will produce excellent rankings for your web pages.

> **NOTE**
> Remember that you should choose two or three of your keywords per page and include them in your title tag, page, and paragraph headings and also the content of your web page. If you run out of keywords, then simply rearrange them to form new phrases.

Referral Traffic

Referral traffic is off-site optimization and is the meat of SEO and is perhaps one of the most important components of SEM. Having a link building campaign that refers to many sites will generate traffic purely through people following the links. But perhaps even more critical is that the number and quality of links to your site is one of the principle factors such engines use to calculate your SERP. So you get two benefits: pure traffic and ranking in the search engines.

Google PageRank

Google particularly emphasizes how many sites link to yours, the *most important* criteria for ranking a website is its link popularity. But what exactly is link popularity and how can you get it? Put simply, link popularity represents the number of sites that link back to your website.

But how is this rank calculated? Quite simply, actually. Google's main criteria for the calculation of relevancy for a page is based on the number of websites that link back to that particular site.

How many sites are currently linking back to your website? If you don't know, it's easy to find out. Just go to google.com and type **link:www.yoursite.com** into the search box (replacing www.yoursite.com with the domain name of your website). Note that Google only displays a small percentage of the true backlink set for any given URL. You can get other estimates by doing the same thing on Yahoo! and MSN. When the search results are returned, look at the text on the right-hand side of the blue bar at the top of the page. It should look something like what's shown in Figure 8.3.

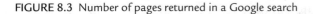

FIGURE 8.3 Number of pages returned in a Google search

Figure 8.3 shows that there are 411,000 websites linking back to this site. If there are only a handful linking back to your website, don't worry—by the end of this section you should be able to increase this number by 5, 10, 20, or even 100 times!

"How many websites should be linking to my site?" I hear you ask. As a general rule of thumb, you want as many sites linking back to your site as those linking back to the site in position #1 for one of your five keywords. Keep in mind that the rate of link growth is very important. Backlinks should be acquired at an even pace and should not be acquired all at once or within a short time frame. This sets off Google filters.

Take one of your five keywords/phrases that we worked out earlier and search for it on Google. Take the www part of the URL for the first search result of this keyword and find the number of websites that link to that website—this should be your goal for the number of websites linking back to yours.

For example, if one of your keywords were "baby names," and the first site that came up when you did a search for this keyword was www.babynames.com, then perform a link popularity check on this site by searching for link: **www.babynames.com** in Google.

When the search results page is displayed, look at the number after "about" in the text on the right-hand side of Figure 8.3. That's the number of sites linking back to this website, and it's also the number that you should be aiming for to link back to your website.

So how do you go about finding sites to link back to *your* website? Spy on your competition using PR Prowler (www.pr-prowler.com). This will tell you exactly who is linking to your competition and how.

As we saw earlier in this chapter, the most valuable links for your site are from other sites that are related by topic to yours. So if you have a site about baby names, a link from a site about baby health would be more valuable than one from a site about computers. So the challenge is not a need to find links, but to find links from sites that have a similar theme or topic to yours.

So to find them, as we just saw in the example, you can use a command link: in the search box to find sites linking to a particular URL. You can also use search engines to find websites that are related to a particular URL. The command to do this is "related:".

So you can go to Google and type in **related:www.babynames.com**, and that will find many sites that are related by topic to www.babynames.com. You can also use the related: command to find sites that are topically related to your competition.

So let's summarize where we are right now:

- You find keywords by finding out how many people are searching for it and how much competition they have using a tool such as yourseobook.com or wordtrackerkeywords.com.

- Succeeding at SEO means you only have to beat your competition. Find out who they are by searching with your keywords in Google.

- Find out how many people are linking to the top results using the link command. That's how many links you need to rank to beat them.

- Use the related command to find sites topically related to yours.

While these four steps are pretty labor-intensive, they are critical to achieving high search engine ranking. There are many software tools out there that can help automate this process. If this were a web document, this might be the place I would have a few affiliate links! Instead, in keeping with the idea of building a website on a low budget, there is a useful tool available for free called Webferret.

Using WebFerret to Find Websites

One tool that many Webmasters (including myself) use is WebFerret, which is a free tool owned by CNet. WebFerret is an excellent tool that you can use to find sites that have similar interests to yours—these are also the perfect websites to ask to link back to your website to build your link popularity!

You can download Webferret at www.ferretsoft.com/download.htm. Once downloaded, click **Start > Programs > WebFerret > WebFerret** to launch it. It should look like what's shown in Figure 8.4.

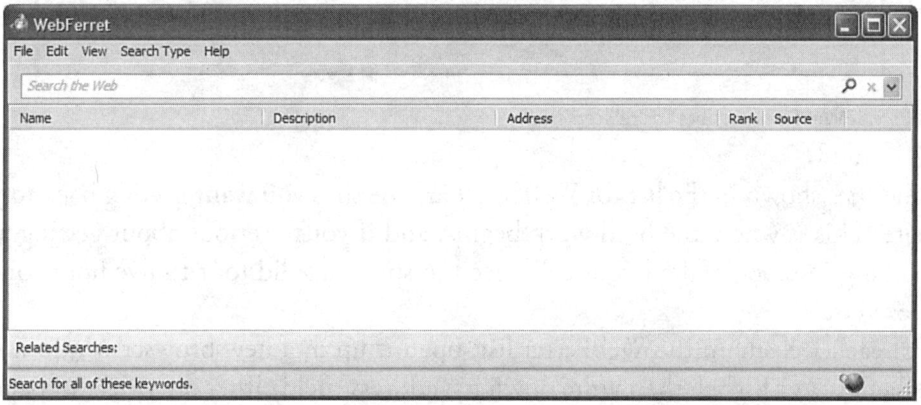

FIGURE 8.4 Using WebFerret to find link partners

Now, do a search in Google and write down the URLs of the top 10 or 20 sites returned. I did a search for baby names, and these were the top five:

1. www.babynames.com
2. www.babynamesworld.com

3. www.ssa.gov/OACT/babynames

4. babynamewizard.com

5. www.babycenter.com

Now you can use WebFerret to find what sites are linking to these. You use the same syntax as Google:

link:www.whateverthesiteis.com

Enter the first site, www.babynames.com, into Webferret (don't forget the link: command) and press enter or click on the Search button. WebFerret will go off and find all sites that link back to the site that you entered. Using www.babynames.com, it should now look something like what is shown in Figure 8.5.

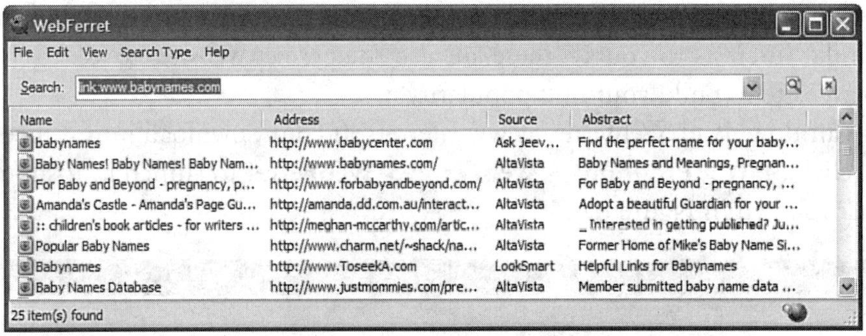

FIGURE 8.5 WebFerret results for related sites

The sites shown in the list for WebFerret are the sites you want linking back to your website. This is where the hard work begins, and if you're serious about getting a top 20 ranking in Google, then you really need to spend a solid four to five hours on this next exercise.

For each website in the WebFerret list, open it up in a new browser window. If its PageRank is 7 or higher, then write down its "address" field either on a piece of paper or in a new word processing document. Repeat this for every site in the WebFerret list.

There could be anywhere from 50 to 5,000 sites in this list, but it's getting these sites to link to your site that will boost both your link popularity and push your PageRank through the roof!

After you've written each address down, start at the top of your list and visit each site. Search the site for both a contact email address *and* a contact name. Write these down next to the websites' addresses on your list.

If you can't find a contact email for some of the sites, then simply put the contact email down as webmaster@sitename.com (replacing sitename.com with the domain name of the website, minus the "www" part). If you can't find a contact name, then just write down "Webmaster."

You'll now have a list of websites, contact email addresses, and first names that looks something like this:

> www.site1.com john@site1.com John
>
> www.site4.com info@site4.com Mary
>
> www.site6.com fsmith@site6.com Fred
>
> ...and so on

You now need to email all the contacts on your list and ask them if they would kindly link back to your website.

Fire up your favorite email program and start at the top of your list and send it to each contact email on your list. You must be creative in your reciprocal link requests and definitely do not put "link swap" anywhere in the email subject. The best way is if you can give them something in exchange for a link.

> **NOTE**
> Google evaluates links back to your site on the actual description that the link contains, so try and include your site's name as well as two to three of your top five keywords in the link description, such as "baby-names.com—Get a great baby name for your boy or girl."

When they reply telling you that they've placed a link from their sites to your site, go to their websites and double-check that the links exist and are working. Send them back a reply email along these lines:

Hi <Contact Name>,

Thank you very much for linking to my site! I've placed a link from my site to yours, and you can see it at <Your Site URL>.

Thanks again!

Regards,

<Your Name>

<Your Site URL>

As you have probably guessed, you will now need to create a page on your site with links to all the sites that are linking back to you. Call this page Partners or something similar and make sure you include its URL as the <Your Site URL> in the sample email.

Last, you want to make sure that Google knows about each site that is linking back to you. You can use the Google submission tool, but it's not terribly effective. Simply getting a link from an indexed site is all that is needed to get yours indexed.

This is a tedious process but absolutely essential to find useful sites to link back to you. It's possible to buy software, that does all of this automatically for you. I use something called PR Prowler. It's simple and pretty effective; if you are serious about trying to rank for competitive keywords, then you might want to look into something like this. It searches for sites related to your keywords and then figures out what boost they will give you based on their PageRank, how many sites link to them, and how few links they have outgoing (the fewer the better). It then sorts all these choices and ranks them by which sites will give the most benefit and outputs it as an HTML file. It not only hunts for potential link partners and assesses their value as link partners, but it hunts down pretty much anything for you, whether it is competitor information or joint venture partners, and gives you several methods to contact them. It is the first SEO tool to show the age of any site, to help find trusted sites. It finds niche markets with little competition.

You can find out more at www.pr-prowler.com.

Other Link-Building Strategies

As well as holistically finding links using the techniques described previously, you can also find links to your site in other ways. Traditionally, this involves submitting your site to all sorts of directories. I do not advocate this anymore as the effect of these directories is diluted, and now they probably take more time to do than the benefit you receive. Definitely make sure you do not pay anyone to "submit your sites to directories;" it's not useful in regard to the amount of money you might spend.

However, having said that, there is one circumstance where submitting to directories can be useful. If you know of industry-specific and topic-specific directories related to your website, a submission can be useful. This is because links from a topic-related site are worth more than just a general one. We discussed the idea in the previous section.

There are a few easy places where you can submit a Joomla site for free.

- The official site, www.joomla.org, maintains a site listing. You can submit your Joomla-powered site at www.joomla.org/component/option,com_submissions/Itemid,75/.
- Also at the official site in the forms there is a board called Site Showcase. You can post your site there, and members of the Joomla community will also give you some free feedback. It's always honest and usually positive! The board is at forum.joomla.org/index.php?board=58.0.
- If you are using a commercial template such as one from Joomlashack, we have our own Site Showcase (www.joomlashack.com/community/index.php/board,9.0.html). Most commercial template vendors have similar places to submit your website.

One last place to put links to your website is in your signature on a forum. For this to be effective, you need to do a couple things:

- Find a forum that is related to your website based on its industry or topic.
- Become an active contributing member of that forum.
- Place a link to your website in your signature, making sure you follow forum rules.

The nice thing about this strategy is that the more you contribute, the more members of the community will see your link. It's a situation where everybody wins.

Internal Linking

As previously mentioned, internal links are often forgotten when people are developing a link building campaign. The truth is that properly constructed internal links on your sight are almost as useful as external links to your site. One tremendous advantage is that you have total control over these internal links. Two efficient ways to leverage Joomla to automatically produce useful internal links are by using the Read More link and by creating sitemaps.

Joomla Linked Titles and Read More

The great thing about Joomla is that a CMS is designed to add lots of content very quickly and to create dynamic pages. So, for example, on your homepage you might designate certain articles to be shown. Joomla will show these in a blog format, with the option of having a linked title that goes deeper into the site to the actual article.

You can control whether titles are linked or not in the Preferences of the Article Manager (to set it globally for the whole site) or by going to the menu item that links to that page for a particular page. The same is also true for the Read More link that is commonly shown on Joomla sites to indicate that a longer article is available.

Linked titles are off by default, and the Read More link is on. Change linked titles to Yes and click Save. If you preview the frontend of the site now, you see that the titles are now links, and there is a Read More link to read the full article. This is shown in Figure 8.6.

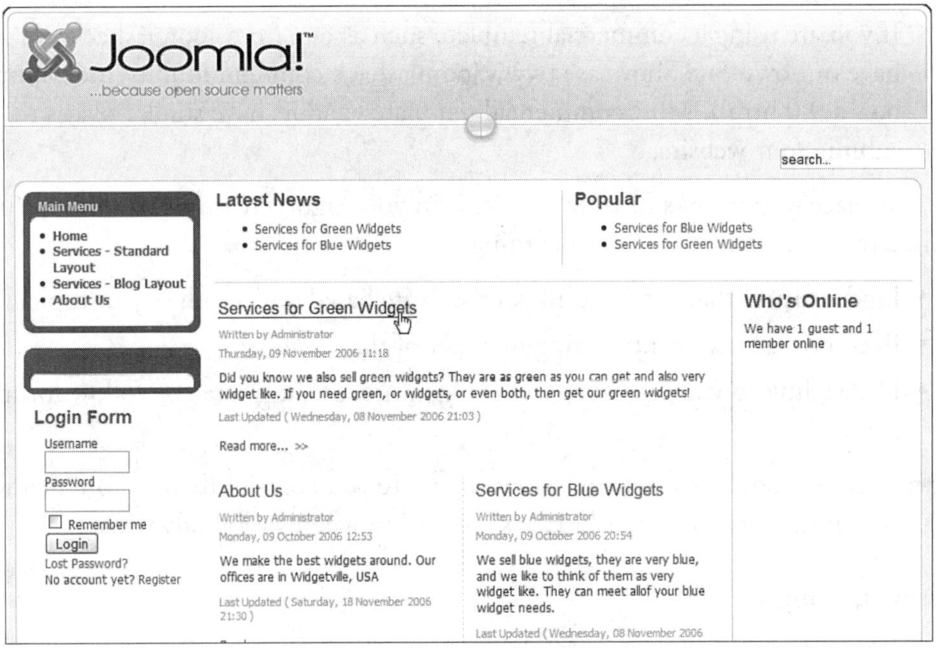

FIGURE 8.6 Frontend view of linked titles and Read More links

Notice a couple of important things here. One is that the linked title is quite beneficial for organic SEO. I carefully chose my article title, "services for green widgets," to contain some useful keywords: services, green, and widgets. This means that I have a great internal link to that article. The Read More link is not nearly so useful. Based on what is in the anchor text here (the part that is the blue link), I am optimizing for the keywords "read" and "more."

If you want to see how common this kind of linking strategy is, go to Google or Yahoo! and do a search for "click here." Astonishingly enough, there are about

1.5 *billion* websites that are trying to optimize their organic traffic for these keywords. Remember, it's the words in the link, called the anchor text, that search engines use to decide what the page being linked to is about. It's absolutely critical that your anchor text represents that page.

If you want further proof of this, do a Google search for "miserable failure." Take a look at the number one search result and you will see the powerful effect of anchor text in search engine optimization. As much as I would like to make a political commentary here, the words miserable and failure are not anywhere in that site!

So how to solve the problem of Read More? Fortunately there is an easy solution. There is a small plug-in from Run Digital that will replace "Read More" with "Read More about Whatever this Title Is." I actually use this on my site www.compassdesigns. net. You can see it working in Figure 8.7.

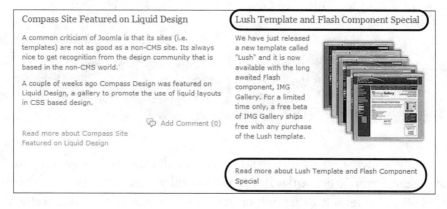

FIGURE 8.7 Expanded Read More links

This is the introduction text shown on my homepage from two of my blog articles. Notice that the title is a link, and also the Read More has been expanded to include the title, which is a link as well. Not only does this make certain that search engine spiders will quickly index those articles, it also provides two immediate internal links for that article.

NOTE
While we're talking about my blog, it's packed full of great news and tips about Joomla. If you haven't already, you should definitely head over and check it out. The direct link is www.compassdesigns.net/joomla-blog.

Last, let's look at one place that should contain useful title links to all the articles on your site—your sitemap.

Sitemaps

A sitemap serves as an internal link to every article on your site. A sitemap also provides a very useful technique to make sure that search engine spiders index your entire website.

The spider is a piece of automatic software associated with a search engine. It goes around the Web to different websites in a process called *indexing*. When it gets to a home page, it analyzes all the words and keywords on it and then follows every single link from that page. It's critical that a spider can easily get to all the articles on a site so that they can be indexed. One easy way to do this is to have a link somewhere on the homepage to something called "sitemap."

> **NOTE**
> This concept of being indexed is one of the reasons why you don't want to use JavaScript for your menus. A search engine spider cannot follow links if they are JavaScript links (or Flash). If your navigation uses JavaScript or flash your site is going to be at a disadvantage for SEO.

Put simply, a sitemap is a web page that links to all other web pages on your site. If you have created your article titles in Joomla carefully, then this step will be very easy. There are several extensions that will create a sitemap for you automatically. On the sitemap page will be a list of all the articles on your site as links using the article titles. In a static website you'd have to create this page manually; in Joomla it's done for you on the fly, and even better as you add articles, they are automatically added to the map. It simply doesn't get any easier than this.

Let's take a quick look at the available extensions for sitemaps:

- **Joomap**. developer.joomla.org/sf/projects/joomap
- **SEF Service Map**. fun.kubera.org/
- **samSiteMap**. developer.joomla.org/sf/projects/samsitemap

You can find out more about these extensions (including their reviews) at extensions. joomla.org/component/option,com_mtree/task,listcats/cat_id,1806/Itemid,35/.

Finally, you need to submit the URL of your sitemap to Google. Go to www.google.com/addurl/?continue=/addurl and submit the link to your sitemap. You will need to copy and paste the link generated by the sitemap component that you chose and use that in your submission.

Google Sitemap

Recently Google started offering a number of Webmaster tools. The first offering was something called Google Sitemaps. The basic idea was that you actually submitted a sitemap to Google and then kept a copy of it in your root directory. As you added pages (or in Joomla's case, articles) you would add them to your sitemap file, and then the Google spider could read that file and know that you had added pages. The concept was that by using the sitemap, pages would get added to the Google index more quickly than if Google was just following links.

You can register for the Google sitemaps and other tools such as diagnostic and statistics by going to www.google.com/webmasters/tools. You will need to create an account and then also place some code on your site to verify that it is yours. Implementing the Google sitemap is quite tricky and is definitely an example of the 80/20 rule. At this point, you are spending 80% of your effort to get the last 20% out of what you are doing. Make sure that you have a sitemap using one of the tools described previously, but don't feel that you need to go ahead and mess with the Google sitemap.

Pay-Per-Click Traffic

If you have a website (Joomla or otherwise), and you have a vague interest in getting traffic, then Pay-Per-Click (PPC) needs to be part of your SEM strategy.

Why is PPC so useful?

If you put an ad in a magazine about your product, you pay the magazine the add fee, and it goes in. At that point you are hoping that the ad is compelling enough to get people to call/email/visit your site. If you get no leads from the ad, then you still had to pay the magazine the fee.

Adwords is an example of a PPC. This means you only have to pay for an ad if somebody clicks it. The equivalent would be that you only have to pay the magazine if you get a sales lead from your advertisement. No magazine in the world is ever going to give you an offer like that—they would go out of business in a heartbeat! On the Web using sophisticated tracking software with this kind of arrangement is possible.

The two leading providers are Google and Yahoo!. Adwords is actually one of the main ways Google makes its money; it had to get the $1.3 billion it paid for YouTube somewhere!

PPC has even more going for it than the manner in which you pay for the ad. It's actually drawing on three ideas:

- You are advertising to people who are looking for your product or service right now.
- You only pay when someone clicks your ad.
- Pricing is based in real time; you bid live against other advertisers.

How Google Adwords Works

When you do a search in Google, the results are based on organic search(the results based on Google's complicated algorithm), and advertising or Adwords, what Google calls *sponsored links*. Let's do a search in Google (see Figure 8.8).

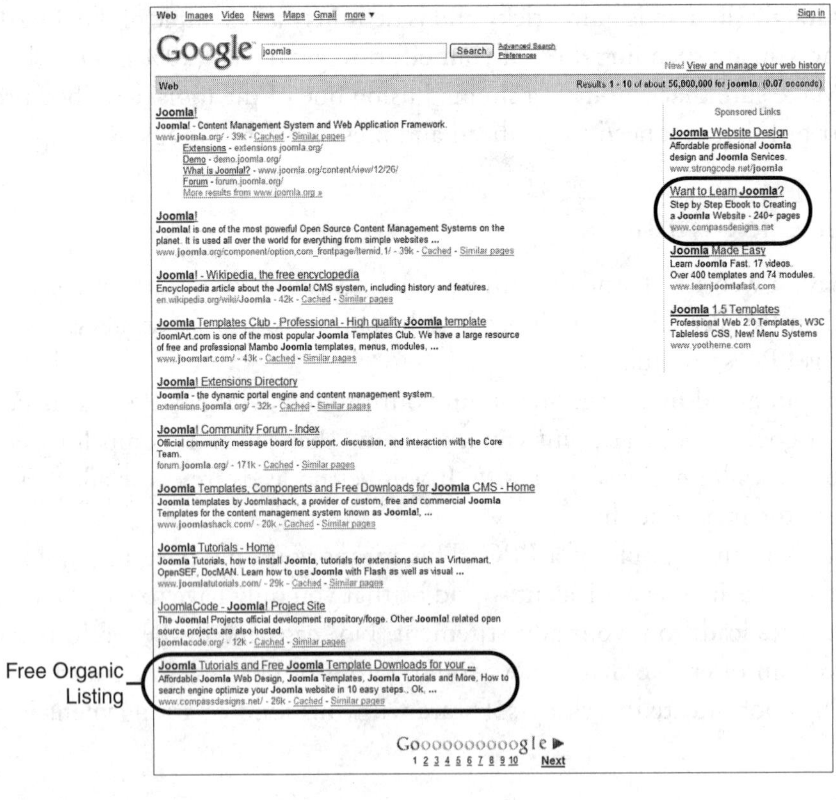

FIGURE 8.8 Paid search results in Google

Here I have done a search in Google for everybody's favorite CMS, Joomla. On the left-hand side are the organic search results. You can see in position number eight a great website for commercial Joomla templates. On the right-hand side you can see smaller listings that are Google's PPC Adwords. Circled in position number eight is an ad I have created for a manual for Joomla.

Here is an important bit: Sometimes people think that organic search on the left is free, and the sponsored link grouping on the right is paid advertising. From your perspective as someone who is trying to market your website, this is not true. You have to pay for *both* listings.

How so? Well, to get listed on the left-hand side, you do not have to pay for the listing itself, but you have to spend time and effort on your site's search engine optimization. To get listed on the right-hand side, it takes much less time and effort, but you have to pay for the listing. Either way, it's a combination of time, effort, and money from your perspective.

Here is another important bit: At the end of the day, one method for your site might end up being more cost effective than the other. However, the reality is you need to do both. In the same way as your retirement plan needs to have a diversified portfolio, so does your SEM strategy.

At this point, I hope I have given a basic introduction to Pay-Per-Click and some suggestions to convince you why you should be adding it to your marketing strategies. There is not much value to me continuing and explaining how to develop a Google Adwords campaign. The reason is because it's already been done. It's generally accepted that there is one leading guide to Adwords, written by Perry Marshall. You can find out more about it at www.perry-marshall.info. I absolutely recommend it and have a copy myself. I have managed to reduce how much I am paying for my Adwords campaigns by half by using his techniques. As you can see in Figure 8.8, I have an ad at position number two for a very competitive search term, and let's just say I'm not paying too much for it!

One strategy I would like to share from the book is Perry's idea of using Google Adwords to test things.

Say you are starting a new product and you're struggling between a couple of slogan ideas. All you have to do is whip up a landing page of some sort to sign-up form and then create a Google Adwords campaign that uses the two slogans in the ads. Then all you need to do is insert the free conversion tracking code from Google, and you can find hard statistics about which slogan converts your customers better. For $5 to $10, you have implemented sophisticated split testing, something normally only within the reach of big companies and expensive marketing budgets.

Joomla and Adwords

So far we have been discussing the usefulness of PPC advertising, which you can apply to any website. Where does Joomla come in?

Google Adwords is a powerful way to drive controlled traffic to your website. Getting it there is only half the story too; you need to know what it does when it gets there so you can have a better picture of whether your advertising money is being well spent. You do this through *conversion tracking*.

After you set up conversion tracking, you are able to see your conversion rate as well as your cost per conversion. Figure 8.9 is a great example of why this is critical. This product only costs $19.99, but I am paying over $21 for every sale—I am losing money! Armed with this information I need to dig out Perry's book and find out how to either lower my bid price or increase my conversion rate. Without this information I would be burning money.

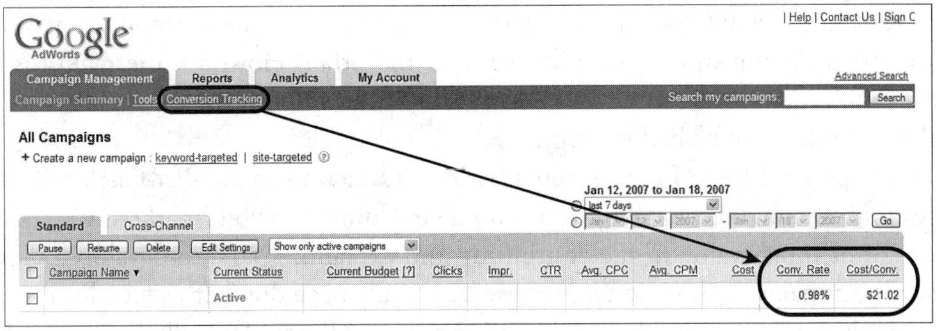

FIGURE 8.9 Google Adwords conversion tracking

Adding the conversion code is relatively simple on a Joomla website. When you click conversion tracking, Google gives you some JavaScript code that you need to insert onto your website. The code will look something like this:

```
<!-- Google Code for purchase Conversion Page -->
<script language="JavaScript" type="text/javascript">
<!--
var google_conversion_id = YOURIDEHERE;
var google_conversion_language = "en_US";
var google_conversion_format = "1";
var google_conversion_color = "FFFFFF";
if (1) {
  var google_conversion_value = 1;
```

```
}
var google_conversion_label = "purchase";
//-->
</script>
<script language="JavaScript"
src="http://www.googleadservices.com/pagead/conversion.js">
</script>
<noscript>
<img height=1 width=1 border=0 src="http://www.googleadservices.com/pagead/conver-
sion/YOURIDEHERE/?value=1&label=purchase&script=0">
</noscript>
```

To figure out what page you need to put it on, you have to decide which page represents a successful conversion. For an e-commerce store it might be the Thank You page. If you are trying to get people to sign up to join an email list, it will be a different page. Whatever your scenario, you have to add the Google conversion code to that page.

One important thing to remember is that you will need to add to the code as HTML. Depending on which editor you are using, in Joomla somewhere there will be a button to edit the raw HTML code, as opposed to working in WYSIWYG mode. Figure 8.10 shows the HTML button and dialog box for the default editor for Joomla 1.5.

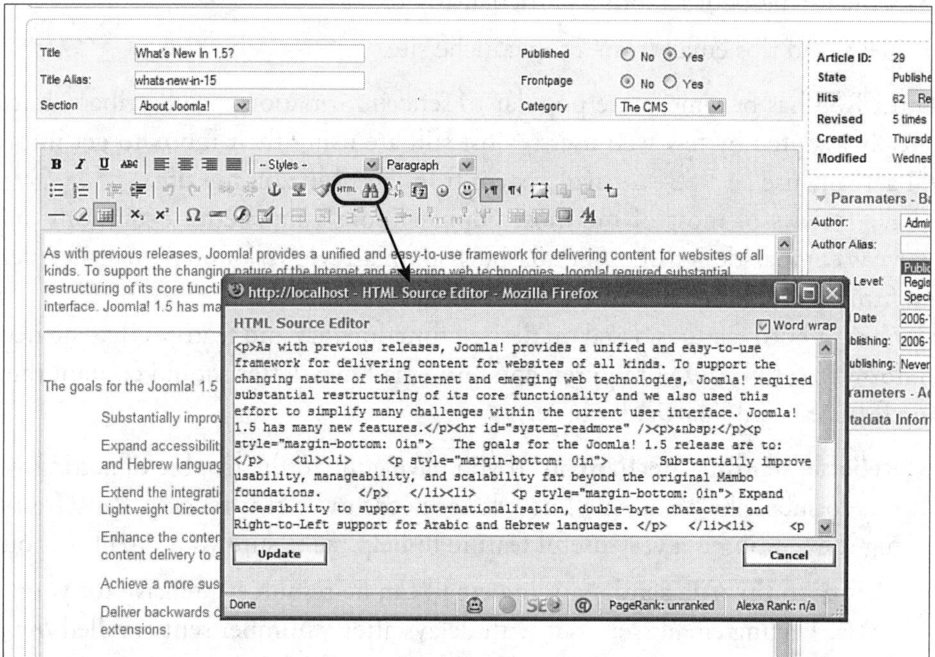

FIGURE 8.10 Editing the HTML source

Much of the work involved in developing a Google Adwords strategy is quite generic to any website. But if you have a Joomla website, it's a website nonetheless. Arm yourself with Perry's book (www.perry-marshall.info) and make sure you are tracking the conversions.

If you are interested in finding out more about how to optimize your Joomla site for organic searches, come over to Joomlashack and check out our forum for Joomla SEO. You can find it at www.joomlashack.com/component/option,com_smf/Itemid,183/board,59.0.

Email Traffic

A modern website should have many tools that allow two-way communication with site visitors. A key part of this communication is the use of email newsletters. Many people associate email marketing just with spam, but email can fill many needs, for example

- Follow-up emails from e-commerce purchases.
- Communicating with family members on a family website.
- Sequential e-books about a particular topic.
- News and tips email from a topic niche site.

Recently, RSS has become more popular to send information to subscribers, but it is only really adopted by few web users. Most still are using their inbox to get information. I actually use an RSS-to-email system from Feedblitz on my site.

I have reviews of most of the most popular Joomla newsletter extensions on my site at www.compassdesigns.net/joomla-blog/joomla-reviews/joomla-email-newsletter-review.html.

I looked at both features based on desired functionality and features that are needed to conform to CAN-SPAM requirements. An email newsletter should contain the following features (in no particular order):

- **Reliable sending mechanism.** If you have gone to the trouble of getting visitors to subscribe, your email newsletter needs to be sent reliably. Pause/resuming the sending is a very useful feature to help make sure your emails get out.
- **Ability to throttle send.** Sending email can be resource-intensive for your server. Having emails sent out with delays after x number sent is called *throttling*. It also can overcome forced web host email sending caps.

- **Unsubscribe mechanism.** For your email to be legal, it must meet the CAN-SPAM Act requirement of having an easy unsubscribe mechanism.

- **Subscribe form.** You need to be able to offer site visitors to subscribe to your email list.

- **Double opt in.** Recognized as an industry best practice, it is advised to ask subscribers to confirm their email subscription by some manner, perhaps clicking a link sent to the given email address.

- **Multiple lists.** Very useful if you have different lists for different topics/ purposes.

- **Bounce handling.** Emails might bounce for many reasons. It's important for these to be automatically removed from your list because repeat bounces from a particular server can get you flagged as a spammer (blacklisted) by ISPs.

- **HTML templating.** Current research indicates that HTML emails have a greater response rate than pure text. They also allow easy tracking of "opens."

- **Import/Export subscribers.** As your needs change, you might need to change your email newsletter system. You'll need to be able to easily import and export your subscriber list. You will also want to have some sort of duplicate handling.

- **Integration into Joomla user database.** Many sites will have registration set up on their Joomla sites for many reasons—e-commerce, private pages, paid subscription, and so on. You will often want to send emails to your user database.

- **Email Statistics.** It's very important to be able to track statistics about your newsletters, such as open and click rates.

This is by no means an exhaustive list, but is what I would consider a minimum list to both meet federal legal requirements for email marketing and for an email marketing solution that compliments Joomla.

One important consideration that you need to immediately take into account is how your website is hosted. Most Joomla Webmasters have their sites on relatively affordable hosting plans that are called "Virtual Hosting" or "Shared Hosting," which cost about $10–20 per month. With this method, your site shares a server with several other sites. Most hosting companies have an email sending cap in place. For example, Bluehost, a very popular host only allows you to send out 200 emails per hour. Obviously, if you have a large list, this is inadequate. You either need a dedicated server, with prices from $200 per month, or a hosted email solution.

To a certain extent, this does immediately question the usefulness of Joomla email newsletters. If you have big lists, or hope that you will, you will need a dedicated server to make use of them.

Joomla Email Newsletter Extensions

There are four main email marketing newsletters available for Joomla as integrated components for the 1.0 version of Joomla:

- Massmail
- Letterman
- YaNC
- Acajoom

> **NOTE**
> Massmail is built into the core of Joomla. It is only included here for the sake of completeness as it is not really an email newsletter component. It is most suited for shooting out a quick email to all your administrators, for example.

There is not too much to separate the Joomla email newsletters at this time. All of them contain more or less the same core features.

If you need something simple for a small (<1000) mailing list, then these might work for you. As mentioned previously, you can find the full reviews at compassdesigns.net.

Third-Party Hosted Email Solutions

If you are serious about trying to monetize your site, email marketing is a key factor. Assuming your plan for this is successful, you hopefully will grow your list. When this happens, integrated email newsletter extensions are not totally adequate.

- Unless you are running on an expensive dedicated server that sends out thousands of emails in one go, it will strain your performance. You can throttle the email sending, but with the email lists in the thousands, it can take up to a day to send out a single newsletter.
- It's possible to get caught by the CAN-SPAM Act by accidentally mixing your subscription and Joomla user databases. If you email somebody that has unsubscribed from your list, you can get penalized.

- Following on from the hosted email solutions we just looked at, work hard to ensure deliverability. This includes such things as white listing their IPs and providing automatic CAN-SPAM compliance.
- Last, third-party email providers usually have very good stats analysis, especially if you are dealing with a large volume of emails.

As with the Joomla newsletter extensions, I have much more detailed reviews of hosted email solutions on my website: www.compassdesigns.net/joomla-blog/joomla-reviews/what-you-need-to-know-about-email-marketing-solutions.html.

There are many hosted email marketing solutions available. I started with a list of about 20 and then reduced them down to my top three:

- Constant Contact
- Get Response
- iContact

If you want the full review, you'll have to head to my site (www.compassdesigns.net/joomla-blog), but here are the summaries of each one along with current pricing. I based the pricing on a list of 5000 subscribers and sending out five emails per month. Comments about support and how many posts are in the vendor's support forum are based on time of writing (November 2006).

Constant Contact

Constant Contact has an easy-to-use interface. Most functions lead you step by step through the tasks in a wizard-like fashion. Clearly, it's targeted at users without advanced computer skills.

Constant Contact is very good at making it simple to build and send an email list. The interface is clear and simple, and the wizards target ease of use. It does have some critical missing features however, including RSS integration, autoresponders, throttling, and any sort of API. Great for small lists, but if you have small lists, you might as well go with a Joomla email newsletter.

Support

Support seems very strong with a wide selection of options, including email, phone, chat, and forums. The forums had 543 posts in 102 topics in 10 forums. I was able to chat with a gentleman called "Edward," and he quickly answered my questions—in very good English.

Integration Into Joomla

Trying to integrate Constant Contact into Joomla might be very difficult. There is no API or database integration and no setting where you can email to a specific email (for example, subscribeme@yoursite.com) and get added.

Pricing

Constant Contact costs about $50 per month.

Get Response

Get Response has a medium level of features, though there are still some critical ones missing. The interface seems to have had a little Ajax thrown in but still seems clunky. An annoyance is the presence of advertising and upselling on the interface.

Get Response seems like a decent enough system, but scratch the surface, and it has some major flaws. Forced confirmation, no export, and upselling in the interface make me believe this solution is more interested in making money than in providing a good product. Having said that, it does feature autoresponders and RSS notification to your subscribers.

Support

Support seemed comparable to Constant Contact. It's available via email, phone, and live chat. I wasn't able to raise anyone on the chat. The forum seemed to be a new one with 4,478 posts in an old forum.

Integration Into Joomla

As with Constant Contact, there is no real integration with Joomla or API available.

Pricing

Get Response costs $17.95 a month.

iContact

Out of all the email systems I reviewed, iContact is the best one out there. It has a very Web 2.0 feel to it and uses Ajax and has some useful features to offer. It now also has an API to integrate into other systems. The interface has recently been revised. The slide-out contextual help was well implemented. It's simple to use, but one complaint I had was its narrow resolution width (Does *anyone* use 800px anymore?).

iContact is a great email marketing solution. It has most of the core features, like autoresponders and flexible importing, that you need. All this is wrapped up in a slick and robust interface. It's one of the more expensive options we have reviewed, but the price is well worth it.

Support

Support seemed comparable to that of other solutions. It's available via email, phone, and live chat. The chat and phone are available 9:00 a.m.–8:00 p.m. EST Monday through Friday. The forum had 235 posts in 102 topics and 758 registered members.

Integration Into Joomla

In October 2006, iContact released its API. Creating integrations into various registration systems is relatively easy. It took me about three hours to create an integration between iContact and our shopping cart, Iono.

Pricing

iContact costs $47 per month.

J!Contact: An Integration of iContact and Joomla

JoomlaShack has partnered with iContact to develop J!Contact, a simple way to integrate the registration process of Joomla into iContact. We have released it free at www.joomlashack.com. It integrates user registration of Joomla and subscribing to email lists at iContact. We are big fans of iContact and actually use it ourselves for our email needs. So we decided to build a complete integration using iContact's powerful API. You can grab it as a free download from my site.

Joomla SEF Extensions

Search engine friendly URLs (SEF) are an option for Joomla that modifies the default URL produced by the CMS. Most of them also have additional functionality such as providing sitemaps, redirecting URLs, and manipulating web page titles.

You'll see much of the discussion about how SEO revolves around various SEF components. These components allow for advanced manipulation of URLs and metatags. Neither of these was identified as a major factor in any studies I have seen. Turn on the default Joomla SEF, but I am not sure there is much evidence that it's very influential after that.

NOTE
Last year sometime on my old blog (2005), I coined the phrase "Human Readable URLs" or "HUF" to describe what people commonly refer to as Joomla SEF. I did this to point out that easily readable and memorable URLs like www.compassdesigns.net/joomla-blog are much more important for humans than they are search engines. Joomla SEF fixes a major usability issue, not an SEO one.

I stand relatively alone in this opinion—many people don't agree. But for further reading, check out www.compassdesigns.net/joomla-blog/joomla-seo/top-10-joomla-seo-tips-for-google.html and www.alledia.com/blog/joomla-urls/in-defense-of-search-engine-friendly-urls/.

Quickstart SEO for Joomla

Looking for a quick punch list of ways you can improve the SEO your site? Check out Appendix C, "A Quick Start to SEO."

Summary

In this chapter, we have gone far beyond search engine optimization (SEO) into the broader field of search engine marketing (SEM). We saw that if you want your website to be successful, it is absolutely critical that you have a balanced marketing plan that addresses four different strategies to get site traffic. Just focusing on one will put you at a disadvantage to competitors that have a more balanced approach.

- **Organic**. What was traditionally known as SEO, organic marketing is the idea of having your website visible in various search engines when people search for keywords.

- **Referral**. Quite simply, this is the idea of having links from other sites to yours. A robust SEM plan will have a comprehensive link building strategy. These can be natural through attracting links to your high-quality content or can be paid links or other techniques.

- **Pay-Per-Click** (PPC). This strategy involves bidding for placement on search results. Submitting an ad to a search engine such as Google will also mean that it appears on its distributed ad network, for example, in Google's case AdSense. Your ads will appear both in search results and on content sites.

- **Email**. Building an email subscription list is a key part of a modern SEM plan. It's important to know who your website viewers are and, if appropriate, to capture emails so you can present them with information that might draw them back to your site.

---

1 You can find out more at www.vaughns-1-pagers.com/internet/google-ranking-factors.htm.

[2] Percentages are based on a study done at www.seomoz.org.

[3] http://www.searchengineworld.com/engine/theme_pyramids.htm

Chapter 9

Creating a Pure
CSS Template

In this chapter, we'll go through the steps of creating a Joomla template. Specifically, we will create a template that uses Cascading Style Sheets (CSS) to produce
a layout without use of tables. This is a desirable goal because it means that the
template code is easier to validate to World Wide Web Consortium (W3C) standards. It also tends to load faster, be easier to maintain, and perform better in search
engines. These issues are discussed in detail later in the chapter.

In This Chapter

- What is a Joomla template? What functions are performed by a Joomla template, and
  what is the difference when a template has no content versus when content is added into
  the Content Management System (CMS).

- How does the localhost design process differ to that of a static (X)HTML web page?

- What are the implications of tableless designs in Joomla and the relationship between
  W3C standards, usability, and accessibility?

- What files make up a Joomla template, and what functions do they perform?

- How do you create a source-ordered 3-column layout using CSS rather than tables?

- What are the basic CSS styles that should be used with Joomla, and what are the default styles that are used by the Joomla core?

- How do you place and style modules, and what are some new techniques for rounded corners?

- What would be a simple strategy to produce lean CSS menus that mimic the effect of those developed with JavaScript?

- How do you control when columns are shown and hide them when no content is present?

- What are the proper steps to create a real Joomla 1.5 template?

What Is a Joomla Template?

A Joomla template is a series of files within the Joomla CMS that control the presentation of the content. The Joomla template is not a website; it's also not considered a complete website design. The template is the basic foundation design for viewing your Joomla website. To produce the effect of a "complete" website, the template works hand in hand with the content stored in the Joomla databases. An example of this can be seen in Figure 9.1.

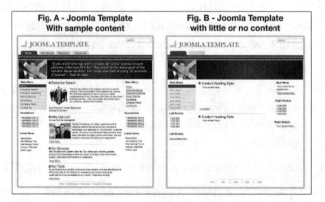

FIGURE 9.1 Template with and without content

Figure 9.1, part A, shows the template in use with sample content. Part B shows the template as it might look with a raw Joomla installation with little or no content. The template is styled so that when your content is inserted, it will inherit the stylesheet defined in the template such as link styles, menus, navigation, text size, and colors to name a few.

Notice that the images associated with the content (the photos of the people) are not part of the template but the header is.

Using a template for a CMS, as Joomla does, has a number of advantages and disadvantages:

- There is a complete separation of content and presentation, especially when CSS is used for layout (as opposed to having tables in the index.php file). This is one of the main criteria for a site that meets modern web standards.

- A new template, and hence a completely new look to a website, can be applied instantly. This can even have different locations/positioning of content as well as colors and graphics.

- If different layouts are called for within one website, it can be difficult to achieve.

Although different templates can be applied to different pages, this built-in functionality is not reliable. Much better is to use conditional PHP and create a layout that dynamically adjusts the number of columns based on what content is published.

> **The Least You Need to Know**
> Modern websites separate content from presentation using a technology known as Cascading Style Sheets (CSS). In Joomla, the template controls the presentation of the content.

Localhost Design Process

The web page you see at a Joomla-powered website is not static. That means it is generated dynamically from content stored in the database. The page that you see is created through various PHP commands that are in the template, which presents some difficulties in the design phase.

It's common now to use a What You See Is What You Get (WYSIWYG) HTML editor, such as Dreamweaver. This means that the designer does not even need to code the HTML. However, this is not possible in the Joomla template design process because WYSIWYG editors cannot display a dynamic page. This means that the designer must code "by hand" and view the output page from the PHP on a served page. With a fast enough connection this could be a web server, but most designers use a "local server" on their own computer. This is a piece of software that will serve the web pages on the designer's computer.

There is no "right way" to create a web page; it depends on the designer's background. Those more graphics-inclined make an "image" of a page in a graphics program like Photoshop and then break up the images to be able to use them for the Web (known as slice and dice). More technology-based designers will often just jump straight into the CSS and start coding. However, as just mentioned, the Joomla template designer is limited in that he cannot instantly see the effect of his coding in the same editor. The modified design process is as follows:

1. Make edits with HTML editor, save changes.

2. Have localhost server running in background to "run" Joomla.

3. View edits in a web browser.

4. Return to step 1.

> **The Least You Need to Know**
> When creating a template, you have to have Joomla "running" on a server so you can make changes and refresh the page output.

Localhost Server Options

In Chapter 2, "Downloading and Installing Joomla," we saw how to install a web server that will run on your computer. We described one for a webserver called WAMP5. To move further along in this chapter, you will need to have this installed. If you haven't yet, go ahead and install it. I'll wait right here.

> **TIP**
> One useful technique to make the design process more efficient is to serve a web page that you are designing and then copy and paste the source into an editor. For example, once your layout CSS is set up, you can use one of these localhost servers to serve a page, then view the source of the page. You then copy and paste the source code into your editor. You can now easily style the page using CSS and not have to go through the cycle of steps described earlier.

> **NOTE**
> **A Free XHTML Editor**
> For those not able to pay for a commercial editor, such as Dreamweaver, some free editors are available. Nvu is a solid choice and has built-in validation—and it is 100% open source. This means anyone is welcome to download Nvu at no charge (nvu.com/down-load.html), including the source code if you need to make special changes.

W3C and Tableless Design

Usability, accessibility, and search engine optimization (SEO) are all phrases used to describe high-quality web pages on the Internet today. In reality, there is a significant amount of overlap between usability, accessibility and SEO and a web page that demonstrates the characteristics of one does so for all three; this is shown in Figure 9.2. The easiest way to achieve these three goals is to do so using the framework laid out in the World Wide Web Consortium (W3C) web standards.

For example, a site that is structured semantically with (X)HTML (the (X)HTML explains the document, not how it looks) will be easily read through a screen reader by someone who has poor vision. It will also be easily read by a search engine spider. Google is effectively blind in how it reads your website, it's as though it is using a screen reader.

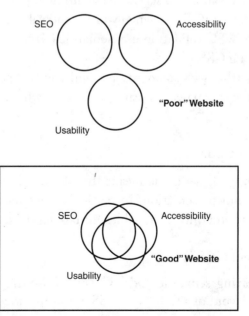

FIGURE 9.2 The overlap between usability, accessibility, and SEO

Web standards put into place a common set of "rules" for all web browsers to use to display a web page. The main organization pushing these standards is the World Wide Web Consortium (W3C), whose Director, Tim Berners-Lee, has the distinction of actually inventing the Web in 1989.

To help you understand where web standards came from, some history is helpful. Many web pages are actually designed for older browsers. Why? Browsers have continually evolved since the World Wide Web started. New ones have appeared, and some old ones have disappeared (remember Netscape?).

Current W3C standards serve to (hopefully) push manufacturers to release more compliant browsers so that designers can design to one common platform.

Another complicating factor is that different browser makers (like Microsoft) tend to have their browsers interpret html/xhtml in slightly different ways. This has lead to web designers having to design their websites to support older browsers rather than new ones. It's often decided that it's important that a web page appear properly to these "legacy" browsers. The W3C standards outlined for web page code have been developed to achieve consistency. A site that incorporates the W3C's web standards has a much better foundation for making itself accessible, usable, and search engine-optimized. Think of these as building codes for your house. A website built with them is stronger and safer and coincides with users' expectations. You can check your pages with the W3C's HTML validation service (validator.w3.org/). It's easy and free (make sure you use the correct DOCTYPE when you try and validate your code[1]). At its simplest, a site that meets W3C validation uses semantic (X)HTML and separates content from presentation using CSS.

Ask five designers what web standards are, and you will get five different answers. But most agree that they are based on using valid code, whether HTML or (X)HTML (or others).

Semantically Correct Code

As mentioned earlier, being semantic means that the (X)HTML in the web page describes only content, not presentation. In particular, this means structured organization of H1,H2 tags etc and only using tables for tabular data, not layout.

Cascading Style Sheets (CSS)

Closely related to having semantic code, is using Cascading Style Sheets (CSS) to control the look and layout of a web page. CSS is a simple mechanism for adding style (that is, fonts, colors, spacing, and so on) to Web documents (source: www.w3.org/Style/CSS/). They exist parallel to the (X)HTML code and so let you completely separate content (semantic code) from presentation (CSS). The best example of this is CSS Zen Garden, a site where the same semantic (X)HTML is shaped in different and unique ways with different CSS. The result is pages that look very different but have the same core content.

Designing Joomla-powered sites currently presents considerable challenges to meet validation standards. In the first series of releases, 1.0.X, the code used a significant amount of tables to output its pages. This isn't really using CSS for presentation, nor does it produce semantically correct code. This problem is compounded by the fact that very few third-party developers are using CSS; most use tables to generate their code too.

Fortunately, the Joomla Core Development team recognized this issue with Joomla. In the 1.5 version, it's possible for template designers to completely override the output of the core (called a view) and strip out the tables or customize the layout—whatever they want.

Regardless, care can still be taken when creating a template to make sure it is accessible (for example, scalable font sizes), usable (clear navigation) and optimized for search engines (source-ordered).

> **The Least You Need to Know**
> Creating valid templates should be a path, not a goal. The idea is to make your template as accessible as possible for humans and spiders, not to achieve a badge of valid markup.

Creating a Simple Template

To understand the contents of a template, we will start by looking at a blank Joomla template.

The Template File Components

The template contains the various files and folders that make up a Joomla template. These files must be placed in the /templates/ directory of a Joomla installation in their own folder. So if we had two templates installed, our directory would look something like the following:

```
/templates/element
/templates/voodoo
```

Note that the directory names for the templates must be the same as the name of the template, in this case element and voodoo. Obviously they are case sensitive and shouldn't contain spaces.

Within the directory of a template, there are a number of key files:

```
/element/templateDetails.xml
/element/index.php
```

These two filenames and locations must match exactly because this is what they are called by the Joomla core script.

The first of these is the template XML file.

```
templateDetails.xml
```

This is an XML format metadata file that tells Joomla what other files are needed when loading a web page that uses this template. Note the uppercase "D." It also details the author, copyright, and what files make up the template (including any images used). The last use of this file is for installing a template when using the admin backend.

Second, we have the engine of the template, the `index.php`:

```
index.php
```

This file is the most important. It lays out the site and tells the Joomla CMS where to put the different components and modules. It is a combination of PHP and (X)HTML.

In almost all templates, additional files are used. It is conventional (although not required by the core) to name and locate them as shown here:

```
/element/template_thumbnail.png
/element/css/template.css
/element/images/logo.png
```

These are just examples. Table 9.1 examines each line.

TABLE 9.1 Core Files Needed for a Template

/templatename/folder/filename	Description
/element/template_thumbnail.png	A web browser screenshot of the template (usually reduced to around 140 pixels wide and 90 pixels high). After the template has been installed, this functions as a "Preview Image" visible in the Joomla administration Template Manager and also the template selector module in the frontend (if used).

/templatename/folder/filename	Description
/element/css/template.css	The CSS of the template. The folder location is optional, but you have to specify where it is in the index.php file. You can call it what you like. Usually the name shown is used, but we will see later that there are advantages in having other CSS files too.
/element/images/logo.png	Any images that go with the template. Again for organization reasons, most designers put this in an images folder. Here we have an image file called logo.png as an example.

templateDetails.xml

The templateDetails.xml must include all the files that are part of the template. It also includes information such as the author and copyright. Some of these are shown in the admin backend in the Template Manager. An example XML file is shown here:

```xml
<?xml version="1.0" encoding="utf-8"?>
<install version="1.5" type="template">
      <name>TemplateTutorial15</name>
      <creationDate>August 2007</creationDate>
      <author>Barrie North</author>
      <copyright>GPL</copyright>
      <authorEmail> compassdesigns@gmail.com </authorEmail>
      <authorUrl>www.compassdesigns.net</authorUrl>
      <version>1.0</version>
      <description>First example template for Chapter 9 of the Joomla Book
      </description>
      <files>
            <filename>index.php</filename>
            <filename>templateDetails.xml</filename>
            <filename>js/somejsfile.js</filename>
            <filename>images/threecol-l.gif</filename>
            <filename>images/threecol-r.gif</filename>
            <filename>css/customize.css</filename>
            <filename>css/layout.css</filename>
            <filename>css/template_css.css</filename>
      </files>
      <positions>
            <position>user1</position>
            <position>top</position>
            <position>left</position>
            <position>banner</position>
            <position>right</position>
            <position>footer</position>
      </positions>
```

```
        <params>
             <param name="colorVariation" type="list" default="white" label="Color
Variation" description="Color variation to use">
                    <option value="blue">Blue</option>
                    <option value="red">Red</option>
             </param>
        </params>
</install>
```

Let's explain what some of these lines mean:

- `<install version="1.5" type="template">`. The contents of the XML document are instructions for the backend installer. The option `type="template"` tells the installer that we are installing a template and that it is for Joomla 1.5.

- `<name>TemplateTutorial15</name>`. Defines the name of your template. The name you enter here will also be used to create the directory within the templates directory. Therefore it should not contain any characters that the file system cannot handle, for example spaces. If installing manually, you need to create a directory that is identical to the template name.

- `<creationDate>August 2007</creationDate>`. The date the template was created. It is a free form field and can be anything such as May 2005, 08-June-1978, 01/01/2004, and so on.

- `<author>Barrie North</author>`. The name of the author of this template—most likely your name.

- `<copyright>GPL</copyright>`. Any copyright information goes into this element. A Licensing Primer for Developers and Designers can be found in the Joomla forums.

- `<authorEmail>compassdesigns@gmail.com</authorEmail>`. Email address where the author of this template can be reached.

- `<authorUrl>www.compassdesigns.net</authorUrl>`. The URL of the author's website.

- `<version>1.0</version>`. The version of this template.

- `<files></files>`. Various files used in the template.

  The files used in the template are laid out with `<filename>` tags:

```
        <files>
             <filename>index.php</filename>
             <filename>templateDetails.xml</filename>
```

```
<filename>js/somejsfile.js</filename>
<filename>images/threecol-l.gif</filename>
<filename>images/threecol-r.gif</filename>
<filename>css/customize.css</filename>
<filename>css/layout.css</filename>
<filename>css/template_css.css</filename>
</files>
```

- The "files" sections contain all generic files like the PHP source for the template or the thumbnail image for the template preview. Each file listed in this section is enclosed by `<filename> </filename>`. Also included would be any additional files; here the example of a JavaScript file that is required by the template is used.

- All image files that the template uses are also listed in the `<files>` section. Again, each file listed is enclosed by `<filename> </filename>`. Path information for the files is relative to the root of the template. For example, if the template is in the directory called 'YourTemplate', and all images are in a directory 'images' that is inside 'YourTemplate', the correct path is: `<filename>images/my_image.jpg</filename>`.

- Last, any stylesheets are listed in the files section. Again, the filename is enclosed by `<filename> </filename>`, and it's path is relative to the template root.

- `<positions></positions>`. The module positions available in the template.

- `<params></params>`. These describe parameters that can be passed to allow advanced template functions such as changing the color of the template.

index.php

What actually is in an `index.php` file? It is a combination of (X)HTML and PHP that determines everything about the layout and presentation of the pages.

First, let's look at a critical part of achieving valid templates, the DOCTYPE at the top of the `index.php` file. This is the bit of code that goes at the very top of every web page. At the top of our page, we have this in our template:

```
<?php
// no direct access
defined( '_JEXEC' ) or die( 'Restricted access' );
?>
<!DOCTYPE html PUBLIC "-//W3C//DTD XHTML 1.0 Transitional//EN" "http://www.w3.org/
TR/xhtml11/DTD/xhtml11-transitional.dtd">
```

The first PHP statement simply makes sure that the file is not accessed directly for security.

A web page DOCTYPE is one of the fundamental components of how a web page is shown by a browser, specifically, how that browser interprets CSS. To give you further understanding, an observation from alistapart.com says

> [Information on W3C's site about DOCTYPEs is] written by geeks for geeks. And when I say geeks, I don't mean ordinary web professionals like you and me. I mean geeks who make the rest of us look like Grandma on the first day of She's Got Mail.

Anyway, you can use several DOCTYPEs. Basically, the DOCTYPE tells the browser how to interpret the page. Here the words "strict" and "transitional" start getting floated around (`float:left` and `float:right` usually). Essentially, ever since the Web started, different browsers have had different levels of support for CSS. This means for example, that Internet Explorer won't understand the "min-width" command to set a minimum page width. To duplicate the effect, you have to use "hacks" in the CSS.

> **NOTE**
> Some say that serving (X)HTML as text/html is considered harmful. If you actually understand that statement you are well ahead of the game and beyond this guide. You can read more at hixie.ch/advocacy/xhtml.

Strict means the HTML (or (X)HTML) will be interpreted exactly as dictated by standards. A transitional DOCTYPE means that the page will be allowed a few agreed upon differences to the standards.

To complicate things, there is something called "quirks" mode. If the DOCTYPE is wrong, outdated, or not there, the browser goes into quirks mode. This is an attempt to be backwards-compatible, so Internet Explorer 6 for example, will render the page pretending as if it were IE4.

Unfortunately, people sometimes end up in quirks mode accidentally. It usually happens in two ways:

- They use the DOCTYPE declaration straight from the WC3 web page, and the link ends up as `DTD/xhtml1-strict.dtd`, except this is a relative link on the WC3 server. You need the full path as shown earlier.

- Microsoft set up IE6 so you could have valid pages but be in quirks mode. This happens by having an "xml declaration" put before the DOCTYPE.

Next is an XML statement (after the DOCTYPE):

```
<html xmlns="http://www.w3.org/1999/xhtml" xml:lang="<?php echo $this->language;
  ?>" lang="<?php echo $this->language; ?>" >
```

The part about IE6 quirks mode is important. In this chapter we only design for IE6+, so we will make sure that it's running in standards mode. This will minimize the hacks we have to do later on.

> **NOTE**
> Making a page standards-compliant, where you see "valid xhtml" at the bottom of the page does not mean really difficult coding, or hard-to-understand tags. It merely means that the code you use matches the DOCTYPE you said it would. That's it! Nothing else.
> Designing your site to standards can, on one level, be reduced to saying what you do and then doing what you say.
> Here are some useful links, which will help you understand DOCTYPE and quirks mode:
> - www.quirksmode.org/css/quirksmode.html
> - www.alistapart.com/stories/doctype
> - www.w3.org/QA/2002/04/Web-Quality
> - http://forum.joomla.org/index.php/topic,7537.0.html
> - http://forum.joomla.org/index.php/topic,6048.0.html

What Else Is in `index.php`?

Let's look at the structure of the header first; we want to be as minimal as possible but still have enough for a production site. The header information we will use is as follows:

```
<?php
// no direct access
defined( '_JEXEC' ) or die( 'Restricted access' );
?>
<!DOCTYPE html PUBLIC "-//W3C//DTD XHTML 1.0 Transitional//EN" "http://www.w3.org/
  TR/xhtml1/DTD/xhtml1-transitional.dtd">
<html xmlns="http://www.w3.org/1999/xhtml" xml:lang="<?php echo $this->language;
  ?>" lang="<?php echo $this->language; ?>" >

<head>

<jdoc:include type="head" />
```

```
<link rel="stylesheet" href="templates/system/css/system.css" type="text/css" />
<link rel="stylesheet" href="templates/system/css/general.css" type="text/css" />
<link rel="stylesheet" href="templates/<?php echo $this->template ?>/css/template.
css" type="text/css" />
```

```
</head>
```

What does all that mean?

We have already discussed the implications of the DOCTYPE statement in the in-dex.php file. The `<?php echo $this->language; ?>` is pulling the language from the site Global Configuration.

The next line is to include more header information:

```
<jdoc:include type="head" />
```

This is all header information that is set in the Global Configuration again. It includes the following tags (in a default installation):

```
<title>Welcome to the Frontpage</title>
  <meta name="description" content="Joomla! - the dynamic portal engine and
  content management system" />
  <meta name="generator" content="Joomla! 1.5 - Open Source Content Management" />
  <meta http-equiv="Content-Type" content="text/html; charset=utf-8" />
  <meta name="robots" content="index, follow" />
  <meta name="keywords" content="joomla, Joomla" />

  <link href="index.php?option=com_content&amp;view=frontpage&amp;format=feed&amp;
Itemid=1&amp;type=rss" rel="alternate" type="application/rss+xml" title="RSS 2.0"
/>
  <link href="index.php?option=com_content&amp;view=frontpage&amp;format=feed&amp
;Itemid=1&amp;type=atom" rel="alternate" type="application/atom+xml" title="Atom
1.0" />
  <script type="text/javascript" src="http://localhost/Joomla-1.5RC2/media/system/
js/mootools.js"></script>
  <script type="text/javascript" src="http://localhost/Joomla-1.5RC2/media/system/
js/caption.js"></script>
```

Much of this header information is created on the fly specific to the page (article) that someone is on. It includes a number of metatags—the favicon, RSS feed URLs, and some standard JavaScipt files.

The last lines in the header provide links to CSS files for the template:

```
<link rel="stylesheet" href="templates/system/css/system.css" type="text/css" />
<link rel="stylesheet" href="templates/system/css/general.css" type="text/css" />
<link rel="stylesheet" href="templates/<?php echo $this->template ?>/css/template.
css" type="text/css" />
```

The first two files, system.css and general.css contain some generic Joomla styles. The last one is all the CSS for the template, here called template.css. The PHP code `<?php echo $this->template ?>` will return the name of the current template. Writing it in this way rather than the actual real path makes the code more generic. When you create a new template you can just copy it (along with the whole header code) and not worry about editing anything.

The template CSS files can have any number of files, for example conditional ones for different browsers. This one targets IE6:

```
<!--[if lte IE 6]>
<link href="templates/<?php echo $this->template ?>/css/ieonly.css"
rel="stylesheet" type="text/css" />
<![endif]-->
```

This example is part of a technique to use a template parameter:

```
<link rel="stylesheet" href="templates/<?php echo $this->template ?>/css/<?php
echo $this->params->get('colorVariation'); ?>.css" type="text/css" />
```

Blank Joomla Template Body

Creating our first template will be very, very easy! Ready?

All we need to do is use Joomla statements that insert the contents of any modules and the mainbody.

```
<body>
<?php echo $mainframe->getCfg('sitename');?><br />
<jdoc:include type="module" name="breadcrumbs" />
<jdoc:include type="modules" name="top" />
<jdoc:include type="modules" name="left" />
<jdoc:include type="component" />
<jdoc:include type="modules" name="right" />
</body>
```

At this point (if you preview it), our site does not look very awe inspiring. The output is shown in Figure 9.3.

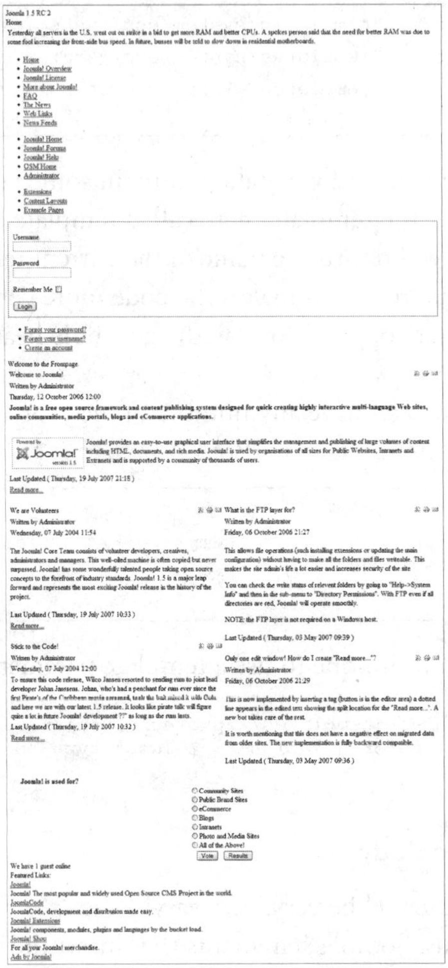

FIGURE 9.3 An unstyled template

The template contains the following in reasonably logical order:

- name of the site
- top module
- left modules
- main content
- right modules

> **The Least You Need to Know**
> The most basic template simply loads the Joomla modules and mainbody (component). Layout and design is part of the CSS, not Joomla.

The goal is to try and come as close to semantic markup as possible. From a Web point of view, it means a page can be read by anyone—a browser, a spider, or a screen reader. Semantic layout is the cornerstone of accessibility.

> **NOTE**
> What we have here really is only the potential for semantic layout. If we were to go ahead and put random modules in random locations, we would have a mess. An important consideration for CMS sites is that a template is only as good as the population of the content. It is this that often trips designers up when trying to validate their sites.

You will notice that we have used the first of a number of commands specific to Joomla to create this output:

```
<?php echo $mainframe->getCfg('sitename');?><br />
<jdoc:include type="module" name="breadcrumbs" />
<jdoc:include type="modules" name="top" />
<jdoc:include type="modules" name="left" />
<jdoc:include type="component" />
<jdoc:include type="modules" name="right" />
```

The PHP echo statement simply outputs a string from the `configuration.php` file. Here, we are using the site name; we could have as easily had the following:

```
The name of this site is <?php echo $mainframe->getCfg('sitename');?><br />
The administrator email is <?php echo $mainframe->getCfg('mailfrom');?><br />
This template is in the <?php echo $this->template?> directory<br />
The URL is <?php echo JURI::base();;?>
```

The `jdoc` statement inserts various types of (X)HTML output from modules of components.

This line inserts the output from a component. What component it will be is determined by the menu link:

```
<jdoc:include type="component" />
```

NOTE
Interestingly enough, you seem to be able to have multiple instances of component output. Not sure why you would want to, but I thought I would let you know! Might be a bug.

This line inserts the output for a module location:

```
<jdoc:include type="modules" name="right" />
```

The full syntax is actually

```
<jdoc:include type="modules" name="LOCATION" style="OPTION" />
```

We look at the various options for styles in the section about modules later in this chapter.

CSSTemplateTutorialStep1

At this point, we have a very bare template. I have created an installable template that is available from www.joomlabook.com: CSSTemplateTutorialStep1.zip.

This will install a template that has only two files, the `index.php` and `template-Details.xml`. I removed references to other files to give a bare bones output with no CSS. This is actually a useful diagnostic template; you can install it and track errors that are occurring with a component or module.

Using CSS to Create a Tableless Layout

We will be using pure CSS to make a 3-column layout for the Joomla template. We will also be making it a fluid layout. There are two main types of web page layout—fixed and fluid—and they both refer to how the width of the page is controlled.

The width of the page is an issue because of the many browser resolutions at which people surf the Web. Although the percentage is dropping, about 17% of surfers are using an 800x600 resolution. The majority, 79%, are using 1024x768 and higher[2]. Making a fluid layout means that your valuable web page won't be a narrow column in the 1024 resolution and will be visible in full on smaller monitors.

A typical design might use tables to lay out the page. They are useful in that you just have to set the width of the columns as percentages, but they have several drawbacks.

For example, tables have lots of extra code compared to CSS layouts. This leads to longer load times (which surfers don't like) and poorer performance in search engines. The code can roughly double in size, not just with markup but also with something called "spacer gifs."

Even big companies sometimes fall into the table trap, as seen by a recent controversy about the new disney.co.uk website[3]:

There are a couple of major problems with a site that uses tables for layout.

- They are difficult to maintain. To change something you have to figure out what all the table tags like td/tr are doing. With CSS there are just a few lines to inspect.

- The content cannot be source-ordered. Many Web surfers do not see web pages on a browser. Those viewing with a text browser or screen reader will read the page from the top left corner to the bottom right. This means that they first view everything in the header and left column (for a 3-column layout) before they get to the middle column, the important stuff. A CSS layout, on the other hand, allows for "source-ordered" content, which means the content can be rearranged in the code/source. Perhaps your most important site visitor is Google, and it uses a screen reader for all intents and purposes.

Let's look at our layout using CSS. You can position elements (stuff) in several ways using CSS. For a quick introduction, a good source is Brainjar's CSS Positioning.[4]

If you are new to CSS, you might read at least one beginner's guide to CSS. Here are a few suggestions:

- Kevin Hale's *An Overview of Current CSS Layout Techniques*
  http://particletree.com/features/an-overview-of-current-css-layout-techniques/

- htmldog's *CSS Beginner's Guide*
  www.htmldog.com/guides/cssbeginner/

- yourhtmlsource.com
  www.yourhtmlsource.com/stylesheets/

The Least You Need to Know
Modern web design uses CSS rather than tables to position elements. It's difficult to learn, but worth the investment. There are many (non-Joomla) resources available to help you.

We will be using float to position our content. At its most basic, the template might look like Figure 9.4.

Still not very exciting, but let's see what the different parts are all about.

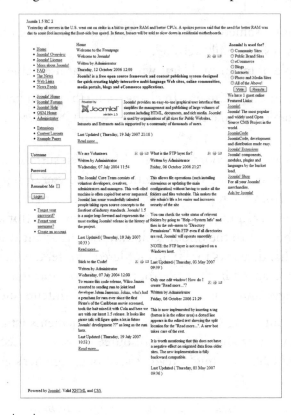

FIGURE 9.4 Basic template layout

In Figure 9.4, the left, middle, and right columns are each given their own element. Each is floated left and given a percent width that together add up to 100%. The `clear:both` style on the footer tells the browser to "stop floating" and makes the footer stretch across all three columns. When we build our second template in this chapter, we will have to use a more advanced clearing technique.

To improve the layout and to add some breathing room to the content, we need to add some column spacing, commonly called "gutter." Unfortunately, there is a problem here. You might know that Internet Explorer does not interpret CSS correctly. One problem is that it calculates width differently. We can solve this problem by not using any padding or borders on something that has a width. To get our gutter, we add another `<div>` element inside the columns.

To the CSS we add

```
.inside {padding:10px;}
```

Our resulting `<body>` code for `index.php` is:

```
<body>
<div id="wrap">
  <div id="header">
    <div class="inside">
        <?php echo $mainframe->getCfg('sitename');?>
      <jdoc:include type="modules" name="top" />
    </div>
  </div>
  <div id="sidebar">
    <div class="inside">
      <jdoc:include type="modules" name="left" />
    </div>
  </div>
  <div id="content">
    <div class="inside">
      <jdoc:include type="component" />
    </div>
  </div>
  <div id="sidebar-2">
    <div class="inside">
      <jdoc:include type="modules" name="right" />
    </div>
  </div>
  <div id="footer">
    <div class="inside">
Powered by <a href="http://joomla.org">Joomla!</a>. Valid <a href="http://valida-
tor.w3.org/check/referer">XHTML</a> and <a href="http://jigsaw.w3.org/css-valida-
tor/check/referer">CSS</a>. </div>
  </div>
</div>
<!--end of wrap-->
</body>
```

Our `template.css` file looks like this:

```
/*Compass Design layout.css CSS file*/
body {
}
#wrap {
```

```
min-width:760px;
max-width:960px;
}
#header {}
#sidebar {float:left;width:20%; overflow:hidden }
#content {float:left;width:60%; overflow:hidden }
#sidebar-2 {float:left;width:20%; overflow:hidden }
#footer {clear:both;}
.inside {padding:10px;}
```

> **TIP**
> **CSS Shorthand**
> It's possible to reduce the amount of CSS code by using "shorthand." One example of this is padding and margin styles applied to an element, where
>
> ```
> margin-top:5px; margin-bottom:5px; margin-left:10px; margin-right:10px;
> ```
>
> can be replaced by:
>
> ```
> margin: 5px 10px;
> ```
>
> There are "shorthand" styles at the beginning of each style definition. After you have figured out the styles, fill the shorthand versions in and delete the long versions. The syntax is
>
> ```
> font: font-size |font-style | font-variant | font-weight | line-height | font-family
> ```
>
> Here is an example. Rather than using this
>
> ```
> font-size:1em; font-family:Arial,Helvetica,sans-serif; font-style:italic; font-weight:bold; line-height:1.3em;
> ```
>
> use this
>
> ```
> font:bold 1em/1.3em Arial,Helvetica,sans-serif italic;
> ```
>
> Read more about this syntax at An Introduction to CSS shorthand properties (http://home.no.net/junjun/html/shorthand.html).

This simple layout is a good one to use for learning about how to use CSS with Joomla because it shows two of the advantages of CSS over table-based layouts, it is less code, and it is easier to maintain. However, it is not source-ordered. For that we must use a more advanced layout known as a *nested float*.

Source-ordered layouts perform better for SEO than ones where the important content occurs late in the code. From a Joomla site perspective, the important content is that which is coming from the component.

Default CSS

So far, all of our CSS has been only about layout, which will make a plain page. So let's add some formatting:

```css
/* layout.css CSS file*/
body {
text-align:center; /*center hack*/
}
#wrap {
min-width:760px;
max-width:960px;
width: auto !important; /*IE6 hack*/
width:960px; /*IE6 hack*/
margin:0 auto; /*center hack*/
text-align:left; /*center hack*/
}
#header {}
#sidebar {float:left;width:20%; overflow:hidden }
#content {float:left;width:60%; overflow:hidden }
#sidebar-2 {float:left;width:20%; overflow:hidden }
#footer {clear:both;}
.inside {padding:10px;}
```

We have centered the page by using a small hack. This has to be done because Internet Explorer does not read CSS accurately. With a standards-compliant browser, we could just say `margin:0` 10%; to center the page, but IE does not recognize that, so we center the "text" of the whole page and then align it left in the columns.

In celebration of IE7's support of min/max width (which IE6 does not), we can add in a minimum and maximum width. Note we have to add a tiny hack for IE6 as it does not understand these. It will ignore the `!important` statement and have a plain, old 960px width.

NOTE

It might seem strange to define our columns in percentage widths and then have a containing `div` that is fixed. Well, a few things are going on here:

- Having fluid columns inside a fixed width container makes the template very flexible. If we add width changer buttons, we only need to change one value.
- We still have a max-width so why not go all fluid? Many viewers on the Web now have enormous screens. Usability research tells us that lines of text over 900px wide are hard to read because the eyes have to go a long way to go to the next line. Limiting the fluidity makes the site more useable/accessible.

We have also added a new style to the columns: `overflow:hidden`. This will make the page "break" more consistent as we reduce its width.

At the beginning of the typography, with CSS we will set some overall styles and have what is known as a *global reset*:

```
/*Compass Design typography css */
* {
margin:0;
padding:0;
}
h1,h2,h3,h4,h5,h6,p,blockquote,form,label,ul,ol,dl,fieldset,address {
margin: 0.5em 0;
}
li,dd {
margin-left:1em;
}
fieldset {
padding:.5em;
}
body {
font-size:76%;
font-family:Verdana, Arial, Helvetica, sans-serif;
line-height:1.3;
}
```

Everything is given a zero margin and padding, and then all block level elements are given a bottom margin. This helps achieve browser consistency. You can read more about the global reset at clagnut[5] and left-justified.[6]

The font size is set to 76%. The reason for this is to try and get more consistent font sizes across browsers. All font sizes are then set in em. Having `line-height:1.3` helps readability. This means that the pages will be more accessible because the viewer will be able to resize the fonts to their own preferences. This is discussed more at "An experiment in typography" at The Noodle Incident (Owen Briggs).[7]

If we add some background colors to the header, sidebars, and content containers, we see something like what is shown in Figure 9.5.

Notice that the side columns do not reach their footer. This is because they only extend as far as their content; where the space is white on the left and on the right, they don't exist.

FIGURE 9.5 Basic template with typography

If we have a template that has a white background for all three columns, this is no problem. We will use this approach and will have boxes around the modules. If we want equal height columns that are colored or have boxes, we have to use a background image that will tile vertically. This technique is called *Faux Columns* and is described by Douglas Bowman[8] and Eric Meyer.[9]

Joomla-Specific CSS

Although Joomla 1.5 has the functionality to override the core output in a template, its default rendering still uses significant tables to output content in the main body. Along with these tables, CSS output is available for a designer to style pages. Based on some research by various community members, Table 9.2 shows the current list. Note, it does not include generic web page styles like H1, H2, p, ul, a, form, and so on.

TABLE 9.2 Legacy Default CSS Styles from 1.0 in 1.5

article_separator	contentpane	outline
adminform	contentpaneopen	pagenav
article_separator	contenttoc	pagenav_next
author	createdate	pagenav_prev
bannerfooter	created-date	pagenavbar
bannergroup	date	pagenavcounter
bannerheader	input	pathway
banneritem	inputbox	pollstableborder
blog	intro	read
blog_more	latestnews	search
blogsection	loclink	searchintro
breadcrumbs	mainlevel	sections
button	message	sectiontable_footer
buttonheading	metadata	sectiontableentry
clr	modifydate	sectiontablefooter
componentheading	module	sectiontableheader
content_email	moduletable	small
content_rating	mosimage	smalldark
content_vote	mosimage_caption	sublevel
contentdescription	mostread	title
contentheading	newsfeed	wrapper
contentpagetitle		

Many designs you might see in Table 9.2 actually have given CSS styles that are more specific in their definitions. Basically, a more specific rule overrides a less specific rule.

For example

```
a {color:blue;}
a:link {color:red;}

.contentheading {color:blue;}
div.contentheading {color:red;}
```

The color on a link and the color of the .contentheading will be *red*, as that rule is more specific (as .contentheading is contained within a <div>)

In the case of Joomla templates, you will often see more specific rules used. This often occurs when the class is on a table. Here are more examples:

```
.moduletable
table.moduletable
```

.moduletable is the name of the <div> that wraps a module. table.moduletable will only apply the style to a table with class="moduletable" on it.

`.moduletable` will apply the style regardless of what element the class is on.

```
a.contentpagetitle:link
.contentpagetitle a:link
```

`a.contentpagetitle:link` will apply the style to any `a` tags with a `.contentpagetitle` class on them that is a link.

`.contentpagetitle a:link` will apply the style to any elements *inside* `.contentpagetitle` that are links.

Specificity is not easy to understand; its often easier to start by using the most general style possible and then getting more specific if the results are not what you expect.

Here are some links to websites that discuss specificity in detail:

- www.htmldog.com/guides/cssadvanced/specificity/
- www.meyerweb.com/eric/css/link-specificity.html
- www.stuffandnonsense.co.uk/archives/css_specificity_wars.html

At the moment, our template is using several tables. As mentioned earlier, this slows the pages down and makes them harder to update. To reduce the number of tables, when we call the modules, we need to use style parameters in the `jdoc:include`.

> **The Least You Need to Know**
> Joomla will output specific elements, ids, and classes in the code of a webpage. These can be predicted and used to style the design using CSS.

Modules in Templates

When a module is called in the `index.php`, it has several options on how it is displayed.

The syntax is

```
<jdoc:include type="modules" name="LOCATION" style="OPTION" />
```

The style is optional and is defined in `templates/system/html/modules.php`. Currently, the default `modules.php` file contains the following layouts.

`OPTION="table"` (default display) modules are displayed in a column. The following shows an example of the output:

```
<table cellpadding="0" cellspacing="0" class="moduletable<?php echo $params-
>get('moduleclass_sfx'); ?>">
<?php if ($module->showtitle != 0) : ?>
 <tr>
  <th valign="top">
   <?php echo $module->title; ?>
  </th>
 </tr>
<?php endif; ?>
 <tr>
  <td>
   <?php echo $module->content; ?>
  </td>
 </tr>
</table>
```

OPTION="horz" makes the modules appear horizontal. Each module is output in the cell of a wrapper table. The following shows an example of the output:

```
<table cellspacing="1" cellpadding="0" border="0" width="100%">
 <tr>
  <td valign="top">
   <?php modChrome_table($module, $params, $attribs); ?>
  </td>
 </tr>
</table>
```

OPTION="xhtml" makes modules appear as a simple div element. The following shows an example of the output:

```
<div class="moduletable<?php echo $params->get('moduleclass_sfx'); ?>">
<?php if ($module->showtitle != 0) : ?>
 <h3><?php echo $module->title; ?></h3>
<?php endif; ?>
 <?php echo $module->content; ?>
</div>
```

OPTION="rounded" makes modules appear in a format that allows, for example, stretchable rounded corners. If this $style is used, the name of the <div> changes from moduletable to module. The following shows an example of the output:

```
<div class="module<?php echo $params->get('moduleclass_sfx'); ?>">
 <div>
  <div>
```

```
<div>
 <?php if ($module->showtitle != 0) : ?>
  <h3><?php echo $module->title; ?></h3>
 <?php endif; ?>
 <?php echo $module->content; ?>
 </div>
 </div>
 </div>
</div>
```

OPTION="none" makes modules appear as raw output containing no element and no title. Here is an example:

```
echo $module->content;
```

As you can see, the CSS options ((X)HTML and rounded) are much leaner in code, which makes it easier to style the web pages. I don't recommend using suffixes of table (default) or horz unless absolutely needed.

Here's the really good bit!

If you examine the modules.php file, you will see all the options that exist for modules. It's easy to add your own; this is part of the new templating power that is in 1.5. We look at this in more detail in our section on template overrides.

To develop our template, we will put a module style of "xhtml" on all of our modules:

```
<body>
<div id="wrap">
  <div id="header">
    <div class="inside">
        <h1><?php echo $mainframe->getCfg('sitename');?></h1>
      <jdoc:include type="modules" name="top" style="xhtml" />
    </div>
  </div>
  <div id="sidebar">
    <div class="inside">
      <jdoc:include type="modules" name="left" style="xhtml" />
    </div>
  </div>
  <div id="content">
    <div class="inside">
      <jdoc:include type="module" name="breadcrumbs" style="none" />
      <jdoc:include type="component" />
    </div>
```

```
    </div>
    <div id="sidebar-2">
      <div class="inside">
        <jdoc:include type="modules" name="right" style="xhtml" />
      </div>
    </div>
    <div id="footer">
      <div class="inside">
        <jdoc:include type="modules" name="footer" style="xhtml" />
      </div>
    </div>
<!--end of wrap-->
</body>
```

Note that we cannot put these module styles on the `<jdoc:include type="component" />` because it is not a module.

> **The Least You Need to Know**
> In 1.5, the output of modules can be completely customized, or you can use the pre-built output. All these options are called module *chrome*.

We have also placed the site title inside an `<H1>` tag. It's more semantically correct and will also help in SEO. Let's also remove the background from the layout `divs`.

We add some CSS to style the modules with a border and a background for the module titles.

Our CSS now looks like this:

```
/*Compass Design typography CSS*/

* {
margin:0;
padding:0;
}
h1,h2,h3,h4,h5,h6,p,blockquote,form,label,ul,ol,dl,fieldset,address {
margin: 0.5em 0;
}
li,dd {
margin-left:1em;
}
fieldset {
padding:.5em;
}
body {
```

```css
font-size:76%;
font-family:Verdana, Arial, Helvetica, sans-serif;
line-height:1.3;
margin:1em 0;
}
#wrap{
border:1px solid #999;
}
#header{
border-bottom: 1px solid #999;
}
#footer{
border-top: 1px solid #999;
}
a{
text-decoration:none;
}
a:hover{
text-decoration:underline;
}
h1,.componentheading{
font-size:1.7em;
}
h2,.contentheading{
font-size:1.5em;
}
h3{
font-size:1.3em;
}
h4{
font-size:1.2em;
}
h5{
font-size:1.1em;
}
h6{
font-size:1em;
font-weight:bold;
}
#footer,.small,.createdate,.modifydate,.mosimage_caption{
font:0.8em Arial,Helvetica,sans-serif;
color:#999;
}
.moduletable{
margin-bottom:1em;
```

```
padding:0 10px; /*padding for inside text*/ border:1px #CCC solid;
}
.moduletable h3{
background:#666;
color:#fff;
padding:0.25em 0;
text-align:center;
font-size:1.1em;
margin:0 -10px 0.5em -10px;
/*negative padding to pull h3 back out from .moduletable padding*/ }
```

> **NOTE**
> Several of the menus in the default installation have a menu suffix in the module properties of _menu. To get everything behaving properly, I deleted that parameter.

This typography CSS now produces the result shown in Figure 9.6.

FIGURE 9.6 Basic template with module title styling

Menus in Templates

We saw in Chapter 5, "Creating Menus and Navigation," that there are a number of settings for how a menu will be rendered.

Again, using CSS lists rather than tables results in reduced code and easier markup. After setting all our menus to lists we have only 12 tables (we see how to remove the rest using the new version 1.5 override feature). Remember, the *list* setting is the new 1.5 version; *flat list* is from 1.0 and will be depreciated. Lists are also better than tables because text-based browsers, screen readers, non-CSS supporting browsers, browsers with CSS turned off, and search bots will be able to access your content more easily.

One of the other advantages of using CSS for menus is that there is a lot of example code on various CSS developer sites. Let's look at one of them and see how it can be used.

A web page at maxdesign.com[10] has a selection of over 30 menus, all using the same underlying code. It's called the Listamatic. There is a slight difference in the code that we need to change in order to adapt these menus to Joomla.

These lists use the following code:

```
<div id="navcontainer">
<ul id="navlist">
<li id="active"><a href=" #" id="current">Item one</a></li>
<li><a href="#">Item two</a></li>
<li><a xhref="#">Item three</a></li>
<li><a href="#">Item four</a></li>
<li><a href="#">Item five</a></li>
</ul>
</div>
```

This means that there is an enclosing `<div>` called navcontainer, and the `<ul>` has an id of `navlist`. To duplicate this effect in Joomla, we need to have some sort of enclosing `<div>`.

We can achieve this by using module suffixes. If you recall, the output of an (X)HTML style option module is

```
<div class="moduletable">
  <h3>modChrome_xhtml</h3>
  modChrome_xhtml </div>
```

If we add a module suffix, that will get added to the `moduletable` class, like this:

```
<div class="moduletablesuffix">
  <h3>modChrome_xhtml</h3>
  modChrome_xhtml </div>
```

So when picking a menu from Listamatic, you need to replace the `navcontainer` class style in the CSS by `moduletablesuffix`.

> **NOTE**
> Module suffixes, to a certain extent, blur the line between site design and site administration. One of the goals of further development of the Joomla core is to clearly separate these roles. The implication is that it is likely they might be depreciated in future versions beyond 1.5.

This use of a module class suffix is helpful. It allows different colored boxes with just a simple change of the module class suffix.

> **The Least You Need to Know**
> It's best to always use the bulleted or flat list for menu output. You can then make use of many free resources for the CSS that are available on the Web.

For our site, we use List 10 by Mark Newhouse.[11] Our CSS is

```
.moduletablemenu{
padding:0;
color: #333;
margin-bottom:1em;
}
.moduletablemenu h3 {
background:#666;
color:#fff;
padding:0.25em 0;
text-align:center;
font-size:1.1em;
margin:0;
border-bottom:1px solid #fff;
}
.moduletablemenu ul{
list-style: none;
margin: 0;
padding: 0;
}
```

```
.moduletablemenu li{
border-bottom: 1px solid #ccc;
margin: 0;
}
.moduletablemenu li a{
display: block;
padding: 3px 5px 3px 0.5em;
border-left: 10px solid #333;
border-right: 10px solid #9D9D9D;
background-color:#666;
color: #fff;
text-decoration: none;
}
html>body .moduletablemenu li a {
width: auto;
}
.moduletablemenu li a:hover,a#active_menu:link,a#active_menu:visited{
border-left: 10px solid #1c64d1;
border-right: 10px solid #5ba3e0;
background-color: #2586d7;
color: #fff;
}
```

We then need to add the module suffix of *menu* (no underscore in this case) to any modules of menus we want to be styled. This produces a menu like what's shown in Figure 9.7.

For any menu we want to be styled this way, we have to add "menu" as a module suffix.

> **TIP**
>
> When trying to get a particular menu to work, here is a useful tip: Create a default Joomla installation and then look at the code that makes up the mainmenu. Copy and paste this code into an HTML editor (like Dreamweaver). Replace all the links by "#," and then you can add CSS rules until the effect you want is achieved. The code for the menu to create the style is as follows:
>
> ```
> <!DOCTYPE html PUBLIC "-//W3C//DTD XHTML 1.0 Transitional//EN"
> "http://www.w3.org/TR/xhtml1/DTD/xhtml1-transitional.dtd">
> <html xmlns="http://www.w3.org/1999/xhtml">
> <head>
> <meta http-equiv="Content-Type" content="text/html; charset=iso-8859-1" />
> <title>Untitled Document</title>
> <style type="text/css">
> <!--
> .astyle {
> ```

continues

```
}
-->
</style>
</head>
<body>
<div class="moduletable">
<h3>Main Menu</h3>
<ul class="mainmenu">
  <li id="current" class="item1 active"><a href="#">Home</a></li>
  <li class="item2"><a href="#">Joomla! Overview</a></li>
  <li class="item3"><a href="#">What's New in 1.5?</a></li>
  <li class="item4"><a href="#">Joomla! License</a></li>
  <li class="item5"><a href="#">More about Joomla!</a></li>
  <li class="item6"><a href="#">FAQ</a></li>
  <li class="item7"><a href="#">The News</a></li>
  <li class="item8"><a href="#">Web Links</a></li>
  <li class="item9"><a href="#">News Feeds</a></li>
</ul>
</div>
</body>
</html>
```

The CSS is embedded instead of linked to make editing easier.

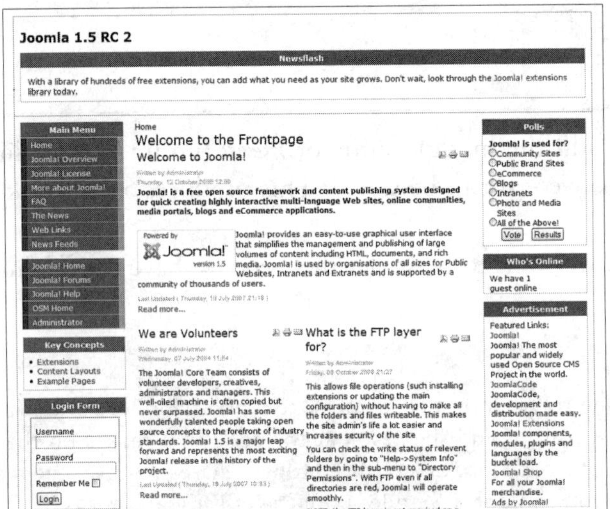

FIGURE 9.7 Basic template with menu styling

Hiding Columns

So far, we have our layout such that we always have three columns, regardless of whether there is any content included. From the perspective of a CMS template, this is not very useful. In a static site the content would never change, but we want to give our site administrators the ability to put their content anywhere they want to without having to worry about editing CSS layouts. We want to be able to "turn off" a column automatically or "collapse" it if there is no content there.

During the development of the Joomla 1.5 templating engine, there were a number of changes and improvements. Quoting directly from the Joomla development blog[12]:

> The changes to the template system in Joomla 1.5 can be divided into two categories. First, there are changes to the way things where done in Joomla 1.0—for example the new way modules are loaded, and second there are also a bunch of extra features, like template parameters…a quick overview:
>
> Changes to the old ways
>
> **mosCountMoules**
>
> The mosCountModules function has been replaced by the $this->countModules function and support for conditions has been added. This allows designers to easily count the total number of modules in multiple template positions in just one line of code, for example $this->countModules('user1 + user2); which will return the total number of modules in position user1 and user2.

> **NOTE**
> More information is also available in the Joomla forum.[13]

So the general use of `mosCountModules` would be

```php
<?php if ($this->countModules('condition')) : ?>
   do something
<?php else : ?>
   do something else
<?php endif; ?>
```

There are four possible conditions. As an example, let's count the number of modules in Figure 9.7. We could insert this code somewhere in the `index.php`:

```php
left=<?php echo $this->countModules('left');?><br />
left and right=<?php echo $this->countModules('left and right');?><br />
```

```
left or right=<?php echo $this->countModules('left or right');?><br />
left + right=<?php echo $this->countModules('left + right');?>
```

- `countModules('left')`. Will return 4; there are 4 modules on the left.
- `countModules('left and right')`. Will return 1; there is a module in the left and right-hand position.
- `countModules('left or right')`. Will return 1; there is a module in the left or the right-hand position.
- `countModules('left + right')`. Will return 7; counting the modules in the left and right-hand positions.

In this situation, we need to use the function that allows us to count the modules present in a specific location. So for example, if there is no content published in the right column, we can adjust the column sizes to fill that space.

There are several ways to do this. We could put the conditional statement in the body to not show the content and then have a different style for the content based on what columns were there. To make it as easy as possible, I have a series of conditional statements in the head tag that (re)define some CSS styles:

```
<?php
if($this->countModules('left and right') == 0) $contentwidth = "100";
if($this->countModules('left or right') == 1) $contentwidth = "80";
if($this->countModules('left and right') == 1) $contentwidth = "60";
?>
```

So we count:

- If there is nothing in left OR right, we are 100%.
- If there is something in left OR right, we are 80%.
- If there is something in left AND something in right, we are 60%.

We then need to change the index.php file in the content div to

```
<div id="content<?php echo $contentwidth; ?>">
```

Change the layout css to

```
#content60 {float:left;width:60%;overflow:hidden;}
#content80 {float:left;width:80%;overflow:hidden;}
#content100 {float:left;width:100%;overflow:hidden;}
```

The PHP conditional statements in the head must appear *after* the line that links to the `template.css` file. This is because if there are two identical CSS style rules; the one that is last will overwrite all the others.

This can also be done in a similar fashion by having the `if` statement import a sub CSS file.

> **TIP**
> While you try to troubleshoot your conditional statements, you can add a line of code into your `index.php`, like this, to show what the value is:
>
> ```
> This content column is <?php echo $contentwidth; ?>% wide
> ```

So we are half-way there, but now we have empty `div` containers where the columns are.

Hiding Module Code

When creating collapsible columns, it is good practice to set up the modules not to be generated if there is no content there. If this is not done, the pages will have empty `<div>`s in them, which can lead to cross browser issues.

To hide the empty `<div>`, the following `if` statement is used:

```php
<?php if($this->countModules('left')) : ?>
<div id="sidebar">
  <div class="inside">
    <jdoc:include type="modules" name="left" style="xhtml" />
  </div>
</div>
<?php endif; ?>
```

Using this code, if there is nothing published in the left, then `<div id="sidebar">` will not be outputted.

Using these techniques for our left and right columns, our `index.php` file now looks like the following code. We will also add an "include for the breadcrumbs module," the module that shows the current page and pathway. Note that this now needs to be included in the `index.php` file and also published as a module.

```php
<?php
// no direct access
defined( '_JEXEC' ) or die( 'Restricted access' );
```

```
?>
<!DOCTYPE html PUBLIC "-//W3C//DTD XHTML 1.0 Transitional//EN"
"http://www.w3.org/TR/xhtml1/DTD/xhtml1-transitional.dtd">
<html xmlns="http://www.w3.org/1999/xhtml" xml:lang="<?php echo $this->language;
?>" lang="<?php echo $this->language; ?>" >


<head>

<jdoc:include type="head" />

<link rel="stylesheet" href="templates/system/css/system.css" type="text/css" />
<link rel="stylesheet" href="templates/system/css/general.css" type="text/css" />
<link rel="stylesheet" href="templates/<?php echo $this->template
?>/css/template.css" type="text/css" />

<?php
if($this->countModules('left and right') == 0) $contentwidth = "100";
if($this->countModules('left or right') == 1) $contentwidth = "80";
if($this->countModules('left and right') == 1) $contentwidth = "60";
?>


</head>

<body>
<div id="wrap">
  <div id="header">
    <div class="inside">
        <h1><?php echo $mainframe->getCfg('sitename');?></h1>
      <jdoc:include type="modules" name="top" style="xhtml" />
    </div>
  </div>
  <?php if($this->countModules('left')) : ?>
  <div id="sidebar">
    <div class="inside">
      <jdoc:include type="modules" name="left" style="xhtml" />
    </div>
  </div>
  <?php endif; ?>

 <div id="content<?php echo $contentwidth; ?>">
    <div class="inside">
      <jdoc:include type="module" name="breadcrumbs" style="none" />
      <jdoc:include type="component" />
    </div>
```

```
  </div>
<?php if($this->countModules('right')) : ?>
  <div id="sidebar-2">
    <div class="inside">
      <jdoc:include type="modules" name="right" style="xhtml" />
    </div>
  </div>
  <?php endif; ?>
  <?php if($this->countModules('footer')) : ?>
  <div id="footer">
    <div class="inside">
      <jdoc:include type="modules" name="footer" style="xhtml" />
    </div>
  </div>
  <?php endif; ?>
<!--end of wrap-->
</body>
</html>
```

> **The Least You Need to Know**
> Elements such as columns or module locations can be hidden (or collapsed) when
> there is no content in them. This is done using conditional PHP statements that are
> linked to different CSS styles.

I would recommend a slightly different way of producing the footer. In the manner shown here, it is hard coded into the index.php file, which makes it hard to change. Right now, the "footer" module in the administrative backend shows the Joomla copyright and can't be easily edited. It makes much more sense to have a custom (X)HTML module placed in the footer location so the site administrator can change it more easily. If you wanted to create your own footer, you would simply unpublish that module and create a custom html module with whatever language you wanted.

In this case we would replace

```
<jdoc:include type="modules" name="footer" style="xhtml" />
```

with

```
<jdoc:include type="modules" name="bottom" style="xhtml" />
```

We must also remember to add this position to the templateDetails.xml file.

> **TIP**
> There are several names associated with modules in Joomla: banner, left, right, user1, footer, and so on. One important thing to realize is that the names do not correspond to any particular location. The location of a module is completely controlled by the template designer, as we have seen. It's customary to place them in a location that is connected to the name, but it is not required.

This basic template shows some of the fundamental principles of creating a Joomla template.

CSSTemplateTutorialStep2

We now have a basic, but functional template. Some simple typography has been added, but more importantly, we have created a pure CSS layout that has dynamic collapsible columns. I have created an installable template that is available from www. joomlabook.com: CSSTemplateTutorialStep2.zip.

Now that we have the basics finished, let's create a *slightly* more attractive template using the techniques we have learned.

Making a Real Joomla 1.5 Template

The first thing we need to start with is our *comp*. A comp is the design that is the basis of the template. We use one kindly donated by Casey Lee, the Lead Designer from Joomlashack[14] for our purposes. It's called "Bold," and we can see it in Figure 9.8.

Slicing and Dicing

The next step in the process is what is known as slicing. We need to use our graphics program to create small sliced images that can be used in the template. It's important to pay attention to how the elements can resize if needed. (My graphics application of choice is Fireworks, because I find it better suited to web design—as opposed to print—than Photoshop).

FIGURE 9.8 A design comp from Joomlashack

Setting Up Module Locations

This template will have some specific locations for specific modules, slightly different from the standard Joomla installation. To make sure the modules are correctly set up as you work through this template, make sure of the following:

- User1=for the search module
- User2=for the top menu
- Top=for newsflash or custom HTML module

Nothing else should be published in these locations.

Header

The header image has a faint swish at the top. We want to retain that, so we put the image in as a background and then assign a color also. That way, the header will scale vertically if we need it to; for example, if the font sizes are resized. We also need to change the colors of any type to white so they show up on the black background.

We also use the background image for the search box. We need to make sure that we target the correct input by using CSS specificity. I have also used absolute positioning inside a relatively positioned element to place the search box where I want it. The image will not scale with text resizing with just a single image. That would require a top and bottom image. That's another exercise for you!

```
#header {
color:#fff;
background:#212121 url(../images/header.png) no-repeat;
position:relative;}
#header h1 {
font-family:Arial, Helvetica, sans-serif small-caps;
font-variant:small-caps;
font-stretch:expanded;
padding-left:20px;}
#header input {
background:url(../images/search.png) no-repeat;
border:0;
height:22px;
width:168px;
padding:2px;
font:1em Arial, Helvetica, sans-serif;
}
#header .search {
position:absolute;
top:20px;
right:20px;
}
```

I did not use a graphical logo here; I used plain text. The reason is mainly because SEOs, as search engines, cannot read images. One could do some nifty image replacement, but I will leave that as an exercise for you to do on your own.

Our header now looks like what's shown in Figure 9.9.

FIGURE 9.9 Header image background

Next, we need to implement a technique used to show a background on a fluid column: sliding doors.

Column Backgrounds

Recall that when we put a color background on the columns, the color did not extend all the way to the footer. This is because the `div` element, in this case sidebar and sidebar-2, is only as tall as the content. It does not grow to fill the containing element.

We have to use a technique called *Sliding Faux Columns*, with which you essentially create two wide images that will slide over each other. We need to create two new containers to hold the backgrounds. Normally, we could apply one to the `#wrap`, but I am using an extra (and wasteful) container for illustration purposes.

For a full description, you can check out these two guides:

- http://alistapart.com/articles/fauxcolumns/
- www.communitymx.com/content/article.cfm?page=1&cid=AFC58

In our case, our maximum width is 960px, so we start with an image of that width. In the image source files, it is `slidingcolumns.png`. We then export two slices (I used the same slice and just hid/revealed the side images), one 960px wide with a 192px background on the left, and one 960px wide with a 196px background on the left.

> **NOTE**
> The left image needs to have a white background, and the right image needs a transparent background. I modified the color of the backgrounds as I exported the images from the source file.

Where does 192px come from? It's 20% of 960, as our columns are 20% wide.

We use the `background-position` property to place the images in the correct place. Here, we are using condensed CSS format so they are part of the background property:

```
#leftfauxcol {
background:url(../images/leftslidingcolumn.png) 20% 0;
}
```

```css
#rightfauxcol {
background:url(../images/rightslidingcolumn.png) 80% 0;
}
```

In our `index.php`, we simply added an inner container inside the wrap:

```php
<div id="wrap">
  <?php if($this->countModules('left')) : ?>
  <div id="leftfauxcol">
    <?php endif; ?>
    <?php if($this->countModules('right')) : ?>
    <div id="rightfauxcol">
      <?php endif; ?>
      <div id="header">
```

We also need to put a conditional on the closing `divs`:

```php
      <?php if($this->countModules('left')) : ?>
    </div>
    <!--end of leftfauxcol-->
    <?php endif; ?>
    <?php if($this->countModules('right')) : ?>
  </div>
  <!--end of rightfauxcol-->
  <?php endif; ?>
```

We must also put a background on our footer and bottom modules/elements; otherwise, the column background would be shown:

```css
#footer {
background:#212121;
color:#fff;
text-align:right;
clear:both;
}
#bottom {
background:#333;
color:#666;
padding:10px 50px;
}
```

We need to clear the floats so that the float container (the faux columns) will extend to the bottom of the page. The traditional method to do this was to use the property `:after`.[15] But with the release of IE7, this method will not work completely. We need to address clearing the floats in Internet Explorer 6 *and* 7, and this is where it all goes down the tubes.

A couple[16] of solutions have been found[17]; we are going to use the *Float (nearly) Everything* option[18] here.

Thus, we add a simple `clear:both` to the `#footer`, and we add floats to the `fauxcol` wrappers. We add these to a *conditional stylesheet* specifically for IE6:

```css
#leftfauxcol {
float:left;
width:100%;
}
#rightfauxcol {
float:left;
width:100%;
}
#footer {
float:left;
width:100%;
}
```

We will have to add some conditional statements to the head of the `index.php` file:

```html
<!--[if lte IE 6]>
<link href="templates/<?php echo $this->template ?>/css/ie6only.css"
rel="stylesheet" type="text/css" />
<![endif]-->
<!--[if lte IE 7]>
<link href="templates/<?php echo $this->template ?>/css/ie7only.css"
rel="stylesheet" type="text/css" />
<![endif]-->
```

Flexible Modules

In our design, we have a large initial module block. We don't know how tall the text will be that is needed. To solve that problem, we put the module `jdoc:include` statement in a containing element and give it a background of the same color as the image. This is the same strategy we used for the header:

```php
<?php if($this->countModules('top')) : ?>
<div id="top">
  <div class="inside">
    <jdoc:include type="modules" name="top" style="xhtml" />
  </div>
```

```
</div>
<?php else : ?>
<div id="top"> </div>
<?php endif; ?>
```

Note, we have also used a conditional comment so that if the top module location has no content, the orange teaser image will not be there. What will be there is an empty container that will contain a little of the background image and 20px worth of vertical padding. This is purely for aesthetics.

The CSS needs to use CSS specificity to override the moduletable styles defined earlier:

```
#top {
background:#ea6800 url(../images/teaser.png) no-repeat;
padding:10px;
}
#top .moduletable h3 {
color:#fff;
background:none;
text-align:left;
font:2.5em Arial, Helvetica, sans-serif normal;
padding:0;
margin:0;
font-stretch:expanded
}
#top .moduletable{
font:bold 1em/1.2 Tahoma,Arial, Helvetica, sans-serif;
color:#fff;
margin:0;
padding:0;
border:0;
}
```

Now we need to focus on some of the typography.

Typography

Many of the links will need to be white, so we will define them as such globally and then modify the color for the center column:

```
a:link,a:visited {
text-decoration:underline;
color:#fff;
```

```
}
a:hover {
text-decoration:none;
}
#content60 a:link,#content60 a:visited,#content80 a:link,#content80
a:visited,#content100 a:link,#content100 a:visited {
color:#000;
}
```

The design has a stylize button. We create this using a background image from the comp. It's a thin slice that is tiled horizontally:

```
.button {
border:#000 solid 1px;
background:#fff url(../images/buttonbackground.png) repeat-x;
height:25px;
margin:4px 0;
padding:0 4px;
cursor:hand;
}
```

For tables, such as FAQ, we can add an easy background by repeating the use of the image we used for the teaser. Reusing the image is thematic and also saves on image download, making the pages load faster.

```
.sectiontableheader {
background:url(../images/teaser.png);
padding:5px;
color:#fff;
font:1.2em bold Arial, Helvetica, sans-serif;
}
```

Modules need just a simple redefinition and adjustments to the padding and margins:

```
/* Module styling */
.moduletable {
margin-bottom:1em;
color:#fff;
font-size:1.1em;
}
.moduletable h3 {
font:1.3em Tahoma,Arial,Helvetica,sans-serif;
background:#000;
color:#ccc;
```

```
text-align:left;
margin:0 -10px;
padding:5px 10px;
}
```

Menus, as always, need a lot of CSS style. Here, we keep it as simple as possible. We slice a single image that includes both the bullet and the underline, not that the styling is turned "on" by applying a module suffix of menu to any list of the links that we want this look applied to:

```
/*Menu Styling*/
.moduletablemenu {
margin-bottom:1em;
}
.moduletablemenu h3 {
font:1.3em Tahoma,Arial,Helvetica,sans-serif;
background:#000;
color:#ccc;
text-align:left;
margin:0 -10px;
padding:5px 10px;
}
.moduletablemenu ul {
list-style:none;
margin:5px 0;
}
.moduletablemenu li {
background:url(../images/leftmenu.png) bottom left no-repeat;
height:24px;
font:14px Tahoma,Arial, Helvetica, sans-serif;
margin:10px 0;
padding:0 0 0 10px;
}
.moduletablemenu a:link,.moduletablemenu a:visited {
color:#fff;
display:block;
text-decoration:none;
padding-left:5px;
}
.moduletablemenu a:hover {
text-decoration:none;
color:#fff;
background:#ADADAD;
}
```

Last is the Tab menu at the top right. As an accessibility advocate, we want to set this up so that the tabs will scale as the font is resizing. Fortunately, a technique has been developed to do this; it's actually the same principle we use for our columns, the sliding doors[19] again!

We will also try and do some speed optimization for the template and use just a single image for the left and right side of the "doors," as well as the on and off state. This is known as using *sprites*.[20]

The CSS is not too hard; we just have to fiddle around with the vertical position of the image background for the "on" state:

```css
/*Tab Menu Styling*/
.moduletabletabs {
font:bold 1em Georgia, Verdana, Geneva, Arial, Helvetica, sans-serif;
}
.moduletabletabs ul {
list-style:none;
float:right;
margin:0;
padding:0;
background:#212121;
width:100%;
}
.moduletabletabs li {
float:right;
background:url(../images/tabs.png) no-repeat 0 -4px;
margin:0;
padding:0 0 0 12px;
}
.moduletabletabs a:link,.moduletabletabs a:visited {
float:left;
display:block;
color:#000;
background:url(../images/tabs.png) no-repeat 100% -4px;
text-decoration:none;
margin:0;
padding:7px 18px 5px 9px;
}
.moduletabletabs #current {
background:url(../images/tabs.png) no-repeat 0 -84px;
}
.moduletabletabs #current a {
color:#fff;
```

```
background:url(../images/tabs.png) no-repeat 100% -84px;
}
```

We also need to add the module suffix of `tabs` to the module for the menu we are using.

If you look back at the original design, you notice that there were icons on these tabs. As we are already using two background images, one on the li and one on the link, we would need a third element on which to place the icon background. You could do this by having a span, but this is advanced CSS Jujutsu. I'll leave that as a homework assignment.

The last thing that remains is to revise the `templateDetails.xml` file. It needs to contain all the files and images used in the template so it will install properly as a zip file. There are a number of tools that will do this automatically for you if you are using 1.0.X, but at the time of writing, none are available for 1.5.

Our finished template should look like Figure 9.10.

FIGURE 9.10 Advanced template with typography

> **The Least You Need to Know**
> Creating a production Joomla template is more a question of graphical design and CSS manipulation than some special "Joomla knowledge."

CSSTemplateTutorialStep3

We now have a template based on a comp (or design). Some simple typography has been added, but more importantly, we have created a pure CSS layout that has dynamic collapsible columns and a slick tabbed menu. I have created an installable template that is available from www.joomlabook.com: CSSTemplateTutorialStep3. zip.

Now that we have the basics done, let's start delving into some of the advanced features possible with 1.5 templates.

Advanced Templating Features

Joomla 1.5 offers a number of advanced template features that significantly expand what is possible with templates. We have already seen one example in this chapter, the ability to create custom *chrome* or output for modules.

Let's examine each of these in turn:

- Template Parameters
- Template Overrides

Template Parameters

New in 1.5 is the addition of template parameters for templates. This allows you to pass variables to the template from options selected in the administrative backend.

We can add a relatively simple parameter function to our template. In the `templateDetails.xml` file, add the following:

```
<params>
<param name="template_width" type="list" default="fluid" label="Template Width"
description="Width style of the template">
    <option value="fluid">Fluid with maximum and minimum</option>
    <option value="medium">Medium</option>
    <option value="small">Small</option>
  </param>
</params>
```

You also need a file called `params.ini` in your template folder. It can be a blank file, but Joomla needs this file to store what settings you have. For example, an INI file for the previous example might look like this:

```
template_width=2
```

You need to make sure that this file is writable so changes can be made.

We also need to add that as a file in the `templateDetails.xml` file.

In the Template Manager for that template, you see the settings for the parameter, as shown in Figure 9.11.

FIGURE 9.11 Template parameters in admin backend

We can see that it is a simple drop-down with three options.

```
<param name="template_width" type="radio" default="0" label="Template Width"
description="Change width setting of template">
<option value="0">800x600</option>
<option value="1">1024x756</option>
<option value="2">fluid (min/max with FF and IE7, 80% with IE6)</option>
</param>
```

Then we change the body tag in our `index.php` to the following:

```
<body class="width_<?php echo $this->params->get('template_width'); ?>">
```

We then add the following to the CSS file:

```
body.width_0 div#wrap {
width: 760px;
}
```

```
body.width_1 div#wrap {
width: 960px;
}
body.width_2 div#wrap {
min-width:760px;
max-width:960px;
width:auto !important;
width:960px;
}
#wrap {
text-align:left;
margin:0 auto;
}
```

This gives us three options: a fixed narrow width, fixed wide width, and a fluid version.

Using template parameters in this way can give the site administrator flexibility in almost any facet of a template, width, color, and so on, all controlled with conditional PHP setting CSS styles.

Template Overrides

Perhaps the most powerful new feature of templates in 1.5 is the ability to easily override core output. This is done with new output files called template files that correspond to the layout views of components and modules. Joomla checks in each case to see if one exists in the template folder, and if one does, uses that one and overrides the normal output.

Override Structure

All of the layout views and templates are in the main core in a `/tmpl/` folder. The location is slightly different for components as for modules because modules essentially have only one view. For example

```
modules/mod_newsflash/tmpl/
modules/mod_poll/tmpl/
components/com_login/views/login/tmpl/
components/com_content/views/section/tmpl/
```

The basic structure of all components and modules is View→Layout→Templates.

Table 9.3 shows some examples; note that modules only have one view.

TABLE 9.3 Example overrides

View	Layout	Templates
Category	Blog.php	blog_item.php
		blog_links.php
Category	default.php	default_items.php
	default.php	
(Newsflash module)	horz.php	_item.php
	vert.php	

There are usually several template files involved for a particular layout. They have a common naming convention (see Table 9.4).

TABLE 9.4 Naming convention of overrides

Filename Convention	Description	Example
layoutname.php	The master layout template	blog.php
layoutname_templatename.php	A child layout template called from the master layout file	blog_item.php blog_links.php
_templatename.php	A common layout template used by different layouts	_item.php

Overriding Modules

Each module has a new folder that contains its templates, which is called tmpl. Inside are PHP files that create the output. For example

```
/modules/mod_newsflash/tmpl/default.php
/modules/mod_newsflash/tmpl/horiz.php
/modules/mod_newsflash/tmpl/vert.php
/modules/mod_newsflash/tmpl/_item.php
```

The first three are the three layouts of Newsflash based on which module options are chosen, and the _item.php file is a common layout template used by all three. Opening that file, we find

```php
<?php // no direct access
defined('_JEXEC') or die('Restricted access'); ?>
<?php if ($params->get('item_title')) : ?>
<table class="contentpaneopen<?php echo $params->get( 'moduleclass_sfx' ); ?>">
```

```
<tr>
    <td class="contentheading<?php echo $params->get( 'moduleclass_sfx' ); ?>"
width="100%">
    <?php if ($params->get('link_titles') && $item->linkOn != '') : ?>
        <a href="<?php echo $item->linkOn;?>" class="contentpagetitle<?php
echo $params->get( 'moduleclass_sfx' ); ?>">
            <?php echo $item->title;?>
        </a>
     <?php else : ?>
        <?php echo $item->title; ?>
    <?php endif; ?>
    </td>
</tr>
</table>
<?php endif; ?>


<?php if (!$params->get('intro_only')) :
    echo $item->afterDisplayTitle;
endif; ?>


<?php echo $item->beforeDisplayContent; ?>

<table class="contentpaneopen<?php echo $params->get( 'moduleclass_sfx' ); ?>">
    <tr>
        <td valign="top" colspan="2"><?php echo $item->text; ?></td>
    </tr>
</table>
<?php if (isset($item->linkOn) && $item->readmore) :
    echo '<a href="'.$item->linkOn.'">'.JText::_('Read more').'</a>';
endif; ?>
```

We could change this to remove the tables to make it a little more accessible:

```
<?php // no direct access
defined('_JEXEC') or die('Restricted access'); ?>
<?php if ($params->get('item_title')) : ?>
<div class="contentpaneopen<?php echo $params->get( 'moduleclass_sfx' ); ?>">
    <div class="contentheading<?php echo $params->get( 'moduleclass_sfx' ); ?>">
    <?php if ($params->get('link_titles') && $item->linkOn != '') : ?>
        <a href="<?php echo $item->linkOn;?>"
class="contentpagetitle<?php echo $params->get( 'moduleclass_sfx' ); ?>">
            <?php echo $item->title;?>
        </a>
     <?php else : ?>
```

```php
            <?php echo $item->title; ?>
        <?php endif; ?>
        </div>
</div>
<?php endif; ?>


<?php if (!$params->get('intro_only')) :
      echo $item->afterDisplayTitle;
endif; ?>


<?php echo $item->beforeDisplayContent; ?>

<div class="contentpaneopen<?php echo $params->get( 'moduleclass_sfx' ); ?>">
<?php echo $item->text; ?>
</div>
<?php if (isset($item->linkOn) && $item->readmore) :
      echo '<a href="'.$item->linkOn.'">'.JText::_('Read more').'</a>';
endif; ?>
```

This new file should be placed in the template directory in a folder called `html` as follows:

`templates/templatetutorial15bold/`**`html`**`/mod_newsflash/_item.php`

We just took the tables out of the Newsflash module—as easy as that!

Component Overrides

Components work almost exactly the same way, except there are several views associated with many components.

If we look in the `com_content` folder, we see a folder called `views`.

```
/components/com_content/views/
/components/com_content/views/archive
/components/com_content/views/article
/components/com_content/views/category
/components/com_content/views/section
```

So these folders would match the four possible views for content, archive, article, category, and section.

Inside a view, we find the `tmpl` folder, and in that, the different layouts that are possible.

If we look in the `category` folder, we see

```
/components/com_content/views/category/blog.php
/components/com_content/views/category/blog_item.php
/components/com_content/views/category/blog_links.php
/components/com_content/views/category/default.php
/components/com_content/views/category/default_items.php
```

Note that in the case of `com_content`, the `default.php` layout is referring to the *standard* layout that presents articles as a link list.

Opening up the `blog_item.php` file we see the tables currently used. If we want to override the output, we put what we want to use in our `template/html/` folder, for example:

```
templates/templatetutorial15bold/html/com_content/category/blog_item.php
```

It's a relatively simple process to copy and paste all these views from the `/components/` and `/modules/` folders into the `templates/yourtemplate/html` folder.

The template override functionality provides a powerful mechanism to customize your Joomla site through its template. You can create output templates that focus on SEO, accessibility, or the specific needs of a client.

> **The Least You Need to Know**
> Joomla 1.5 offers new features for templates that allow designers to completely control the code and presentation of a Joomla website.

Tableless Joomla

The Joomla download also contains a template called Beez that is a developed example of the template overrides in action. The Design and Accessibility team have created a full example set of overrides as contained in the `html` folder. Our final example is a template that uses these overrides to remove all tables from the output of Joomla.

CSSTemplateTutorialStep4

We now have a template based on a comp (or design). More visual typography has been added, but more importantly, we have used our pure CSS layout to create a template that has dynamic collapsible columns and a slick tabbed menu. We have then overridden the output of Joomla so that no other tables are used. I have created an installable template that is available from www.joomlabook.com:

CSSTemplateTutorialStep4.zip

Summary

In this chapter, we worked through four examples of templates, each time building the complexity and features.

- Modern websites separate content from presentation using a technology known as Cascading Style Sheets (CSS). In Joomla, the template controls the presentation of the content.

- When creating a template, you have to have Joomla "running" on a server so you can make changes and refresh the page output.

- Creating valid templates should be a path not a goal. The idea is to make your template as accessible as possible, for humans and spiders, not to achieve a badge for valid markup.

- The most basic template simply loads the Joomla modules and mainbody (component). Layout and design are part of the CSS, not Joomla.

- Modern web design uses CSS rather than tables to position elements. It's difficult to learn but worth the investment. There are many (non-Joomla) resources available to help you.

- Joomla will output specific elements, ids, and classes in the code of a web page. These can be predicted and used to style the design using CSS.

- In 1.5, the output of modules can be completely customized, or you can use the pre-built output. All of these options are called module chrome.

- It's best to always use the bulleted or flat list for menu output. You can then make use of many free resources on the Web for the CSS.

- Elements such as columns or module locations can be hidden (or collapsed) when there is no content in them. This is done using conditional PHP statements that are linked to different CSS styles.

- Creating a production Joomla template is more a question of graphical design and CSS manipulation than some special "Joomla knowledge."

- Joomla 1.5 offers new features for templates that allow designers to completely control the code and presentation of a Joomla website.

---

[1] This article at Compass Design helps explain this more: www.compassdesigns.net/tutorials/joomla-tutorials/installing-joomla-doctype-and-the-blank-joomla-template.html

[2] www.upsdell.com/BrowserNews/stat_trends.htm#res

[3] www.compassdesigns.net/joomla-blog/general-joomla/what-makes-a-good-designer.html

[4] www.brainjar.com/css/positioning/

[5] www.clagnut.com/blog/1287/

[6] http://leftjustified.net/journal/2004/10/19/global-ws-reset/

[7] www.thenoodleincident.com/tutorials/typography/template.html

[8] www.stopdesign.com/log/2004/09/03/liquid-bleach.html

[9] www.meyerweb.com/eric/thoughts/2004/09/03/sliding-faux-columns/

[10] http://css.maxdesign.com.au/listamatic/index.htm

[11] http://css.maxdesign.com.au/listamatic/vertical10.htm

[12] http://dev.joomla.org/component/option,com_jd-wp/Itemid,33/p,210/

[13] http://forum.joomla.org/index.php/topic,101825.msg535479.html#msg535479

[14] www.joomlashack.com

[15] http://positioniseverything.net/easyclearing.html

[16] http://www.quirksmode.org/css/clearing.html

[17] http://www.sitepoint.com/blogs/2005/02/26/simple-clearing-of-floats/

[18] http://orderedlist.com/articles/clearing-floats-fne/

[19] www.alistapart.com/articles/slidingdoors/

[20] www.fiftyfoureleven.com/sandbox/weblog/2004/jun/doors-meet-sprites/

Chapter 10

Creating a School Site with Joomla!

School websites tend to be medium to large in size. One of the defining characteristics of Joomla is that it is very powerful and flexible, but can be quite time-intensive to set up. This chapter is an extensive guide to creating and setting up a school website using the Joomla Content management System (CMS).

In this chapter

- Why do we need a school website?

- What features do we need on a school site?

- Where can we get a school template from?

- What is the best way to organize the content structure for a school website?

- What is the relationship between sections and categories and our menu?

- How can I best use the Front Page component?

- What extra functionality can be easily added to the default Joomla installation?

Why Do We Need a School Website?

I actually started my Internet career as a teacher and the technology coordinator for a small school in Vermont almost ten years ago. One of the things I was responsible for, of course, was the school website. When I think of the time and effort that could have been saved had a CMS like Joomla been available back then, it makes me realize how lucky schools are today. I wonder how many realize that such an astonishingly powerful tool to build a website is available virtually free.

A school perhaps is the perfect organization suited for having a comprehensive website. As I have mentioned elsewhere, twentieth-century websites were about one-way communication between the website and the readers. In the twenty-first-century Web 2.0 world, websites need to be about interaction and two-way communication. What makes a school website interesting is that there are very clearly defined stakeholder groups, each with their own needs with respect to this communication.

What is unusual perhaps about a school website is that there is a clearly defined body of content and also different groups you need to get to it. The key to a successful school website is having different paths to this information based on the user group. Let's look at these groups and their needs.

Students

Sometimes students are relegated to a lesser user on a school website. This is a critical mistake, not only because students are the group most invested in the school (it's their education after all), but they also are the group most likely to adopt web technology.

Student's lives frequently revolve around three areas: academics, athletics, and activities. Students need easy access to these areas of the site. There should also be key information that the school wishes to make sure is easy to find, such as guidance help or graduation requirements.

Students are probably primarily consumers of information on the website. As just mentioned, a healthy website should also have mechanisms for interaction.

Teachers and Administrators

A school website can make a huge difference in the way a teacher can communicate and educate. The list is endless. For example, publishing course notes, homework, events, and for the more adventurous (with appropriate security), class grades.

The biggest challenge for teachers is that adding the Web to their toolbox can be overwhelming. Always busy, they need time and help from the IT staff to help them successfully use it. There will be early adopters and those who will probably always struggle, but critical to implementing a successful school website will be a commitment to professional development for the teaching staff.

Parents

The third leg of this stool is the parents. A brief look through research on the topic will tell you that the school that is able to engage the parents into its community is one where the students are more successful. To that end, a website can be a powerful tool.

The initial goal should be to make a website as sticky and useful as possible for the parents. Principal's blog, e-mail news, calendars of events, and student work are only examples of many things that would keep parents coming back to the site. Ultimately the goal is to have parents contributing to the site, initially focusing on early adopters and those already involved, such as parent associations.

> **The Least You Need to Know**
> A website for a large organization, such as a school, needs to meet the needs of diverse groups. This can make organizing its content and functions a challenge.

What Features Do We Need on a School Site?

With over 2000 extensions available on the official Joomla extension site, it's very easy to add everything and the kitchen sink. There are even specialized components for lunch menus! However, a key consideration for a school website is security, but some components are not 100% secure, and care should be taken with which ones are chosen.

What follows is a discussion of potential solutions for common features for a school website. Please bear in mind that this list is not a guarantee of security. School webmasters that are using Joomla should subscribe to the security boards at the official Joomla forum:

http://forum.joomla.org/index.php/board,372.0.html

http://forum.joomla.org/index.php/board,267.0.html

http://forum.joomla.org/index.php/board,296.0.html

In no particular order, a brainstorm of common functionality/extensions might include

- User Registration
- Event Calendar
- Downloadable Documents
- Polls
- Staff Directory
- Email Newsletter
- RSS
- Random Images
- Sitemap

We look at each of these in turn at the end of the chapter, consider options, and then briefly explain a possible solution for each.

Before we get too far ahead of ourselves, let's create a fresh Joomla installation with *no sample content.* The first step will be to install a template.

Downloading and Installing a School Template

At www.joomlashack.com, you can grab a free template that we'll be using in this chapter. It's called Education. It's a relatively simple template with a horizontal drop-down menu, three collapsible columns, and then three equal-height module blocks at the bottom, as shown in Figure 10.1.

You can grab the template from either joomlashack.com or compassdesigns.net.

Got it? Great. You should now have a template zip file that we need to install into Joomla. Go to **Extensions > Install/Uninstall** to get to the Extension Manager. We looked at how extensions are installed and managed in Chapter 6, "Extending Joomla."

We next need to browse to the template zip file and click the Upload File and Install button. We get a message that says, "Install Template: Success." We then need to make this template our default template. This is done through the Template Manager.

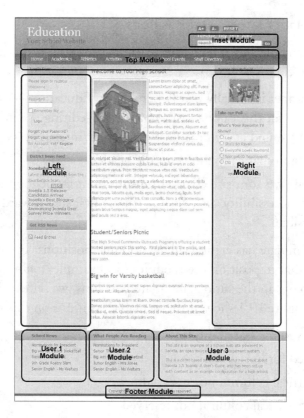

FIGURE 10.1 The Education template

Go to **Extensions > Template Manager** and select the new JS_education template and click the Default button to make it the default template. Viewed in the frontend, our site (empty of content) should look like the screen shown in Figure 10.2.

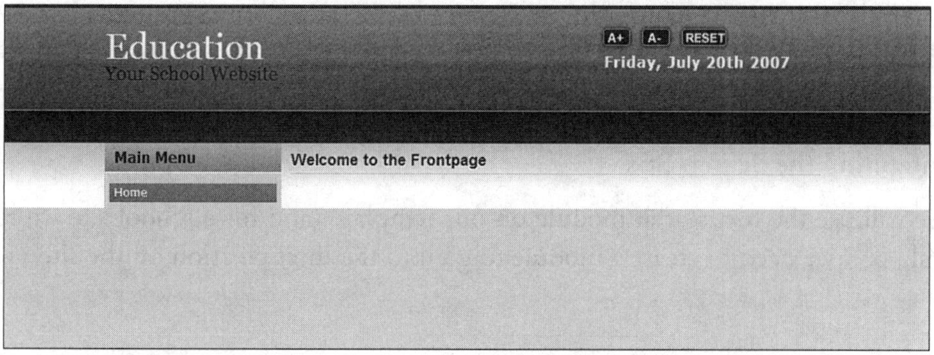

FIGURE 10.2 The Education template empty of content

Education Template Features and Positions

This particular template has three main features, along with the usual functionality such as collapsible columns.

- The logo/header is actually text (where it says Education—Your School Website). The test for this can be easily changed by editing the index.php template file. It can be found at /templates/js_education/index.php.
- The date is automatically shown in the header.
- The template has font size changer buttons built in. Schools are often concerned with accessibility, and this is a simple first step toward making a site more accessible.

The Education template has eight available module positions. In looking at this template, we can see that to position the modules (for example, main menu, login, syndicate, polls, and so on) in the various template positions, we set the Position parameter in each module. Figure 10.1 showed the available positions on this template.

- **inset**: reserved for search module
- **top**: reserved for horizontal menu
- **left**: left vertical column, not reserved
- **right**: right vertical column, not reserved
- **user1**: left column between main content and footer
- **user2**: middle column between main content and footer
- **user3**: right column between main content and footer
- **footer**: footer

Most of these are pretty generic in their potential use. Two, however, were placed with specific locations in mind. The inset module location is really intended for a search box. The top module location is intended for a horizontal navigation.

Configuring the Search Box

If we will use the text search module on our template (and for a school site we really should be), we need to create a module to go into the inset position on the site.

Go to **Extensions > Module Manager > New**. Find the module titled "Search," select it, and click Next.

Give the module a title but make sure the title parameter is set to not show. From the Position parameter drop-down menu, select "inset." In the Module Class Suffix parameter, type a hyphen (or dash) followed by the word "search" so it looks like this "**-search**" without the quote marks. Also enable a search button and use "Go" as the button text. The Module Edit screen for the search module is shown in Figure 10.3.

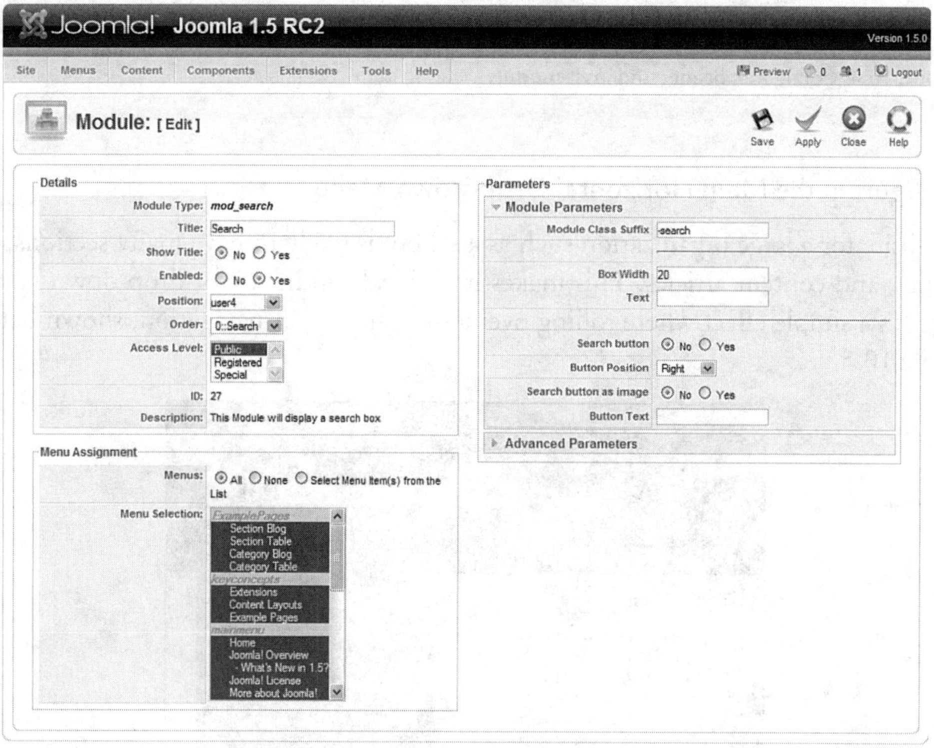

FIGURE 10.3 Search Module Parameters

We add a module suffix to be able to use some specific Cascading Style Sheet (CSS) styles that are targeted at that module suffix.

Save your changes.

The page should now look like the screenshot in Figure 10.4.

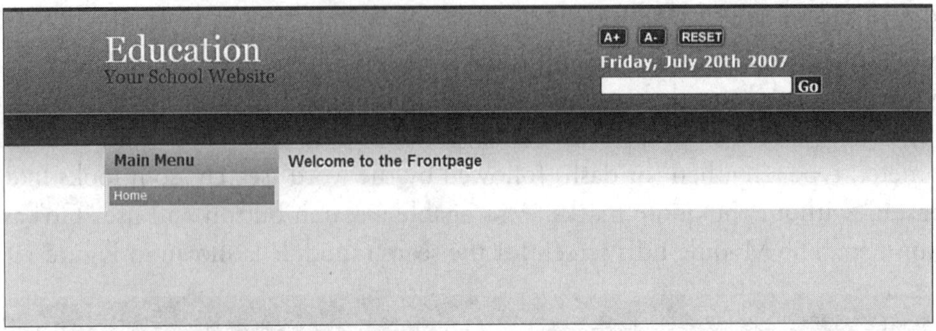

FIGURE 10.4 Configured header and inset module

Configuring the Main Horizontal Drop-down Menu

A website for a large organization such as a school is likely to have many sections, categories, and content articles. This makes it an ideal candidate for drop-down navigation. It's a simple effect where rolling over a link shows sub-navigation, shown here in Figure 10.5.

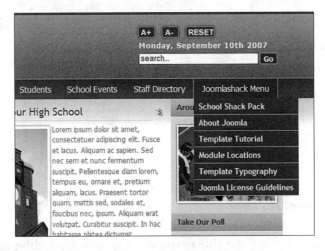

FIGURE 10.5 Example menu drop-down

Many options exist to achieve this effect using JavaScript. However, there are big problems with this approach. JavaScript links are more difficult to navigate if you are not using a browser or have JavaScript turned off. This has big implications for a website's accessibility (viewers using screen readers for example) and for search engine optimization (SEO)/search engine spiders.

It might not seem as if a school website needs to worry about SEO, but they do. Schools would want their content to be well indexed by search engines so that people seeking information can find it easily.

The solution to JavaScript is to use pure CSS to get the same effect. On a screen reader or with JavaScript turned off, these links will look like a simple flat list:

- <u>Academics</u>
  - <u>Science</u>
  - <u>Mathematics</u>
  - <u>Foreign Language</u>
  - <u>History/Social Studies (SS)</u>
  - <u>Fine Arts</u>
  - <u>English</u>

> **The Least You Need to Know**
> A pure CSS drop-down menu, sometimes called a *Suckerfish menu*, is a highly accessible and SEO-friendly way to organize complex navigation.

When Joomla is installed, it starts with the mainmenu and a single home link as shown in Figure 10.4. However, the default location given for it is *left*, so we need to move that module into the correct spot for a horizontal menu as determined by the Education template. In this case it's top.

Go to **Extensions > Module Manager > Main Menu** and change the position to top. While here, we need to set some parameters for our drop-down to work correctly.

- In the Module Parameters, set the Always Show Submenu Items to Yes.
- Set Show Title to No.
- In the Advanced Parameters, make sure the Menu Class Suffix and the Module Class Suffix are both blank.

Configuring the menu as outlined now moves it to the horizontal position and prepares it for drop-downs, as seen in Figure 10.6.

FIGURE 10.6 Horizontal menu with no content

Let's now take a detailed look at perhaps the most important part of setting up a complex site like this, how to set up the site structure—or in terms of Joomla, the sections, categories, and navigation.

Organizing Content on a School Website

It is important that you understand some of the basics of how Joomla organizes its content and the structure it uses. If you haven't already, make sure you read through Chapter 4 "Content is King: Organizing Your Content.".

As previously mentioned the different groups (students, parents, and teachers) represent paths to the same core content of Academics, Athletics, and Activities to a certain extent. There will be much more going on in each user group's area, so this structure will form the core of our school website.

As we think about our site design, we try and use the following principle, which has as its goal to effectively manage a large site with a large number of contributors:

- Each group/person should have a single main page on the site that is his. So whether it's Mr. Hardy's English class, the Guidance Counselor, or the varsity basketball team, we try to have a one-to-one relationship between people and pages.

One of the main reasons to do this is to distribute content generation. This solves two problems: If more people are involved in the content of the site, more people will use the site. Additionally it means that one person, usually the Technology Co-ordinator or Webmaster, is not responsible for generating huge amounts of content. So these roles become gatekeepers, as they should be, rather than whole-site creators/maintainers.

Using the English Department as an example, let's examine how we can set up a page. Our goal is to have a departmental page that shows the various classes/courses, has a link to that departmental page, and shows some news about the department.

In the drill-down, we want to make sure each course has its own page. This enables teachers to have meaningful input into what is on pages that relate to them. Thus, the site organization here is

Section = Academics

Category = English

Page 1 = Freshman English—Mr Hardy

Page 2 = Sophomore English—Mr Stevenson

(and so on...)

Let's set up this single section, category, and the two articles:

1. Go to **Content > Section Manager > New**.

2. Create a section called Academics.

3. Go to **Content > Category Manager > New**.

4. Create a category called English.

5. Go to **Content > Article Manager > New**.

6. Create an article called Freshman English—Mr Hardy and another called Sophomore English—Mr Stevenson. The Article Manager should look like Figure 10.7 (note the section and category columns).

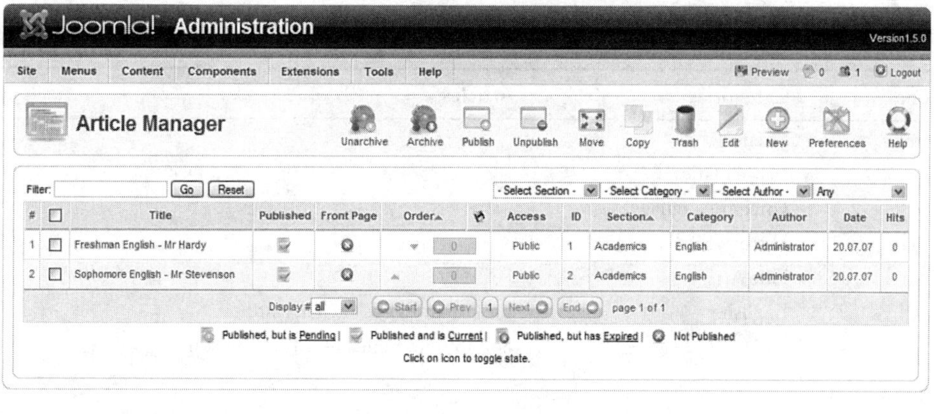

FIGURE 10.7 English Department articles in the Article Manager

It should be easy to see how this structure can be extended to other parts of the site. Here are two more examples—Athletics and Administration:

> Section = Athletics
>
> Category = Basketball
>
> Page 1 = Ninth Grade Girls
>
> Page 2 = Tenth Grade Boys
>
> (and so on...)

> Section = Administration
>
> Category = High School Team
>
> Page 1 = Mrs P Rincipal
>
> Page 2 = Mr V Ice Principal
>
> (and so on...)

NOTE

The articles have to be created in a specific order. The one you want to appear at the top of the page needs to be created first. So for example, for an academic subject you would create first ninth grade then through twelfth. This is important to have the news function properly later.

Let's set up the rest of the content sections and categories. Use Table 10.1 and make sure you select the correct section when you create the categories.

TABLE 10.1 Section/Category content hierarchy

Sections	Categories	Articles
Academics	Science	
	Mathematics	
	Foreign Language	
	History/SS	
	Fine Arts	
	English	Freshman English—Mr Hardy
		Sophomore English—Mr Stevenson

Sections	Categories	Articles
Athletics	Football	
	Volleyball	
	Track and Field	
	Hockey	
	Basketball	
Activities	Community Outreach	
	Band	
	Student Council	
	Yearbook	
	Chess club	
Students	Administration	
	Teachers	
	General Info	
	Guidance	
	FAQs	

This is a complex organization but one that allows a big site like a school to organize its articles. Key to this example is that we have chosen to make a single article be the responsibility of a single individual, whether a teacher or coach.

> **The Least You Need to Know**
> There is always more than one way to organize content. It often helps to decide what the articles will be and then build backwards into categories and sections.

After we have set up all of our sections and categories, the Category Manager should look like Figure 10.8.

Some of the placement of categories might not look immediately obvious, such as the Teachers category in the Students section. I did this because I am considering who wants to find the information. I could have created a section called Staff, but from a navigation point of view, teachers don't need to find out about themselves—they know who they are! They might want to have that information available for another stakeholder, however. In this case I chose Students.

This organizational structure was developed based on two things:

- The concept of trying to have (in so far as possible) one person responsible for one page.

• The sections and categories are chosen based on navigation. (You'll see how this develops in the next section.)

We now need to go and create the rest of the horizontal main menu.

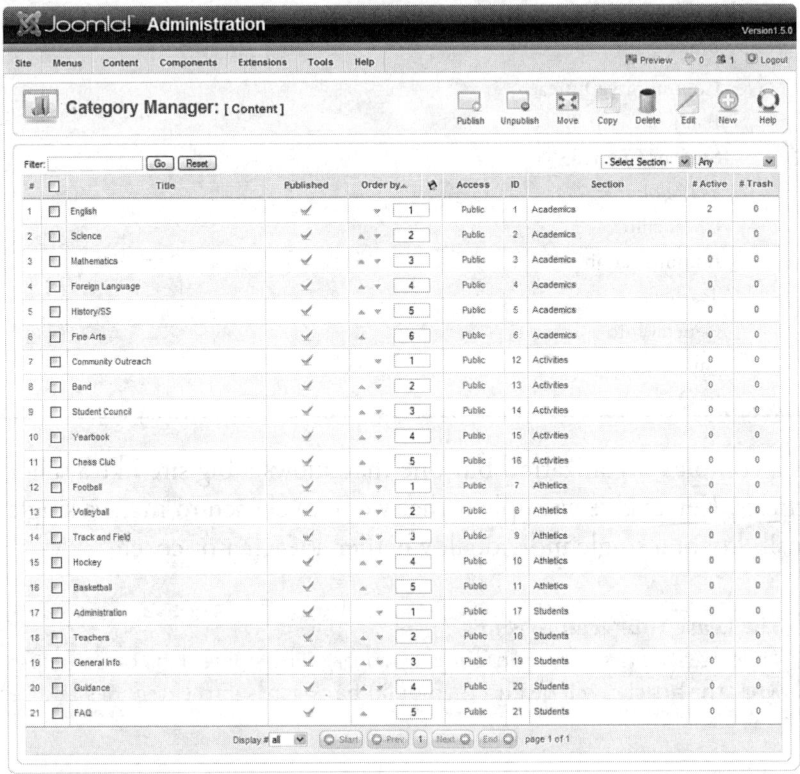

FIGURE 10.8 Completed school sections and categories

Creating the Menus

Our main horizontal navigation menu has links to the sections along the top level and then links to the categories as drop-downs. Let's work through an example to see how to set this up.

Going back to our English department, let's create a link to the Academics section. Go to **Menus > Main Menu > New**.

Create a menu item that links to the Academics sections and call it Academics. This menu item should be a *standard section layout* and link to a page that has a list of all the categories in that section.

> **The Least You Need to Know**
> When creating larger, more complex sites, it's sometimes easiest if the navigation mirrors the sections and categories.

Create a menu item that links to the English category and call it English. This link should be a *category blog layout*. When we create this second link, we need to make sure that its parent item is the Academics menu item we just created.

This shows all the content articles in the English category as a blog, that is, with the introductory text shown and a link to read more. Our mainmenu should now look like Figure 10.9.

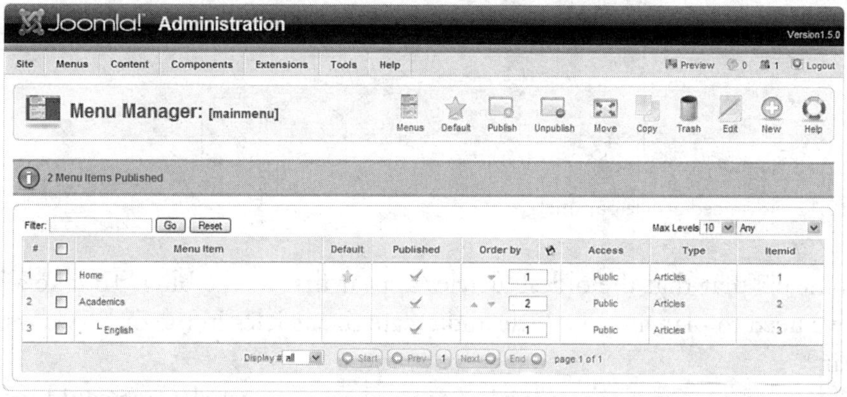

FIGURE 10.9 Example submenu item

It's important that in our link parameters, we have some key settings, shown in Figure 10.10.

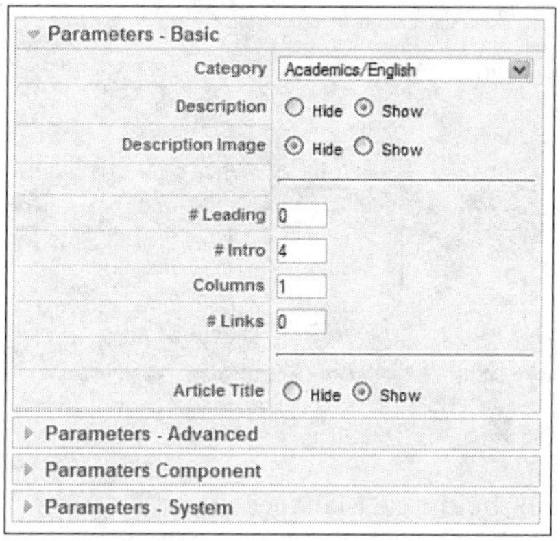

FIGURE 10.10 English menu item parameters

Here we have # Intro set to 4. This means that there will be four articles with the introduction text shown. In our case, for four years of English—the number of classes/courses.

Though we could change it, we only have one column and no articles shown as links. The order is set as oldest first in the Advanced Parameters (shown in Figure 10.11).

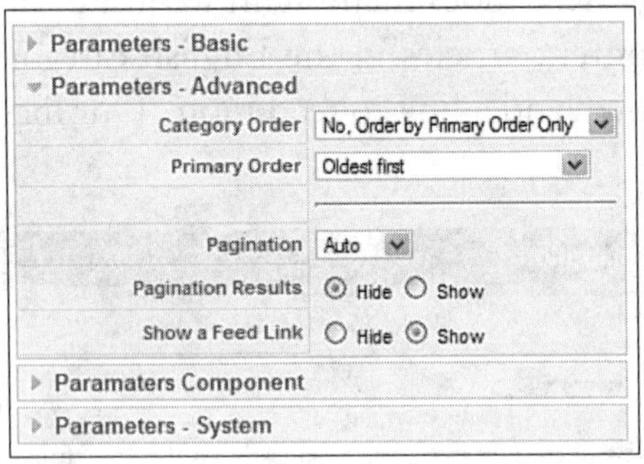

FIGURE 10.11 Advanced article parameters

This means that that the oldest articles appear first in the blog. To take advantage of this, we need to plan ahead a little and create the articles in the order we want them to appear.

If we wanted to have finer control of the order or the articles, we could set the primary order to Ordering and then arrange the articles as we choose in the order column in the Article Manager. The ordering column is circled in Figure 10.12.

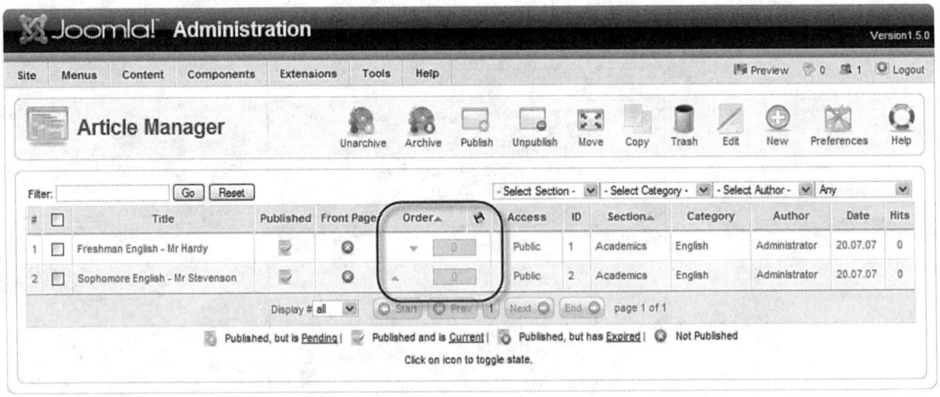

FIGURE 10.12 Ordering articles in the Article Manager

The English category page is shown completed in Figure 10.13.

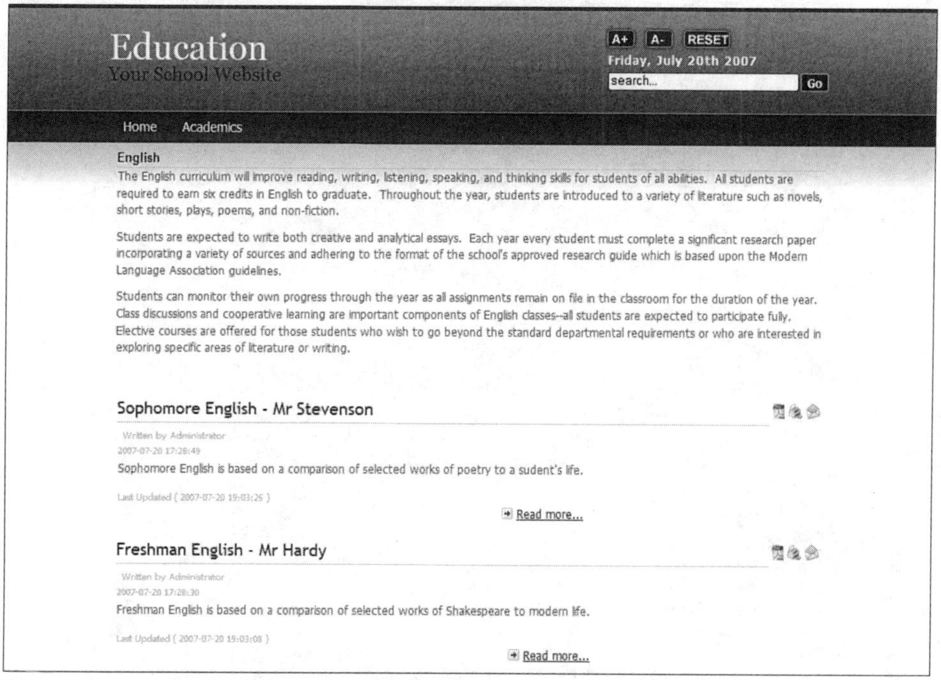

FIGURE 10.13 Screenshot of English department page

The first area of text under the department header, English, is the category description. We are using this so we have content on the page before the course descriptions. This could be as long or as short as needed. This is created by editing the category itself: **Content > Category Manager > English** in this example. An additional step is also required to show it. We need to go to the menu link for this page: **Menu > mainmenu > English** and set Description to Show.

In the same way, we can create menu items that link to each of our sections as standard section layouts and then menu items (with the section as parent) that link to our categories as blog category layouts. After we have done this, our mainmenu should look like Figure 10.14.

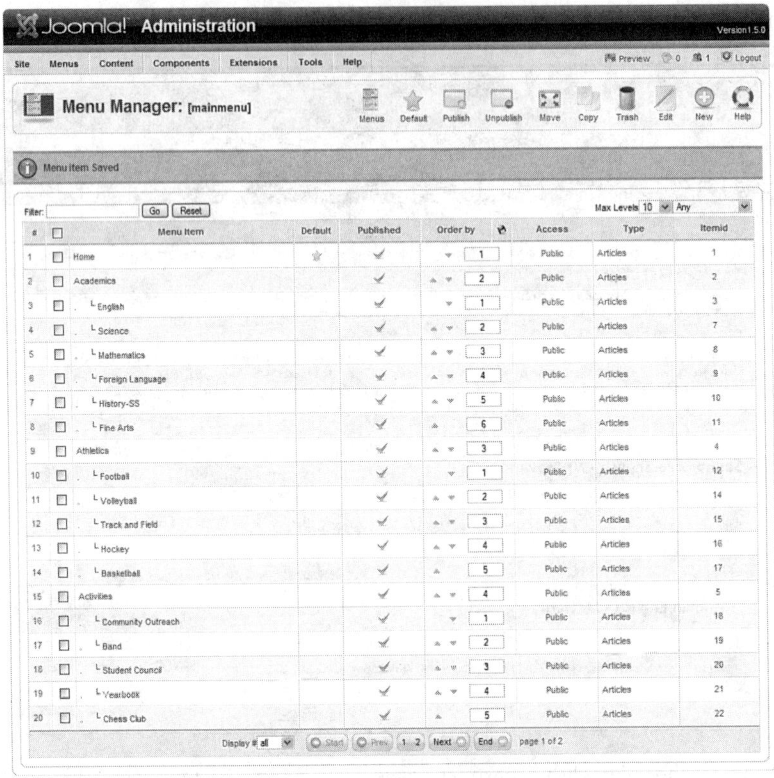

FIGURE 10.14 Development of submenu items in main menu

Building Out Content

Now that we have our sections and categories and links to them in the main menu, we need to start adding some content for our articles.

We'll be making use of that standby of web designer's everywhere, Lorem Ipsum! You have probably seen this text before; it reads something like

> Lorem ipsum dolor sit amet, consectetuer adipiscing elit. Aenean mollis, erat nec ultrices lacinia, tellus lectus lobortis sapien, vel vehicula lacus dolor feugiat magna. Duis sollicitudin malesuada enim. Suspendisse bibendum odio in ante. Mauris mollis auctor enim. Aliquam cursus. Fusce aliquam nonummy dui.

The point of using Lorem Ipsum is that it has a more-or-less normal distribution of letters, as opposed to using "Content here, content here," making it look like readable English. You can generate chunks of this filler text at sites such as www.lipsum.com. From our perspective it means we can quickly create articles with text to build out structure and then go back in to edit it to be more meaningful.

> **The Least You Need to Know**
> Using Lorem Ipsum is a useful technique to create articles that will form the structure of a Joomla site so you can check the navigation for it as you go along. The pages/articles can be edited later.

For each category, create an article and add some Lorem Ipsum as the text.

Creating Subnavigation

A site such as a school will have many articles, and we should have plenty of pathways for site visitors to drill down to that content. To achieve this we use the left-hand column to place some links of increasing specificity down the page.

The concept is to have the most general links at the top; these would be ones that link to other categories in the current section.

Looking at the basic page again, in this example of the English department, we've actually carefully chosen what is in the left column, shown here in Figure 10.15.

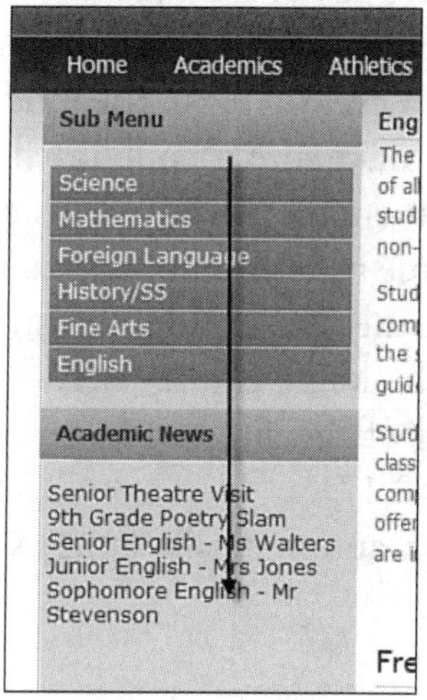

FIGURE 10.15 Eye tracking of visitor on the left column

The top menu, "Academics," contains links to all the departments.

The next module shows links to articles that are new in the Academics section. This means from a hierarchical point of view, these links are the next level down from the Academics menu.

The effect of this for the site visitor is seeing a continuum of information starting from a broad level and going down to a narrow one (as shown by the arrow). Studies that track eye movement on websites have shown that a visitor will tend to start in the top left, so the movement of the eye down the page matches a changing organization from broad and narrow. A technique like this is important for usability.

Let's look at each of those modules in turn.

Academics Submenu

As shown in Figure 10.15, the goal is to have a submenu at the top of the left column that shows links to all the other categories that are in that section. For each section you are in, the submenu should change to reflect that.

Fortunately, this is easier than it sounds. All we have to do is create a copy of the mainmenu and then set it to show sublevels only (as we just defined a few paragraphs earlier). Joomla figures out which section we are in and automatically shows the correct categories.

First let's make a copy of the Main Menu. In the Module Manager (**Extensions > Module Manager**), select the checkbox for the mainmenu module and then click Copy. Then open the module we just created to edit it.

We now need to change the name (to Sub Menu).

Set the Start Level and End Level to "1" in the module parameters. This will show only the sublevel menu items. Make sure it's published in the left location.

Select only the menu assignment for the pages we want the module to appear on (in this case everything but the home page). To do this, we click the Select From List radio button and we are able to click the menu selection list.

The edited module should look like Figure 10.16.

The result on the frontend of the site can be seen if we navigate to the English department, shown in Figure 10.17.

Notice how the left column automatically appears and the main column shrinks when we put content there.

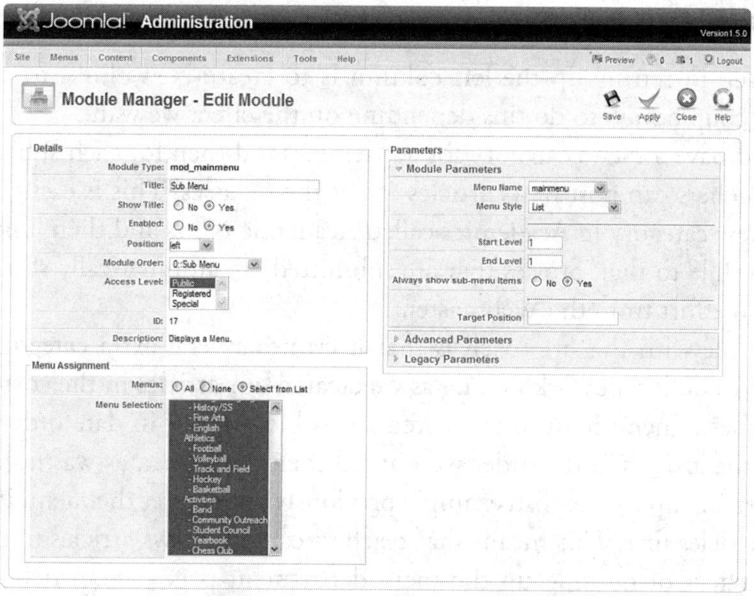

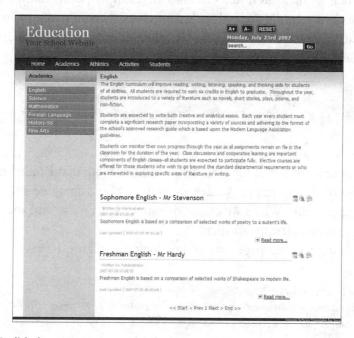

FIGURE 10.16 Module parameters for the submenu

FIGURE 10.17 English department page with left-column submenu

Creating News Links for a Section

Our next step in setting up the left column is to create News links to that section. There are a couple ways to do this depending on the effect we want.

We could have a News category for academics (and then for each subject)—somewhere all teachers can post news articles about their classes. This is easily achieved by creating a new category in Academics called Academic News and then linking our latest news module to that. Stories that are submitted are automatically shown dynamically with no effort from the Webmaster.

The trouble with this approach is that it creates several extra categories. A more elegant way to do it will work as long as we created our articles in the correct order.

You can set a menu item to show items in a blog layout in date order. As long as we created the articles in the order we wanted them to appear, as was noted when we described setting up the English example previously, we can set the menu item to show the oldest articles first. This means that teachers can add news articles to their categories without fear of messing up the main department page. The articles are hidden because we are only showing four.

We could then set up a latest news module that simply points to the Academics section. Then the most recently created or modified article would appear in the list.

Create a latest news module for the Academics section (**Extensions > Module Manager > New > Latest News**), shown in Figure 10.18.

> **TIP**
> Print out your section and category managers so you can easily reference the IDs.

Make sure the module is assigned only to that section.

Create latest news modules for each other section. Note that I called my latest news module for the students section Academic News. I could imagine that global school news might appear here. When we create this module let's also add the home page to its menu assignment so it appears there.

The English department page would now look like Figure 10.19.

> **The Least You Need to Know**
> Deep sites with many content articles need to provide several opportunities (subnavigation and links) for site visitors to find that content.

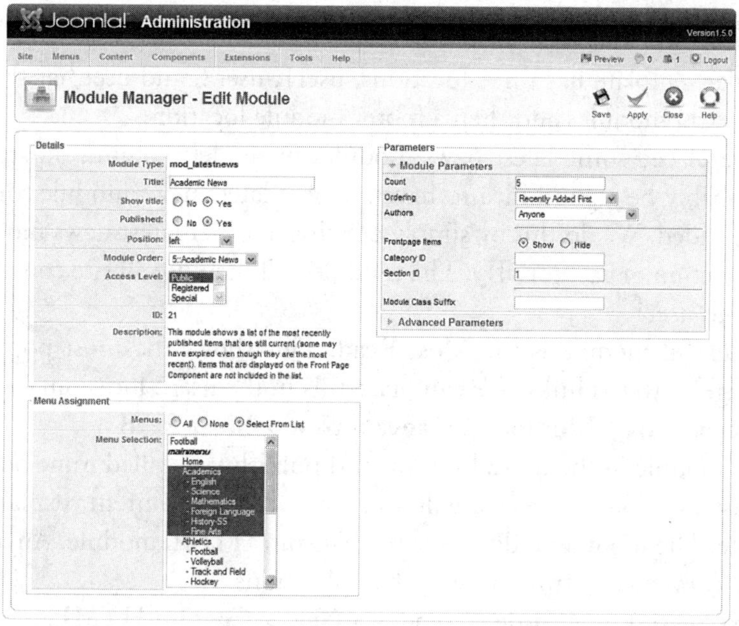

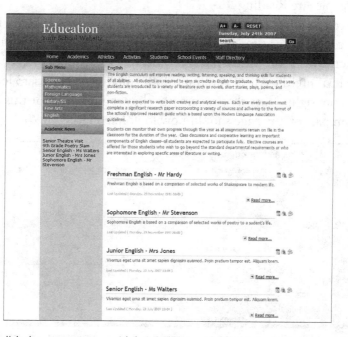

FIGURE 10.18 Latest news module parameters

FIGURE 10.19 English department page with latest news module added

Setting Up the Footer

This particular template has three locations, user1, user2, and user3 at the bottom of the page for extra modules and then a footer module location.

Earlier we placed some latest news modules in the left column on specific pages. It would probably be a good idea to have a global latest news module for all content that is being added. We do this by simply creating another latest news module but not specifying a section or category ID. The module will then use all site content. Let's put that module in user1.

Another useful module is the Most Read. This shows the most popular content (based on page views) as links. We can place this in the user2 location.

Go to **Extensions > Module Manager > New > Most Read**.

Place the module in the user2 location and publish it. I called mine School News.

In the last location, user3, we will add some custom content, explaining a little about the site. The module to do this is the Custom HTML module. Anything can be placed in here, even code from other web applications.

Go to **Extensions > Module Manager > New > Custom HTML**.

Add some text into the editor and publish the module to the user3 location. I called mine What People Are Reading.

Next we need to add a footer. This is simply just another Custom HTML module with relevant content, this time published in the footer module location.

Go to **Extensions > Module Manager > New > Custom HTML**.

Add some text into the editor and publish the module to the user3 location. I called mine Footer Copyright. Note that we are not showing the title for this module.

The bottom part of our page should now look like Figure 10.20.

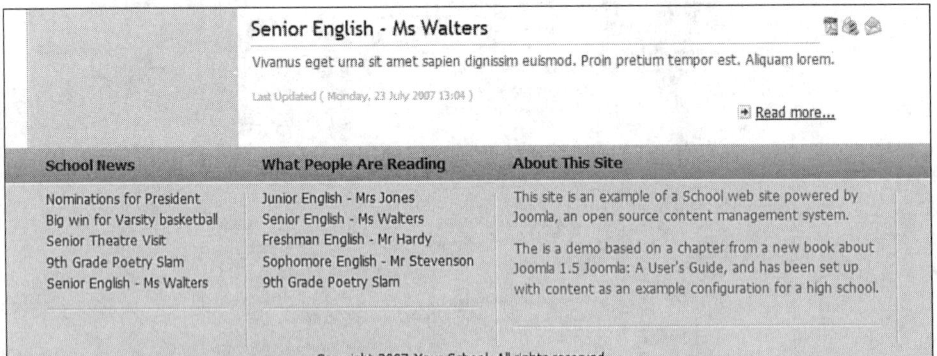

FIGURE 10.20 Setting up the bottom module blocks

So now we have a site that has a robust content organization and a rich network of links to find that content. Let's move on and do a little more with our home page...it's a bit blank.

Setting Up the Home Page

The home page for a school site should follow a portal type concept. As previously mentioned, there are various stakeholder groups in a school, so the home page needs to have a little something for everyone.

A school site, as an example of a large organization, is an ideal candidate for using the FrontPage component. As we saw in Chapter 5 "Creating Menus and Navigation," the Front Page component allows the Webmaster to select articles from anywhere on the site and post them to the home page, which allows him to take the role of content manager rather than content producer.

> **TIP**
> Even though the Front Page Manager does the work, an organization should still develop a policy of how content will be created and published to the home page.

First, let's create an uncategorized article that will be the first article shown on the home page. Go to **Content > Article Manager > New**.

Create an article suitable for the home page and make it uncategorized for its section and category (we can also add an image, as we've done here). Also make sure it is published to the Frontpage.

Now if we go to our Article Manager, we can pick out a couple articles to appear on the home page along with our main welcome article.

Go to **Content > Article Manager**. Publish a couple of the articles to the Front Page by clicking on the icons in the Front Page column in the Article Manager.

We now need to make sure the articles are in the order in which we want them to appear. We can adjust this in the Front Page Manager.

Go to **Content > Front Page Manager**. Adjust the order using the up/down arrows until the Welcome to Your High School article (the uncategorized one) is listed first. The Front Page Manager should look like Figure 10.21.

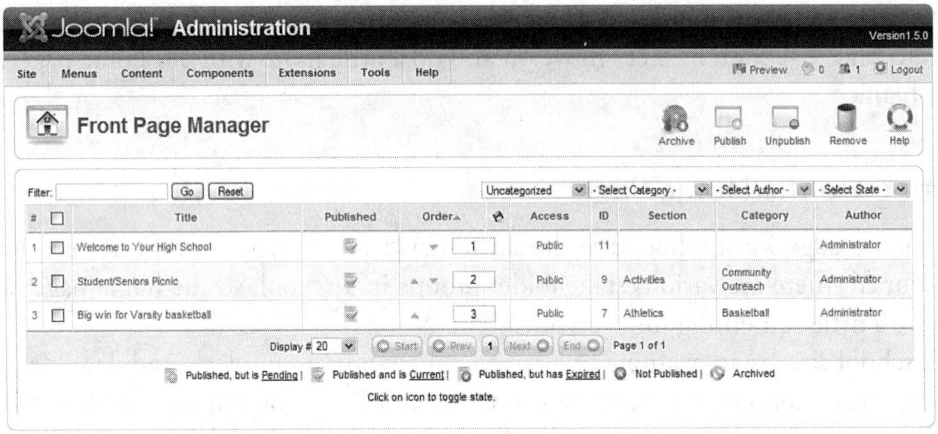

FIGURE 10.21 Front Page Manager

Last, we want to modify the menu item parameters. Go to **Menus > mainmenu > Home**. In the Basic Parameters, we should set the following:

Leading = 0

Intro = 4

Columns = 1

Links = 10

In the Advanced Parameters, the Category Order should be set to Ordering and Pagination to Hide.

In the Component Parameters we set the Author name, Created date, and the email/PDF/print icons to Hide. In the system parameters we also set the title to Hide. The home page should now look like Figure 10.22.

Depending on our needs, we could leave the home page as it is. We will be adding some useful modules to the left and right columns as we look at how we can add functionality to the site through core Joomla extensions and third-party add-ons.

> **The Least You Need to Know**
> The Joomla Front Page component is an excellent way for a site to manage its home page content when there are several individual contributors.

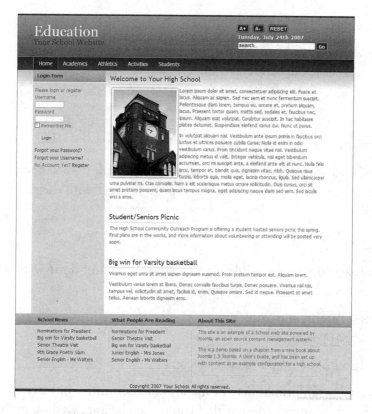

FIGURE 10.22 Completed front (home) page

Adding Basic Functionality to a School Website

At the beginning of this chapter, we brainstormed a list of possible functionality we would like our site to have. At the time of writing, the 1.5 version of Joomla is still in Beta, so many third-party developers are still working to update their extensions from 1.0.X to 1.5. For the purposes of considering our school website, we will look at resources for 1.0.X. Where possible, I'll give more than one alternative so you can use whichever you need based on their update timeline to 1.5.

Let's examine each one in turn and see what options are available.

User Registration

One of the most powerful features of Joomla is that it allows several layers of permission. At the most basic, these are

- Guests
- Users
- Administrators

When setting up a school website, we need to think a little about the needs and size of the school and how we want these user groups to interact with the site. Let's look at a few examples.

A Small School

If we have a few people responsible for adding content and don't want much student interactivity, we might use the following structure:

- Guests = Parents and Students
- Users = Teachers
- Administrators = Webmaster

This structure allows information to be made available only to the teachers. It would also allow them to easily submit content that could then be approved by the Webmaster.

A Medium-sized School

If we want to get more involvement from students in the site, we might move them up a level:

- Guests = Parents
- Users = Teachers and Students
- Administrators = Webmaster

This structure allows more involvement and interaction between the teachers and students behind a private, registered security wall. For example, teachers and students could collaborate on assignments and then submit content that could then be approved by the Webmaster.

A Large School

If we want to have significant involvement from all stakeholders in the school community, we might use

- Guests = Public
- Users = Students, Teachers, Parents
- Administrators = Webmaster

This structure is one that intends to leverage the website to increase communication between all the groups. It opens the door for projects such as a student digital portfolio that can be shared privately online with parents, teachers, and peers.

Note that to illustrate the differences, I have used the size of the school as a delineator. We could just as easily replace this with "Desire to adopt web technology."

As you can see there is a philosophical decision here as well as a technical one. For now let's add a login module to the home page.

Go to **Extensions > Module Manager > New > Login**. Create a login module and set it to be assigned to the Home menu item only.

Events Calendar

JCal Pro (developed by Anything-Digital.com) is an excellent choice for a calendar. You can download it at extensions.joomla.org/component/option,com_mtree/ task,viewlink/link_id,1401/Itemid,35/ or from the developer website.

Figure 10.23 is from a demo of the 1.0.X version of Joomla.

Once the component is installed, we can add a link to it in the mainmenu (**Menus > mainmenu > New > Component**), which leads to a full-page calendar, shown in Figure 10.23.

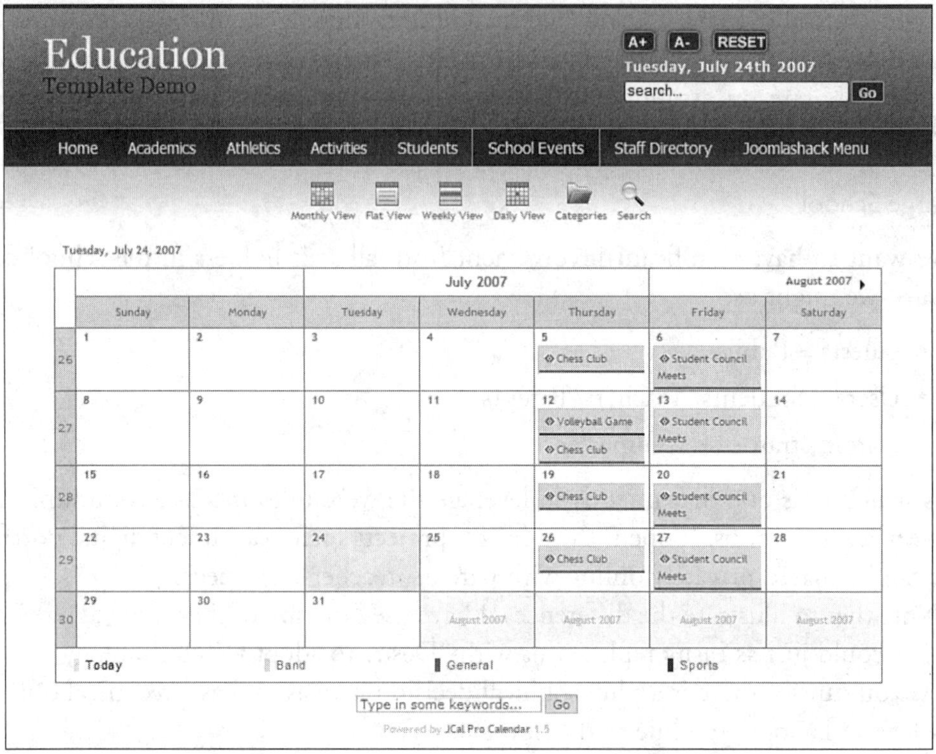

FIGURE 10.23 Full page display of JCalPro

Downloadable Documents

A school website is likely to have many documents that might be in PDF form available for easy downloading. Examples might include:

- Course descriptions
- Meeting minutes
- Hard copy of newsletter
- Hard copy of forms
- Student work (digital portfolio perhaps)

An excellent extension for Joomla that gives the potential for document management is ReMOSistory, which Martin Brampton (et al) developed. You can download

ReMOSistory at extensions.joomla.org/component/option,com_mtree/task,viewlink/
link_id,83/Itemid,35/ or from the developer website, www.remository.com/.

Polls

Basic poll functionality is built into the default installation of Joomla. There is nothing
more to do here than craft the questions and post the poll to the pages you want it to
be on through the module settings.

Remember that you can make multiple polls so that each area can have its own.

Let's create a new poll and publish the module for it to the home page in the right-
hand column. Go to **Components > Polls** and enter the title and some questions.
Next we need to create a module to collect the votes. Go to **Module Manager > New >
Poll**.

Publish the module to the home page right–hand column and select the poll you
just created in the module parameters.

Staff Directory

For medium-sized to small schools, this is probably most easily achieved through the
core Joomla contacts component. First we need to create contacts and associate them
with users.

Go to **Components > Contacts > Categories > New**. Create a category called
Staff.

To do the next step, it's easiest if we have already asked the staff to register on the
site. We need to create contacts, and for each one, associate him/her with the appropriate registered user.

We can then create a menu item that will link to our contacts component.

Go to **Menus > mainmenu > New > Contacts > Contact Category Layout**.

This creates a link to the category we just created, forming an instant staff directory
(shown in Figure 10.24). It is possible to create a content article to hold this information. But doing it this way has the advantage that the task of creating/editing the
content is passed onto the staff themselves, reducing the burden on the Webmaster to
type everyone's name in.

For larger schools, you might want to consider using a more complete directory
component. There are a few available; my recommendation would be Mosets Tree
available at www.mosets.com. It's priced (at time of writing) at $99.

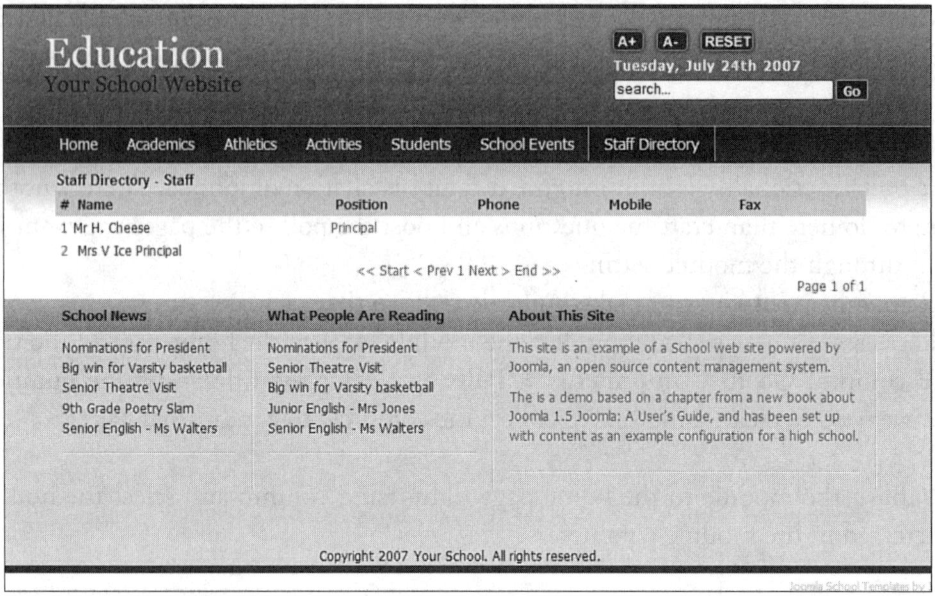

FIGURE 10.24 Default Joomla directory/contacts component

Email Newsletter

An email newsletter is a very important part of the school website. Schools often push out newsletters to stakeholder groups, students, teachers, or parents. Being able to migrate this traditional paper-based communication to electronic e-mail can mean big cost savings for the school.

Two basic Joomla email components are Acajoom or YaNC. If we need to do lots of segmentation (for example, because we have several lists based on athletics or clubs), we might need something with robust segmenting, like J!Contact.

- **YaNC** (developed by Adam van Dongen). Download from extensions.joomla. org/component/option,com_mtree/task,viewlink/link_id,172/Itemid,35/ or the developer website joomla-addons.org.

- **Acajoom** (developed by Joobi). Download from extensions.joomla.org/ component/option,com_mtree/task,viewlink/link_id,964/Itemid,35/ or the developer website acajoom.com.

- **J!Contact** (developed by joomlashack.com). Download from the developer website.

Once a suitable newsletter has been installed, we can publish a module containing the signup to our home page (and on any other pages we want it to appear).

RSS

Another tremendously useful feature of Joomla is its ability to work with Real Simple Syndication (RSS).

Joomla has two main functions. One is that it can provide an RSS from content from the website; second, it can display RSS feeds from other places.

In the demo, we have the Syndication button on the home page in the left column. In Joomla, RSS syndication comes from content that is in the page that is published. To provide content from other categories deeper in the site, a third-party component has to be used. For our purposes, the target audience is probably site visitors that want to use RSS to get the latest news. For that, syndication of the home page only is adequate.

Let's create an RSS syndication module. Go to **Extensions > Module Manager > New > Syndicate**.

Give the module a name and publish it to the left column with a Home menu item assignment.

Displaying an RSS feed provides interesting possibilities for a school site. Imagine a scenario of a school district with perhaps half a dozen schools in it. Each school and the school district itself could have a website, maybe even powered by Joomla, and each site could provide RSS feeds to be published on the others. So an example of what this might look like would be a school website showing news from the district's website—all automatically without any extra effort needed.

On our demo site, we show the feed capability not with the RSS feed that loads in the main column, but a small module feed that loads in the left column. To demonstrate how it loads links, I have linked the feed to Joomlashack.com. The module then appears as shown in Figure 10.25.

These links are all generated dynamically. If the news changes on the other website, these links are automatically updated.

FIGURE 10.25 Example of RSS newsfeed in a module

Random Image

A school is likely to have many images generated by its community, from photos to student art work. A great way to share these is with Joomla's random image module. The module randomly displays an image taken from a designated directory.

Go to **Extensions > Module Manager > New > Random Image**. Give the module a name and publish it to the right-hand column and assign it to the Home menu item.

Sitemap

A sitemap is a very important part of the website, especially a larger one like a school. Usually it contains links to all pages that are in the website.

To generate this by hand would be monstrously time-consuming, but again this is where the dynamic nature of a CMS like Joomla saves the day. An excellent third-party sitemap is available as an extension: Joomap.

Joomap was developed by Daniel Grothe, and you can download it from /extensions.joomla.org/component/option,com_mtree/task,viewlink/link_id,202/ Itemid,35/ or from the developer website http://www.koder.de/joomap.html.

As shown in Figure 10.26, Joomap produces a sitemap. (Figure 10.26 is from a demo of the 1.0.X version of Joomla.)

FIGURE 10.26 A sitemap created by the Joomap extension

A menu item needs to be added to link to the sitemap.

Now that we have extended some of the basic functionality, our home page is now a much richer experience for the site visitor, as shown in Figure 10.27.

> **The Least You Need to Know**
>
> Even a site heavily based on content has to have interactive functionality to make the visitor's experience richer. Without this, visitors have little motivation to return.

FIGURE 10.27 Home page with newsletter, polls, RSS feeds, and syndicate

Extending the School Website Beyond the Basics

If you want to extend your Joomla-powered school website, we have set up a forum at joomlashack.com especially for school Webmasters to meet and swap ideas and get help with problems.

Registration is free, and you can find it at http://www.joomlashack.com/community/index.php/board,74.0.html. There are also some specific Joomla extensions especially for schools at the Joomla extension site (extensions.joomla.org/component/option,com_mtree/task,listcats/cat_id,1852/Itemid,35/), such as the following:

- Joomla LMS
- E-Portfolio component for Joomla
- School Lunch Menu Component

User's Guide Chapter 10 Demo Site

A demo of this site is available at www.joomlabook.com. It is an exact copy of what you should have if you follow all the steps in this chapter. You can log in to the administrative backend so you can see the site framework and the sections, categories, and menus that were set up.

Summary

In this chapter we looked at using Joomla to develop a large site that would have several contributors, like a school, and that needs to organize its content and extensions to produce a site that meets multiple needs. We saw that

- A website for a large organization, such as a school, will need to meet the needs of diverse groups. This can make organizing its content and functions a challenge.

- A pure CSS drop-down menu, sometimes called a Suckerfish menu, is a highly accessible and SEO-friendly way to organize complex navigation.

- There is always more than one way to organize your content. It often helps to decide what the articles would be and then build backwards into categories and sections.

- When creating larger, more complex sites, it's sometimes easiest if the navigation mirrors the sections and categories.

- Using Lorem Ipsum is a useful technique to create articles that will form the structure of a Joomla site so you can check the navigation for it as you go along. The pages/articles can be edited later.

- Deep sites that have several content articles need to provide many opportunities (subnavigation and links) for site visitors to find that content.

- The Joomla Front Page component is an excellent way for a site to manage its home page content when there are several individual contributors.

- Even a site heavily based on content has to have interactive functionality to make the visitor's experience richer. Without this, the visitors have little motivation to return.

Chapter 11

Creating a Restaurant Site with Joomla!

This chapter looks at the entire process of creating a small business website, in this case for a restaurant, from scratch. Starting from a needs analysis, this chapter shows you how to organize possible content all the way through adding photos and considering further extensions.

In This Chapter

- Why do small businesses like restaurants need websites?

- What website features does a restaurant need?

- How can I organize my content?

- What's the easiest way to build the content of my site?

- How should I set up the navigation of a restaurant site?

- How should I set up the home page of a restaurant site?

- Where can I get quality photos?

- How can I extend the functionality of my restaurant site?

Why Does a Restaurant Need a Website?

A restaurant is an excellent example of a business website that needs to communicate its brand and business information. These type websites are often called *brochure websites*. They function as brochures but from an online platform.

As I have discussed elsewhere in the book, the standards for websites are changing. Visitors are becoming increasingly less apt to accept (and visit) sites where the content rarely changes, and they want to be able to interact with sites.

The example of a restaurant is a good one for us to generalize. It represents any small business that has relatively fixed content but wants to add enough interactivity to be able to make the site interesting and worth revisiting. For a restaurant, this means regularly updating menus and event information.

Ultimately, the example of a restaurant in this chapter represents a baseline for all small businesses today. The question is not, "Why does a restaurant want a website?" Rather, the question should be, "How can I make a professional site that's easy to update and very extendable?"

> **The Least You Need to Know**
> The modern business must have a Web presence that communicates its brand and information about the company.

Enter the modern Content Management System (CMS).

What Features Does a Restaurant Website Need?

Most restaurants have a number of key facets they need to communicate through their websites. Most visitors will want to know one of five things:

- Menus
- Specials/News
- Hours
- Directions
- Contact Information

All five of these can easily be handled with the core default Joomla installation.

With usually rather small websites, most restaurants are unlikely to need many additional third-party extensions to add functionality. As just discussed, a key function for a restaurant website is the ability to add and change content, such as menus, frequently and to provide PDF printouts of menus. Both of these are core features of Joomla out of the box.

> **The Least You Need to Know**
> The key features needed for a small business site are taken care of by a default Joomla install: easily edited content and flexible menu configuration.

One of the most powerful things about Joomla is the ability to easily add functionality as the site grows and needs updated.

Several restaurant owners identified several "nice to have" extensions they would like to see for their sites:

- **An Image Gallery**. An important part of a restaurant's branding is the imagery present in its décor and food. Being able to provide an image gallery of these would be a useful tool in projecting that brand onto the Web.

- **Calendar**. Many restaurants have various events, such as bands or tastings held at their venues. Although this could easily be presented through content articles, more control and ease of management would be possible with a calendar component.

- **Email Newsletters**. Any business that has a Web presence needs to include email marketing in its mix of customer communication. For restaurants, this can be a very timely way to drive virtual traffic to their sites and foot traffic to the restaurants. Combined with the tradition of specials, it's easy to set up customer loyalty programs where regulars can be emailed offers to return. This has become a very common practice.

- **Google Maps**. Directions are OK, but a map is so much better. You'll find that many websites use Google maps to provide some sort of geographic data. This kind of option increases the ease of the visitor (to the site and the restaurant) experience.

As we work to develop a restaurant website, we incorporate the basic functionality we need, and we also take a look at how we might add some of these "nice to have" features.

First, we need to find a decent looking template that a restaurant can use.

Downloading and Installing a Restaurant Template

At www.joomlashack.com (or compassdesigns.net), you can grab the free template we use in this chapter. It's called Ready To Eat. It's a relatively simple template with a horizontal menu, a single large column, and then three equal height module blocks at the bottom, as shown in Figure 11.1.

FIGURE 11.1 Ready To Eat template

Downloaded the template yet? Great. We should now have a template zip file to install into Joomla:

1. Go to **Extensions > Install/Uninstall** to get to the Extension Manager. We looked at how extensions are installed and managed in Chapter 6, "Extending Joomla."

2. Next we browse to the template zip file and click the Upload File and Install button. We get a message that says, "Install Template: Success." We then need to make this template our default. This is done through the Template Manager.

3. Go to **Extensions > Template Manager** and select the new Ready To Eat template and click the Default button to make it the default template. Viewed in the frontend, the site (with no content) should look like Figure 11.2.

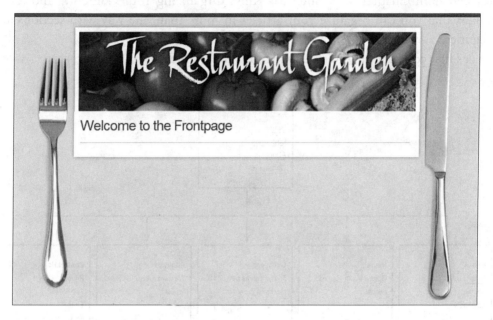

FIGURE 11.2   Ready To Eat template empty of content

The Ready to Eat template has three main features:

- The header image can be used as the logo header for the site. The image can be easily replaced by any 638px×155px image. To do this, we simply replace the file /templates/js_ready_to_eat/images/header.png with one of our own.

- The two images (here, the fork and knife) are equally as easy to replace. (Maybe you need chopsticks to fit the restaurant theme!) These are the images: /templates/js_ready_to_eat/images/fork.png and /templates/js_ready_to_eat/images/knife.png.

- The three bottom columns, designed for modules, use some javascript to give the containing `divs` equal height.

Now that the template is installed, let's add content. As we have already seen, it's best to first create the sections and categories and then to create the menus/navigation that link to them.

Organizing the Content on a Restaurant Website

This example restaurant site will not have many pages. Before going any further, go back and skim Chapter 4, "Content Is King: Organizing Your Content," and revisit the idea that you can organize your articles in more than one way with sections and categories.

Let's first consider our sitemap, which is shown in Figure 11.3.

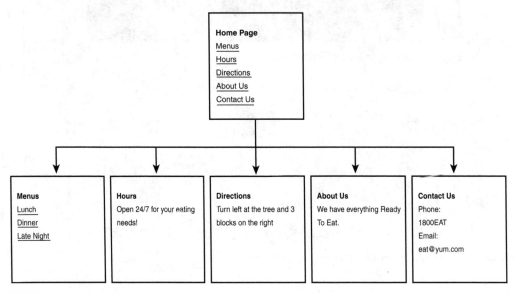

FIGURE 11.3 A simple restaurant sitemap

As we saw in Chapter 4, there is always more than one way to organize articles. The main thing to consider is what will be the basic content building block of the site? What is the article?

Looking at this example for the menus, we need to think about how this would be structured. Let's consider the following two different examples.

Content Level	Example 1	Example 2
Section	Menus	Content
Category	Lunch Dinner Late Night	Menus
Article	A Lunch Menu A Dinner Menu A Late Night Menu	Lunch Dinner Late Night

In Example 1, there would be a redundant layer in the hierarchy. We touched on this problem in Chapter 4. The redundant layer is not there in Example 2, but the section used is a bit global and unspecific.

The decision comes down to asking, "Will there be any other articles at the menu level or deeper?" For example, if we have lunch menus for different days of the week or a drill-down that provides information about a specific menu item (that's as in what the chicken salad looks like, not a Joomla menu item), then we should plan for that and use a structure that can grow. This is reflected in Example 1 of the table.

If we do not expect much growth to occur in this content area, only the ongoing revision (changing the menu listings), then a simpler structure can be used—Example 2.

For the purpose of this chapter, I'll assume that the restaurant owner is more interested in a simple structure that's easy to update (Example 2), rather than a more complex one that would call for several articles (Example 1).

With this assumption in mind, let's build the site with the following structure.

Sections	Categories	Articles
Content	Menus	Menus* Lunch Dinner Late Night
	About	About Us* Directions Hours
	Specials	Lunch Specials Dinner Specials Late Night Specials
	Reviews	Review 1 Review 2

Here are a couple points about this organization:

- The articles with asterisks are needed to hold content for the "top level" of the menu. This probably doesn't make sense right now, but will in a few pages!
- The sitemap in Figure 11.3 didn't have any specials or reviews included. We will use these categories to hold articles we'll use in modules. That will make more sense in about 10 pages!

> **The Least You Need to Know**
> A small website does not need a detailed section/category structure. Often just a single section can be used for all of the content articles.

Let's set up the structure. First, we go to the Section Manager (**Content > Section Manager**) and create a single section called Content. After saving, the Section Manager should look like Figure 11.4.

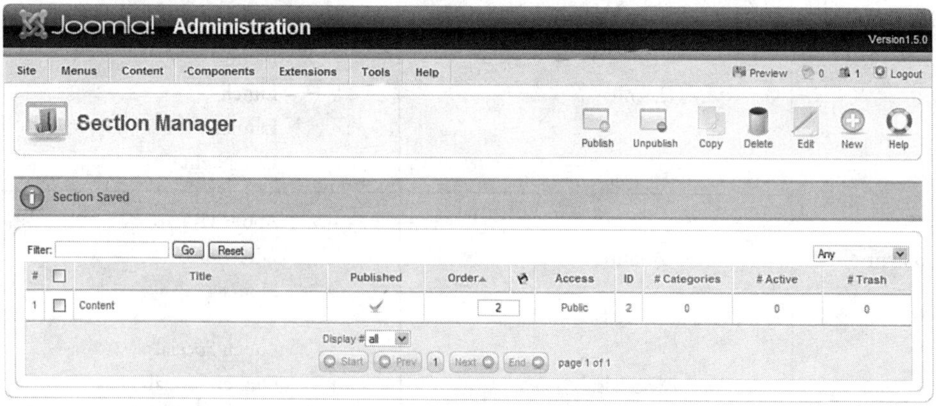

FIGURE 11.4 Simple restaurant section configuration

Now we create our four categories. Go to the Category Manager (**Content > Category Manager**) and create categories called Menus, About, Specials, and Reviews. After you have created these, the Category Manager should look like Figure 11.5.

Now that our organizational structure is complete, we need to create some articles.

The plan here is that the top menu will link directly to articles rather than categories. This means we must create these articles first, so we link to them when we create the links in the Menu Manager.

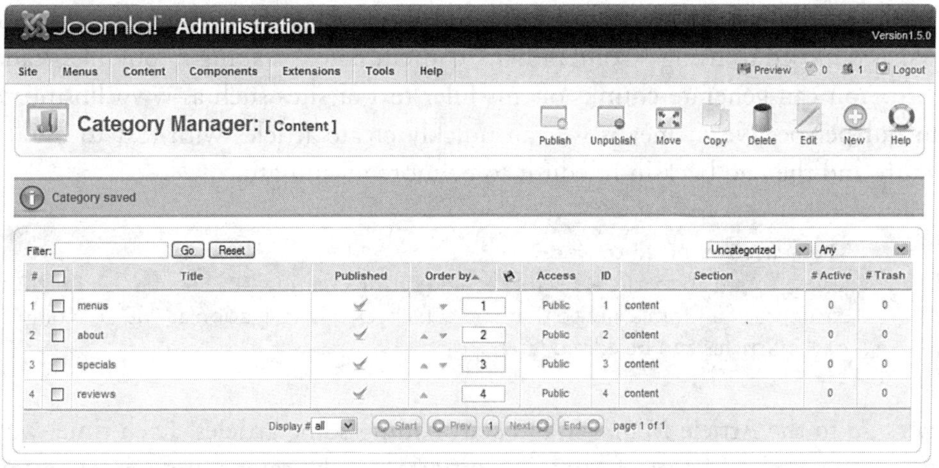

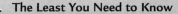

FIGURE 11.5 Simple restaurant category configuration

The Least You Need to Know
In most cases, it's easiest to create a site in the following order:
1. Create sections
2. Create categories
3. Create articles as placeholder content
4. Create menus/menu items
5. Go back and enter more detailed content

Now that we have our sections and categories, we need to start adding some content for our articles.

Building Content Articles with Lorem Ipsum

We'll be making use of that old standby of web designers everywhere, "Lorem Ipsum!" You have probably seen this text before; it reads something like this:

Lorem ipsum dolor sit amet, consectetuer adipiscing elit. Aenean mollis, erat nec ultrices lacinia, tellus lectus lobortis sapien, vel vehicula lacus dolor feugiat magna. Duis sollicitudin malesuada enim. Suspendisse bibendum odio in ante. Mauris mollis auctor enim. Aliquam cursus. Fusce aliquam nonummy dui.

The point of using Lorem Ipsum is that it has a more-or-less normal distribution of letters, as opposed to using "Content here, content here," making it look like readable English. You can generate chunks of this filler text at sites such as www.lipsum.com. From our perspective, it means we can quickly create articles with text to build out structure and then go back in to edit it to be more meaningful.

> **The Least You Need to Know**
> Using Lorem Ipsum is a useful technique for creating articles that will form the structure of a Joomla site so that you can check the navigation as you go along. The pages/articles can be edited later.

Let's go to the Article Manager and start adding some articles. Each time, we add a simple paragraph of Lorem Ipsum. It's important to be careful and select the correct section and category for that article to belong. When we're finished, the Article Manager should look like Figure 11.6.

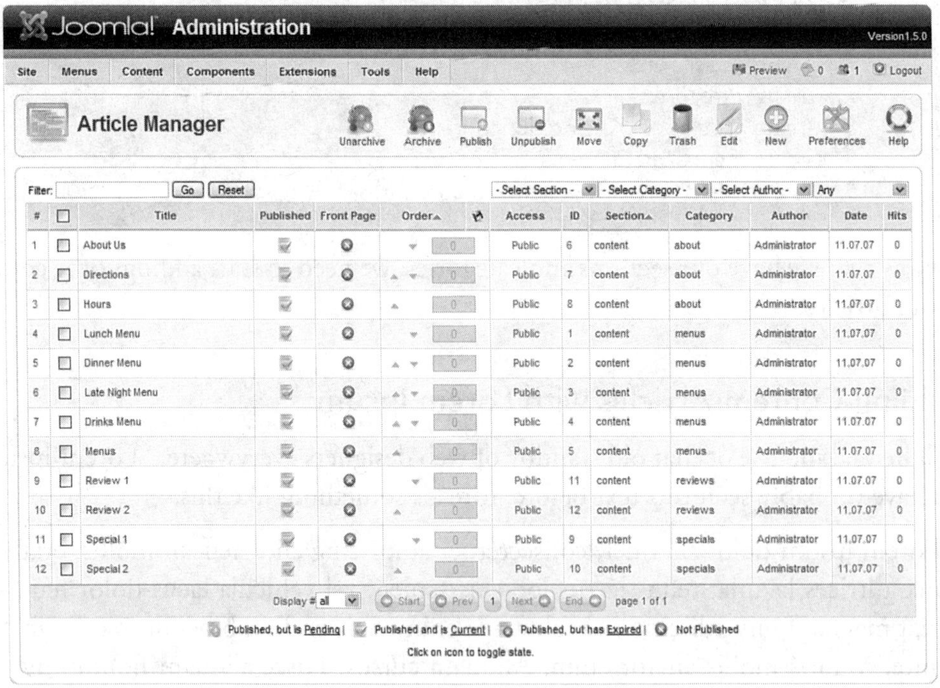

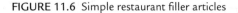

FIGURE 11.6 Simple restaurant filler articles

Note carefully the sections and categories that the articles are in. In a moment, we develop meaningful content for these articles, but first, we need to create some menus.

Creating Menus

Looking back at Figure 11.1, we can see the intent is to have a horizontal menu that extends across. Let's start creating it now:

1. First we need to create a top link to Menus and submenu links to the different "time of day" menus. Go to **Menus > Main Menu**.

2. We click New to create a new menu item and create a link to the Menus content article by drilling down to **Internal Link > Article > Standard Article Layout**. This takes us to the Edit Menu Item page. We name the link (Menus) and select the correct article to link to with the button on the right-hand side.

3. We then do the same for Lunch Menu, Dinner Menu, Late Night Menu, and Drinks Menu. Main Menu now looks like Figure 11.7.

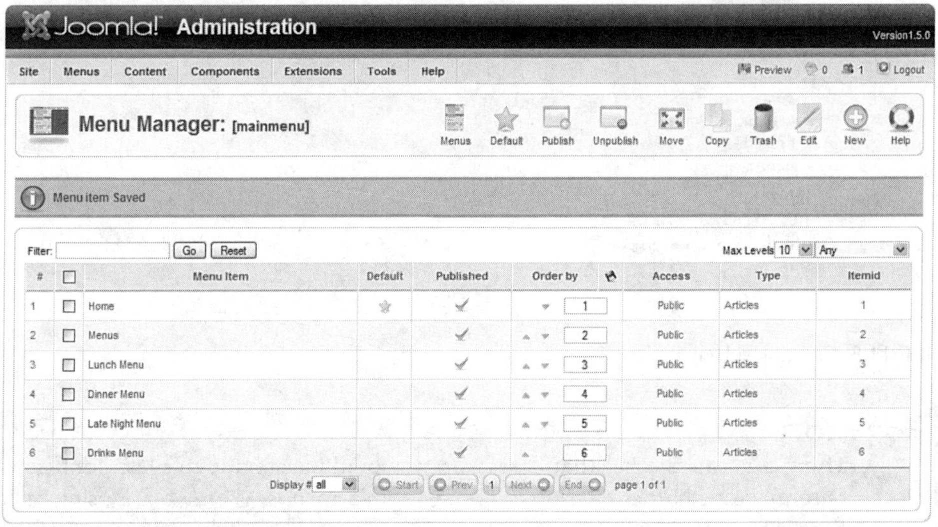

FIGURE 11.7 Creating the main menu

Viewed from the backend, our site looks like Figure 11.8. Notice that the menu items are not showing properly as a drop-down menu. Although our template provides for this functionality, we need to tell Joomla to take advantage of it by adjusting these menu items for the lunch menu, dinner menu, etc to be children of the top menu item, menus.

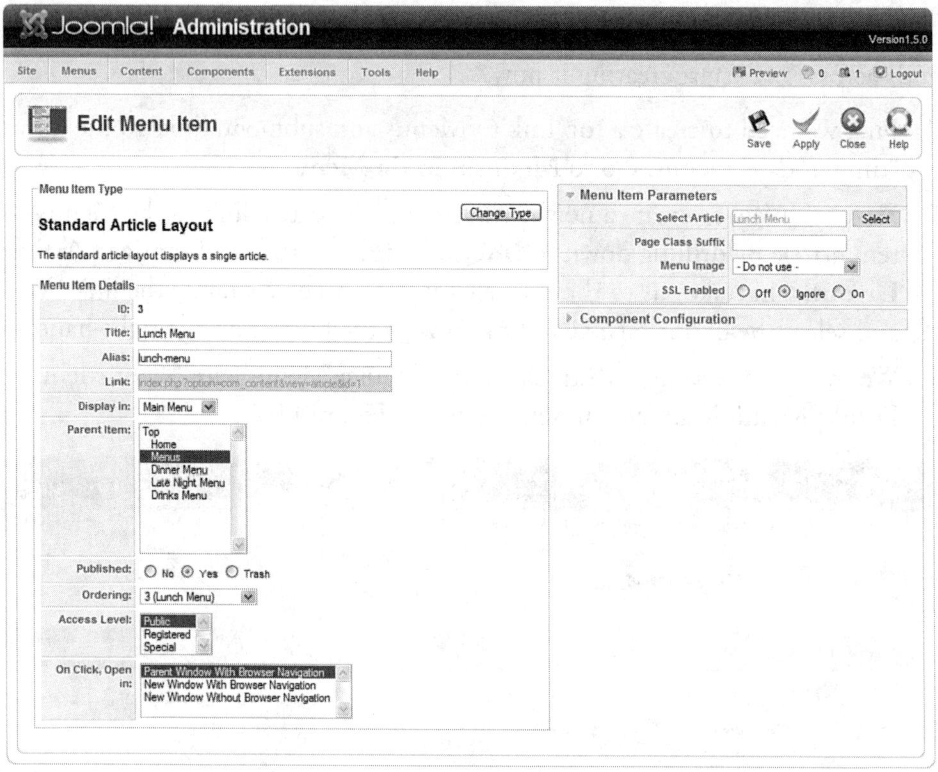

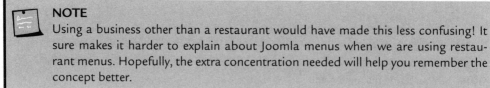

FIGURE 11.8 Creating sub-menu items

> **NOTE**
> Using a business other than a restaurant would have made this less confusing! It sure makes it harder to explain about Joomla menus when we are using restaurant menus. Hopefully, the extra concentration needed will help you remember the concept better.

Moving on, we need to set the correct parent menu item for each of the four menu items we want in the drop-down. When finished, our Menu Manager should look like Figure 11.9.

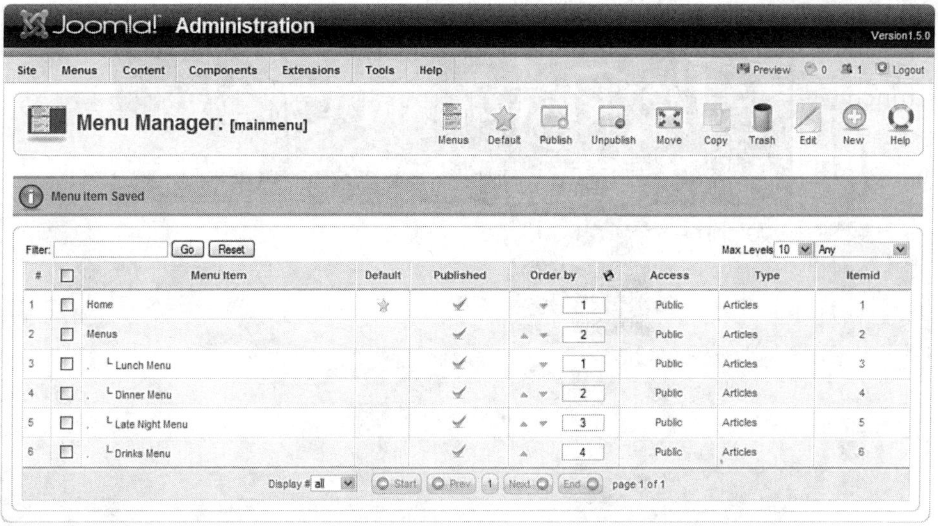

FIGURE 11.9 Completed main menu with sub-menu items

When we created the menu, a module was automatically created for it. However, the default location given for it was "left." This particular template does not have a left position for modules, so we need to move that module into the correct spot for a horizontal menu as determined by the Ready To Eat template. In this case it's "top." To do this, we follow these steps:

1. Go to **Extensions > Module Manager > Main Menu** and change the position to top. While here, we need to set some parameters for our drop-down to work correctly.

2. In the Module Parameters, we set the Always Show Submenu Items to Yes.

3. In the Advanced Parameters, we need to make sure the Menu Class Suffix and the Module Class Suffix are both blank.

Creating these submenu items will now give us a drop-down menu as seen in Figure 11.10.

Looking back at our sitemap, we wanted to have links in the Main Menu for Directions, Hours, and About Us. We can add these through the Menu Manager by linking to the appropriate articles; each time, we must make sure that we select the correct article to link to.

FIGURE 11.10 The drop-down menu from the frontend

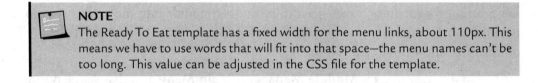

NOTE

The Ready To Eat template has a fixed width for the menu links, about 110px. This means we have to use words that will fit into that space—the menu names can't be too long. This value can be adjusted in the CSS file for the template.

The last page that was called for in the sitemap was a Contact Us page. As this is a narrow width template and there is not much room left in the main horizontal menu at the top, let's place this menu item in a smaller menu in the footer, another location available in this template.

First, we need to create another menu. While in the Menu Manager, click New and create a menu called Footer Menu. Create a single menu item in that menu that points to the contact form (**Internal Links > Contacts > Contact > Standard Contact Layout**).

NOTE

Because we started with a Joomla installation that had no sample content, we will have to go and create a contact for this menu item to link to. Do this as described in Chapter 4.

Let's make it even easier for the site owner to edit his content by giving him a front-end login link in the footer so he can edit without going to the backend:

1. Go to the Footer Menu and create a new menu item (**Menus > Footer Menu > New**). Link the menu item to the login page, (**Internal Link > User > Login > Default Layout**).

   We then need to go to the module for that menu and make sure it's published in the correct location.

2. Go to **Extensions > Module Manager > Footer Menu** and publish it in the footer location. Make sure that the Show Title Parameter is set to No.

The home page of our site should now look like Figure 11.11.

FIGURE 11.11 The Front Page with the footer menu

Although our menus are as intended, the home page is blank. Let's configure that as we need it.

Setting Up the Home Page

Referring to Figure 11.1, we see that the basic concept for the home page is to have some central content and then three blocks at the bottom. Setting up the main content is easiest, so let's start with that.

Home Page Alternative to the Front Page Manager

In Chapter 4 I covered different ways to organize content and that Joomla has a special component called the Front Page Manager that allows you to pull content from anywhere else on the site and have it displayed on the home page. This type of function is useful for a site that might have the main content of the home page changing frequently, for example a blog or a news site. Conceptually, the content of the main section of this restaurant site home page is not meant to change; the bottom teaser boxes will do that.

While discussing the Front Page component in Chapter 5, I mentioned that you can have any other menu item (which means any article, section, category, or component) shown on the home page simply by making it the default on in the Menu Manager.

Let's use this approach on our restaurant website. First we need to create an article that we will use as our home page. Create a new article in the Article Manager (**Content > Article Manager > New**). I gave mine the title of "Welcome to Ready To Eat." For now, fill it with some of that good old Lorem Ipsum (www.lipsum.com).

Here is an important bit—give the article an uncategorized section and category.

Now we create a menu item to this new article in the Main Menu (**Menus > Main Menu > New**) and have it link to the article (**Internal Link > Articles > Standard Article Layout**). Select the correct article to link to on the right-hand side by clicking the Select button. Give the menu item a title of *Home*.

After creating this link, the Menu Manager should look like that shown in Figure 11.12.

We now have two menu items (link) for Home. The top one goes to the Front Page component, and the bottom link is our new one. We need to do the following:

1. Make the new item the default by clicking the checkbox and clicking the Default button in the toolbar.

2. Unpublish the original Home item.

3. Place the new item first on the list by either clicking its up arrow icon in the order column or entering "1" into its field and clicking the Save icon at the top of that column.

4. Last, we just need to set up the menu item parameters so the author and date are not shown. To do this, open the new Home menu item and expand the Component Configuration tab on the right. Set the following:

- Author Names: Hide
- Created Date and Time: Hide
- Modified Date and Time: Show
- PDF Icon: Hide
- Print Icon: Hide
- Email Icon: Hide

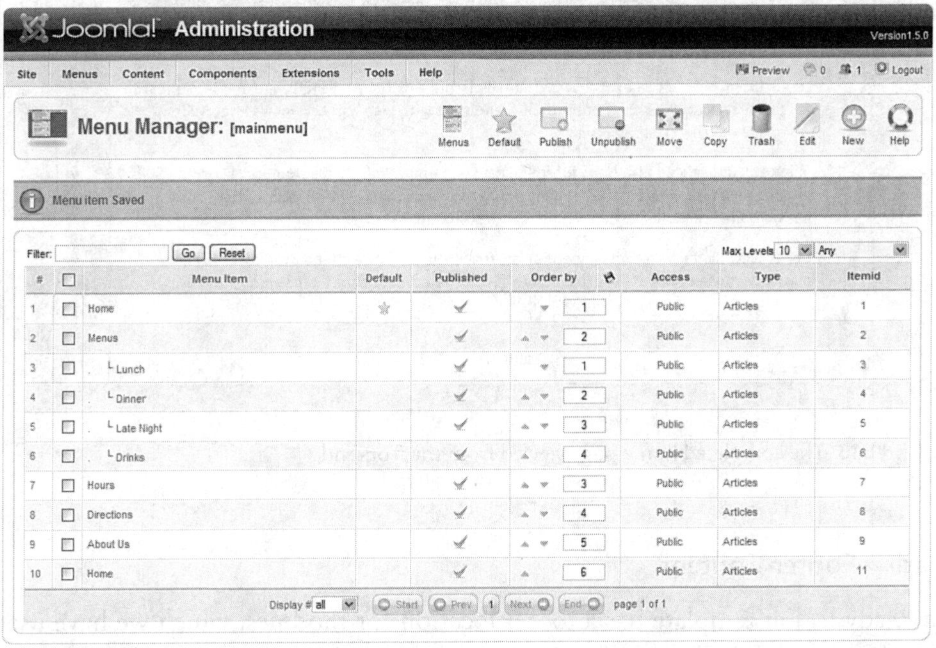

FIGURE 11.12 Building out the main menu

NOTE
You can choose other options here; these are my own personal preferences as I think the home page content should be relatively clear of this distraction.

The home page should now look like the screen shown in Figure 11.13.

So now we have home page content that can easily be updated. The site owner can just log in and edit live on the home page or any other page she needs to.

We should probably add the ubiquitous footer text that you see on most websites. Let's add those things now.

FIGURE 11.13 The completed home page viewed from the frontend

Creating Footer Content

The Ready to Eat template has a footer location for modules, which we have used already to place the small menu for the Contact Us and the Login links. Let's add some content there.

As described in Chapter 1 "Content Management Systems and an Introduction to Joomla," the concept of a module location is simply a placeholder, or bucket if you like, for Joomla to drop content into, in this case modules. You can have as many modules as you like in a particular module location. How the modules are presented (vertically, horizontally) is determined by the module style. This is a more advanced concept regarding templates that was discussed in Chapter 9, "Creating a Pure CSS Template."

Let's put some copyright text in the footer. To do this, we need to create a custom HTML module: Go to **Extensions > Module Manager > New** and select a Custom HTML module. This brings up a module editing screen shown in Figure 11.14.

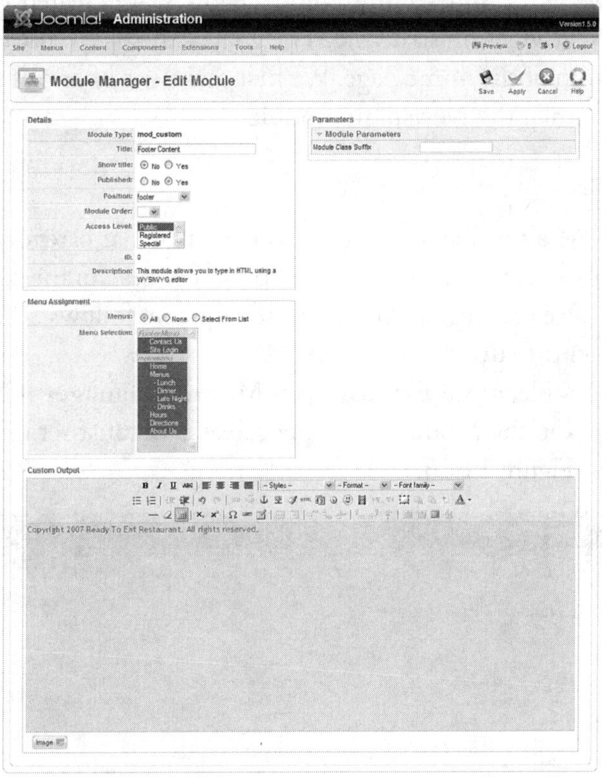

FIGURE 11.14 Creating a custom HTML module

We enter a simple copyright statement and make sure it appears in the correct location, and the title is set to not be shown.

When first saved, the module is set to appear in last place. We can adjust that by using the up/down arrows in the Module Manager in the same way we changed menu item placement in the Menu Manager (handy how all these managers function the same way!)

Last but not least, we need to set up the three blocks of content at the bottom.

Creating Module Teaser Blocks

The concept of what I call a teaser block is using modules across two to three columns at the top or bottom of the page. The idea is that the content of the blocks has something compelling in it that will have the site visitor click and go deeper into the site. You will frequently see this technique used on websites.

Earlier when we set up our sections and categories, we created two categories that were not part of the navigation structure. The goal of these is to use them in our "teaser blocks" at the bottom of the home page. We first make use of one of the dynamic modules available in Joomla, the Newsflash module.

Newsflash Module

This module displays a number of articles from a particular category. With every page refresh, it randomly selects new ones to be shown. For restaurant content, this is ideal for reviews. We can select various ones, and if someone follows a link, she will see all the ones we have on the site.

To create the module, go to **Extensions > Module Manager > New** and select the Newsflash module. On the Module Manager screen, we must set up the Module Parameters as shown in Figure 11.15.

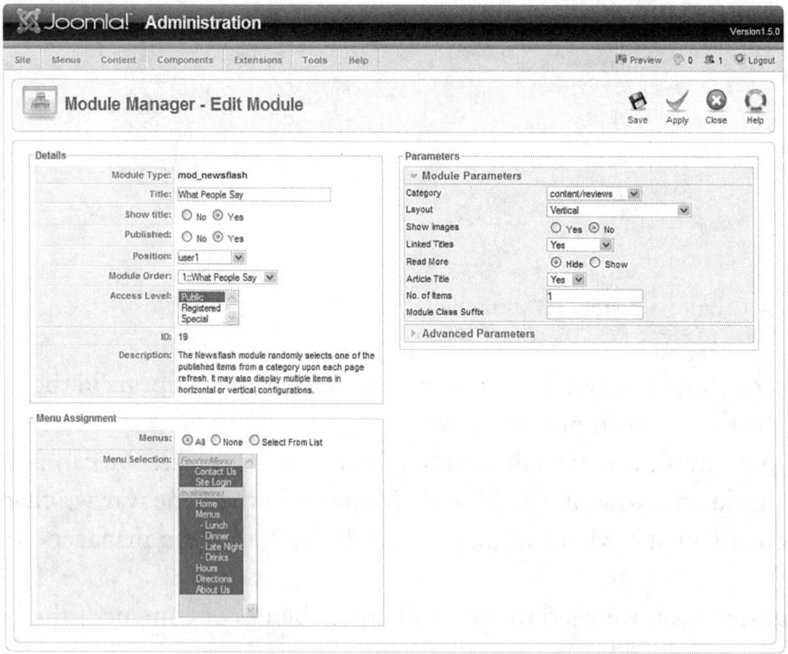

FIGURE 11.15 Setting up the Newsflash module

The following are some items to note:

- The location is user1.
- We will assign it to all menus so it shows on all pages.
- The category is reviews.
- The alignment is vertical.
- Select to show the titles as links.
- Choose to only show 1 item.

Viewed from the frontend, our site should now look like the screen shown in Figure 11.16.

FIGURE 11.16 The Newsflash module from the frontend

Note that the module is stretching across the page. As we add more modules, the template is set up so Joomla dynamically adds columns as needed and contracts/expands the module content as needed. This collapsible column functionality is a common feature of professional commercial templates—and this one!

Now let's add some links to our specials.

Linking to Articles from Within Content

Most restaurants have a changing menu of specials that they offer to diners. In our site, we might have specials for each of the menus that our example restaurant has: lunch, dinner, and late night. We could have a simple menu module that would show links to these three articles, but it would show as a list and would be difficult to customize. What I want to do here is to create a custom HTML module and then have some links/text in it to the relevant articles. The problem is, there is no easy way to add a link to another article as you are writing content.

If you recall, in Chapter 1, I explained the nature of a dynamic CMS. Pages don't exist until a menu item link is created to point to them. This means that an article, such as Review 1, has no independent existence. I have to first create a menu item to link to it, and then I can use that link in content articles.

So first, we need to create a menu. We won't even publish it but will use it to create links and then use the URLs elsewhere in the site.

Create a new menu. Call it Link Holder (**Menus > Menu Manager > New**).

Then create three menu items, one linking to each of the articles we have in the Specials category.

If we open up one of the menu items, we now see a URL that we can use in content items to link to this article; the URL is circled here in Figure 11.17.

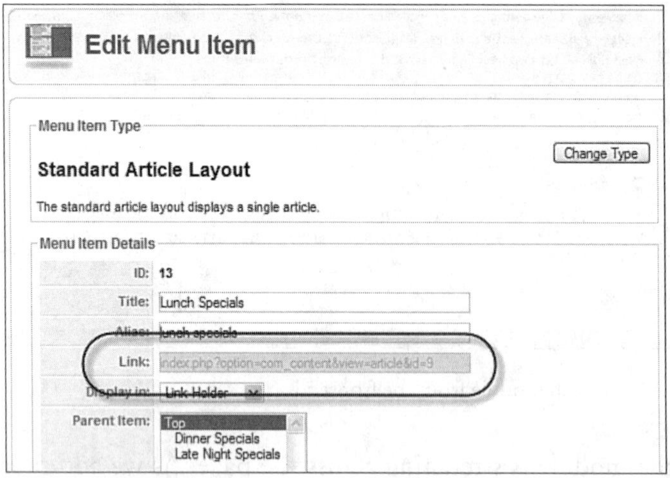

FIGURE 11.17 The URL from the menu item

We might ask ourselves, "Hey, we know the item ID for this article by looking in the Article Manager; why can't we just write the URL following this format? Why do we need to create a menu item?"

We actually don't, but a problem would occur if we wanted to change any of the page parameters, such as whether the PDF/Email icons are shown. These are all set in the menu item, so we would not be able to control any of them.

So now we can create a custom HTML module to describe our specials and place it in the user2 module location. We can use the URLs from the Link Holder menu for links embedded in the text. The module I created is shown in Figure 11.18.

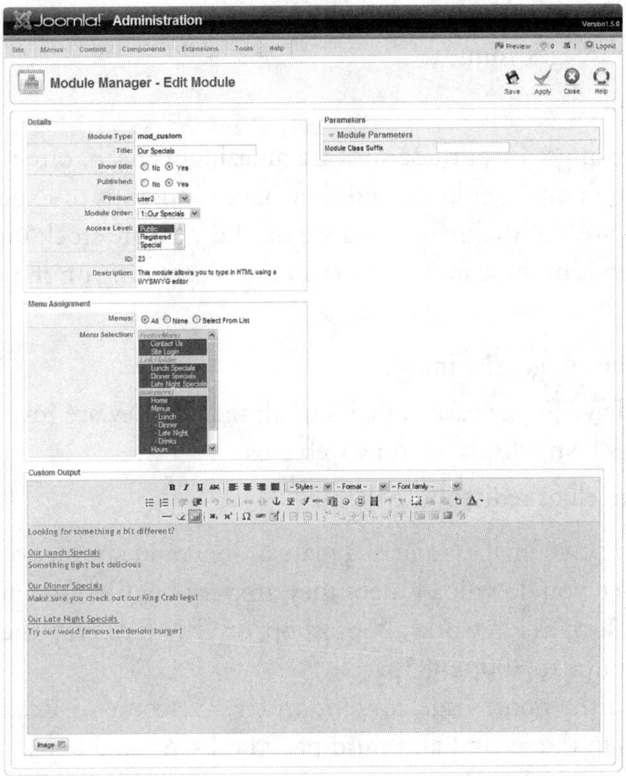

FIGURE 11.18 A custom HTML module with links

One last step to take is to swap the Specials and Review modules around. More people will probably be looking for the Specials menus, and the closer content is to the top left corner; the easier it is to find and the more important it is perceived to be by the site visitor.

Our site is starting to get into shape. It still looks a bit bland, though; we need some images and photos.

Using Stock Imagery

One of the best kept secrets of web designers is the use of stock photos and imagery when they create websites for their clients. There are many websites where you can get royalty-free images to use on a single site. Examples include the following:

- www.dreamstime.com
- www.istockphoto.com
- www.GettyImages.com
- www.sxc.hu

The images you can get from these sites are amazingly cheap, often as low as a dollar per image for a high quality photo, and they have thousands to choose from. I would imagine that 80–90% of the images you see on the Web are stock images.

The license terms of these images are typically (depending on the source) characterized by

- You pay once to get the image.
- You don't have to pay each time it's used; that is, they are royalty-free. Being used means being displayed on a web page.
- You can't resell or redistribute them.

I have downloaded two images: one of a plate of food and another of some drinks and a wine glass. When you download them they are very big files, so you will need to use a graphics editor such as Fireworks, Photoshop, or GIMP to crop them to the size you need. I cropped mine to 200px×85px.

Going back to the home page content article, Welcome to Ready to Eat, I'll add these two images in the second and third paragraphs. Several key points to remember are

- Use the Joomla Image button at the bottom to upload and insert the images.
- Remember to set the alignment of the images to left.
- Add some white space/margin. I did this by adding the style of imagemargin to the images in the editor. This appears in the drop-down for the editor styles because it is in the template CSS.
- Add the style of clearing to the second paragraph. This is in the template CSS.

Our editor will look like Figure 11.19 after the images are inserted and the styles are added.

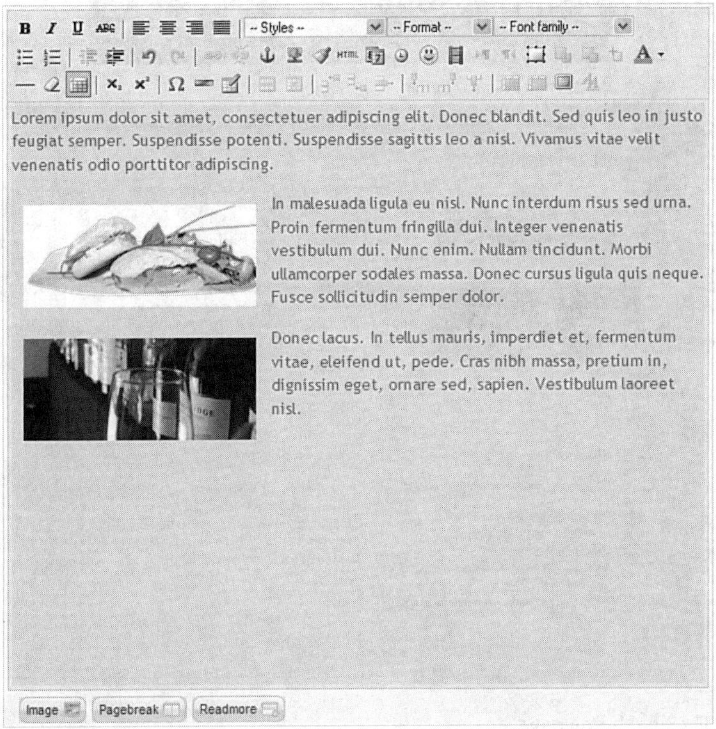

FIGURE 11.19 Inserting stock imagery

The Least You Need to Know

Web designers around the world use stock images to easily add rich graphical content to their sites.

When adding content, some manipulation of the HTML or CSS is usually needed to achieve the result you want. Often, styles can be created in the template CSS and used in articles.

Our home page now looks like what's shown in Figure 11.20.

Not bad. Now let's look at some of that extra functionality we want to add.

FIGURE 11.20 The final home page

Extending a Restaurant Website

At the beginning of the chapter, we looked at four potential areas in which the basic functionality of a restaurant website could be extended:

- Image gallery
- Calendar
- Email marketing
- Google maps

At the time of writing, Joomla 1.5 is still in Beta, so many third-party developers are still working to update their extensions from 1.0.X to 1.5. For the purposes of considering our restaurant website, we will look at resources for 1.0.X. Where possible,

I'll give more than one alternative so you can use whichever you need based on their update timeline to 1.5.

Image Gallery: JPG Flash Rotator 2

The concept of an image gallery is to show attractive photos or images that the visitor can browse through. For a restaurant website, unlike, say, a photographer website, the images are being shown for effect as a whole rather than there being a need to view specific ones individually. What I mean by that is the site visitor doesn't specifically need to be able to navigate the individual images like SlideshowPro might, but the images can just scroll or rotate.

A very simple but effective tool for this is the JPG Flash Rotator. JPG Flash Rotator 2 was developed by Joomlashack.com and you can download it at extensions.joomla.org/component/option,com_mtree/task,viewlink/link_id,437/Itemid,35/. You can also download it from the developer website.

You upload half a dozen images of the same size and the component rotates the images with various flash effects, like fade or swipe. This extension is a module, so you need a module location to place it in.

Calendar: JCal Pro

As with the subject of the previous chapter, school websites, JCal Pro is an excellent choice for a calendar. JCalPro was developed by Anything-Digital.com, and you can download it at extensions.joomla.org/component/option,com_mtree/task,viewlink/link_id,1401/Itemid,35/ or from the developer website.

If the restaurant needs to have several dates and be able to post dates for future events, JCal Pro is a robust component to manage this content.

Email Marketing

There are several choices when it comes to marketing a website via email. In Chapter 8, "Getting Traffic to Your Site," when we looked at a global marketing strategy for any website, we looked at email newsletters as a useful tool. For a restaurant, there might well be more specific needs based around highly targeted emails to different segments based on information about your regulars. Based on this, I might suggest two options. If the restaurant owner just needs to do general emails, he could use a Joomla email component, say Acajoom or YaNC. If lots of segmentation is needed, for example targeting customers who come later in the evening or frequently attend live music, something with robust segmenting, like J!Contact, would be required.

- **YaNC**

  YaNC was developed by Adam van Dongen, and you can download it at extensions.joomla.org/component/option,com_mtree/task,viewlink/link_id, 172/Itemid,35/ or from the developer website joomla-addons.org.

- **Acajoom**

  Acajoom was developed by Joobi, and you can download it at extensions. joomla.org/component/option,com_mtree/task,viewlink/link_id,964/ Itemid,35/ or from the developer website acajoom.com.

- **J!Contact**

  J!Contact was developed by joomlashack.com, and you can download it at the developer website.

Google Maps

If you have never used this tool on a website, it's a great interactive way to give people both clear visual information as to the location of your business and dynamic directions from wherever they are to you. There are currently only two real alternatives:

- **Google Maps API**

  Developed by David Pollack, you can download it at extensions.joomla.org/ component/option,com_mtree/task,viewlink/link_id,377/Itemid,35/ or from the forge joomlacode.org/gf/project/com_google_maps/.

- **Googlemaps**

  For a useful Google Map plugin, download Plugin Googlemap, which was developed by Mike Reumer. You can download it at extensions.joomla.org/ component/option,com_mtree/task,viewlink/link_id,1147/Itemid,35/, or from the forge joomlacode.org/gf/project/mambot_google1/.

User's Guide Chapter 11 Demo Site

A demo of this site is available at www.joomlabook.com. It is an exact copy of what you should have if you followed all the steps shown in this chapter. You can log in to the administrative backend so you can see the site framework and the sections, categories, and menus that were set up.

Summary

In this chapter, we tackled one of the trickiest parts of creating a Joomla site, how to take your sitemap and content and organize it into Joomla's content hierarchy.

- The modern business must have a Web presence that communicates their brand and information about their company.
- The key features needed for a small business site are taken care of by a default Joomla install: easily edited content and flexible menu configuration.
- A small website does not need a detailed section/category structure. Often just a single section can be used for all of the content articles.
- In most cases, it's easiest to create a site in the following order:
  1. Create sections.
  2. Create categories.
  3. Create articles as placeholder content.
  4. Create menus/menu items.
  5. Go back and enter more detailed content.
- Using Lorem Ipsum is a useful technique to create articles that will form the structure of a Joomla site so you can check the navigation for it. The pages/articles can be edited later.
- Web designers around the world use stock images to easily add rich graphical content to their sites.
- When adding content, some manipulation of the HTML or CSS is usually needed to achieve the result you want. Often styles can be created in the template CSS and used in articles.

Chapter 12

Creating a Blog Site with Joomla!

It seems as if everyone has a blog these days. Technorati.com (a web service that tracks blogs) estimates that 500 blogs are started every day. Many people still think of blogs as personal diaries, but more and more organizations and companies are using blogs as a way to shape perception of who they are and what they do. Chances are, if you go to a website today, you will find a link to their blog somewhere on their site. What is becoming more common on websites now is a section of the site that is dedicated to the blog.

The ways blogs are used is an important distinction. The traditional view of the blog is one where the entire website is the blog. Short posts are shown on the home page along with links to the rest of the article. You might find links to other blogs or popular blog posts in a side column. This chapter talks about blogs in a more general sense: a dynamic communication medium for a person or organization to interact with their stakeholders.

In This Chapter

- What is a blog?

- Why do you need a blog?

- What features does a blog need?

- How should we organize the content on a blog?

- How can we extend the functionality of a blog?

What Is a Blog?

At the most fundamental level, a blog is a communication medium. Typically it has frequent brief posts about a particular subject (sometimes the subject is the author). Almost all blogs incorporate some sort of system to allow site visitors to leave comments. This shapes the characteristics of the communication; rather than being one-way communication, such as advertisements, a blog is two-way communication that aims to engage the reader actively.

The second defining characteristic of modern blogs is that they are a communication style. What I mean by that is they are most effective when written in an honest first-person voice. A blog that is written as old-school, third-person press releases will die a lonely death. One implication of this is that frequently, a blog will be written by one person so that the writing voice clearly comes through in the posts.

My third and last defining characteristic of a blog is frequent posting. It's quite easy to find heated debate about how often you should post. Some are convinced it needs to be daily, others weekly. All will agree, though, that you need to make regular posts to build a sustainable readership. Usually these posts are brief, and only introductory text is shown on the main page along with a Read More link.

I also want to mention what a blog is *not*. It's not TrackBacks, pings, Digg It buttons, blog rolls, permalinks, or Google ad sense. You will see all of these things on a blog (hopefully not all at once), but these are just features of a blog.

You can have a successful blog, even the top 50 heavyweight, without any of these. As you create your blog, make sure you don't let the trees get in the way of seeing the great potential of the woods.

> **The Least You Need to Know**
> A blog is a modern communication vehicle that is becoming more and more important in today's Web-connected world.

Why Have a Blog?

As blogs become more mainstream, they are providing a highly cost-effective medium for organizations to communicate with their stakeholders. They help organizations engage in two-way dialog, which can take many forms. For example

- A software company updating users about new development
- A nonprofit describing new outreach projects
- A CEO communicating his or her vision to company employees
- A political candidate rallying his base
- A bike lock company dealing with a product defect

Okay, so the last one is a red herring. It's actually the complete opposite. Kryptonite, a popular bike lock manufacturer, had a small lock defect last year. It was possible to open one of the high end bike locks with a ballpoint pen. Somebody posted the story on the Internet, and it spread. For reasons yet unknown, Kryptonite did not respond to the story. Within a few days, the story spread and got picked up by major news outlets. The result was a class-action suit against Kryptonite. The interesting point here is that blogs significantly magnified the speed at which the story spread. If Kryptonite had been on its collective toes, it could have used blogs to respond to the issue. Blogs are a two-edged sword; they can both help and hinder your organization.

> **The Least You Need to Know**
> News and information moves faster than ever in smaller and smaller news cycles. A blog that is easy to update is an important tool for any organization to communicate with its stakeholders.

What Options Are There for Blogging?

There are many places on the Web where you can create a blog; some are free, and some are paid services. Here are a few:

- Blogger (www.blogger.com)
- Typepad (www.typepad.com)
- Wordpress (www. wordpress.org)
- Moveable Type (www.sixapart.com/moveabletype)

The 800-pound gorilla in the room here is Blogger. Part of the Google world, it by far hosts the most blogs. This is probably because it is very easy to set up and free.

A quick look at some Alexa rankings (rough estimate of traffic) show that Joomla is not a very popular platform for a blog, shown here in Figure 12.1.

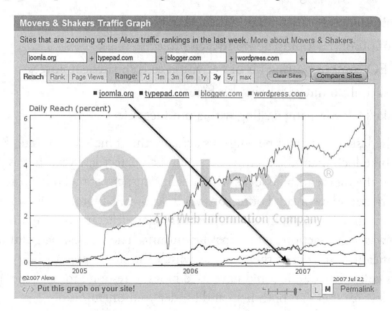

FIGURE 12.1 Alexa traffic trends of blog platforms

So why would we want to use Joomla for blogs? Aren't there already much easier solutions?

Well, first off, this is a book about Joomla, not Blogger, so I want to try and show how you can use Joomla to blog, sell products, build community sites, make your coffee, and so on. But there is a real reason too: *Blogs are closed systems.*

What I mean by that sentence is this: The software that powers many of these blogs is basic. That's perhaps part of Blogger's huge popularity. But if a moment should come that you want to extend the features of your blog, you are stuck. Maybe you want to add a forum, a shopping cart for your e-book, or a subscription part of your blog. You can't add any major functionality in a service like Blogger at this time. This is even true about some of the high-end blog platforms such as Wordpress. The platform itself is not designed to be extensible, so you can't add anything.

A big theme of this book has been how amazingly extendable Joomla is with its GPL and commercial extensions. With that in mind, if Joomla can mimic the basic functions of a blog, it can be a basic foundation for all you bloggers out there on which to build a super sticky blog site.

What Features Are Needed on a Blog Site?

Let's pause from our headlong rush into joining the blogosphere and consider what essential features are needed for a successful blog. Each one is given a brief description of what solutions are available for Joomla:

- **Flexible Layout**. Been to one Blogger blog, and you have been to them all. Being able to make yours look different to the other 27 million blogs out there is a good thing.

  Joomla is best-of-breed here. It's recognized as being one of the most "skinnable" open source Content Management Systems (CMS) available. What controls a Joomla site's look and feel is called the *template*. There are many templates available that have a definite blog look to them.

- **Browser-based Editing**. You have to get your content on the Web fast and easy.

- **Automated Publishing**. FTWho? You don't want to have to mess with complicated file transfer; you want to click a button and have your posts appear. Text formatting and spell checking is a bonus too.

- **Categories**. Part of having a usable site is being able to split your posts into categories that will make them easier to find.

- **Search Engine Optimized URLs**. If you have written a post, you don't want your URL to be www.myblog.com/9823749.html?myleftleg. You want to be able to squeeze every ounce of search engine optimization (SEO) out of your post. So having a URL that includes keywords about the post is useful in this regard.

- **Comment Systems**. A critical feature. The comment system is the number one way your site becomes sticky (how likely a visitor will return). Free for all commenting is something bloggers have embraced and has led to their explosion in popularity. Many corporate sites that have blogs are afraid to tread this path. So Web 1.0.

- **Syndication Feeds**. RSS and ATOM are XML applications that can push your posts onto other RSS readers. Email clients such as Thunderbird come with RSS readers, as do personal sites like Yahoo. Perhaps a more important point is that a website can read RSS, you can have your posts appear automatically on someone else's website, where (hopefully) it will get even more readership. It's kind of like automatic and dynamic real-time article syndication.

- **Email Notification**. If you make a post, wouldn't it be good if you had an email list that got notified that you did? If you are a web business, you will soon start building a list of emails. This is a whole other subject beyond blogging, however, involving CANs of SPAM.

- **Search**. As a prolific blog poster, you will soon have your archive bursting. You will need a robust search tool that can help site visitors find your posts. Steve Krug maintains that some visitors will automatically look for a search as the first thing they do; people are either searchers or browsers.

- **Trackback**. Trackbacks are complex. The bottom line is you read a post, and you comment about it on your blog. You place the URL to the post in yours, and the blog picks up your post and leaves it as a comment in the other's post.

> **The Least You Need to Know**
> A blog isn't about widgets and gizmos; it's about the quality of the content. You need a tool that can help you organize and present your blog posts as easily as possible.

Downloading and Installing a Blog Template

At www.joomlabook.com, you can grab a special commercial template that we'll be using in this chapter. It's called *Aqualine*. It's a pure CSS-based template design with some nicely integrated SEO features. It's designed to be as easy as possible to set up. It's shown in Figure 12.2.

FIGURE 12.2 Screenshot of Aqualine template

Got the template? Great. You should now have a template zip file to install into Joomla.

Go to **Extensions > Install/Uninstall** to get to the Extension Manager. We looked at how extensions are installed and managed in Chapter 7, "Expanding Your Content: Articles and Editors."

Browse to the template zip file and click the Upload File and Install button. The message, "Install Template: Success," should be displayed.

We then need to make this template our default template. This is done through the Template Manager.

Go to **Extensions > Template Manager** and select the new JS_Aqua template and click the Default button to make it the default template. Viewed in the frontend, our site (empty of content) should look like that shown in Figure 12.3.

FIGURE 12.3 The Aqualine template empty of content

Aqualine Template Features and Positions

This particular template has three main features, along with the usual functionality such as collapsible columns:

- The logo/header can be text of a logo. If you put text into the user1 module, it automatically detects and shows it. Otherwise it will use a logo taken from /templates/images/header.png.
- It uses pure CSS to lay out the content rather than tables. This has significant advantages for making the site meet W3C standards and for SEO.
- It has the ability to use a pure CSS Suckerfish drop-down menu.
- An easy to adjust the custom CSS file—customize.css

The JS Aqualine template has seven available module positions.

To position your modules (for example, main menu, login, syndicate, polls) in the various template positions, you set the Position parameter in each module. Figure 12.2 showed the available positions on this template:

- **user1**. Reserved for text instead of logo.
- **top**. Reserved for horizontal menu.
- **left**. Left vertical column, not reserved.
- **Banner**. Banner position, not reserved.
- **user4**. Bottom left teaser location, not reserved.
- **right**. Bottom right teaser location, not reserved.
- **footer**. Footer position, reserved for footer information.

Most of these are generic in their potential use. Two, however, were placed with a specific purpose in mind. The user1 module location is really intended for a text logo. The top module location is intended for a horizontal navigation.

Configuring the Logo

There are two ways you can configure the logo. By far the easiest is to just add some text in the user1 location. If it is given an H1 tag, then the template CSS styling will give it some appropriate formatting. This can easily be adjusted in the customize.css file.

Let's create an example for the text.

Go to **Extensions > Module Manager > New > Custom HTML**. Give the module a name (I called mine Header Logo Text) and put it in the user1 position. Make sure the title is set to not show. Then add some text as desired. This was mine:

```
<a href="index.php">
<h1>A User's Guide to Joomla 1.5</h1>
<h2>Creating a Blog site with Joomla</h2>
</a>
```

This snippet produces a header as shown in Figure 12.4.

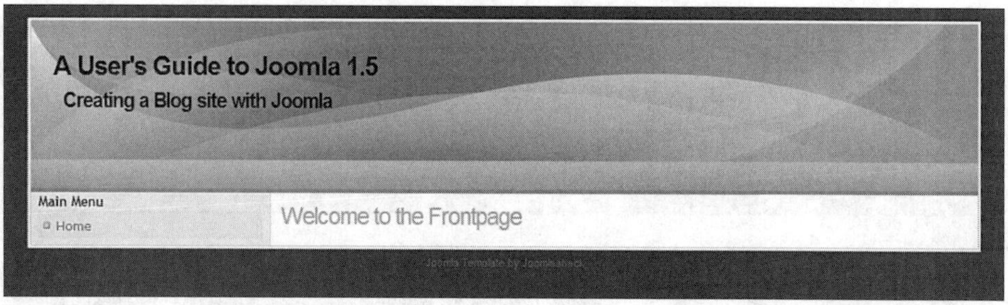

FIGURE 12.4 Configuring the logo in the heading

It's important to provide that link back to the home page with the text. As we saw in Chapter 8 "Getting Traffic to Your Site," the anchor text is very important. We have a link called Home in the menu, but that doesn't do much for our SEO. Now we have a link on every page with some important keywords in it.

If we want a more graphical logo, we simply don't have a user1 module and upload our logo to /templates/images/header.png. We need to make sure to use the same dimensions.

This template automatically detects which method we are using and dynamically adjusts as needed.

Configuring the Main Horizontal Drop-down Menu

JS Aqualine has a built-in drop-down menu in the template CSS.

When installed, Joomla starts with the main menu and a single Home link as shown in Figure 12.4. However, the default location given for it is *left*, so we need to move that module into the correct spot for a horizontal menu as determined by the Aqualine template. In this case it's top.

Go to **Extensions > Module Manager > Main Menu** and change the position to top.

While here, we need to set some parameters for our drop-down to work correctly.

1. In the Module Parameters, set the Always Show Submenu Items to Yes.

2. Set the Title to *not* show

3. In the Advanced Parameters, make sure the Menu Class Suffix and the Module Class Suffix are both blank.

Configuring the menu as outlined now moves it to the horizontal position and prepares it for drop-downs, as seen in Figure 12.5.

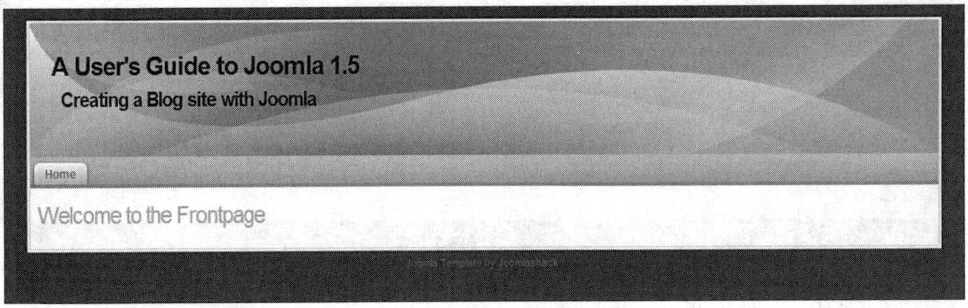

FIGURE 12.5 Configuring the horizontal menu

Let's now take a detailed look at how to set up the site structure, or in terms of Joomla, the sections, categories, and navigation.

Organizing Content on a Blog

It is important that you understand some of the basics of how Joomla organizes its content and the structure it uses. If you haven't already, make sure you read through Chapter 5, "Creating Menus and Navigation."

We started in the introduction to this chapter discussing two types of blog sites: a pure blog that would have little other content and an organization's blog that might be part of the bigger site. These two slightly different types of sites would need different section/category hierarchies to organize their articles. Let's look at each of them in turn.

Organizing a Blog Within a Larger Site

A good example of this is my own site, compassdesigns.net. I have a number of sections for templates, services, and so on and then a section for my blog posts. Each section has a menu link as shown in Figure 12.6.

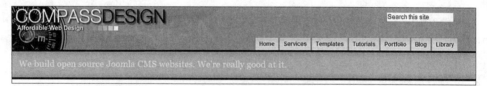

FIGURE 12.6 Example menu of a blog

We can see that the blog is a link in the main menu. This concept of having the blog be part of a larger site is very common; it's most applicable when the blog is supporting the main goal of the site. In this scenario, the section would be the blog, and we could have categories inside it.

Let's take an example of a restaurant site (refer to Chapter 11, "Creating a Restaurant Site with Joomla"). As a business, it's definitely a good candidate for having a rich blog to communicate to site visitors. Our sections and categories might be

Section	Blog
Categories	Recipes
	Cooking Tips and Tricks
	News

With this as our structure, we would create a menu item that links to the section in a blog layout. This would show all the articles in that section in the order we wanted, probably by date, most recent first. If we wanted to, we could then have more menu items linked to the specific categories so people could browse a single category if they wanted.

To do this we need to create a new menu and in it, create menu items that link to each category. We can then publish the module for that menu in the location we want. I do this on my own blog on compassdesigns.net, as shown here in Figure 12.7.

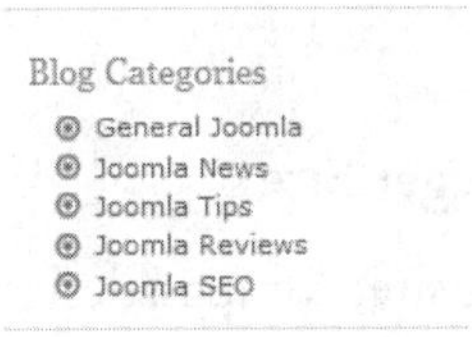

Blog Categories
- General Joomla
- Joomla News
- Joomla Tips
- Joomla Reviews
- Joomla SEO

FIGURE 12.7 Using Joomla categories in a blog

The example we work with throughout this chapter is the kind in which the blog actually *is* the site.

Organizing a Standalone Blog

This is the type of blog that has been popularized by tools such as blogger.com. The home page shows the most recent blog entries, usually in the order of most recent first. An excellent example is copyblogger.com, shown in Figure 12.8.

> **NOTE**
> I am using copyblogger as an example because it's a really great resource. If you are building a blog, you should have this site on your RSS feed for daily reading.

In the example we are going to work through, let's make a blog about parenting. Heck, with 3 boys myself, I could use all the parenting tips I can get!

At this point, flip back to the previous chapter about creating a restaurant. When we discussed organizing our sections and categories there, we faced a similar problem—there were two alternatives. We are actually going to be using a very similar concept here; we will have a section that holds all of our content. In the restaurant example, it was called Content; here we call it Parenting Blog. The article organization will be like what's shown in the following table.

FIGURE 12.8 Screenshot of www.copyblogger.com

Sections	Categories	Articles
Parenting Blog	Parenting	Various blog posts
	Vacations	Various blog posts
	Money	Various blog posts
	Home	Various blog posts
	Family	Various blog posts
	Other Stuff	Various blog posts

Lets set up this structure.

Go to **Content > Section Manager > New** and create a section called Parenting Blog. Next Go to **Content > Category Manager > New** and create the six categories shown in the table.

> **The Least You Need to Know**
> How you organize your sections and categories will depend on what type of blog you have. Standalone blogs can have all of the posts under a single section of the site.

It's important to remember that our sections and categories are merely buckets for us (the Webmaster) to organize our content. From the user perspective, they might view articles in other ways, such as by date. For blogs, this brings us to an important feature—the ability to use tags to organize content.

About Tagging

If you have been to a blog, you might have seen a box that showed several keywords, often in different sizes. These are known as *tags* and are a common feature on a blog.

A tag is basically another way of organizing the visitor's experience with your content. You have an article, say in the Parenting category, but then add tags such as bedtime, reading, and bath time (maybe it was a story about getting your kids to bed after bath time). These tags are then shown on the page and present an alternative path to content from the categories.

In my review of the literature on tags (most of it from bloggers), there seems to be no real consensus whether tags are critical to blogs. When used carefully and in moderation I think they can help, if just simply through the anchor text internal link benefits they can bring (see Chapter 8). I would have them on my "nice to have" list for a Joomla site.

If you do want to try out tags for your site, there are a few extensions available (currently only for 1.0.X):

- www.phil-taylor.com (Joomla Tags)
- www.azrul.com (MyBlog component)

Creating the Menus

We will have two menus, the first will be a horizontal one across the top, our Main Menu. The second will be links to the categories in a side column.

Creating the Main Menu

With our standalone blog about parenting, configuring the menu will be relatively easy. We just have to pay attention to correct settings for the parameters.

As we said about our restaurant site in Chapter 11, we don't really want to use the Front Page component. We want everything to appear automatically. In the same way as before, we need to create a new menu item that meets our needs, make it the default menu item, and then unpublish the Home menu item.

Go to **Menus > Main Menu > New > Articles > Section Blog Layout** and give it a name (I called mine Blog) and link it to the Parenting blog section. We then need to set the following parameters:

- Basic Parameters
    - # Leading = 10
    - # Intro = 0
    - Columns = 1
    - # Links = 10
- Advanced Parameters
    - Primary Order = Most recent first
- Component Parameters
    - Title Linkable = Yes
    - Author Name = Hide
    - Modified Date = Hide
    - PDF/email/print = hide
- System Parameters
    - Show Page Title = Hide

We then need to make the new menu item the default and unpublish the old Home menu item (in the Menu Manager).

So we can properly see the effect of setting these parameters, let's add a few content articles using Loerum Ipsum, as we have done in the last couple of chapters. With this in place, our home page now looks like Figure 12.9.

If you look around most blogs, you usually find a few other links in the Main Menu. Let's add the standard About Us and Contact Us links. The About Us page is a simple uncategorized article. Let's make that first.

Go to **Content > Article Manager > New** and create an uncategorized article. I called mine About Me. Create a menu item to that article. Next, go to **Menus > Main Menu > New > Articles > Standard Article Layout** and give it a name (I called mine About Me) and link it to the article we just created.

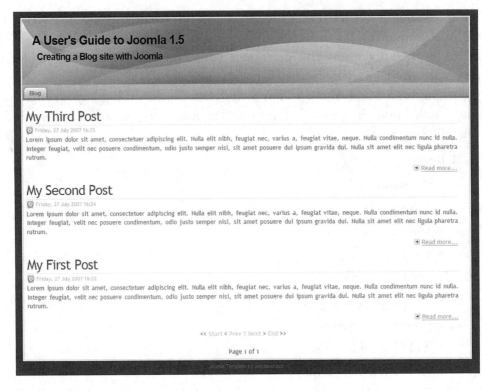

FIGURE 12.9 Initial posts showing on the home page

Now, let's create the Contact Us form. As we have seen in the previous two chapters, installing with no sample content means that you have to create the Contact category and the contact first. (Flip back to Chapter 11 to see how to do this.)

To create a link to the contact, go to **Menus > Main Menu > New > Contacts > Standard Contact Layout**, give it a name (I called mine About Me), and link it to the contact just created.

Now we need to create that side menu.

Creating a Submenu to Categories

To create the side menu, we need to create a whole new menu.

Go to **Menus > Menu Manager > New**. I called mine Blog Categories, as shown in Figure 12.10. Remember, when we create this menu, it automatically creates a module for it.

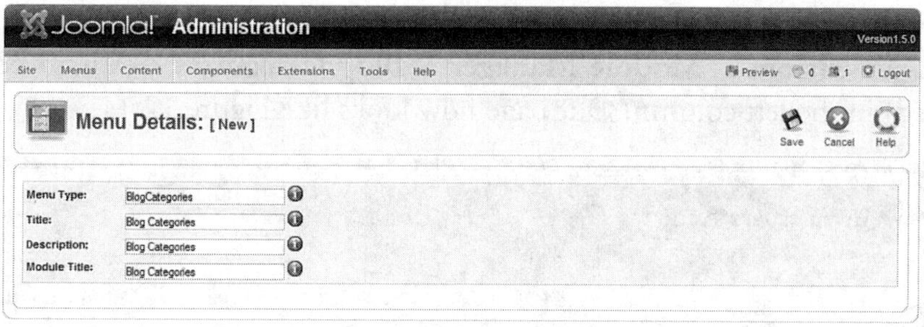

FIGURE 12.10 Creating the submenu for categories

We then need to add the menu items for this menu. Go to **Menus > Blog Catego-ries > New > Articles > Category Blog Layout**. Give it a name (Family to correspond to the exact name of the category) and link it to the Family category. Give it the same parameter settings as the home page link:

- Basic Parameters
  - # Leading = 10
  - # Intro = 0
  - Columns = 1
  - # Links = 10
- Advanced Parameters
  - Primary Order = Most recent first
- Component Parameters
  - Title Linkable = Yes
  - Author Name = Hide
  - Modified Date = Hide
  - PDF/email/print = hide
- System Parameters
  - Show Page Title = Hide

Do this for each of the other categories.

> **TIP**
> A quick way to do this is to copy the original menu item. That way you don't have to keep setting those parameters and just need to change the name and the category to where it links.

We now need to publish our module for the menu in the correct location.

Go to **Extensions > Module Manager > Blog Categories**. Set it to be enabled (published) in the left column. Our page now looks like Figure 12.11.

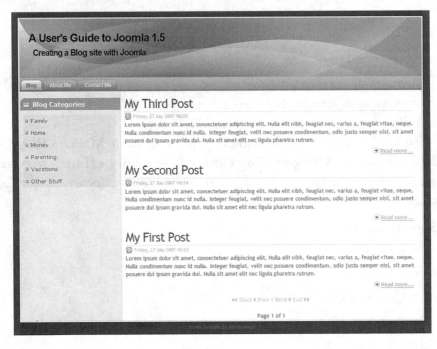

FIGURE 12.11 The home page with category submenu

While we are adding modules, let's create some more modules for some of the other functionality we want to achieve.

Adding Dynamic Modules

Joomla has many features that allow you to automatically generate page content that is continuously updated. We will add three modules to our left column that do this and are commonly found in blogs.

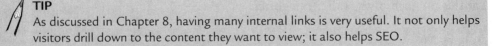

TIP

As discussed in Chapter 8, having many internal links is very useful. It not only helps visitors drill down to the content they want to view; it also helps SEO.

For our blog we are going to make use of three default Joomla modules:

- Latest News
- Most Read Content
- Related Items

To see the full effect of these modules, we need to add some more content. We also need to enter some meta data for the article.

Create the following articles with Lorem and enter the metadata keywords as indicated.

Category	Article Title	Keywords
Family	Family 1	1,2,3
Home	Home 1	2,3,4
Money	Money 1	3,4,5
Parenting	Parenting 1	4,5,6
Vacations	Vacations 1	5,6,7
Other Stuff	Other Stuff 1	6,7,8

After we do this, the Article Manager should look something like Figure 12.12.

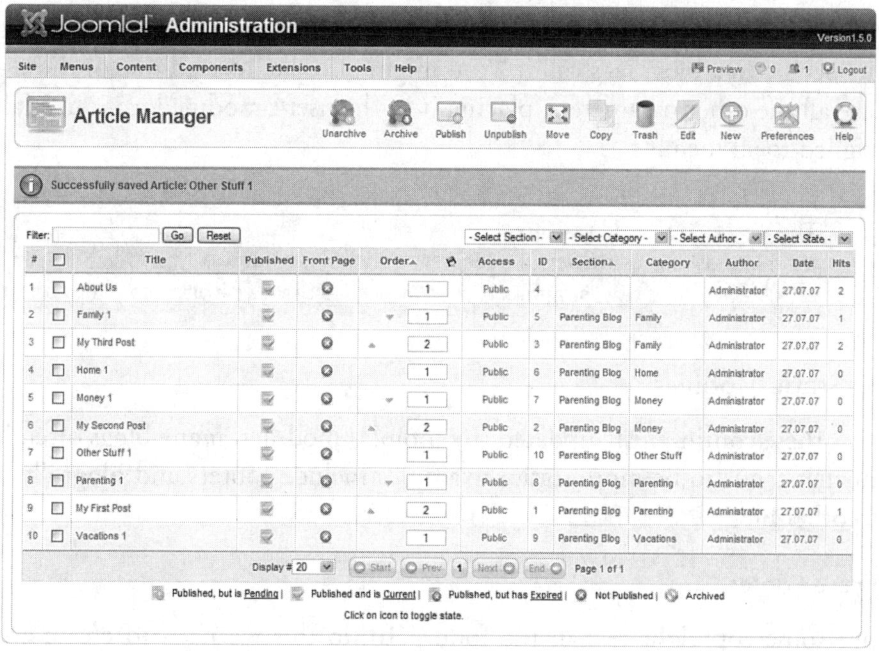

FIGURE 12.12 Building out the articles in the Article Manager

The reason we have carefully added the metadata is for the Related Items module. It uses this information to figure out what to show. As we discussed in Chapter 8 about getting traffic to a site, it is best to add two to six *specific* keywords for any article. Don't add the same keyword to everything; otherwise the Related Items module will just list the whole site!

First let's create a Latest News module.

Adding Latest News Module

Go to **Extensions > Module Manager > New** and select the Latest News module. To make it specific to a blog, let's call it Latest Blog Posts and leave all the other parameters, placing it in the left column. Make sure it is assigned to all menus.

Adding Most Read Content Module

Go to **Extensions > Module Manager > New** and select the Most Read module. I called mine What People Like. To make it specific to a blog, let's call it Latest Blog Posts and leave all the other parameters, placing it in the left column. Make sure it is assigned to all menus.

Adding Related Items Module

Go to **Extensions > Module Manager > New** and select the Related Item module. To make it specific to a blog, let's call it "You might also like to read one of these posts," and leave all the other parameters, placing it in the user4 module location. Make sure it is assigned to all menus.

> **The Least You Need to Know**
> Joomla has some powerful features that will dynamically show links to more articles in your site. Using this is a great way to draw visitors into your content.

Adding Static Modules

As well as these continuously updated (by Joomla) modules, many blogs often include content that tends to be more static. Examples include footers and blogrolls (lists of links to other blogs).

Adding the Footer

Let's put some copyright text in the footer. To do this we need to create a custom HTML module.

Go to **Extensions > Module Manager > New** and select a Custom HTML module. We have entered a simple copyright statement and made sure it appears in the correct location and the title is set not to be shown.

Adding a Blogroll

The idea of a blogroll is a very common one. The basic premise is the easiest way to get links to your blog is if you link to other blogs. This builds an informal web of linking between a group of blogs. In Joomla, a blogroll would be a simple Custom HTML module where you have links to the other blogs in question.

Go to **Extensions > Module Manager > New** and select a Custom HTML module. Enter a name (blogroll) and enable in the left column. In the editor area, enter in the site URLs you want to link to. After adding these modules, when we navigate to a particular article, we should see a screen like Figure 12.13.

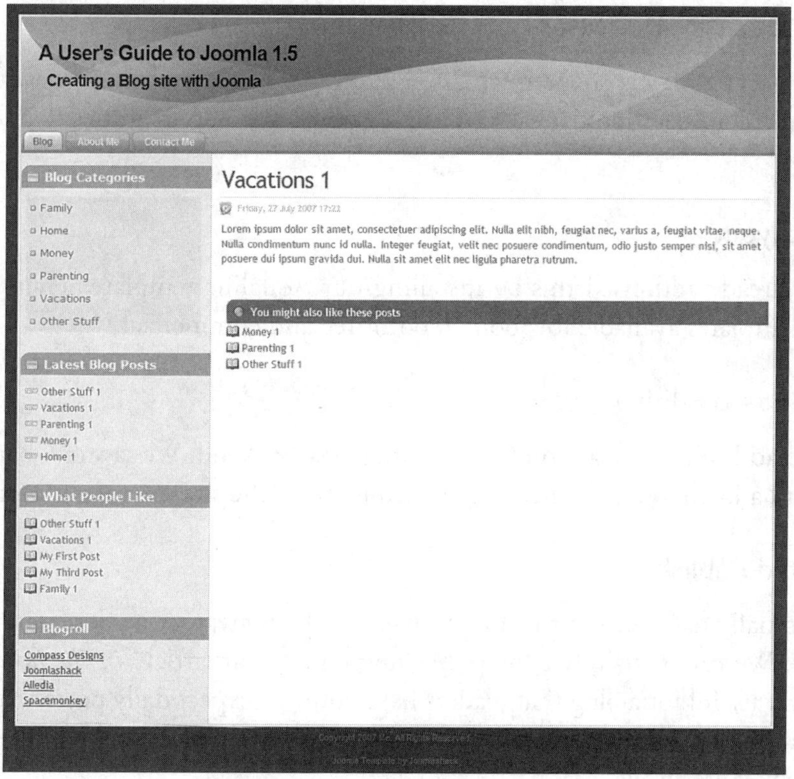

FIGURE 12.13 The frontend with left column modules

Here we have our latest blog posts and what the most popular blog posts are in the left column. We also have a mechanism for people to browse deeper into the site with the related items module.

> **NOTE**
> A common concept in blogging is the idea of classic content. As you begin to write articles, you will usually find you will write a bunch articles that will prove to be popular. People will link to them and comment on them, and they will form the backbone of your blog. Its important for visitors to be able to find them quickly and easily, hence the use of the Most Read module on all pages.

Now we need to start adding some of that basic functionality that will increase the stickiness of our blog.

Adding Basic Functionality to a Blog

At the beginning of this chapter, we listed a number of features that we would like to have in our blog. Let's look at each one and explore the opportunities to add them to Joomla.

Flexible Layout

We have already addressed this by installing our Aqualine template. There are thousands of templates available for Joomla, both free and commercial.

Browser-based Editing

It's easy to add content to a Joomla site through the backend. We saw in Chapter 7 that we can add a login and user menu to the frontend of the site to make it even easier.

Automated Publishing

Joomla actually has a nice bit of functionality hidden away in its date parameters for an article. We can actually set the publishing date for an article *in the future*. This is particularly useful for a blog that readers have come to expect daily posts. Heading out on a vacation? Just pre-write your blog posts and have them set to be published every day while you are away.

Categories

We already set up our blog into themed categories for our articles. We then created a subnavigation module that links to these categories.

Search Engine Optimized URLs

With the default installation of Joomla, the URLs given are difficult to understand. For example

```
index.php?option=com_content&view=article&catid=2:vacations&id=9:vacations-
1&Itemid=4
```

A phrase has been coined in Joomla for a feature that makes these easier to read called Search Engine Friendly URLs (SEF). In the chapter about getting traffic and SEO, I suggested that these might have less to do with search engines and more to do with being Human Friendly (something I like to call "HUF").

In the global configuration there are two options for SEF, as shown in Figure 12.14.

FIGURE 12.14 Enabling SEF in the global configuration

Turning on the basic SEF takes the link we're talking about and turns it into this:

```
index.php/blog/2-vacations/9-vacations-1
```

This is in the format of index.php/section/category/article. If your web host is running on Linux (for example, Apache), you can take advantage of mod_rewrite and get URLs like this:

Go to **Site > Global Configuration** and set Search Engine URLs to Yes.

Comment Systems

There are several comment extensions available for Joomla (1.0). As we have already mentioned, having site visitors able to leave comments is essential for blogs.

J! Reactions

J! Reactions was developed by S. A. DeCaro, and you can download it from http://extensions.joomla.org/component/option,com_mtree/task,viewlink/link_id,1595/Itemid,35/ or from the developer website http://jreactions.sdecnet.com.

Jomcomment

Jomcomment was developed by Azrul, and you can download it from http://extensions.joomla.org/component/option,com_mtree/task,viewlink/link_id,676/Itemid,35/   or from the developer website www.jom-comment.com.

This developer also makes an extended blog component called MyBlog. It integrates with Jomcomment and has additional functionality similar to many Wordpress features.

ComboMAX

ComboMAX was developed by Phil Taylor, and you can download it from http://extensions.joomla.org/component/option,com_mtree/task,viewlink/link_id,357/Itemid,35/ or from the developer website http://www.phil-taylor.com.

Syndication Feeds

More and more people are starting to use RSS as a means to gather their favorite blogs. Many RSS readers exist, and people take the feeds of the blogs they like to read and pull them into a single place—the RSS reader they like to use. (I use Thunderbird.) However, we need the ability to actually produce RSS feeds of our content.

Joomla 1.5 produces these out of the box. All we have to do is create a Syndication module and enable/publish it on a page. Joomla then creates an RSS syndication feed of that page. So if it's published on the home page, the feed will be of that page. If it's on an interior page, then the feed will be of that page (say, the Family category on our site).

Let's create a syndication module. Go to **Extensions > Module Manager > New** and select a Syndication module. Assign it to the home page only and use the parameters I have set up as shown in Figure 12.15.

This will now show an RSS link in the left column, as we can see in Figure 12.16.

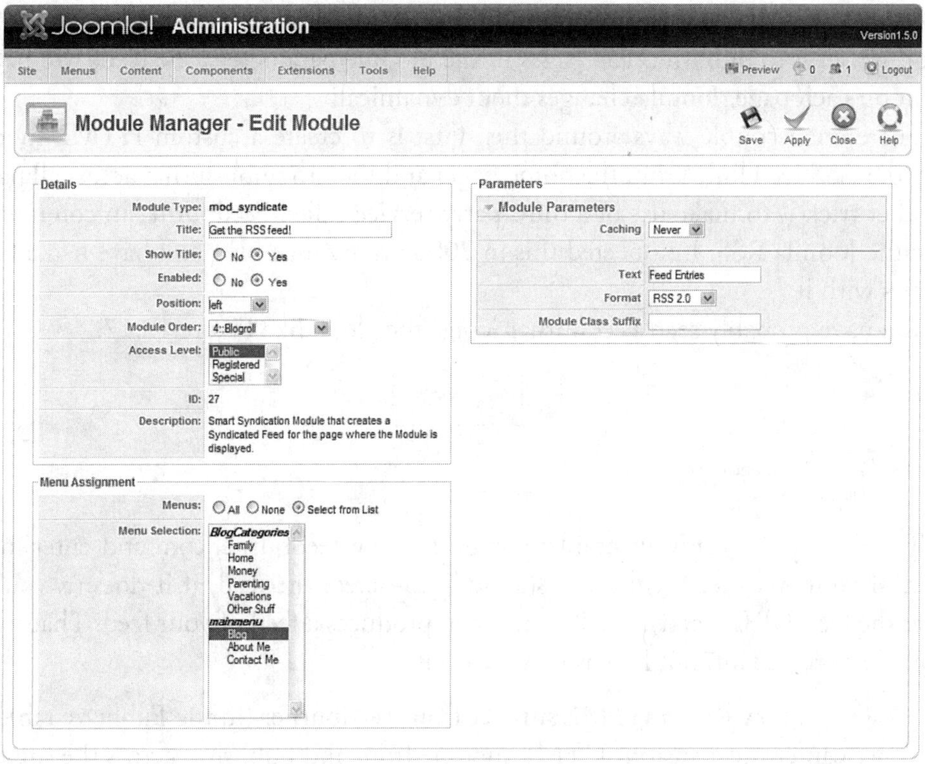

FIGURE 12.15 Editing the syndication module

FIGURE 12.16 The syndication module from the frontend

Now, ideally we would want to offer this RSS feed link on all the pages in the site. But if we set it to publish on all pages in the module parameters, the feeds will be different on each page. Joomla changes them dynamically.

There are a couple ways around this. First is to create a custom HTML module with the RSS feed link (from the home page) and then to publish that across all pages. Another trick is to make use of a third party service called Feedburner in conjunction with the Joomla RSS. I pioneered this in 2006 on my own blog and have had a lot of success with it.

You have probably seen Feedburner icons, they look like Figure 12.17.

FIGURE 12.17 The Feedburner icon

The concept is relatively simple; you go to www.feedburner.com and enter in the URL of your website. Feedburner should auto-detect the feed; if it doesn't, you can enter the feed URL exactly. Feedburner then produces a feed of your feed. That might seem a bit redundant, but here is why we do it:

- We can now get an HTML snippet from Feedburner (in the Publicize tab) that we can create a custom HTML module from and publish it across the site.

- We can add the Feedcount feature of Feedburner (that shows the number of subscribers).

- We can get global and details stats of who is subscribing to our feed, as shown in Figure 12.18.

FIGURE 12.18 Feedburner stats

- Last, and most usefully, we can take advantage of an email subscription service called Feedblitz.

The site I have been developing here as an example is running on a localhost, and as such, Feedburner would not be able to find it. To illustrate this example I will use the first method I described of creating a custom HTML module from the source of the home page.

If we view the home page source, we see the following code:

```
<div class="moduletable">
<h3>Get the RSS feed!</h3>
<a href="?option=com_content&amp;view=section&amp;format=feed&amp;id=1&amp;type=rss&amp;Itemid=4">
<img src="images/M_images/livemarks.png" alt="" align="top" border="0" />
<span>Feed Entries</span>
</a>
</div>
```

The `<div>` tag is created by Joomla. We need to copy everything inside that tag and paste it into a custom HTML module. After we have done that, we can unpublish the real Joomla syndication module. We now have a feed link on all the pages of our site.

Email Notification

Pushing out blog posts via email through an opt-in list is a great way to build readerships. RSS technology is still relatively new, and many people still prefer email as their subscription vehicle.

If we are using Feedburner, there is another service that Feedburner offers called Feedblitz. This allows people to subscribe to an email list of the feed. When new posts are made, subscribers automatically get an email with the post. This is a great way of building readership and traffic. It even can supply posts via Skype! I use this on my blog as an alternative to a traditional email newsletter.

To set this up we go to www.feedblitz.com and create an account and then a subscription. We can then create a custom HTML Joomla module with the simple sign up form or icon from Feedblitz.

If we look closely at the Copyblogger blog used as an example earlier (www.copyblogger.com), we see he is using both Feedburner and Feedblitz.

Search

Joomla has a very robust search function built into the core. To use it, we need to create a search module.

Go to **Extensions > Module Manager > New** and select a Search module. Give it a suitable title and then enable/publish it in the left column.

Trackback

There is currently no extension for Joomla that adds Trackback functionality to a Joomla site. There is a (1.0) extension that has this functionality as part of a bigger extension called MyBlog.

Social Bookmarking

You might have noticed that I have not mentioned a very popular blog topic these days, *social bookmarking*. I would not go so far as to say that there are not benefits to be found in social bookmarking sites such as Digg or del.icio.us, but I don't think it's as critical as people make it out to be—for several reasons.

First is information overload. It's very common to see blogs with a whole row of social bookmark tags. I think that these are going the way that banner ads have over the last few years; site visitors have a blind spot for them.

Second, if someone wants to bookmark your site with one of these other sites, they can do it anyway; they don't need your insistent icon asking them to do so.

Last, according to Digg itself, 94% of Digg users are male. 88% of Digg users are in the 18–39 year age range, and 52% of them are "IT professionals, developers, or engineers." That's a very narrow demographic. Unless you have a blog that is targeted at this demographic, none of the ensuing traffic you might get will do much good anyway. It's unfocussed, untargeted, and will not convert very well.

We now have a basic blog site ready to which we can add lots of high-quality articles and blog posts. Our home page now looks like Figure 12.19.

> **The Least You Need to Know**
> Comments and syndication are critical features of a blog.

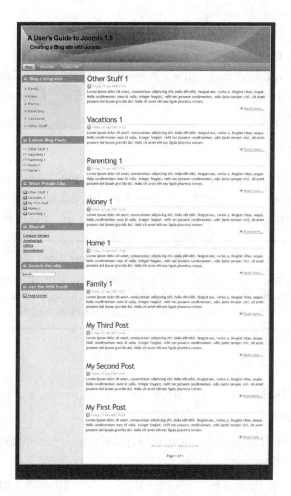

FIGURE 12.19 The completed blog site

Extending a Blog Website Beyond the Basics

One of the main reasons we would want to power a blog site using Joomla is that we want to use it as a foundation for other efforts. A classic example might be authors or consultants who might well want to offer further products or services.

There are a couple of obvious features with which we might want to extend our site.

Forums

Comments are fine for having visitor interactivity on blog posts, but a forum is a great mechanism for a community to come around the topic of a website. It allows the site visitor to initiate conversation. An excellent choice for a forum is Fireboard (www.bestofjoomla.com).

Ecommerce

If you have a few digital goods, perhaps an e-book, then there are a couple of good alternatives. A mature extension that is based on paypal is MosIPN from phil.taylor.com. A more robust solution is a recent offering from ijoomla.com called DigiStore.

User's Guide Chapter 12 Demo Site

A demo of this site is available at www.joomlabook.com. It is an exact copy of what you should have if you followed all the steps in this chapter. You can log into the administrative back-end so you can see the site framework and the sections, categories, and menus that were set up.

Summary

In this chapter, we looked at how Joomla can be used to create a basic blog that can be extended as a site grows. In particular we saw that

- A blog is a modern communication vehicle that is becoming more important in today's Web-connected world.

- News and information moves faster than ever in smaller and smaller news cycles. A blog that is easy to update is an important tool for any organization to communicate with its stakeholders.

- A blog isn't about widgets and gizmos; its about the quality of the content. You need a tool that can help you organize and present your blog posts as easily as possible.

- How you organize your sections and categories will depend on what type of blog you have. Standalone blogs can have all of the posts under a single section of the site.

- Joomla has some powerful features that will dynamically show links to more articles in your site. Using this is a great way to draw visitors into your content.

- Comments and syndication are critical features of a blog.

APPENDIX A

Getting Help

Community Forums

One of the great things about Joomla, like many open source projects, is the enormous community that surrounds the project. To give a sense of the number of users, we can take a snapshot of the membership levels of some of the biggest forums.

Forum	URL	Posts (Sept 2007)
Joomla!	http://forum.joomla.org	989,241
Community Builder	http://www.joomlapolis.com	44,750
Joomlashack	http://www.joomlashack.com/	24,693
Joomlart	http://www.joomlart.com	26,637
Joomlahacks	http://www.joomlahacks.com/	19,143

Most of these are the forums for commercial products, but they are a great resource for getting help. Make sure you clearly communicate your problem and be patient for answers.

Note, these don't include Joomla sites specific to countries. Most have a Joomla-sanctioned site with a forum. For example, in Germany you will find www.joomla.de.

Help Sites

There are a number of websites that have good (original) guides and tutorials about Joomla. I say original as there are many sites that tend to jump on the Joomla bandwagon, put up a couple of tutorials, and then cover the site in ads.

A selection of the better quality websites include

> http://www.compassdesigns.net/
> http://www.howtojoomla.net
> http://www.thejoomlauniversity.com/
> http://www.alledia.com/

and obviously the Mother Ship

> http://help.joomla.org/ (for end users)
> http://dev.joomla.org/ (for developers)

Getting Help from Google

With such a large community, it's likely that someone might have come across a problem you are experiencing before you. Try searching in Google with a phrase that describes your issue or, even better, the error you are getting (if any). For the best results, enclose the phrase in quotes.

APPENDIX B

Joomla! Case Studies

Joomla powers millions of websites. One of the amazing things is the range of sites that you can find it on. This Appendix gives you some of the results from a Joomlashack survey and also six case study interviews from various types of websites.

Six Case Studies for Organizations That Use Joomla

In May 2007 Joomlashack conducted a survey of Joomla users. Over 3,600 users responded. One of the questions asked in this survey was, "What type of site do you use Joomla for?" The results are shown in Figure B.1.

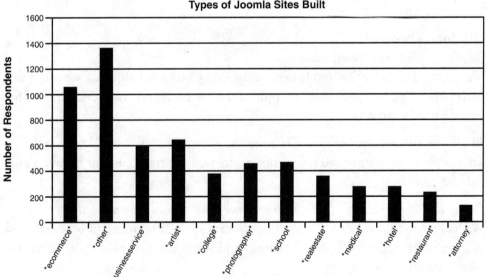

FIGURE B.1 Results from the Joomlashack survey

Clearly, Joomla enjoys widespread use. To provide some insight into these Joomla-powered sites, six Joomlashack clients generously agreed to take part in a brief interview to offer case studies in how real organizations use Joomla. They represent (I hope) a broad sample of the spectrum of organizations and users that are using Joomla.

The six case studies include

- a magazine publishing company
- a medium-sized municipality in Florida
- a public library in metro Detroit
- an interconnectivity service company
- a community/news site about Macs
- a community site about smartphones

www.yourwedding.com.au (MP Media)

Welcome to Your Wedding (www.yourwedding.com.au) helps brides in Australia find resources they need (see Figure B.2) and is a companion site to their offline magazine publication. It combines many resources, such as directories, a blog, shopping, a planner, and forum, all tied together with Joomla. It also serves as the online presence for its offline magazines.

John Paoloni, Owner

Q: *Briefly describe your organization.*

A: We are traditional print publishers, publishing our own titles of wedding and parenting magazines plus contract publishing for clients. A small company of five aimed at niche markets.

Q: *Briefly describe the goals of your Web presence.*

A: To complement our printed titles plus ensure we have fresh content between publication dates.

Q: *Briefly describe the status of your Web presence prior to using Joomla.*

A: We had a good basic HTML website that was OK for the time and was well used, but we realized the Web was changing, and we needed to provide a better and more modern presence.

Q: *Why did you use Joomla to create your site?*

A: To take advantage of Content Management System (CMS) to keep track of a rapidly growing website and avoid trying to link about 1000 static HTML web pages. A friend recommended it, and I remember recoiling in horror when he showed me the backend, etc. and thinking there was no way I had room left in my brain for another software learning curve.

Q: *What third-party extensions do you have installed?*

A: We have experimented with most of the commercial add-ons but mainly use

Joomcloner	Mosets Tree	Letterman
Simple Pro gallery	Front page slideshow	WYSIWYGPro
Docman	JomComment	

FIGURE B.2 www.yourwedding.com.au

Q: *What parts of Joomla do you struggle with the most? Which features do you like the most?*

A: I found it hard at first with the menu structure and its relationship with modules.

    The overall management of the CMS is great, ability to use a subscriber newsletter function from within site, the ability to change templates fairly easily; a great feature of Joomla overall is that it seems to be maturing in terms of well supported availability of templates/components and other add-ons.

Q: *How has Joomla changed how your organization uses your website? Has it changed your Web goals?*

A: We update the site(s) more regularly; we are now more confident with using and updating and improving our site as it is just simpler to do it from the backend in real time. We don't dread updates like we used to.

Q: *How (if it has) has Joomla made it easier to reach your Web presence goals?*

A: As a print publisher, I remember thinking that the last thing I wanted to do was change the way we did things—i.e., we had perfected our print production/workflow for CMYK printed material. Then the Web came along and demanded new ways of working. (At the early stage, I agreed with Homer Simpson when he said, "The Internet? Is that thing still around?")

    It is now a vital component of our business. I doubt our two wedding magazines would have survived without our early adoption of this new medium and our integration of print/Web. (Interesting some of the big print publishers are now playing catch-up as they denied this new medium and just tried to protect the print side of their business)

    Joomla, with its great array of add-ons, has allowed us to take the lead in giving our clients (advertisers) a great website to promote their business and link to them. It gives us a tidy way of controlling our pages in a database-driven site and manages our data and design as separate beasts.

www.longwoodfl.org (City of Longwood, Florida)

The City of Longwood is a medium-sized municipality in Florida. Seeking to update an old site, it carefully examined various CMS options including open source alternatives. Figure B.3 shows the site.

FIGURE B.3 City of Longwood website

Ryan I. Spinella, Executive Assistant

Q: *Briefly describe your organization.*

A: The City of Longwood is a municipality in Florida with 14,000 residents and 150 employees.

Q: *Briefly describe the goals of your Web presence.*

A: We aim to keep citizens informed of official business, provide contact information, an events calendar, and other various local information.

Q: *Briefly describe the status of your Web presence prior to using Joomla.*

A: We had an outdated site that was difficult to update and poorly designed.

Q: *Why did you use Joomla to create your site?*

A: The open source concept appealed to the City Commission, and price was less than for proprietary options.

Q: *What third-party extensions do you have installed?*

A: WYSIWYGPro   DocMan

    PHP Auction   Thyme 1.3

Q: *What parts of Joomla do you struggle with the most? Which features do you like the most?*

A: The most difficult part in the beginning was figuring out the program structure, but after a few months of working with it, things became quite clear. By far the best feature of Joomla is the ease of updating pages once the site has been built.

    After the initial training for myself and staff, several departments worked together to initiate a plan to build content for the site. This process was very dynamic in that each department could work simultaneously on their particular pages, and I could do final editing and layout once they were finished.

Q: *How has Joomla changed how your organization uses your website? Has it changed your Web goals?*

A: Joomla has enabled several people within the organization to maintain their own pages. It has also provided a much more comprehensive way for the City to share documents, photos, and other materials with the public. It has not changed our Web goals, but it has certainly enhanced them.

    Joomla has also provided great improvements to how we inform the public through the Thyme 1.3 calendar component. I should also mention, the auction site the City was able to implement through PHP Auction allows us to sell surplus items to willing buyers. These are all great improvements to the way Longwood uses its website to achieve its ultimate goal of connecting with and providing information for the public.

Q: *How (if it has) has Joomla made it easier to reach your Web presence goals?*

A: Joomla has firmly established our Web presence through robustness and design. Furthermore, commercial Joomla developers greatly assisted the City in achieving this goal through dedicated support, a sleek design, and valuable industry knowledge.

Joomla is truly a powerful competitor in the world of CMS, and that has been proven once again through this project. Key to creating the City's website has been the user-friendly features of Joomla, a dedicated city staff, and the quality of professional Joomla third-party companies.

www.ropl.org (Royal Oak Public Library—Michigan)

The public library in Royal Oak, Michigan, has a great website for the community, shown in Figure B.4. It includes many interactive features made possible with Joomla.

FIGURE B.4 Royal Oak Public Library website

Eric Hayes. Technology Specialist

Q: *Briefly describe your organization.*

A: Royal Oak Public Library (www.ropl.org) is a public library in metro Detroit serving 60,000 residents. We have about 112,500 books and audio-visual materials in our collection. We provide 36 computers for public use. We receive about 1200 hits to our website every day.

Q: *Briefly describe the goals of your web presence.*

A: Our goal for our web presence is to convey current and updated information about programs and events at our library, book reviews and recommendations, a portal for research databases and a seamless transition to our collection catalog.

Q: *Briefly describe the status of your web presence prior to using Joomla.*

A: Prior to using Joomla, our website was comprised of basic HTML and tables and nearly every page had a different look and feel to it. This included the layout, color scheme, and font attributes. One person was designated to add content.

Q: *Why did you use Joomla to create your site?*

A: We decided to use Joomla because we were fascinated with the flexibility, usability, third-party extensions, and ability to have all our staff members add content when they want.

Q: *What third-party extensions do you have installed?*

A: Attend Events (program registration)
    Bookmarks (portal for research database)
    Extended Menu (menu structure and pathway)
    FacileForms (advanced forms)
    Fireboard (forum)
    JCal Pro (calendar)
    JCE (WYSIWYG editor)
    Jom Comment (allow for public comments on content)
    Jombackup (daily, automatic backup of Joomla database)
    MyContent (allows staff to add content to website without admin privileges)
    Opening Times (flexible display of hours of operation)

Q: *What parts of Joomla do you struggle with the most? Which features do you like the most?*

A: We struggled with how to organize our Sections and Categories to form our navigation menus. This wasn't due to Joomla, though. What is a limit in Joomla is the ability for staff members to add images/media to the content that they publish with the third-party extension, MyContent. Joomla requires someone with admin privileges to upload images/media to their web server before another staff member can display it in their content.

Q: *How has Joomla changed how your organization uses your website? Has it changed your web goals?*

A: Joomla has allowed all staff members to add content in a blog format to our website easily. It has freed up our webmaster to concentrate on other performance and design issues. We now accept online registration for programs that require it, online volunteer forms and comments on content from visitors. Joomla helped us realize what our web goals should be. One week of playing with Joomla and you'll be amazed at what you can do with it.

Q: *How (if it has) has Joomla made it easier to reach your web presence goals?*

A: Our web goals have been met by having flexible content be displayed on our website without much management. Our programs and events are displayed and removed automatically, we can keep track of the usage of our research databases and some visitors to the website have left comments on content which opens up communication between them and our staff.

www.telx.com (The Telx Group, Inc.)

The Telx Group's site, shown in Figure B.5, is an excellent example of the next generation of company brochure sites that use a CMS. Joomla makes it possible to have a coherent look (the template) across the site and makes it easy to add and maintain content.

Michael Di Martino, Director of MIS

Q: *Briefly describe your organization.*

A: Telx provides an interconnect facility to, primarily, the telecommunications industry.

    Each customer is provided a panel in our "Meet Me Rooms" so they can quickly and cheaply cross connect with other companies. We are carrier-neutral.

Q: *Briefly describe the goals of your Web presence.*

A: To provide industry-related news and trends within our industry as well as company information.

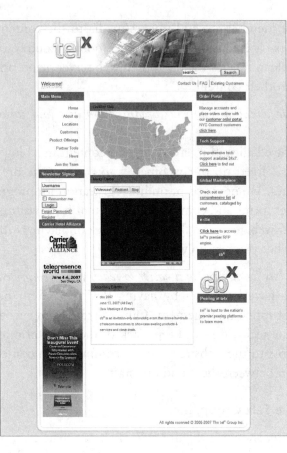

FIGURE B.5 Telx Group website

Q: *Briefly describe the status of your Web presence prior to using Joomla.*

A: Static XHTML pages

Q: *Why did you use Joomla to create your site?*

A: We needed to create a WEB 2.0 site with a sophisticated CMS system on a very small budget. Joomla fit these requirements perfectly.

Q: *What third-party extensions do you have installed?*

A: Docman (Extended Menu)

Q: *What parts of Joomla do you struggle with the most? Which features do you like the most?*

A: Adding links to content on other sites. Cross Browser Style Sheets

Q: *How has Joomla changed how your organization uses your website? Has it changed your Web goals?*

A: We no longer need a dedicated individual to handle site updates. Now each department is in charge of updating their own content.

Q: *How (if it has) has Joomla made it easier to reach your Web presence goals?*

A: The CMS and templating has enabled us to keep the format of our site intact as we add and edit content.

www.nzmac.com (NZMac.com)

NZMac.com is a high-traffic community news site. It leverages Joomla to bring a community of Mac users together online. The site is shown in Figure B.6.

FIGURE B.6 NCMac.com website

Philip Roy, Webmaster

Q: *Briefly describe your organization.*

A: NZMac.com is a website owned and operated by Philip Roy and dedicated to supporting the New Zealand Macintosh community. It includes the latest New Zealand Macintosh news, discussion forums, international news and reviews. NZ Mac events, businesses, user groups, and Mac items for sale are all featured on the site.

Q: *Briefly describe the goals of your Web presence.*

A: Mac users worldwide are an enthusiastic and obsessive bunch of people. With NZMac.com, the focus is specifically on developing a sense of community within New Zealand and the Macintosh user base. Although the site is owned by Philip Roy, many facets of the site are developed through consensus and through gauging the needs of sites users. It is hoped that NZ Mac users, User Groups, companies, and institutions will take an active part in using the site and contribute to it. Through the use of discussion forums, buy/sell areas, NZ news and information with a specific New Zealand flavour, it's hoped to provide a website that Mac users in New Zealand will look to as their main source of all things Macintosh.

Q: *Briefly describe the status of your Web presence prior to using Joomla.*

A: With the exception of the discussion forum (which has always been a database-driven form system) NZMac.com began its life as HTML pages (see http://www.nzmac.com/previous_site_designs.html), managed using Dreamweaver. RSS feeds of news from overseas sites lessened the amount of work required to update the site at the time, but more was needed.

Q: *Why did you use Joomla to create your site?*

A: I explored a number of CMS systems and had used Xoops for some time. The decision to move to Mambo (and then Joomla) was for a variety of reasons:

- I wanted to be able to be anywhere at anytime and have the ability to update the site.

- I wanted to allow users to contribute news and interact with the site more.

- I wanted an easy templating system for site design.

- Features such as RSS feeds for the site were of importance.

- Its modular approach meant that I could easily add new features and functionality with little difficulty over time.

- StaticXT was a component that allowed an easy way to use existing HTML files until such time that I brought content into the database, so migration was quick at first and then built upon later.

- Compared to other open source systems, Mambo/Joomla was easy to understand and (despite the Mambo-Joomla split that eventuated) had a large community that wasn't being affected by individual users' politics.

Q: *What third-party extensions do you have installed?*

A: **Components**
Bookmarks component (www.tegdesign.ch)
Community Builder (www.joomlapolis.com)
eXiT-Poll (www.phpprojects.net)
Google Maps (www.atlspecials.com/index.php?option=com_google_maps&Itemid=36)
JA Submit (www.joomlart.com)
JCal Pro (dev.anything-digital.com)
JCE Editor (http://www.cellardoor.za.net/jce/)
JomComment (www.azrul.com)
joomlaXplorer (http://developer.joomla.org/sf/projects/joomlaxplorer)
Knowledgebase (www.phil-taylor.com)
mosDirectory (www.phil-taylor.com)
OpenSEF (www.j-prosolution.com)
OpenWiki (www.j-prosolution.com)
Phil-A-Form (www.phil-taylor.com)
RSS XT (www.nodetraveller.com)
SMF Bridge (www.simplemachines.org)
YaNC (www.joomla-addons.org)

Mambots of Interest
TagBot (www.fijiwebdesign.com)

Modules of Interest
mod_kl_evalphp—used to pull in PHP code for OpenAds advertising (www.idealagent.com)

Q: *What parts of Joomla do you struggle with the most? Which features do you like the most?*

A: My biggest issue has been anything that isn't directly integrated into Joomla. The best example of this is the SMF forum, which is bridged…meaning that items of information (i.e., user information) are shared but not truly combined. This has caused users a few headaches with logging in and out, so I am planning to move to the forthcoming Fireboard (www.bestofjoomla.com) forum component, as it is truly integrated.

At the same time, Joomla still does not cater for true control over who accesses what or can submit items and so on, so access control and functionality has taken a long time to sort out and is still crude in many respects.

I also find the concept of archived stories very confusing. I archive nothing because this seems to suggest the item is no longer accessible.

Q: *How has Joomla changed how your organization uses your website? Has it changed your Web goals?*

A: It has just made life so much easier, made control and organizing the site so much simpler, whilst allowing new functionality to be added in and tested much more quickly.

I may not be the tidiest of people, but I insist that my websites are tidy and exceptionally well structured. It has meant that developing content for Joomla has been so much quicker than traditional web creation.

This means I can respond to news stories, users' requests, and site use in a much more immediate and dynamic way, and it has allowed the site to reach out to the web community far better, through the advanced functionality and through a web presence that is far more functional and professional than I was providing previously.

Q: *How (if it has) has Joomla made it easier to reach your Web presence goals?*

A: Through something that Joomla and NZMac.com see as vital to their existence— Community! The vibrancy, support, enthusiasm, passion, and pure talent that is out there…and the fact that these people so willingly give their time to help others is overwhelming and should never be discounted as such an important factor in why Joomla is such a superb web system. It's not just about the fantastic software…it's about the community around it.

www.everythingtreo.com (Everything Treo)

Everything Treo is another example of a community site focused on technology. It is actually part of a series of sites all with a similar theme. The site is shown in Figure B.7.

FIGURE B.7 Everything Treo website

Christopher Meinck

Q: *Briefly describe your organization.*

A: Our organization, Smart Phone Resource, Inc., runs a family of niche website communities that provide information for specific smartphones including the Palm Treo, Motorola Q, and Apple iPhone.

Q: *Briefly describe the goals of your Web presence.*

A: Our primary goal was to create websites that offer a wealth of information specific to a particular mobile device. In addition to offering news, our focus was to create an interactive site that allowed for our members to download software, submit reviews, and take part in our discussion forums. Most importantly, it was critical to have brand consistency throughout the end user experience.

Q: *Briefly describe the status of your Web presence prior to using Joomla.*

A: The site used static HTML, and each page needed to be hand-coded. The site was relatively small due to the time-consuming process of updating the architecture and pages. Our forums acted as a completely separate entity from our main site and lacked cohesiveness.

Q: *Why did you use Joomla to create your site?*

A: In order for the site to experience growth, we needed a CMS. As the site had started to grow, it had become increasingly difficult to manage. One of the requirements in selecting a CMS was to find a system that allowed for rapid deployment of dynamic pages and content.

Our primary reason for selecting Joomla was the capability to integrate membership databases with our vBulletin forums. Although we had discussion forums, there had been an obvious disconnect between the main site and the forums. By integrating membership from our forums to our Joomla site, we were able to create a seamless end user experience.

Another key factor in the decision had been the SEO capabilities inherent in the Joomla architecture. There were also a number of available extensions and patches that allowed for the further optimization of the sites for search engines.

After researching other solutions, it was clear that Joomla offered the best in class when it came to content management, membership integration, and SEO capabilities.

Q: *What third-party extensions do you have installed?*

A: We currently have the following third-party extensions installed:

SEF Advance	jReviews
SEF Patch Extended	JomComment
DocMan	MosKnowledgebase
BBPixel jvbPlugin	Social Bookmarker Mambot
JoomlaXplorer	

Q: *What parts of Joomla do you struggle with the most? Which features do you like the most?*

A: At times, we struggle with the compatibility of third-party software. Joomla upgrades can become increasingly difficult when you rely on a host of third-party extensions that also require updating. We have found varying levels of support for the products utilized on the sites. We normally test a product on one site and will then roll it out to the other two once confirmed that it works properly on the test site.

The extendibility is what our organization likes most about Joomla. Our company is constantly looking at other sites and how they are using new technologies to offer a more user-friendly and interactive experience. If it's being done on the Internet, you can count on a Joomla developer to offer similar functionality through an extension of some type. Our sites recently launched review sections that are on par with enterprise-level sites at a fraction of the cost. This will allow us to offer an expansive review section and a new level of interaction with our site visitors. Joomla empowers us as website developers, and more importantly it empowers our visitors.

Summary

Several common themes emerge about Joomla from these case studies and seem to be the hallmarks of what Joomla can offer to an organization:

- Most sites were previously in separate pages of HTML. Keeping them all coherent was difficult. The common template of Joomla has allowed a common graphical design site-wide that is on autopilot. The organization can focus much more on content.
- All of the sites added third-party extensions to a lesser or greater extent to achieve the functionality they needed. Almost all of them took advantage of a commercial component.
- The effectiveness in adding new content to the site was greatly enhanced. Organizations were able to make updates in real time, and many found they were able to greatly expand their base of people contributing to the content of the site.
- Taking advantage of some core Joomla features and third-party functionality, many of these sites have a rich interactive user experience. Being able to allow site visitors to participate in creating content is the next threshold in the development of the Web.

Clearly, Joomla has helped these organizations create a Web presence that was previously only possible for big companies and/or big budgets. Open source software such as Joomla, along with a wide availability of commercial and GPL extensions, extends this opportunity to everybody, big and small, alike.

APPENDIX C

A Quick Start to SEO

I thought I would provide a much shorter version of Chapter 8, "Getting Traffic to Your Site" here. Use this if you already have a site ranked and want to see what you can implement to get your ranking higher.

Much of the information here is based on two 2007 studies about ranking in Google from SEOmoz.org[1] and Sistrix[2].

1. Keyword Use in Title Tag

The number one factor in ranking a page on search engines is the *title tag*. These are the words in the source of a page in `<title>` and appear in the blue bar of your browser.

Choose the title of an article very carefully. Joomla will use the title of the article in the title tag (what appears in the blue bar).

2. Anchor Text of Inbound Link

Anchor text appears underlined and in blue (unless it's been styled) for a link from one web page to another.

Try to get some inbound links to your article using the keywords you want to be ranked for. Two ways to do this are through online press services such as PRweb.com or simply by networking.

3. Global Link Popularity of Site (PageRank)

How many pages are linking to your page is called *link popularity*, or in Google, *PageRank*.

The more sites that link to you, the better. Joomla is a Content Management System (CMS) that helps you add content quickly. Create one quality content page per day. Quality content is the most important factor to getting inbound links. For a site that will perform well, you eventually need 200-odd pages of content. This is the important point: *Quick SEO is dead!*. The only way to perform well in SEO now is to have a rich content site.

4. Age of Site

When was the domain of the site registered?

There's nothing you can do about this, but there is evidence that suggests that how long you have your domain registered makes a difference (spam sites are not registered for long). Go and extend your domain registration for a couple years.

5. Link Popularity Within the Site

This is the number of links to the page from inside your own domain.

Because of #2, it's critical that you link to articles from within your site using the right anchor text. Make sure that you

- Use the linked titles setting.
- Make good use of the Most Read, Related Items, and Latest News modules.
- Have a sitemap component linked to directly from your home page.

6. Topical Relevance of Inbound Links and Popularity of Linking Site

It's important that you get quality inbound links. This means they have to be from a site that is topically related to yours and one that has a high PageRank. It's worth submitting once to directories (then forget about it).

- Type **related:www.yoursite.com** into Google and contact the top 20 returns for links.

7. Link Popularity of Site in Topic Community

Make sure you have a blog on your site and network with others in your topical community. Make sure you frequently link to other blogs in your topical community as well.

8. Keyword Use in Body Text

You need to make sure you have a high keyword density of the phrase you are optimizing for in the content of the page. Still important, the German study from Sistrix identified some interesting results:

- Place targeted keywords in the first and last paragraphs. There is a simple trick here—write your quality content and then use the tool of your choice to find the keyword density. *Then*, take the top three words and add them to the meta keywords in the parameters part of the page (in Joomla admin). This is somewhat backwards for some maybe, but it optimizes a page for what you actually wrote, rather than making you write a page optimized for certain words (which I always find difficult).

- Keywords in H2–H6 headline tags seem to have an influence on the rankings, while keywords in H1 headline tags seem to be getting less valuable. Modify the output of the core content component through a template override file.

- Using keywords in bold or strong tags—slight effect, same with img alt tags and filenames.

> **NOTE**
> The two SEO studies identified some other factors of measured/estimated influence on search results that had some impact, but not as much as the first seven listed.

9. File Size

The file size doesn't seem to influence the ranking of a web page on Google, although smaller sites tend to have slightly higher rankings. Optimize those images!

10. Clean URL

Although keywords in the file name (URL) don't seem to have a positive effect (based on the German study), a URL with few parameters (?id=123, and so on) is important. Turn on Joomla SEF but don't get anal about it.

11. Utilize Your Error Pages

Too often, companies forget about error pages (such as 404 errors). Error pages should always re-direct "lost" users to valuable, text-based pages. Placing text links to major site pages is an excellent practice. Visit www.cnet.com/error for an example of a well-utilized error page. To make the error page fit with the rest of the theme of your site, create an uncategorized article and then copy the source as viewed on a web page, and put that into the 404 file.

What's Not Here?

You'll see much of the discussion about SEO revolving around various SEF components. These components allow for advanced manipulation of URLs and meta tags. Neither of these were identified as a major factor in either SEO analysis. Joomla's default SEF does a good job at removing extra URL parameters. Once turned on, you can concentrate on the much more important factors influencing your search engine rank, such as quality content and link building campaigns.

If you are more interested in Joomla SEO, I recommend Steve Burge's *Joomla SEO* ebook. You can find out more about it at www.joomla-seobook.com.

---

[1] http://www.seomoz.org/article/search-ranking-factors

[2] http://www.free-seo-news.com/newsletter265.htm

APPENDIX D

Installing WAMP5

WAMP5 is a complete package of PHP5, Apache, and MySQL for Windows that allows you to run a website from your "local" desktop/laptop computer running the Windows operating system.

WAMP5 is free to use (GPL license), but you can make a donation on the developer's site. You can obtain a copy of WAMP5 from http://www.wampserver.com/en/.

This page is shown in Figure D.1.

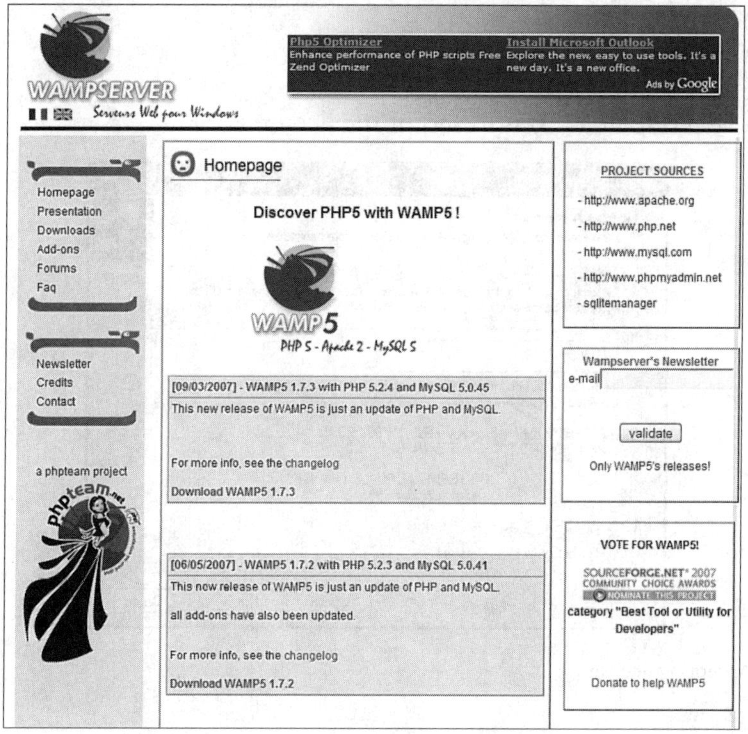

FIGURE D.1 Web page from which to download WAMP5

Clicking the download link takes you to the download page (http://www.wampserver.com/en/download.php), which has the latest version of WAMP5.

After downloading, run the download package, and you start the Setup Wizard (Figure D.2).

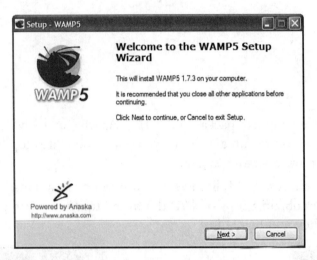

FIGURE D.2 Start of WAMP5 install

The next step (Figure D.3) is to accept the license.

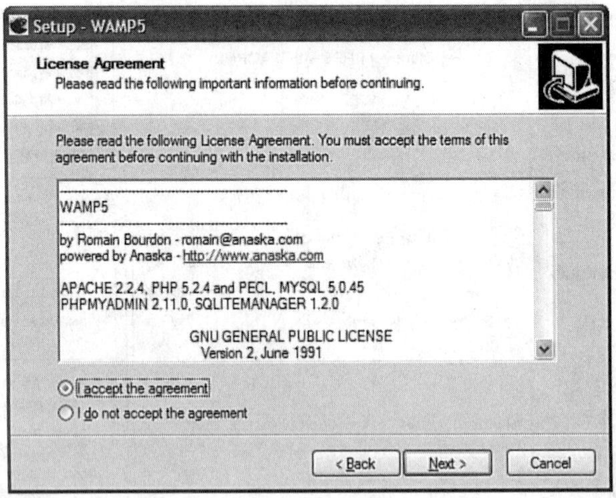

FIGURE D.3 Accepting license

You now need to select the installation folder (Figure D.4).

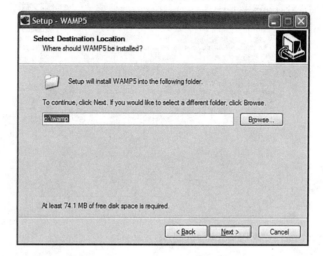

FIGURE D.4 Selecting installation folder

Next you must choose the Start Menu link name (Figure D.5).

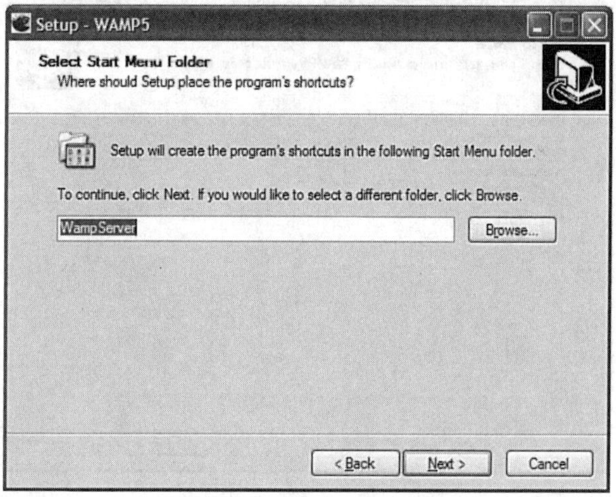

FIGURE D.5 Select Start Menu name

You now have an option to have WAMP5 start automatically (Figure D.6). I usually don't enable this and run it manually.

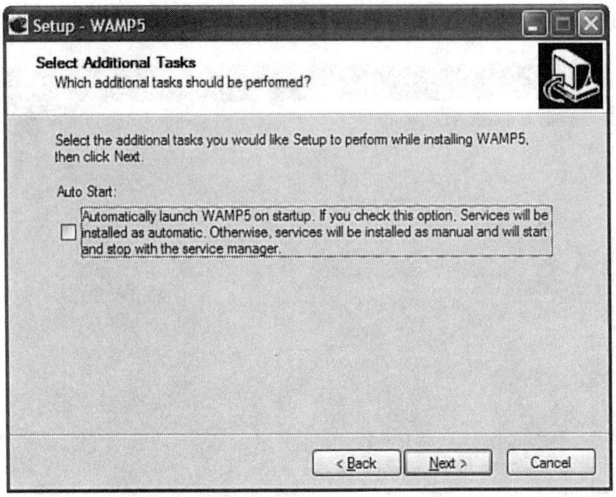

FIGURE D.6 Option to start WAMP5 automatically as a service

The Wizard now shows you the settings you have chosen (Figure D.7), and you're ready to install.

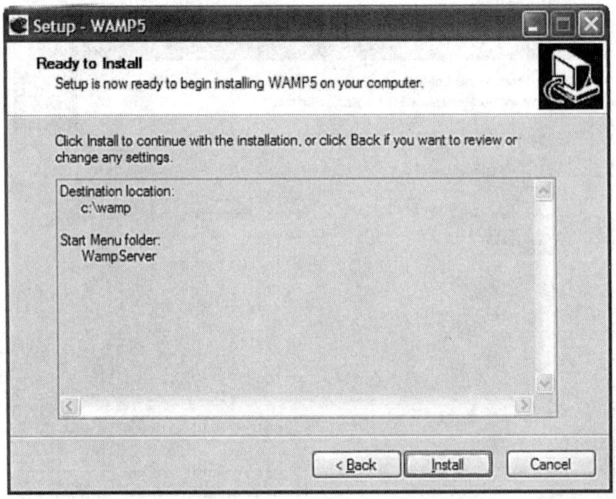

FIGURE D.7 Installation options ready

You now need to choose a folder that will be the location for all the sites you want to work on (Figure D.8). I usually just accept the default: \www\.

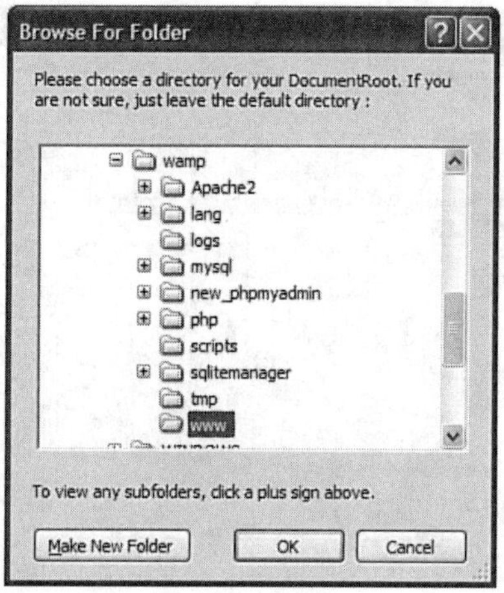

FIGURE D.8 Website folder

WAMP5 is now installed on your computer. Next, you are taken through a series of screens that set up WAMP5. First (Figure D.9) is what to call the SMTP server for email. On a test Joomla site, this really doesn't matter, so you can leave it as is.

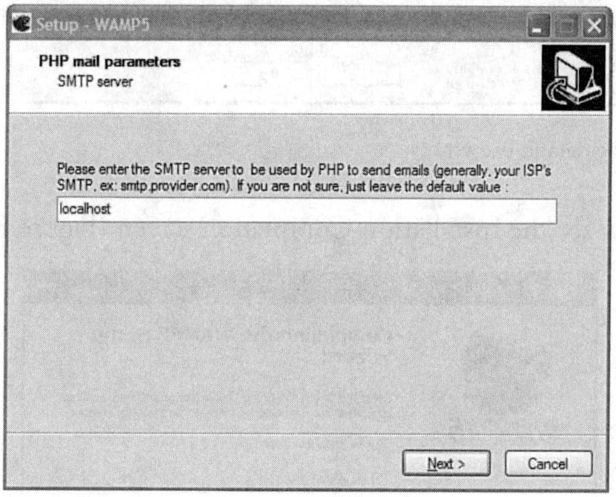

FIGURE D.9 SMTP server name selection

The default email address is next (Figure D.10). Again, for local test Joomla sites, this isn't used, so we can leave as default.

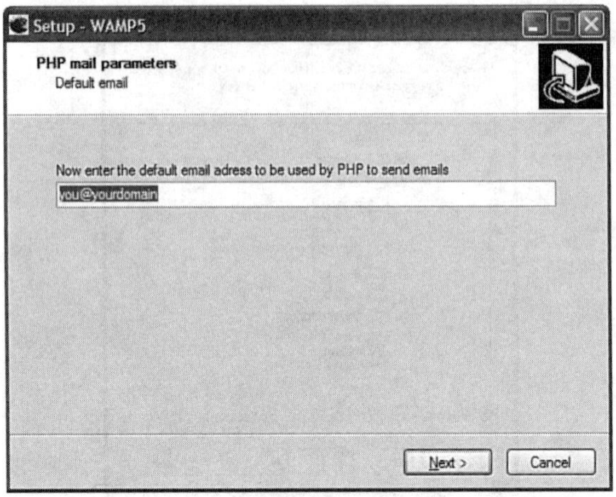

FIGURE D.10 Default PHP email address

You should now see a dialog box asking what browser you wish to use. In Figure D.11, I am accepting my default browser, Firefox.

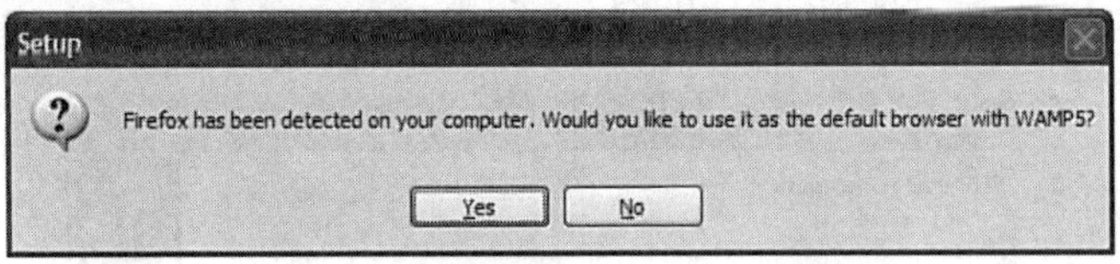

FIGURE D.11 Choosing default browser

You should now see the Installation Completion screen (Figure D.12).

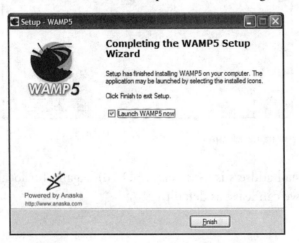

FIGURE D.12 Installation complete

When you run WAMP5, you see a small icon in your system tray. This is the row of small icons at the lower right portion of your screen.

If you left-click the icon, you see an option to Start All Services, as shown in Figure D.13.

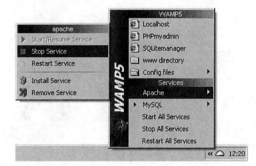

FIGURE D.13 Left-clicking the WAMP5 icon

You will now see the icon go red, then yellow, and then white, indicating that the two services, Apache and PHP, are starting. This is shown in Figure D.14.

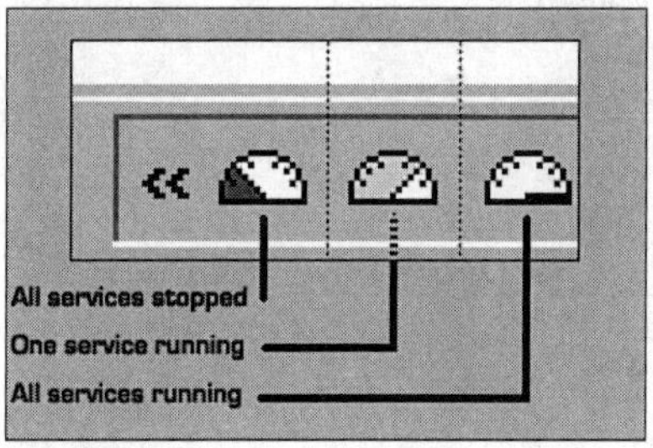

FIGURE D.14 The three stages of starting services

If the icon does not go all the way to white, it means there has been an error. The most common problem is a conflict with Skype. If you use Skype (and who doesn't?!), you will need to quit it first, then start WAMP5, and then start Skype back up.

After you have it running, you will have a folder (I used c:\wamp\www in this example) that is your web folder. Anything you put here, like a Joomla installation, will be accessible as a website. It's best to put a site into a new folder, like c:\wamp5\www\mysite or something similar.

If you left-click the WAMP5 icon, you open the main WAMP5 server as a web page, shown in Figure D.15.

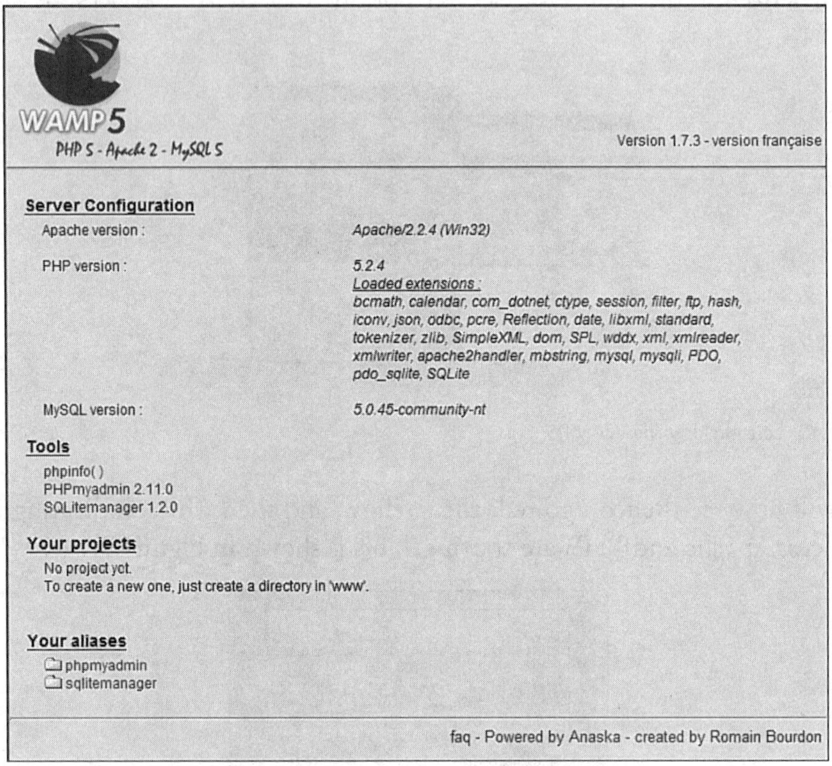

FIGURE D.15   Root level of WAMP5

In the section, "Your projects," you see any folders/websites you have created. If you click one, you go to that site.

When installing Joomla, on the Installation Wizard page about the database configuration (see Chapter 2, "Downloading and Installing Joomla"), you need to provide the SQL details for WAMP5, which are

- Host name = localhost
- User name = root
- Password = [none/blank]
- Database name = [Put anything you like here]

WAMP5 will then be able to create a database for the Joomla site you are installing.

Index

BOOKS ONLINE

ENABLED

THIS BOOK IS SAFARI ENABLED

INCLUDES FREE 45-DAY ACCESS TO THE ONLINE EDITION

The Safari® Enabled icon on the cover of your favorite technology book means the book is available through Safari Bookshelf. When you buy this book, you get free access to the online edition for 45 days.

Safari Bookshelf is an electronic reference library that lets you easily search thousands of technical books, find code samples, download chapters, and access technical information whenever and wherever you need it.

TO GAIN 45-DAY SAFARI ENABLED ACCESS TO THIS BOOK:

- Go to **http://www.prenhallprofessional.com/safarienabled**

- Complete the brief registration form

- Enter the coupon code found in the front of this book on the "Copyright" page

If you have difficulty registering on Safari Bookshelf or accessing the online edition, please e-mail customer-service@safaribooksonline.com.

PRENTICE
HALL